3124300 568 4922

Lake Forest Library
360 E. Deerpath
Lake Forest, IL 60045
847-234-0636
www.lakeforestlibrary.org

D0848524

Ernest Hemingway

Ernest Hemingway

A NEW LIFE

JAMES M. HUTCHISSON

The Pennsylvania
State University Press
University Park,
Pennsylvania

Material from selected unpublished letters by Ernest Hemingway (pp. 89, 92–97, 100, 112–13, 127–28, 175–77, 180, 187, 193, 201, 203, 205, 218–19, 221–44, 247) is reprinted with the permission of Scribner, a division of Simon & Schuster, Inc. Copyright © Hemingway Foreign Rights Trust. All rights reserved.

Quotations from the unpublished correspondence of Ernest Hemingway © 2016 (pp. 89, 92–97, 100, 112–13, 127–28, 175–77, 180, 187, 193, 201, 203, 205, 218–19, 221–44, 247). Printed with the permission of The Ernest Hemingway Foundation.

Library of Congress Cataloging-in-Publication Data

Names: Hutchisson, James M., author.
Title: Ernest Hemingway : a new life / James M. Hutchisson.
Description: University Park, Pennsylvania : The Pennsylvania State University Press, [2016] | Includes bibliographical references and index.
Identifiers: LCCN 2016011792 | ISBN 9780271075341 (cloth : alk. paper)
Subjects: LCSH: Hemingway, Ernest, 1899–1961. | Authors, American—20th century—Biography.
Classification: LCC PS3515.E37 Z643 2016 | DDC 813/.52 [B] —dc23
LC record available at https://lccn.loc.gov/2016011792

TYPESET BY
———
Regina Starace

PRINTED AND
BOUND BY
———
Sheridan Books

COMPOSED IN
———
Baskerville 10 Pro

PRINTED ON
———
Glatfelter Offset
B18 Natural
and Flo Matte

BOUND IN
———
Arrestox

Copyright © 2016 The Pennsylvania State University
All rights reserved
Printed in the United States of America
Published by
The Pennsylvania State University Press,
University Park, PA 16802–1003

The Pennsylvania State University Press is a member of the Association of American University Presses.

It is the policy of The Pennsylvania State University Press to use acid-free paper. Publications on uncoated stock satisfy the minimum requirements of American National Standard for Information Sciences—Permanence of Paper for Printed Library Material, ANSI Z39.48–1992.

FOR MY SONS

Samuel Keen Hutchisson

William Lawrence Hutchisson

I have always had the illusion it was more important, or as important, to be a good man as to be a great writer. May turn out to be neither. But would like to be both.

—ERNEST HEMINGWAY, letter to Buck Lanham

———

He loved everything up to a certain point, and then nothing was any good any more.

—LEICESTER HEMINGWAY, *My Brother, Ernest Hemingway*

CONTENTS

LIST OF FIGURES

ACKNOWLEDGMENTS

My thanks to those libraries and manuscript archives that helped further my research on this book, especially Susan Wrynn and her able staff in the Hemingway Collection of the John F. Kennedy Presidential Library and Museum. Winifred C. "Bo" Moore, dean of the School of Humanities and Social Sciences at The Citadel, provided crucial support and funding, as did The Citadel Foundation. I am also grateful to the staff at Penn State Press, especially to Suzanne Wolk and her fine editorial skills. The early reviewers of the manuscript provided me with many insightful comments; helpful suggestions also came from Kirk Curnutt, James L. W. West III, John Jebb, Hal Bush, Jean Bartholomew, and Lauren Rule Maxwell. Michael Wright and I had many wonderful conversations about Hemingway over many lunches and many cigars; I am grateful for his friendship. And, as always, I cannot conceive of being able to do the work that I do without the support of my wife, Rachel. She has enriched me beyond measure.

J. H.
Charleston,
February
2016

Introduction

Ernest Hemingway is probably the most famous literary figure of all time. Some might argue that Hemingway wasn't the greatest American writer, or even the creator of the best American book. But Ernest Hemingway certainly is *the* American writer. He was the perfect blend of literary talent and iconic personality, and the contours of his life have become deeply etched in the American popular consciousness—from his vibrant, fledgling self in patched jacket and sneakers on the boulevards of 1920s Paris to his white-bearded, barrel-chested eminence in khaki shorts and long-billed fishing cap off the waters of 1950s Cuba. "Papa" still walks among us and looms large on the literary horizon—just as he wanted it to be.

Hemingway is also one of the most written-about authors, in terms of both his life and his art. Yet, surprisingly, there has not been a single-volume biography of Hemingway published in almost twenty-five years.[1] Most of his biographers have seemed to veer from one pole of critical approval to the other, either accepting wholesale—or with exaggerated winks and nods—the self-created legend of the hypermasculine hero, or disapproving of Hemingway by emphasizing the superficial image of him as a mean-spirited, alcoholic womanizer.

Carlos Baker's "official" biography of 1969, *Ernest Hemingway: A Life Story,* laid the groundwork for all further writing on the author, but even Baker, as the authorized scribe, many times expressed true disdain for his subject. (Jack Hemingway, the author's eldest son, once complained that Baker had made his father out to be "a son of a bitch.") Jeffrey Meyers's 1985 *Hemingway: A Biography,* while clearly written and accessible, is openly disapproving. Kenneth Lynn's controversial 1987 psychobiography of Hemingway advances the fascinating argument that the greatest trauma of Hemingway's life was a consistent pattern of gender confusion, but it does not do full justice to the other material of Hemingway's life and work. James Mellow's 1992 book reads nearly everything that Hemingway wrote in the context of the homoeroticism within Hemingway's circle. Unlike previous biographers, I see Hemingway as someone who became many things to many people—sometimes opposite things. He was the war hero, the foreign correspondent, the expatriate, the consummate artist, the marlin fisherman and lion hunter, the womanizer, the drinker, the father and husband, the overbearing egotist, the tragic figure whose thoughts of self-destruction trailed him for nearly his entire life.

Hemingway's keystone subject was violent death. Plagued by depression and a history of mental illness in his family, Hemingway fought constantly against the insidious slow descent of what he called "the black ass," which could envelop him in an instant in a fog of despair. The adventuring, the risk taking, the life lived large, was collectively a way of avoiding the dark places that he tried to steer clear of in his life, so that he could explore them with some measure of safety in his art. His writing was a means of connecting with deep, raw emotion; to him, this meant being truthful about what is real—true to what is. The dark call to die, yet the insistence upon continuing, like the offering and withdrawing of emotion in his fiction, is an essential rhythm of Hemingway's life and art, just as are the silences that sit in his short, declarative sentences—a kind of concession to dread and, ultimately, mortality. It might not be too much to say that he was in some ways a nexus for death, for among the people whom he became close to, or who were part of his family, many were suicides. The psychic terrain that he lived in must therefore have been very hard for him to navigate while still remaining sane.

It is often said that one of Hemingway's best fictional creations was Ernest Hemingway himself. But what has not been traced through his life and work is how he discovered (or created) different identities through his writing, or how he used his writing to try to reconcile the contradictory elements within himself. I thus tend to see Hemingway more sympathetically than many earlier writers have; I believe he thought that if he could see himself clean and whole—what he thought of as the "true gen"—his writing might be useful to others who also lived their lives as journeys into themselves. Like most people, Hemingway changed over the course of his life. He was not the static figure that he has often been made out to be.

Hemingway had unusually high standards for his work, for others' work, and for others' friendships. So great a talent as his, and the concurrent fame and celebrity status that accompanied it, created huge difficulties in his personal life that he could never overcome, although he tried mightily to do so. Having the mantle of fame put on his shoulders while he was so young, he was always looking over his shoulder at the competition. He therefore developed a competitive streak that often made it impossible for him to praise fellow writers or to feel that anybody was as good a writer as he was. His relationships were often tempestuous, like a summer storm crossing the bay. His high standards created an almost suffocating anxiety in him; it is actually something of a miracle that he survived that pressure as long as he did. He also had a deeply ingrained sense of character, which he often, all too humanly, failed to live up to. This seems forgivable in most people, but many found it unforgivable in Hemingway. As Edmund Wilson once snidely put it, Hemingway had an inviolable code of honor that he was always breaking.

Hemingway also had an insecurity about all things physical. He was perpetually trying to impress people with his athletic skill, his sexual prowess, his stamina, his muscle tone, and his ability to participate competitively in physically challenging activities like sportfishing and boxing. His obsession with the body led him to explore the physical in his fiction in ways that no one had ever done before, although that interest did not come into focus until after the period of his greatest productivity, 1926–1940. After 1940, he pondered this theme in his fiction—though he could never push through and actually publish most of this work, perhaps for the very reasons that drove his own physical insecurities. His obsession with the physical also probably accounted for his often harsh treatment of his wives and lovers, since all of those relationships—with the exception of his first wife, Hadley—were based largely on sexual attraction. His letters to his wives and wives-to-be are among the most passionate and heartfelt in all of literary history. He thought that love was both the sine qua non of human existence and the greatest deceiver. When his marriages collapsed, he spun downward each time, powerlessly caught in an inner cyclone of guilt, anxiety, and even grief. By the time his emotions were spent, he was spiritually and psychically empty, hollowed out like a drum.

In this book, I pursue several specific angles of entry into understanding Hemingway. One is the pattern of how his writing was influenced by women and by place. I offer an organized look at the sequence of results produced in his work by his various wives, lovers, and mistresses. Each major novel gestated in Hemingway's consciousness and was brought to fruition during a relationship—whether sexual or not—with a woman. Hemingway's relationships with women were also inextricably bound to geographic locale. The battlefield seems to have been the most recurrent setting, but he also adopted a series of spiritual homes that became stimuli to creativity—most of all Spain, which he said in the second sentence of *The Dangerous Summer* that he loved more than any place on earth.

I also emphasize Hemingway's interest in medicine (his father was a physician, and his third son became one) and analyze his complex medical profile. I take into account his family health history, his recurrent vision problems, and the pattern of accidents, injuries, and illnesses that plagued him throughout his life. As John Dos Passos once said, he never knew an athletic, vigorous man who spent as much time in bed as Hemingway did. Hemingway had a complicated medical history that helps explain his emotions and attitudes, his public behavior, his fictional themes and preoccupations, and his ability or inability to write. Medical records among his personal papers show that for much of his life Hemingway took medications that conflicted chemically with one another and eventually produced disastrous results. It is my strong belief that it was this condition, much more than the idea that he was felled by fame or corrupted by the allure of celebrity, that propelled him down the slope into suicide at the end of his life. With his family history of mental illness, it is not surprising that Hemingway was obsessed with suicides, real and imagined. Trying to stare down the dark facts of a difficult world was something that had been part of him since youth.

The portrait of Hemingway that emerges in this book is neither tragic nor heroic, but is instead a balanced assessment that shows the ambition that drove him, and the anxieties, both real and imagined, that destroyed him.

The Midwest

CHILDHOOD AND YOUTH

When, in the 1850s, Joseph Kettlestrings subdivided the 172 acres he had purchased just west of Chicago into building lots and named the community Oak Park, he advertised it as a place where "good" families could escape the sin and dirt of the city and lead clean, pure lives. Very soon, the village of Oak Park, Illinois, came to be known as the place where the saloons ended and the churches began, and it acquired a reputation as a stronghold of conservativism. As the decades went by, its character changed very little. Until 1973, no alcohol was sold within the village limits, and there were no stand-alone bars or saloons there until 2005.[1]

Religious life was central. Religious denominations—from Presbyterians to Congregationalists—built so many houses of worship there in the 1870s that Oak Park was sometimes called "Saint's Rest." A village pastime involved counting the number of church steeples visible from different locations. Most all of the residents were Protestant; there was only one Roman Catholic church in town. The Hemingway family subscribed to the pieties and conservative attitudes of the community. They attended the First Congregational Church, which boasted a famous pastor, William E. Barton. Barton was a native midwesterner who became an authority on Abraham Lincoln, the author of numerous books about the Civil War, and the creator of a series of homespun advice pamphlets featuring a character called "Safed the Sage." Barton's son, Bruce, became even more famous than his father as the author of the best-selling book *The Man Nobody Knows* (1925), which depicted Jesus as a great salesman and a role model for the successful businessman. The younger Barton went on to found one of the largest advertising agencies in the country; his most famous marketing creation was Betty Crocker.[2]

What the families of Oak Park heard from the pulpit of the First Congregational Church was an unalloyed doctrine of individualism, self-improvement, and optimism that issued forth without pause, even when war came to Europe and American boys were sent to die on foreign soil. A favorite hymn among Oak Parkers at the turn of the century was "Some Day the Silver Cord Will Break (And I No More as Now Shall Sing)," by the blind lyricist Fanny J. Crosby, who wrote more than eight thousand hymns. The song evoked the Victorian concept of the beautiful death, which focused on the melodrama of death rather than its brute realism, an unsubtle but effective way of putting one in mind of reassurance, like picturing a loved one cradled by angels in heaven and resting peacefully on billowy clouds. Oak Park was a protective environment in which the young Hemingway, like most boys his age, did not think about mortality or have much interest in the dead or the dying. Later, however, death would become his chief fictive subject.

The villagers kept a keen eye on their young. They encouraged achievement but restricted freedom, creating an insular, sometimes high-pressure community. Young people were lectured routinely on the evils of dancing and drink, and boys were warned not to become too intimate with girls. Going to movies and smoking cigarettes were sinful activities, and there was always a curfew. Oak Parkers also put heavy pressure on their youths to succeed. Hemingway was a lackluster student and did not excel as an athlete, but he grew up with the awareness that nothing less than a perfect performance in everything was acceptable. He was raised from an early age to be competitive, perhaps even to embrace stress and anxiety as a way of accelerating achievement.

As a civic center, the village was in the forefront of most everything new and developing in twentieth-century America. Each month the library hosted lectures by local speakers who showed magic-lantern slides and talked about such exotic topics as the Orient and the pyramids. There were ice-cream socials and a community chorale, but the town was also very progressive when it came to embracing the modern conveniences of daily life. Automobiles quickly outnumbered horses and carriages when the first "machines" were produced. The telephone supplanted the telegraph, just as the wireless would later become a fixture of family parlors. Oak Parkers were solid, clear-thinking, responsible citizens. Most were progressive Republicans; nearly the whole town voted for Teddy Roosevelt on the Bull Moose ticket in 1912.

Although Hemingway became a revolutionary in many respects, rebelling against this type of safe, jovial conformity in the same way that he broke with the genteel tradition of writing, he also retained many of these Victorian values in his adult life. There was often a tension in Hemingway's life and work between the Victorian morality with which he was raised and his modernist drift toward ethical relativity. During his expatriate years in Paris in the 1920s, he struck some, like the outlandishly unconventional Gertrude Stein, as "ninety percent Rotarian."[3] He believed in hard work and had a strong inner drive, especially when it came to writing. He could be surprisingly genial, jokey, and sentimental. He loved animals, especially cats, and grieved unabashedly when they died. He was always keen to own the latest gadgets and technology. He loved cars as much as he did pets and favored the wide-bodied American showboats to the more streamlined and urban-style European runabouts. He had sophisticated and varied tastes in literature and painting, but in other arts, like music, for instance, his preferences were bland. One scholar visiting Hemingway's Cuban home, Finca Vigía, was surprised to find that the author's classical record collection, still preserved there, was of the "greatest hits" variety and not at all interesting, even to someone with no great knowledge of musical history.[4]

――――

The house on North Highland Avenue, where Hemingway was born on 21 July 1899, belonged to his maternal grandfather, Ernest Hall, and his wife, Caroline. Hall, a deeply religious man, had been born in Sheffield, England, in the West Yorkshire dales, in 1840, and as a teenager had worked in the family cutlery business before emigrating to America in 1860. As a young man in Iowa, Hall ran away from the family farm after he drove some horses into a river; the horses were swept away in the current. Once the news of the Civil War reached him, however, he returned home, contrite, and enlisted. He signed on with the First Iowa Volunteer Cavalry and left the war with a bullet lodged in his leg. When the government offered him a military pension, he refused it. "I gave my services to my adopted country," he said. "I did not sell them."[5] After the war, Hall started a wholesale cutlery business in Chicago. He soon became wealthy and built a large house in the smart Chicago suburb of Oak Park.

Grandfather Hall was known as "Abba" to his grandchildren (the word comes from a German mealtime prayer), and he was strict in his religious beliefs.[6] A prayer was said before each meal, and Hall conducted a family religious service six days a week that everyone was required to attend, including the household help. Hemingway's sister Marcelline recalled the daily ritual in her memoir: "After Abba had read the lesson for the day, we would all rise, turn, and kneel down on the carpet in front of our chairs, resting our elbows on the black leather seats, while Abba knelt at the center table. But instead of closing his eyes or bowing his head as the rest of us did, he raised his head, his eyes upward, as though he was talking to God, right above him. I can still see Abba's shiny pink and white head, his white muttonchop whiskers and the white fringe of his neatly center-parted hair, his beaming smile and those lovely deep blue eyes looking up to God as he prayed."[7]

Hemingway's paternal grandfather, Anson Hemingway, was also of English ancestry, having descended from seventeenth-century Doncaster immigrants. He lived with his wife, Adelaide, and their children in a large white-frame house across the street from Hall's. Like Hall, Anson was a straitlaced, morally upright man, and he too had served in the Civil War. Hemingway grew up watching his grandfather Anson marching in Memorial Day parades decked out in full military regalia.

Anson Hemingway filled his grandson with a fascination about the Civil War. The grandfather hoarded newspaper clippings and other mementos, including the pistol he carried in battle (the same gun with which Hemingway's father took his own life in 1928). At an early age, Hemingway became fascinated with warfare and with the generals and other figures who became famous by leading troops into battle. He read extensively about the Civil War throughout his life, and he would live either to participate in or to chronicle the events of four major wars: World War I, the Spanish Civil War, the Sino-Japanese War, and World War II.

When the Civil War ended, Anson became a successful realtor.[8] However, there were significant differences between the two households. Anson Hemingway, a fervid Congregationalist, presided over a home of many restrictions; he had no interest in literature or the arts but a deep fascination for the sciences, especially astronomy and botany. The house was comfortable but relatively spartan. Ernest Hall, a contented Episcopalian, cared little for science but filled his home with art, music, and literature. The carpet he knelt on each evening at prayer was a rich Belgian weave with gilded silk fringe. The blend of interests and beliefs presented by his two grandfathers made a significant impact on Hemingway.

Hall's daughter, Grace, had known their across-the-street neighbor, Clarence Edmonds Hemingway, since they attended Oak Park High School together, but they didn't begin courting until after graduation. On 1 October 1896, they married. Ernest was the second child, after his older sister, Marcelline. The family would eventually grow to include six children—three more sisters, named Carol, Madelaine ("Sunny"), and Ursula, and a younger brother, Leicester. Ed Hemingway was a good-looking young man with strong features and an athletic frame. More than six feet tall, Ed had a smooth, angular face with a sharp, hawklike nose. Born on 4 September 1871, in Oak Park, Ed graduated from Oberlin College in 1893 and later received his medical degree from Rush Medical College. While studying to be a physician, he had struck up a relationship with Grace, as she was caring for her mother during an illness that eventually led to her death. Grace, who was born in Chicago in 1872, had led a somewhat pampered childhood that included a good many indulgences, like trips to England to trace the family heritage. Her awareness of her British ancestry, drilled into her by her father, made her something of a snob. Her father fancied himself the country squire; Grace, in like fashion, led a life of privilege and genteel comfort. Hemingway's younger sister Carol noted that her mother was "very much an English gentlewoman. . . . She liked to be waited on and expected her children to be well behaved. She thought of us as English as well, though of course we were all born in Oak Park."[9]

Grace grew into an attractive woman. Statuesque, with blond hair, blue eyes, and a ruddy but not unappealing complexion, Grace had presence. Her buxom, voluptuous figure was striking, her silk blouses and wide-brimmed hats were haute couture, and she could fill a room with an air of importance. Although generally healthy, Grace had suffered through a bout of scarlet fever at age seven that had left her blind for several months. It was thought that this illness accounted for weak eyesight in her adulthood, although there is actually no medical connection between the two conditions. Still, Hemingway would recall that when he was a young boy his mother would often complain of sensitivity to light and, pleading discomfort, would frequently withdraw to her bedroom, blinds closed and lamps dimmed, much like someone suffering from a migraine. Hemingway inherited his mother's weak eyesight (it kept him from enlisting in the army during World War I) and seems to have believed much of the family lore surrounding the condition. He once claimed that he always woke at dawn because the sunlight shined through his "thin eyelids"—hence his habit of writing early in the mornings.[10]

Since her childhood, the great love of Grace's life had been music. Her mother, Caroline, had been the proud owner of the first organ in Oak Park, a melodeon. When she left her hometown, Dyersville, Illinois, and traveled to Chicago to get married, Caroline carried the organ with her. Then, during the Great Chicago Fire of 1871, she dragged it to safety from her burning home. Caroline directed her daughter's progress toward what she hoped would be a successful operatic career, in part to show Grace that she did not have to conform to gender stereotypes. Caroline told her daughter that if she could become a professional musician, she would be able to stay out of the kitchen, and Grace, who upon marriage to Ed hyphenated her surname and always signed herself Grace Hall-Hemingway, followed this plan. Grace had been given private voice lessons since early childhood and through high school was groomed for a career in opera.

Caroline died in the fall of 1895, and Grace lived out her mother's wishes. Shortly thereafter, she went to New York to study with Madame Luisa Cappiani at the Art Students' League. Cappiani believed that Grace had a great opera career ahead of her as a contralto and arranged an audition at the Met. During this time, however, Grace was also receiving frequent letters from Ed, imploring her to return home and proposing marriage. There was tension between her and her teacher, too. Although it's not certain, she may have had a lesbian fling with Cappiani; if so, it was short-lived. By 1896, despite her family's financial support, Grace found that she owed Cappiani more than $1,000—a considerable sum. She no longer wanted a career in music, but she was offered the opportunity to perform at Madison Square Garden. She did so to pay off her debt, and during the concert, which received generally positive reviews, Grace claimed that the footlights hurt her eyes and said she could not perform again. Family lore had it that Grace was even offered a contract by the Met—but whatever the case, she returned to Oak Park, and to Ed. She chose marriage and her hometown over a career, travel, and fame.

This did not mean that Grace sacrificed her interest in music. She directed the church choir, and she encouraged Ernest and his sister Ursula to join the high school orchestra. Marcelline took violin lessons, Madelaine the harp, and Ernest the cello. Grace also maintained a successful stay-at-home business giving voice lessons. At one time, she taught more than fifty pupils and far outearned her husband, whose medical practice was just then getting off the ground. In contrast to Ed's paltry monthly income of $50, Grace, charging $8 an hour for lessons, could bring in as much as $1,000 a month. Ernest did not stick with the cello for very long, and he seems to have had something of a tin ear for music. The poet Delmore Schwartz was among the first to notice that his 1940 novel, *For Whom the Bell Tolls,* has a contrapuntal structure, which some have attributed to his study of the cello.[11] But most of the time Hemingway's themes and metaphors referred to sports and the outdoor life, not music.

Grace's relationship with her children was loving but, as is usually the case, complicated. Like most of her son's future wives, Grace was not maternal in a tangible, biological sense. (Of all of Hemingway's four wives, only his first, Hadley Richardson, had a nurturing disposition.) Leicester, Grace's youngest child, recalled, "From the start there was a succession of nurses and mother's helpers in the Hemingway household. For beyond singing lullabies and breast-feeding, our mother lacked domestic talents. She abhorred didies, deficient manners, stomach upsets, house-cleaning, and cooking."[12] Like two of Hemingway's later wives, Pauline Pfeiffer and Martha Gellhorn, Grace's view was unconventional for the time. She wanted to be free of housework to pursue her own interests. But this doesn't mean that she felt no devotion to her children. She kept meticulously annotated photo albums and memory books for each of her sons and daughters. She read to Ernest from hundreds of books and taught him to memorize Latin and German phrases and lines of poetry. She took each child to the opera, to the theater, to museums. And she heaped praised on her children for their accomplishments, a fact that accounts for Hemingway's desire to be the first in any group to do something daring or original and to be the best at everything he attempted. He was born an overachiever, and he would treat his own children the same way. Each of his three boys—Jack, Patrick, and Gregory—would at one time or another have Papa bestow on them the much-coveted title of "top dog" at shooting, fishing, or skiing. Each lived to please his father, and competitiveness ran in the Hemingway bloodline.[13]

Bernice Kert, in *The Hemingway Women,* and other writers have made much of Grace's dominance in the marriage. Hemingway himself, of course, advanced this view of his mother in some of his more extreme public displays of bravado and hypermasculinity. He often cast her as a bully in opposition to his father's natural unassertiveness, and he made some outlandish statements, as when he told Robert Coates that if his mother was a bird and flew in a straight line, he wouldn't hesitate to shoot at her.[14] But the view of Grace as a tyrant and of Ed as a cowardly weakling has come about mainly from the portraits of husbands and wives in Hemingway's fiction.

In several of the stories Hemingway wrote featuring his fictional alter ego, Nick Adams, the character of Mrs. Adams is presented harshly. At times shrewish, at other times unbearably sanctimonious, she is rarely depicted in a positive light. As a Christian Scientist in "The Doctor and the Doctor's Wife," Mrs. Adams puts no store by her husband's considerable medical accomplishments. And as a society lady, she has no admiration for Dr. Adams's skill at living in the outdoors. In "Now I Lay Me," Nick Adams recalls his mother burning her husband's prized collection of Indian arrowheads, snakes, and other specimens, which have been preserved in Mason jars. When Dr. Adams comes home and finds the debris, he asks Nick to get a rake and help him try to salvage something. Together, they comb from the ashes stone axes, skinning knives, pieces of pottery, and shattered arrowheads. Nick's mother goes into the house and Nick and his father are left alone to ponder the ruined collection.

Grace, by contrast, may have been headstrong, but she does not seem to have been mean. Her relationship with Ed was not one-sided but rested on a subtle balance of power from which Hemingway probably learned a good deal. Grace's letters to her children, preserved at the Harry Ransom Center at the University of Texas at Austin, are full of tender solicitude and present a picture of a temperamental but concerned mother who thought of her children daily. Hemingway loved her and appreciated what she had done for him as a child. He took care of her after Ed's death. And he recognized that she was out of place in her time, a woman not made to fit the traditional mold of a Victorian marriage. When she later lived with a companion, Ruth Arnold, he supported both women financially and looked after their welfare. When he became a writer associated with masculinity and male-oriented pursuits, he naturally deflected attention from his relationship with his mother, not wanting to detract from his public image. Hemingway lived, for the most part, in a world of men without women, and, surrounded most of the time by men, he was insecure about his virility. The contemptuous remarks he allegedly made about his mother to people like Charles "Buck" Lanham, the army colonel whose regiment he was embedded with in France during World War II, were what he thought was expected of him by those who equated him with his hypermasculine characters.[15] He did partly blame Grace when his father committed suicide in 1928—which he felt was caused in part by her inattention to Ed's emotional needs—but he certainly did not hate her.

———

In contrast to Grace's pampered upbringing, Ed Hemingway was a man of spartan needs and grudging pleasures. As a young man, Ed abided strictly by the codes of the Sabbath. He did not smoke or drink and disapproved strongly of dancing and playing cards. He tried to lead the clean, pure life that his Sunday school teachers told him was the Christian way—and probably did so to a fault, for Ed seems to have enjoyed little happiness in his life and did not regard pleasure as something to be sought. Neither of Ernest Hemingway's parents was extravagant or hedonistic, but Grace was given to self-indulgences that never remotely crossed Ed's mind. Their marriage was a study in contrasts in other ways as well. Grace preferred to be indoors, surrounded by creature comforts, basking in the pleasures of music and other arts, a mostly sedentary life. She took her cultural responsibilities to the children seriously. Ed lived his life mostly outdoors.

He thrived on physical activity and bristled when forced to attend concerts and plays. As a boy, watching birds and tracking animals, he had whiled away hours alone out on the Des Plaines River searching the old Native American mounds for artifacts. He loved to fish and hunt. He was an amateur naturalist as well as a collector of stamps, coins, Indian arrowheads, and snakes, which he kept preserved in glass jars in his downstairs study.

Ed taught Ernest how to hunt and build a fire. A skilled cook, Ed showed his son how to handle small game—how to clean it, prepare it, and cook it. Ed could make just about anything from scratch; he taught his children that wild onions with bread and butter were great sandwiches for long hikes. Ed was also a good shot; unlike Grace, he had very sharp vision. There was another, more philosophical difference between Ernest's parents. Ed was raised to value the fundamental drive to serve. His father had taught him that no life was complete without service to others. Ed thus spent much of his young adulthood, including his early years of marriage, looking after the needs of others. This sense of duty may explain in part why Ed did not fit the Victorian stereotype of the paterfamilias and allowed Grace to appear to have the "upper hand" in the marriage. His daughter Marcelline said that Ed attended to most all of the housework—despite his full-time career as a physician—and that his innate desire to serve others would not allow him to "neglect home duties."[16] He obviously wanted to please Grace and gave himself over to her desires. Ed's constant busyness was perhaps his defining trait, something hard to ignore in such a sedate village as Oak Park. In photographs from the period, Ed looks somewhat haggard, and despite his meek manner, many remembered him as nervous and high-strung. This was probably due to his unrelenting schedule, which ran the gamut from domestic chores to seeing patients in his office, performing surgery, making his rounds at the hospital, and serving as president of several local societies, such as the Agassiz Club, a society devoted to natural history. He also taught Sunday school and provided free medical services to local orphanages. Ed ran hither and yon, clattering around town and out to the countryside in a well-used horse and buggy, often operating on very little sleep. When Hemingway had the Italian priest in *A Farewell to Arms* declare that loving someone meant sacrifice and service (70), he could have been writing about his father.

Ed was a reliable and well-liked physician. When he returned to Oak Park from his medical studies, another doctor in town took him into his practice and Ed became his assistant, training for the day when he could strike out on his own. As his reputation grew, he always put his patients' needs ahead of his own and was purposely lax about collecting fees, telling Grace, when she pressed him, that good people always paid their bills eventually, and that he was not one to be aggressive about it. He gave free medical care to many patients who he knew could not afford to pay. Like many country doctors, he was also frequently called out in the middle of the night, sometimes to attend to one of the many Native Americans in outlying camps around the area—a scene Hemingway would later fictionalize in "Indian Camp."

Some of Ed Hemingway's medical adventures might even be called heroic.
When Grace was in labor with their first child, Marcelline, on 15 January 1898,
Ed was called home in a snowstorm in order to take over from the attending
physician, who had suffered a heart attack. Ed ran into Grace's room, administered first aid to the fallen doctor, restarted his wife's anesthetic, and performed
a stressful, high-forceps delivery of their baby girl. But all this, of course, took
its toll. The start of Ed's battle with depression can be traced to the stresses of his
professional life and the heavy demands he put on himself. At low moments, Ed
considered giving up his practice and often daydreamed, Walter Mitty–like, of
taking flying lessons, sailing the Mediterranean Sea alone, or being a missionary
in Guam.

When Ernest Hall died in May 1905, Grace received a hefty inheritance.
Oddly, for the time, the bulk of the estate came to Grace, a smaller portion going to her brother, the male heir. Citing her need for more room for music lessons, Grace decided to use the money to build a new house. She was exacting
in overseeing the project, as she was about everything. The result, executed by
the architect Henry George Fiddelke, was a prairie-style residence that boasted
fifteen rooms in two stories of gray stucco and wood trim. Ed's medical office—a
serviceable space for seeing patients and filling in medical charts—was located on
the second floor. But Grace's new music room was more impressive. Thirty feet
square by fifteen feet high, the room had a small balcony and a raised platform
on which stood a new Steinway piano. Galvanized tin drums full of water were
suspended by wire from the ceiling in order to provide the proper humidity to
keep the instrument in tune.

————

Oak Park was the domain of Hemingway's mother. His father's domain was the
open countryside just west of town and, when summertime came, the wilds of
northern Michigan. Every summer, from the time Hemingway was an infant, the
family would leave Oak Park for Walloon Lake, a small outpost eleven miles from
Petoskey, on the southeastern shore of Little Traverse Bay off Lake Michigan. It
was an idyllic place: "Petoskey," named by the Odawa Indians, the first inhabitants of the region, means "where the light shines through the clouds." Michigan,
far more than Oak Park, influenced Hemingway's imagination and made him
deeply aware of himself—they were "the parts . . . which stuck," as Philip Young
wrote.[17] Here, Hemingway learned to hunt and fish, and here he began his informal studies in natural history. By the time he was a teenager, Hemingway
could identify nearly every variety of flora and fauna in the area. He spent more
time there than in any other place in the world. Hemingway would write about
Michigan, too, more than almost anywhere else, except perhaps Spain. It is the
setting for ten published stories, sections of several other tales, one high school
story, and a short novel.

Grace and Ed first visited Walloon Lake in the summer of 1900. According
to their son Leicester, they were "seized with a strange sense of destiny" from

the moment they first laid eyes on the land.[18] They bought two acres of shoreline property about four miles from the foot of the lake and soon started construction on a small cottage there, which was completed in 1904. Then the annual hegira began. Early each summer, Grace—bustling with efficiency—would initiate a massive campaign of organizing the household for the change of venue and mobilize the children and servants with her natural sense of authority. Once packed up, the family would journey by lake steamer from Chicago to Harbor Springs, alighting at a small-frame railroad station there. The spur of the railroad connected Harbor Springs with Petoskey, eleven miles around the bay. There, the family would transfer again, to the train going to the village at Walloon Lake.

At the turn of the century, this area was just starting its transformation from a chock-a-block patch of lumbering camps to an up-and-coming resort. In the East, financial moguls from New York built summer mansions in Newport. The titans of industry from Chicago, Detroit, and St. Louis did the same in Harbor Springs. Yet when the Hemingways built their cottage there, the terrain was still beautiful and unspoiled. Rolling hills passed them by on the train trip, shaded by dense forests filled with pine, maple, and birch. Clear lakes and clean ponds dotted the landscape. Wildlife was everywhere. The children went hunting with Ed and often pretended that they were explorers or Indians.[19]

In keeping with her British heritage, Grace christened the modest cabin Windemere, after the lake in England (minus the "r"). The name was a misnomer, for instead of the stately dwelling that one might expect, the cottage was only slightly more spacious than a shack. It had two bedrooms, a dining room, and a kitchen. There was also a large fireplace, a woodstove, and an iron pump for well water. Marcelline described the dwelling as rustic and remote: "There was a roofed-over porch with a railing, and a hooked, hinged double gate across the front steps, which led down to the lake. The outside was white clapboard and the interior white pine. No plumbing, of course. A well was dug to the right of the cottage in the front yard. Visiting and communication were by water."[20] The family had two rowboats and later a motorboat to help get them around the lake. Ed raised ducks and pigs.

Later, the family added to its property in Michigan, buying a forty-acre tract across the lake from Windemere that they named Longfield Farm. Grace had another small cottage built there on top of a hill. She used the place as an escape from the family and spent time on her own there working on her music. Ruth Arnold, the family's live-in caregiver and housekeeper, accompanied Grace to the new cottage. This cottage, however, like the new home in Oak Park, became a source of some tension within the family—did Grace really need a second, private summer home all to herself? The children also wondered if she was distancing herself from their father. Hemingway once complained that in building the second cottage, his mother had spent the money that could have sent him to college. But he must have forgiven her eventually, because he took good care of her later in life.

In Michigan, Hemingway became a young naturalist. At the age of four, he amazed Grace by being able to identify seventy-three species in the family's *Birds of Nature* volume. At the lake on his third birthday, Grace wrote that he was already an expert fisherman, knowing when he had a bite on his hook and when to reel in his line. "He is a natural scientist," Grace wrote in one of many scrapbooks she kept about her children, "loving everything in the way of bugs, stones, birds, animals, insects, and blossoms."[21] As a boy, he was always observing, appraising, categorizing, and recording the world around him. Like his father, he was a born collector. One "Inventory of Personal Property," in a pocket account book he kept at about age fifteen, lists what he owned, what he knew, and what he wanted to do: "pioneering or exploring work," the young writer said; he intended to study science and "join some expedition."[22] Outdoor work, he believed, would build self-sufficiency.

Hemingway eventually grew to regard nature as possibly the most important force in one's life, a fount of healing and rejuvenation from the scars of a difficult life. He would use nature this way in key scenes in many of his books, as when Frederic and Catherine in *A Farewell to Arms* seek respite from war in the snowcapped mountains of Switzerland, or when Jake Barnes in *The Sun Also Rises* fishes in the mountain streams of Burguete, a momentary escape from the angst of postwar life in Paris. Moreover, Hemingway's first great style (for there were several)—the terse and methodically precise style in which he wrote his early stories and novels—was due first to his training in the Agassiz method of field observation[23] and only later to his work as a cub reporter on the crime beat in Kansas City. And Hemingway's "elegiac stance," as Susan F. Beegel puts it, toward life in general was due as much to the rape of nature he witnessed in his youth as to the later trauma of battle in Italy during World War I: at the time, his beloved Michigan woods were under siege from industrialists who removed four billion board feet of timber per year—an alarming trend.[24] Even in Oak Park, the "back-to-nature" movement was gathering momentum, as evidenced by Frank Lloyd Wright's prairie-style architecture, which found its most concentrated expression in Hemingway's own neighborhood.

Hemingway's outdoor education in Michigan was conducted by his father, who was a stickler for form and always insisted on doing things properly. He used only the correct rifles, rods, and tackle. He would not use a fly that had not been tied to precise specifications, nor would he tolerate laxity when it came to handling guns. "Accidents don't happen to people who know how to handle guns," he would tell his children over and over. "Treat a gun like a friend. Keep it clean. Oil it, clean it after every use, but always remember, it's an enemy if it's carelessly used."[25] Ed also taught his son that one ate everything that one killed, without exception: once, when Ernest went hunting with his friend Harold Sampson and shot a porcupine, the doctor forced the two boys to make a meal of it. Ernest admired his father and respected his knowledge, the dignity of his well-earned expertise. He emulated him both in manner and in dress, donning buckskin shirts, trousers, and a straw hat. (In a photograph from the period, he bears a fine resemblance to Huck Finn.) In adulthood, as Jeffrey Meyers notes, Hemingway always went to experts to learn what he wanted to know, following his father's example. He learned about bullfighting from Juanito Quintana, about deep-sea fishing from Bra Saunders, about big-game hunting from Philip Percival. In turn, he handed down this knowledge and taught these skills to his sons, wives, and friends.[26]

Not very far from Windemere was a small cluster of homes known as Horton Bay, surrounded by a school, a blacksmith's forge, a general store, a post office, and a Methodist church. Hemingway became friends with a local family named the Dilworths. Jim Dilworth ran the forge across from the school, while Liz, his wife, ran a small restaurant called Pinehurst Cottage by the lake; the Hemingway family often ate there. In Michigan, Hemingway also met the orphaned siblings Kenley, Bill, and Katy Smith. Bill would become a good friend and room with Hemingway in Chicago. Katy would marry John Dos Passos, a friend who would later become a rival novelist. Sometimes Hemingway would take Oak Park friends up to Michigan with his family. They would fish at Horton's Creek and eat at Pinehurst Cottage. But the more lasting friendships seem to have been those he made with the locals.

In fact, the most interesting contribution that Ed and northern Michigan made to Hemingway's education concerned Native American culture. The young Hemingway was far more interested in Native Americans than in his own peers. Ed, who served as a physician to the locals, had great friends among them. As an expert marksman, he had been given the name Ne-teck-ta-la, or "Eagle Eye," by Indian friends. Ed was proud of this connection, and Hemingway would later exaggerate it by claiming that his father had Indian blood from the Edmonds side of the family.

Once a year, a tribe of Ojibway would come down from the Garden River area of Ontario to give an outdoor performance of Longfellow's "Song of Hiawatha" at Round Lake, near Petoskey. Hemingway always looked forward to these dramatizations. (One member of the visiting tribe even claimed that his grandfather had been Longfellow's guide.) Ever observant, Hemingway made a careful study of the customs and character of the Ojibway who worked for the nearby mill as tanners or sawyers. He wrote a juvenile tale, "Sepi Jingan," published in his high school literary magazine, in which he refuted the popular stereotypes of Native Americans: they were "not the redskin[s] of the popular magazine," Hemingway wrote. They never said "ugh."[27] Neither did he see them as the noble savages of western lore. They were surrogates for the spirit he found lacking in Oak Park: people of nature, renegades at heart, unconnected with the orthodoxies or false pieties or prejudices of white society. In an unpublished play written in his teens, Hemingway had two boys discuss sexual adventures. One tells the other about an Indian girl he wants to take to bed. The friend warns him off: "Ain't any mixed up with Indians. Fuck'um say goodbye, you never see 'em again."[28] This is a crude satire of white society, but as Hemingway matured into an adult, he held to his belief that Native Americans were more honest with themselves, more in tune with their souls, than conventional white society.

A Native American girl named Prudence Boulton played a curious role in Hemingway's youth and in his fiction; Hemingway later named her as the girl to whom he lost his virginity.[29] Hemingway first met Prudence on one of the trips he made with his father to the Ojibway camps, where Ed's medical services were needed. She became an overt symbol of sexual wantonness and self-indulgence and could be said to have initiated the connection in Hemingway's imagination—played out over and over again in his major works—between sex and death. She is also connected to Hemingway's depiction of his father in fiction; manuscript versions of his works show Hemingway struggling with his true feelings toward Ed. Prudence first appears as Prudence Mitchell in the story "Ten Indians," where she breaks Nick Adams's heart. The news is delivered by Dr. Adams, who tells Nick, coming home late from a Fourth of July celebration at a friend's farm, that he had stumbled upon Prudence and another boy having "quite a time" together in the woods (433).[30] In the published version of the story, Dr. Adams delivers the news of the girl's infidelity with merciless bluntness, even taking his time so as to increase the cruelty. But in manuscript versions of the story, a saturnine Dr. Adams wrestles with the problem of how to tell his son this painful information. In one scrapped episode, he kneels beside his bed and prays that God will restrain him from "telling a kid how things are."[31]

Prudie next appears in another story about the loss of sexual innocence, "Fathers and Sons," where she is called Trudy Gilby. The story is about the natural competition between a man and his father, told through Nick's reminiscences of going hunting as a boy with his Indian friends. The published version focuses on his father's trite advice about living a clean Christian life. As Nick recalls, his "father had summed up the whole matter by stating that masturbation produced blindness, insanity, and death, while a man who went with prostitutes would contract hideous venereal diseases and that the thing to do was to keep your hands off of people" (589). In a passage not used in the story, Dr. Adams appears less one-dimensional. Nick reflects on something darkly sexual about his hypermasculine father, who asks him to take the oars as they row in the lake because "it was too uncomfortable."[32] The evidence suggests that in the published forms of some of Hemingway's fiction, his father is stereotyped, yet the manuscripts show that Hemingway's view of what his father represented was not so black-and-white.

The real Prudence Boulton met a dark end, as naturally as any Hemingway character, male or female. She later took up with a man, Richard Castle, by whom she became pregnant at age sixteen. They committed suicide together, taking strychnine in his father's house at Charlevoix, and thereby acquired dubious fame in the local papers, which reported on the scandal as an object lesson in immorality. Their screams, as local lore had it, were heard across Susan Lake for hours.

Michigan meant summer, fun, and freedom. Oak Park signified winter, school, and responsibility. Hemingway was a lackluster student, but he appears to have done well enough in school, and he became more involved in the school community as he grew older. Oak Park boasted one of the best public school systems in the country, and it offered Hemingway many advantages, both academic and extracurricular, that he might not otherwise have had. When he entered Oak Park and River Forest Township High School in 1913, there were plenty of opportunities to play sports, but Hemingway was no great athlete. He professed no interest in team sports like baseball and football. He made the junior varsity football team but was a reluctant recruit: he later said that if you could play football, then everyone at the school expected you to do so. Unlike other famous writers who went on to play sports in college (such as Stephen Crane and Jack Kerouac), Hemingway had no ambition to be an athletic hero.[33] He later distinguished between "sports" like motor racing and mountaineering and "games" like baseball and football. He did cover sports for the school newspaper, but the importance of these pieces lies mostly in their style and technique. Other comments about American sports are flatly satirical, as in *The Torrents of Spring,* when the simpleton Yogi Johnson compares football to warfare and finds them "much the same thing, intensely unpleasant" (52). In *The Sun Also Rises,* Jake Barnes is unimpressed when he notes that Robert Cohn had been middleweight boxing champion at Princeton (3).

Hemingway was well liked by his classmates. He was daring and slightly rebellious (as when a teacher acquired a toupee, and he wrote about it satirically in the school newspaper). The other students also admired him because he seemed to do exactly what he wanted and resented authority. But he was not a problem youth by any means. In an interview with one of Hemingway's biographers, the literary critic Edward Wagenknecht, who was a classmate, recalled him as "handsome, friendly, and courageous" and debunked the idea that Hemingway had been a loner in school or was regarded as a "tough guy": "There was nothing in my contacts with Hemingway to cause me to suspect this," Wagenknecht said.[34] Hemingway also dabbled in a large variety of extracurricular activities, competing on the swimming team, managing the track team, participating in the debating club, and even acting in some school plays.

Like any typical student, Hemingway found some classes to his liking and others not. He started off with the expected regimen of algebra, Latin, and general sciences, all of which he struggled through; Latin he found so difficult that in his first year he hired a tutor to help him pass the course. English classes, on the other hand, were a pleasure. The school, a massive structure of yellow brick, had an English Club room that resembled a British gentleman's study: floor-to-ceiling bookshelves lined the oak-paneled walls; overstuffed leather armchairs and ottomans were clustered before a fireplace; expensive carpets covered the wood floors.

Hemingway was the darling of all of his English teachers, but he showed no strong interest in writing. Unlike many authors, Hemingway did not yearn to be a writer at a young age, although he was inspired by two teachers in particular. The first was Margaret Dixon. She was physically strong, dark-complexioned, and somewhat mannish-looking. Dixon was an outspoken liberal, sounding a nonconformist note in an otherwise complacent community, and she was up to date on the latest literary trends. By nature somewhat temperamental and bursting with energy, Dixon directed the class plays and school theater performances. Fannie Biggs, on the other hand, was tall, slender, and somewhat prim, her hair done up in pompadour style and her nose and face a thin, angular shape. Biggs was unmarried, and her main interest was creative writing. Both women encouraged Hemingway's early literary efforts.[35]

Hemingway read mostly British literature—the standard texts by Chaucer, Spenser, Shakespeare, Milton, Scott, and Dickens. There were not many American writers on the school syllabus. He read Benjamin Franklin's *Autobiography,* which was required for freshmen, but he professed a profound lack of interest in Emerson, Hawthorne, Whittier, and other classic American writers. Surprisingly, given his interest in nature, he was not drawn to Thoreau, either. And only much later would he become interested in American realist writers like Theodore Dreiser and Frank Norris.

The author he liked best as an adolescent was Ring Lardner, the sportswriter and playwright whose satirical columns Hemingway had probably grown up reading in the *Chicago Tribune.* Lardner was a prolific writer of stories for mass-circulation magazines. Hemingway emulated Lardner in the satirical, sports-themed pieces he wrote for the high school magazine, the *Trapeze.* A feature of Hemingway's writing from this era that would carry through his first novel, *The Sun Also Rises,* and through later short stories, was the cynical, satirical, and at times off-puttingly smart-aleck tone that he evolved from reading Lardner. Although we do not tend to think of Hemingway as a satirist, this mode of expression is common to all of his work.[36] When Hemingway wrote for the *Kansas City Star,* the *Toronto Star,* and the Chicago-based *Cooperative Commonwealth,* his prose style was a blend of irony, critique, and mimicry. Later, he followed up *The Sun Also Rises* with a parody of his mentor, Sherwood Anderson, titled *The Torrents of Spring.*

Hemingway also learned the importance of dialogue from Lardner. Hustling to turn out seven columns a week, Lardner had hit on the idea of hanging around ballplayers—in hotel lobbies, dugouts, and clubhouses—and listening to their idiomatic speech: slang and singular nouns and plural verbs, all mixed together. He then reproduced these natural-sounding conversations in his stories, and readers grew used to the innovation. Lardner's technique was important enough that H. L. Mencken, in his famous work *The American Language,* claimed that the discovery of the speech of the masses could be attributed entirely to Lardner, who reported "the common speech . . . with the utmost accuracy."[37] Although

Hemingway would later claim that modern American literature began with Mark Twain's *Adventures of Huckleberry Finn,* he could well have made the same case for Lardner's books.[38]

Hemingway's talents for mimicry and close observation developed quickly, and he thought it would be worthwhile to see if he could make a go of it as a reporter. This first career would help Hemingway find an authentic voice as a writer, as would his experiences on the battlefields of Italy in World War I.

Italy and
Agnes von Kurowsky

His father wanted him to become a doctor, but Hemingway wasn't interested in a medical career. He did plan to go to college—to Oberlin, as Ed had done before him, or perhaps to the University of Illinois, but he wanted to work for a year or so on a big city newspaper before going to fight in the coming war. His uncle Tyler lived in Kansas City and had connections that helped Hemingway land a job as a cub reporter on the *Kansas City Star*. He moved there in October 1917.

Kansas City was something of a rough-and-tumble place at that time, and Hemingway embraced the life there. He lived for the moment, acted spontaneously, and welcomed any new experience. Initially, he lived with his uncle, but he soon decided that that kind of life was too much like Oak Park, so two months later he took up with a friend who had an attic lodging in a somewhat dodgy part of town. There, for $35 a month, he had a room and two meals a day. One of the areas Hemingway regularly visited was the red-light district; the locals crudely called it Woodrow Wilson Avenue, because there you could get "a piece at any price." Hemingway loved the thrumming energy of the newsroom and racing around the city to beat his competition in reaching a story first. Working long days, from about eight in the morning to around six at night, he rode in ambulances and called in at the police station, the railroad depot, and the hospital. He got an eyeful of violence and corruption in gangland America.[1] Once, he had to jump underneath a car for safety when city detectives got into an unexpected gunfight with IRS agents, mistaking them for criminals.[2] He saw several deaths in the hospital emergency room, and also reported on a suicide.

He was deeply affected by the other reporters—aggressive journalistic cowboys who lived recklessly and showed little restraint on the job. They did not so much report the news as attack it—they were symbolized by people like Lionel

Calhoun Moise, "a big, brutal son-of-a-bitch" whom Hemingway admired for his ability to make a story into "something alive."[3] Moise, who could have been the prototype for any number of Hemingway's tough-guy characters, was a wise-cracking cynic who never hesitated to weigh in on any topic. (He was fond of remarking on the lamentable state of the literary taste of a nation that would choose a national anthem that began, "Oh, say.") Most of all, the broad-shoul-dered, hard-living Moise flouted danger. One night—in circumstances that were never made clear—he got into an argument with a woman. They were parked in Moise's car on a deserted highway, and the woman stabbed him with a knife. As Hemingway later heard the story, Moise calmly took the knife away from her, hit her in the face, breaking her jaw, and then drove her back to Kansas City. He then wrote up the incident for the front page of the *Star*. Hemingway marveled at this kind of individualism and spirit. He began to court danger and use it to his advantage. Another night, a huge fire engulfed a Kansas City apartment building, and Hemingway turned the incident into a lucky break. Evading the patrolman who had cordoned off the area, Hemingway got inside the fire lines, where he could see everything clearly, and wrote it all down while sparks fell on his brand-new brown suit. When he emerged from the conflagration, the suit was full of holes, but Hemingway took away from the incident a lesson that he later imparted to his brother, Leicester: "Never risk anything unless you are prepared to lose it completely."[4]

Hemingway also witnessed government corruption. Always interested in health care, he frequently came upon the abominable living conditions of the poor and saw the lack of proper medical care for indigents. A major scandal erupted when the local hospital board embezzled tens of thousands of dollars. As a result, the hospital ran short of critical supplies, and smallpox and meningitis epidemics broke out. Hemingway studied them and the conditions in which they flourished with his naturalist's eye for detail. He also acted when prompted by his social conscience: encountering a smallpox victim who was being ignored by everyone in a crowded train station, Hemingway "picked up the man in [his] strong arms and carried him out of the station. Then he ordered a taxicab and took him personally to the General hospital, charging the expense to The Star."[5] Another time, he was called in to report on a workers' uprising and ended up helping quell the riot.

Like so many American authors—Crane, Twain, Dreiser, Whitman, and many more—Hemingway's early literary training took place at the city desk. The *Star* was particularly influential because of the style sheet it issued to new reporters on their first day on the job. Its guidelines for writing clear, clean copy read: "Use short sentences. Use short first paragraphs. Use vigorous English. Be positive, not negative." Hemingway later said that these "were the best rules I ever learned for the business of writing. I've never forgotten them."[6]

Many of the stories he filed concerned such topics as death (especially by suicide), heroism, and the military, a subject that always fascinated him. Yet even in his straight reportage, there is a satirical streak. Hemingway experimented with understatement, undermining the climax of a story, and conclusions full of ironic implications. A good example is a story he later singled out as one of his best from the period, "Mix War, Art, Dancing," which concerns a woman who is barred from attending a dance. The implication is that she is a prostitute, but nowhere in the story does Hemingway say so directly. In the middle of the story, he raises the possibility in his readers' minds that the woman is there for business purposes by showing her standing next to another woman, who is young and free of suspicion. He thereby implies "by omission," as Scott Donaldson writes, "a comparison between innocence and experience."[7] He was learning the art of omission, the idea that a skilled writer could achieve more force of impact by implication than by overt description, a theory he would later depict as writing "on the principle of the iceberg": "There is seven-eighths of it underwater for every part that shows."[8]

The most action, however, came from the anticipation of war. In the spring of 1917, Kansas City, like the rest of the country, was seized by war fever. Confronted with the mounting tide of Allied defeats and fearing that Kaiser Wilhelm could become unstoppable, the United States declared war on Germany on 6 April and rushed to mobilize troops to send to Europe. "Orders to All US Naval Forces to Mobilize at Once," read the banner headline on the *Kansas City Star*, and soon, all over the city, the ubiquitous poster of an American doughboy protecting a woman and child from a villainous German soldier could be seen. "Halt the Hun!" became a rallying cry and an iconic image of vanquishing evil.

In this hyperpatriotic atmosphere, Hemingway, like just about everybody else, was eager to enlist. He had been in Kansas City only a few weeks when he signed on with the Seventh Missouri Infantry of the National Guard. He had wanted to join the regular army, but he knew that his poor eyesight would dis-qualify him. This, he thought, would be the next-best thing, and although he boasted to his family back home that the drills, formations, and training exercises were all "regular army stuff," they weren't, and Hemingway knew it.[9] A good friend at the *Star*, Ted Brumback, was also ineligible to serve because of vision problems. Brumback had lost one of his eyes in a golfing accident many years before but, wanting to support the war in some capacity, had spent the summer of 1917 driving ambulances for the American Field Service in France. Brumback had told Hemingway of his experiences abroad, and so, when, by coincidence, representatives of the Italian government arrived in Kansas City in February 1918 to recruit drivers for Red Cross ambulances in Italy, Hemingway and Brumback signed on.

The Red Cross ambulance service was an immediate way for the United States to aid Italy in the interval before it could actually put troops on the ground there.[10] The Italians had been devastated by the German-led attack on Caporetto on 24 October 1917 (which Hemingway later depicted in a signature passage in *A Farewell to Arms*). Mass desertions had followed in its wake, and morale was low. Hemingway knew that driving ambulances would put him directly on the battlefield, even near the front. He was elated at the opportunity, and his youth and romanticized notions of war—inherited from his grandfathers and their tales of derring-do—shielded him from fear of the dangers that might befall him in a global conflict. He could hardly wait to ship out.

In part to pass the time, he and some of his friends from Kansas City took a brief vacation up in Michigan. The woods were always something of a siren call to Hemingway; he loved wading through the brush-choked creeks and pebble-bottomed streams in search of the elusive trout. Nature was solace and purity. In early May he took off to fish and loaf by the lake. At the end of the week, a telegram arrived in Oak Park notifying Hemingway that he was to report in New York on 13 May. Ed read it and wired his son in Seney, Michigan, that he had to get home right away. Hemingway's party, however, was nowhere near Seney at the time, and one of the local Native American guides had to be dispatched to find them. It took three days, and Hemingway got back to Oak Park just in time to pack up his things and head out.

In New York, Hemingway met up with Ted Brumback, and the Red Cross put him up at a hotel on Washington Square. During the ten days that Hemingway was there, he toured all the attractions, from the Statue of Liberty to the Wool-worth Tower—an Oak Parker agog at life in the metropolis. He and his friends also took full advantage of access to less reputable parts of town, doing plenty of things he could never have done back home.

Sowing oats, Hemingway decided to play a joke on his parents. On 14 May 1918 he wrote them a letter saying that he had met Mae Marsh, the actress, and that he and his "Mrs." had decided to get married at the "Little Church Around the Corner" before he shipped out.[11] The tone was straightforward enough, and Ed and Grace took him literally and immediately spiraled into anguish, figuring that their innocent boy had been played by a wanton woman in the big city. Never mind that Hemingway would scarcely have had time to find a woman, woo her, and then decide to marry, given his schedule of medical appointments, exams, and other duties. Ed replied earnestly to his son, "Marriage is a beautiful and wonderful thing; but it is sacred in proportion to the prayerfulness with which it is entered into. Such marriage as you suggest, would be unnatural and apt to bring great sorrow and misunderstanding."[12] Hemingway had to cable back that he was just joking. Nonetheless, his parents had been seriously concerned that he had fallen into the oldest trap around; Ed told him that Grace had lost five nights' sleep over the incident.

He was clearly enjoying himself in New York, and his enthusiasm for getting abroad didn't slacken. The Red Cross gave him two hundred dollars' worth of uniforms and supplies, as well as a steamer trunk, which, in his eagerness, he packed up right away. All the Red Cross recruits marched down Fifth Avenue a few days later in a show of unity, and Hemingway swelled with pride when he told his parents that President and Mrs. Wilson were in the reviewing stand.

"I went because I wanted to go. My county needed me, and I went and did whatever I was told."[13] So Hemingway soberly replied to a local reporter's question about why he had gone to war. The truth was probably less high-minded. The eighteen-year-old Hemingway went to war to get away from Oak Park and from the stultifying conformity of his parents' world, to savor something of life outside the bounds of a safe, complacent existence. But whatever the reasons, he could never have predicted the enormity of the outcome. Hemingway's experience in World War I was the most important of his life. It taught him that the universe was indifferent to human suffering and that fate was unalterable. It brought him face to face with the carnage of battle and gave him an unromanticized view of the human body in all its vulnerability—a contrast to the mysteries of organisms in which he had delighted while observing his father's medical practice and his specimens collection. Moreover, war taught him—as he would show again and again in his fiction—that dying was easy but living was hard. And it created the conditions for his first serious love affair, inaugurating a pattern in his life of associating romantic attraction with warfare. It would also later serve as the inspiration for one of his greatest novels, *A Farewell to Arms*.

He traveled to France on an ancient steamship called the *Chicago,* a castoff from the U.S. fleet that been leased to the French for the duration of the war. The first few days out were smooth, but the weather then turned stormy, and the ship started to heave and roll. Hemingway and his new friends shot craps, drank cheap wine, and played cards—in between dashes to the head when the rocking motion of the old boat overcame them. Still, in the midst of discomfort, Hemingway was jubilant. He thrilled to the idea that there were possibly German submarines around them, and when he wrote his parents at sea, he divulged the ship's approximate location, even though, as he said in his jocose manner, it "may be revealing a military secret to tell you."[14]

He first set foot on foreign soil at Bordeaux on 3 June 1918. The countryside was beautiful, rustic; the food was plain, simply prepared, and delicious. After a few days, he and his fellow recruits boarded a train and stepped out into the dark, dirty Gare du Nord in Paris, the steel trusses of its arched roofline a stopping place for thousands of noisy pigeons. Hemingway may have felt a slight prick of more serious purpose when the group was greeted crisply by French military officers, but it was soon on to more fun. As he had in New York, Hemingway sampled all that was on offer in Paris—the Tuileries, the Champs-Élysées, and the Folies Bergère. The city was being shelled from as close as fifty miles away, but since no one seemed to be afraid, Hemingway remained complacent. "Nothing but a dull boom," he reported in a letter home.[15]

On the evening of 4 June, the recruits took the overnight Paris-Lyon Mediterranée Express, across the French Alps and through the Fréjus Tunnel to Milan. His train steamed into Garibaldi Station the following morning. That afternoon, before even formally joining the unit, Hemingway was initiated into death in another country. But it had naught to do with the war, at least not directly. The drivers were called to the scene of an explosion at a munitions factory twelve miles outside the city. A co-worker, Milford Baker, described the grisly scene in his diary: "A terrible sight greeted us. . . . In the barbed wire fence enclosing the grounds and 300 yards from the factory were hung pieces of meat, chunks of heads, arms, legs, backs, hair and whole torsos. We grabbed a stretcher and started to pick up the fragments. The first we saw was the body of a woman, legs gone, head gone, intestines strung out. Hemmie and I nearly passed out cold but gritted our teeth and laid the thing on the stretcher. . . . One place we found a perfect body of a nude woman with only the head gone."[16] Later, Hemingway would use the repulsive process of picking human remains from a wire perimeter fence in his story "A Natural History of the Dead."

He was on the job after two days' training. As a Red Cross ambulance driver, Hemingway was attached to the Italian army with the assimilated rank of *sotto-tenente*, or second lieutenant. His unit, ambulance section 4, was based in Schio, a town in the northern province of Vicenza. The railway lines sliced across the rich fields of Lombardy to the snow-capped Alps in the distance. It was tedious work. They drove ancient, blunt-nosed Fiats, bringing casualties back to the field hospital, down hazardous roads pockmarked by craters caused by falling shells. Hemingway recalled how "they used to burn out their brakes going down the mountain roads with a full load of wounded and braking in low and finally using the reverse, and how the last ones [that is, the ambulances] were driven over the mountainside empty," so that they could be replaced by new ones just as fresh recruits were cycled into battle.[17] Amid the dusty, choking air of the plains and foothills, the vehicles looked like big, gray elephants lumbering up and down the mountainside.

There was not much to do around camp, but Hemingway made friends easily.[18] He contributed a story to the camp newspaper, *Ciao,* that was a parody of Ring Lardner, but, restless after a couple of weeks, he requested a transfer from section 4 to what was called the "field kitchen service"—basically a canteen on wheels stationed closer to the front. There were twenty-seven such kitchens in the danger zone. The soldiers called them "American bars," and their purpose was to have chocolate, cigarettes, coffee, and other comforts within reach of the soldiers doing the heavy fighting, an easy way of shoring up the steadily eroding morale. Hemingway was doubtful about the effect this would have; in "A Way You'll Never Be," Nick Adams remarks sardonically, "if they see one American uniform that is supposed to make them believe others are coming" (503). But he was thrilled to be closer to the action. "War," he later wrote Scott Fitzgerald, "groups the maximum of material and speeds up the action and brings out all sorts of stuff that normally you have to wait a lifetime to get."[19]

The canteen he took charge of was in Fossalta, a little village at a bend in the meandering Piave River northeast of Venice. He billeted at an old stone country house with Ted Brumback and fellow volunteers Bill Horne and Howell Jenkins, all later to become lifelong friends. The house had been lived in by the same family since the early 1700s. Hemingway would visit the trenches, but only during lulls in the fighting; he didn't think about the danger. He wrote jaunty letters to friends in Oak Park and made wisecracks about "ye olde village." "If anybody had told me . . . last year that . . . I would be sitting out in front of a dug out in a nice trench . . . 40 yards from the Austrian lines . . . I would have said, 'Take another sip.'"[20] Hemingway was oblivious to the threats surrounding him.

All of that changed in an instant. On the afternoon of 7 July, Hemingway rode out on his bicycle with rations of black coffee, chocolate bars, and peanut butter for the men at the front, only a few miles away. When he got there, he heard a rumor that there was going to be an offensive that night. He talked the troops into letting him come back to the line that evening to see for himself. At about 12:30 in the morning, 8 July, hunkered down in the trenches, Hemingway saw a flash in the sky. An Austrian mortar shell sped toward them—basically a can full of pieces of junk steel that burst on contact. The shell hit the post where Hemingway was standing. He was knocked down by the hot blast and temporarily lost consciousness.

When he recovered, he did a very brave thing. The precise details have varied over time as the teller of the tale (often Hemingway himself) alternately exaggerated or mangled attempts to relive history; because of Hemingway's inherent boastfulness, many have also doubted some of his claims. But there is no question that what Hemingway did next was heroic. His friend Ted Brumback told Hemingway's parents what happened in a letter: "The concussion of the explosion knocked him unconscious and buried him in earth. There was an Italian between Ernest and the shell. He was instantly killed, while another, standing a few feet away, had both his legs blown off. A third Italian was badly wounded and this one Ernest, after he had regained consciousness, picked up on his back and carried to the first aid dugout."[21] The X-rays later showed that, in addition to being hit by shrapnel from the mortar shell, Hemingway's legs had also been raked with machine-gun fire, which he variously compared to being stung repeatedly by wasps or getting smacked in the leg with an icy snowball.[22] When he was blown up, he later recalled, he felt life go out of him and go off and then come back.

Medics took him to a barn where the roof had been shot off. He lay there in agony for two hours, staring up at the night sky and wondering if he was going to die. Then he was transported to a first-aid station at Fornaci and given morphine for the pain. A priest passing by assumed he was near death and administered last rites. Then he was moved yet again: first to the town hall and then to a dressing station in the local school, before finally being carried away by ambulance to a field hospital in Casier, in the Treviso province. There, doctors removed 227 pieces of shrapnel from his body. The bullets from the machine guns, however, had to remain lodged in his right kneecap until he could be sent to Milan for surgery. For his actions, Hemingway earned a formal commendation from the Red Cross and a citation from the Italian government, along with its second-highest decoration, the Medaglia d'Argento al Valore Militare. The citation read: "Gravely wounded by numerous pieces of shrapnel from an enemy shell, with an admirable spirit of brotherhood, before taking care of himself, he rendered generous assistance to the Italian soldiers more seriously wounded by the same explosion and did not allow himself to be carried elsewhere until they had been evacuated." Although a noncombatant, Hemingway nonetheless became a bona fide war hero. He was not, however, the first American wounded in Italy, as some have believed.[23]

He felt guilty about the medal, thinking he did not deserve it. His feelings of survivor's guilt would carry over, some years later, into such stories as "Soldier's Home," about the shell-shocked Harold Krebs, and "Now I Lay Me," in which Nick Adams lies awake at night in the hospital with the feeling that if he shut his eyes he would never wake up and that his soul would leave his body. Hemingway began to appreciate the uncertainty of the unknown, of what lay beyond him on the other side, if indeed there was another side. He began to recognize that living with the anticipation of death was truly horrifying; it made life arduous and at times seemingly unendurable. Dying, however, was an easy solution to stress and pain. He began to believe that it took great force of will not to bend to the power of the seductive siren call of death. This perspective became the bedrock of Hemingway's philosophy.

His letters home during his recuperation, therefore, are full of a jocosity meant to hide his guilt at not being obliterated in the blast. In his first letter, Hemingway called the incident "getting bunged up," and detailed with great enthusiasm all of the "really swell" collection of battlefield souvenirs that he had amassed. He then went on to say, "It's the next best thing to getting killed and reading your own obituary," "Well I can now hold up my hand and say I've been shelled by high explosive, shrapnel, and gas. . . . Maybe I'll get a hand grenade later," and "So we took off my trousers and the old limbs were still there."[24] Some have argued that these letters are disingenuous—deliberately couched in a cavalier tone in order not to upset his parents about his brush with death. But with the advantage of hindsight, one can see this as the beginning of Hemingway's pattern of deflection and deflation—of diverting his true feelings and replacing them with audacious indifference, of describing momentous experiences with casual understatement.

———

After several days in Treviso, he was sent to Milan on a rickety train, "complete with flies and gore," for surgery and physical therapy.[25] He arrived in Milan on 17 June and was driven to the Ospedale Maggiore, the first medical and surgical institution ever to be operated by Americans on Italian soil. It was a beautiful, elegant place—a regal stone mansion on the Via Manzoni in the fashionable Piazza della Scala district, near the Duomo and the Galleria. More like a hotel than a hospital, the building contained drawing rooms, a library with a piano and Victrola, single bedrooms for the patients, offices for the nurses, and a professional kitchen with, as one patient recalled, "a beautiful set of utensils containing enough copper to make the German High Command copper-green with envy." A wide rooftop terrace opened up to the sun. Striped awnings shaded wide wicker chairs and chaises, flower boxes and potted plants adorned the deck, and two singing canaries, named George and Martha Washington, were kept in a cage near the entryway.

Just the week before, the hospital had greeted another new recruit, this one a nurse named Agnes von Kurowsky. Born near Philadelphia on 5 January 1892, she was the daughter of an exiled Polish count, Paul Moritz von Kurowsky, and a pretty American debutante from Washington, D.C. Agnes's father had served in the U.S. Army as a civil service language instructor, and the family had lived in Alaska and Vancouver. Agnes had known danger, uncertainty, and grief. As a young girl, she had been stricken with diphtheria and had nearly died. Her sister, not so lucky, had perished from scarlet fever at the tender age of seven. Paul requested a transfer to Washington, D.C., but succumbed to typhus soon after relocating there. Agnes and her mother, in much reduced circumstances, moved into an apartment and Agnes started working at the Washington Public Library. When the war broke out, she wanted to serve, and trained as a nurse at Bellevue Hospital in New York. She applied to the Red Cross Nursing Service in early January 1918 and was accepted for service overseas. She had sterling credentials— in addition to a private education, she could speak French and German fluently. The "von" in her surname did give the government momentary pause, but her father's background in international affairs seems to have allayed any concerns about her loyalty to the United States.

Agnes was twenty-six and alluring, her pale complexion offset by blue-gray eyes and soft chestnut hair. She was gentle-looking, kindly, and loving, but her gaze could be penetrating as well. She seemed to be able to take the measure of a person with speed and precision. She knew what she wanted out of life and had come to Italy for adventure.

She soon made friends with her fellow nurses and the patients. Henry Villard, an ambulance driver from section 1 who had been hospitalized with a decidedly unheroic case of jaundice, recalled that when Agnes came into a room, "the entire place seemed to brighten because of her presence." She was "the most glamorous of the nurses" there, he said, "kind, quick, intelligent . . . and blessed with a sense of humor that verged on the mischievous." Agnes knew how attractive she was. She had had an affair with a physician in New York but had suddenly backed away when it became too serious. She did not like being alone, and she flirted with the officers in Milan, who felt grateful merely to be in her presence—to have the honor of escorting her on carriage rides and sharing candlelit dinners in expensive trattorias.

When Hemingway arrived in Milan, Agnes was involved with an Italian army officer, but by late August, about two weeks after Hemingway's surgery on the tenth, she had begun to take an interest in him. At first, she called him "the

Kid," as if to underscore their seven-year age difference, but her vanity made her encourage Hemingway in his affections. She allowed him to take her out to dinner, and they apparently began seeing each other surreptitiously, mostly at night, when Agnes had volunteered to take a shift—perhaps so that she could be near "the Kid."

_____

As Hemingway's relationship with Agnes progressed, he became friends with some of his fellow hospital patients—in particular, three officers whom Hemingway admired for their worldliness and sense of style: Henry Villard, Nick Nerone, and Chink Dorman-Smith. All were older than he was, and Hemingway saw them as father figures, people who could teach him about life. Hemingway always needed the companionship of other men. A pattern of emotions developed where he would pour out romantic solicitude toward a woman he was in love with, such as Agnes, and then pull back, withdrawing his feelings into himself, in terse, objective discussions of other matters with male "comrades." Hemingway's relationships with Villard, Nerone, and Dorman-Smith became a counterbalance to his emotional immersion in Agnes.

Villard, who arrived in Italy shortly before Hemingway, had been a freshman at Harvard College when, consumed with patriotic fervor, he joined a group of classmates signing up to serve in the ambulance corps. Descended from William Lloyd Garrison, the abolitionist newspaper editor, Villard, who later became a U.S. ambassador to four different countries, was the grandson of Henry Villard, the financier and publisher. His family was well known in New York for the landmark Villard Houses on Madison Avenue (now part of the New York Palace Hotel). Villard and Hemingway quickly became inseparable. They lolled around the hospital terrace "like privileged brothers of a small fraternity," smoking pipe tobacco and endless packs of Macedonia cigarettes as they played low-stakes poker games and rehashed the war news. Villard was struck by Hemingway's eagerness for male company—Hemingway wanted to know every detail of Villard's boyhood and his time in college—all the places he'd traveled to and experiences he'd had. He wanted to know everything.

Villard, in turn, was mesmerized by Hemingway and the cavalier poses he would strike: he remembered him once lying in bed picking bits of shrapnel out of his leg with a pen knife. Hemingway's stagey attitude succeeded in making acolytes of the other patients. Villard recalled, "We and a few other guests formed a nucleus around the chief guest . . . visiting him in turn" and talking through the tedious hours of sedentary recuperation. Hemingway bribed the night porter to smuggle in flasks of whisky; the nurses alternately pampered him and scolded him like a naughty child for being "'smarty' and uncooperative. But he got away with such unruly behavior . . . because everyone melted before his youthful, seemingly unaffected, and spontaneous charm," as Villard put it. He quickly became like the boy in grammar school that all the other kids wanted to be around.

Nick Nerone was an Italian soldier who had had volunteered in 1916 and
fought on the Alpine front, where he was wounded several times. Hemingway
admired Nerone's bravery and his humility, for he was not once to boast of his
battle experiences. Nerone was decorated for his heroism in the battles at Gorizia
and the Isonzo. Later, Nerone was in the mountains along the Piave River in October 1917 when Austrian forces poured through the mountain passes into Italy
and threatened Venice—the humiliating defeat at Caporetto depicted in *A Farewell
to Arms*. In early manuscript versions of that novel, the chief character, Frederic
Henry, was modeled closely on Nerone, a true war hero. As Hemingway came
to doubt the idea of heroism, however, and as the world became disillusioned in
the aftermath of the world-scale conflict, Hemingway remade Henry into a much
different character—cynical, sarcastic, and embittered.

Perhaps the most important and lasting of these friendships was with Eric
Edward "Chink" Dorman-Smith, an acting major in the Royal Northumberland
Fusiliers. Hemingway met Dorman-Smith at the Anglo-American Club in Milan
on 3 November 1918, the Italian armistice day. Chink, born in 1895, was from a
family of squires in County Cavan, Ireland, and had been educated at Upping-
ham School and the Royal Military College at Sandhurst. His family had had
an illustrious military history; his father had been a major in the Boer War, and
Chink, when Hemingway met him, had sustained serious wounds in three different battles since December 1914.

Chink was everything that Hemingway wanted to become. He was the very
model of the citizen-soldier, the man of dignity and emotional restraint—a type
that Hemingway had always admired. Chink was physically fit, with a lean frame,
a long face, and a sharp, angular nose. He looked like the sort of introspective
English gentleman of leisure whose life was spent managing the family estate,
except when his country called him to soldiering, at which he would take up arms
at once, never questioning his patriotic duty. Chink liked skiing, hunting, hiking,
and fishing but was, as John Dos Passos remarked, "chary of words."[26] In fact,
Chink's dry sense of humor was a signature trait that surely affected Hemingway
as he began to model his first public persona—the man with a quiet burden,
jaded by the experience of battle. In Milan, the two friends strolled through the
city like young princes. They ate out at Biffi's, Milan's oldest and best-known
restaurant, and went drinking at the Cova, one of Italy's swankiest cafés, near the
fashion district. People who knew him said that Chink put himself in dangerous
situations simply because it never crossed his mind that he should do anything
differently. He had a suave éclat about him, too, that Hemingway must have
envied. While Chink was dining with Hemingway one night, a waitress rushed
in with the news that the war against Austria was over. Chink looked up from his
drink, cast a glance around the room, and mused, "So we are to go on living!"

Chink's privileged background and bravery under fire made Hemingway feel
embarrassed that he hadn't actually been involved in the fighting, despite his
heroic act and his having the wounds to prove it. Another pattern that emerged

in Hemingway's life was his massaging of the truth of his experiences into compensatory lies—just enough prevarication so that he seemed to be the equal of his peers in love and war. When he returned to Chicago, Hemingway found himself marching in a parade in honor of the Italian army with Nick Nerone. He led Nerone to believe that he had been transferred from the ambulance brigade to the army's Ancona Brigade and had received his wounds there, not while working for the Red Cross. Similarly, Hemingway told Chink that he had been wounded leading elite Arditi storm troopers on Monte Grappa. (The troop's name derives from the Italian verb *ardire*—to dare—and translates as "the braves.") To that fiction Hemingway added a romantic element, bragging that all he'd seen of Sicily had come through a bedroom window because the proprietress of his hotel had hidden his clothes and kept him as her lover for an entire week.

Chink and Hemingway maintained close ties after the war ended. Chink was godfather to Hemingway's first child, and the two men met up several times in Europe after Hemingway returned there in the early 1920s as a journalist and writer. Chink's continuing effect on Hemingway's imagination can be seen in the numerous characters whom he modeled in part on his friend—especially Wilson, the white hunter in "The Short Happy Life of Francis Macomber," and Colonel Cantwell in *Across the River and into the Trees*.[27] Chink fueled Hemingway's desire to be seen as a war hero and influenced how he behaved after leaving Italy in 1919 and returning home to Oak Park.

———

At the same time, Hemingway's relationship with Agnes, or "Ag," as he called her, developed into a serious love affair. Part of it was the exoticism of being in a European capital, squiring about an older woman of aristocratic descent. She thought of him tenderly, lovingly, as "mia ammalato" (my patient). She took him on carriage rides around the ancient city, visiting its famous sites. Strolling through the Galleria, Hemingway looked up and was enchanted with its magnificent blue glass ceiling. The same, too, with the Duomo, its fairyland façade and petrified forest of spires reaching up toward the heavens. Around Agnes, Hemingway was sheepish, grinning, playful—and quite seriously in love.

The progress of their relationship can be charted by Agnes's letters to Hemingway, which she saved and later gave to Henry Villard. The letters are bold and ardent. In many of them, Agnes refers to their future together as husband and wife. Her closing salutations almost always include some variant of "I love you." (Sometimes she even playfully signed a letter "Mrs. Kid.") At one point, Agnes gave Hemingway a ring, which he can be seen wearing in one of the photos of him in his Italian army uniform.

That October, Agnes had to leave Milan for three months to work in Florence and Treviso. She carried his photograph with her and wrote him every day. On returning to Milan, their affair continued apace. Some say it accelerated—that Agnes and Hemingway had a sexual relationship. As would be true in many cases in his life, Hemingway started the speculation with a boastful remark to

Dorman-Smith about how "it takes a trained nurse to make love to a man with one leg in a splint."[28] Presuming that a worldly veteran like Chink must have had lots of sexual experiences, Hemingway did not want to seem inferior. But whether Hemingway's relationship with Agnes was sexual doesn't really matter. The important fact is that he developed an emotional dependence on her, even as his self-confidence grew dramatically from his ability to seduce an older woman.

Agnes later resented the fact that she was the model for Catherine Barkley in *A Farewell to Arms,* but she and Hemingway were closer to the fictional Catherine and Frederic Henry than one might think. At the time, at least, Agnes felt that she loved him; he, younger, responded in kind and felt that they were destined to be married. Bill Horne later described Agnes as "very, very much" in love with Hemingway.[29] They planned to marry when he recovered and return to the United States. Her letters seem to confirm this, for they are full of sincere sentiment. As she had earlier confided to her diary, "Once written you can't take back what you have said."[30] As it turned out, she would eventually do just that, but the language in which she told Hemingway that she loved and wanted to marry him remains. It was that language and sentiment that Hemingway took into his heart and carried with him when he returned home in January 1919.

Agnes's feelings for Hemingway actually grew deeper when he left Italy. In December 1918, she wrote him that if he received her letter around Christmastime, "just make believe you're getting a gift from me (as you will some day) and let me tell you how I love you, & wish that we could be together for our first Christmas." In January: "just remember I'm looking to you for my future life." And later, she opened with "Dear Old Man" because "I want to see how it's going to sound." But by February of the new year she was referring obliquely to "ups and downs" in her life and how "the future" was "a puzzle" that she was not sure "how to solve."[31] One might argue, as some have, that Hemingway half-expected to be jilted, but that is doubtful given Agnes's earlier letters. She hinted at confusion over her emotional state and her plans once she left the Red Cross, but did not say anything explicit. Then, on 7 March, she abruptly announced that she had fallen in love with an Italian army officer, Domenico Caracciolo, a Neapolitan duke, and that they expected to marry in the spring.

When Hemingway received the news, he fell apart. He was so devastated that he took to his bed for several days and lay there, sullen, uncommunicative, and morose. As the mind controls the body, Hemingway's thoughts, anxieties, and nightmares caused him to become physically ill, and he had to rely on his sister Marcelline to nurse him through the ordeal. After a few days, he mustered the courage to write Bill Horne and bare his grief: "I'm just smashed by it," he said, adding that if he hadn't left Italy, the breakup would never have happened. If only he could go back and handle things differently, if only the circumstances could be changed, he thought, his heart would not have been broken. But there was no way to turn back the clock. To Hemingway's credit, he accepted the "sad truth" with stoicism and resolve.[32] In fact, Agnes's engagement to Caracciolo dissolved a few short months later, when the duke's mother refused to permit his marriage to an "American adventuress."[33] Agnes wrote Hemingway in June to tell him what had happened. She hinted that she now wished to renew their romance, but Hemingway did not reply. He began to adhere to an ascetic regimen of never discussing casualties.

But Hemingway never got over Agnes—just as Charles Dickens never got over Maria Beadnell or Thomas Hardy over Tryphena Sparks. Like those writers, Hemingway kept the memory of Agnes alive in the wish-fulfillment elements of his fiction. In *For Whom the Bell Tolls, Across the River and into the Trees,* and other works, a strong theme is an older man's dominance of an innocent younger girl. To assuage his wounded pride, Hemingway would satisfy himself with respect to Agnes in his imagination, if not in reality.

When the war ended, Agnes was transferred to another part of Italy, where she nursed orphaned children who had been injured by bomb explosions. She returned briefly to New York but after six months volunteered to go to Romania to serve the Red Cross there. In 1926 she again enlisted as a Red Cross nurse in Haiti, where she was married for a brief time, but after her return permanently to the United States in the early 1930s, the marriage dissolved. Agnes then married a widower with three children, left nursing, and moved to Virginia Beach, Virginia, where she and her husband ran a motel. She kept her diary and her letters to Hemingway safe until her death in 1984. She often thought about the young soldier who went on to become the world's most famous writer. But she had vowed to herself that she would maintain her privacy and not announce to the world that she had been Hemingway's first serious love. In their old age, she and her husband often vacationed in Florida and visited Cuba. Agnes thought from time to time of looking Hemingway up but never did.

Michigan, Chicago, and Hadley

A hero's welcome awaited Hemingway when his steamer docked at New York Harbor on 21 January 1919. News of the supposed first-wounded boy in the war had reached the States ahead of him, and, to Hemingway's surprise, waiting at the pier was a reporter from the *New York Sun*. Hemingway surely could not have anticipated this and must not have known what he was expected to say. He recovered quickly, however, and described the attack in which he'd been wounded. The reporter took it all in, nodding eagerly, waiting for more. And then, probably caught up in a whirlwind of emotion, Hemingway embellished the story, figuring that the brush with death gave him license to exaggerate a bit. Someone so young surely enjoyed the novelty of being an instant celebrity as well.

The false additions were, as one might expect from a nineteen-year-old, not very credible, but the press, eager for a good story, loved it, and Hemingway started to realize what good copy he could make if he stretched the truth. So he told the reporter that after the medics had pulled thirty-two pieces of shrapnel from his head and body, they told him he would need perhaps a dozen more operations over the coming year. Hemingway said that he didn't think this would be necessary—that the doctors were worrywarts and were exaggerating his potential incapacity—and that, bored after lying about the hospital, he had returned to the front and kept fighting until the armistice. Seizing a good opportunity, Hemingway then announced that he was looking for work. In addition to his wartime adventures, he touted his experience as a newsman in Kansas City and said that any New York paper that "wants a man who is not afraid of work and wounds" should let him know what was on offer. No opportunities came his way, however, despite the page 8 headline that appeared the following day: "Has 227 Wounds, but Is Looking for Job: Kansas City Boy First to Return from Italian Front."[1]

From a public show to a private moment: at the Lasalle Street station in Chicago a few days later, where Ed and Marcelline met his train, the mood could not have been more different or more subdued. An anxious parent waited on the cold platform. As the train rolled in, Ed caught a glimpse of his son wearing a khaki uniform and a black cape, and he rushed to the stairs that descended from the side of the car. His father and sister saw not the returning hero but the young boy who had stepped into an arena of ugly, traumatizing violence. "Here boy!—Here," Ed said, "lean on me!"[2] And they started out of the station, down another long flight of stairs. Hemingway shrugged off the pain, but his father, the physician, knew that he was hurting, and when they arrived home in Oak Park, Hemingway gave in.

Hemingway was suffering from post-traumatic stress disorder. It was called shell shock at the time, but the name was not the only difference. Shell-shocked soldiers were thought to be mentally able to pull themselves out of their depression, that it was an emotional rather than a medical condition. Soldiers were left to fight their own mental battles. As a result, many never recovered. More than eighty thousand cases of shell shock were reported during the war, and by 1927 there were still more than sixty-five thousand men in mental hospitals worldwide as a result of the condition.[3] Today, victims of PTSD are treated pharmaceutically. No such option existed for Hemingway, and he suffered from the effects of nearly dying for the rest of his life. He lost his emotional balance, developed conflicting and ambivalent relationships with friends, family members, and lovers, and suffered great insecurity about his noncombatant role in the war.

PTSD is an anxiety disorder that develops after one is exposed to a terrifying event that presents grave physical danger. It is severe and can continue to the point that the person affected is plagued by widespread psychological trauma. Hemingway manifested the key symptoms: he was unaffectionate, especially with people he used to be close to, such as his sisters; he was irritable and aggressive; he was easily startled; and he had trouble sleeping. (If he went out at night, Ursula faithfully waited up for him, knowing that he would be frightened in the darkness of his bedroom. She sometimes even slept with him to calm his anxiety.) Today, many victims of PTSD undergo counseling in which they relive the experience in a therapeutic setting, sometimes involving trusted friends or family members in reliving the event with them. Hemingway kept to himself and did not talk about the event in honest, straightforward terms. When he did talk about it, he made it into the stuff of fiction. Because he never received proper treatment, Hemingway battled depression, insecurity, aggression, and—later in life—paranoia. Lingering physical injuries from the blast went unnoticed and eventually, in combination with other injuries, evolved into serious physical and mental illnesses. These were all factors that finally drove him to suicide at a relatively young age.

As Michael Reynolds notes in *The Young Hemingway,* no one at the time with mental illness would have gone to see a doctor, as this would have been seen as a sign of weakness. Moreover, depression and mental instability ran in the family. Ed twice left the family for short stays in New Orleans to repair his shattered nerves (in 1903 and again in 1908). Moreover, as Reynolds puts it, "Insomnia, erratic blood pressure, blinding headaches and severe depression were the genetic inheritance of Ernest Hemingway, his sisters and brothers."[4]

Neither Ed nor Grace recognized the severity of their son's illness. Then, when Hemingway received the shocking news from Agnes that she was engaged to someone else, he grew worse. For the next several months, he more or less took to his bed. In the mornings, bundled up in the Red Cross comforter he had brought home as a souvenir, he would sleep and read. In the afternoons, he would take a bit of exercise, then return to his third-floor retreat after an early supper. According to his sister Madelaine ("Sunny"), then fourteen, he would stow bottles of various liqueurs behind the books on the shelves and imbibe when he felt the need. The alcohol, combined with the natural depressive effects of his trauma, made things worse. He would even press a drink on Sunny when she came upstairs to check on him. When she refused, he would drop the matter, but he told her again and again not to let the conformity of Oak Park keep her from experiencing life. "Don't be afraid to taste all the other things in life that aren't here in Oak Park," he would say. "There's a whole big world out there full of people who really feel things. . . . Sometimes I think we only half live over here." And then he would seem to trail off, back into his depressive stupor. Marcelline understood what her brother was thinking and feeling: "For Ernest it must have been something like being put in a box with the cover nailed down to come home to conventional, suburban Oak Park living, after his own vivid experiences."[5]

The effects of Hemingway's brush with death cannot be overestimated. Being wounded, leaving Italy, returning home, losing Agnes, and having to go through a painful physical and emotional recuperation—all of these things constituted the formative period in Hemingway's life. They produced two overarching and contradictory results; the first was the primal wound that never went away psychologically and that would manifest itself in various iterations throughout his life, leading eventually to his clinical depression and suicide.[6] But they also, ironically, gave him a boost that he would not otherwise have had. Like the love affair with Agnes, Hemingway's being wounded provided him the opportunity to shape himself in an image that would prove enduringly appealing, and it gave him something to write about that would appear over and over again, in different symbolic forms, throughout his career. The stress produced by these conflicting impulses exacerbated some of his worst characteristics: his anxiety and insecurity, his harshness toward himself, and his snap judgments and mistreatment of others. It also gave him a taste for violence and danger that would never abate.

The extent of Hemingway's celebrity became clear to him during this time, when parties and gala celebrations were held in his honor. He launched himself into lengthy rounds of public appearances, telling his story, showing off his medals, and talking about what he'd seen on the battlefield. Hemingway wore his Red Cross uniform, and he polished these performances into engaging narrative accounts. Speaking to church groups, social clubs, high school societies, and literally anyone who invited him, Hemingway would show up in his field uniform and pass around his torn, bullet-riddled trousers, urging his listeners to count the number of holes in them.[7] He made a sobering impression on his audiences. Frank Platt, his former English teacher, recalled that "it was a very impressive evening" when Hemingway spoke to a school assembly: "they felt that this man had been through the war and these were the dents of his armor."[8]

Yet Hemingway continued to doubt the extent of his heroism because he had not been, technically, a soldier. Time and again he would seize opportunities to serve near battle—in the Spanish Civil War, in China, and in World War II—as if to make up for his noncombatant status in the Great War. Occasionally, however, he would let down his guard and confide to his male friends more honestly how he felt. "You know and I know," he wrote his former commander, Jim Gamble, two months after returning to Oak Park, "that all the real heroes are dead. If I had been a really game guy I would have gotten myself killed off."[9] But Hemingway never let such candor penetrate the finely filamented scrim in which he wrapped his public image. It was a defensive measure to which he clung tightly for the rest of his life.

____

Hemingway spent the summer of 1919 in Michigan, fishing, hunting, and camping with friends. Keeping company with other men was always a means by which Hemingway retreated from physical and emotional stress. One extended expedition, near Seney, fishing the Big and Little Fox Rivers, would inspire one of Hemingway's best stories, "Big Two-Hearted River," in which Nick Adams returns home from the war and restores himself through the orderly and methodical rituals of fishing. (It is also a great example of Hemingway's tutorial instinct, for it is a story about teaching that illustrates Hemingway's need to do things the "right" way.) The woods and river satisfy Nick's "need for thinking, the need to write, other needs." "It was all back of him," Hemingway wrote, asserting that the past could be put to rest—at least in fiction (308).

Just when it seemed that he could sink no lower, Hemingway's depressive condition took another hit when his parents' marriage looked like it was about to disintegrate. The beginnings of Ed's depression took place when he began to vacation less with the family in Michigan, staying behind in Oak Park instead. He was conscientious about his patients and he worried constantly about money; he felt that he had to work all the time in order to keep the wolves at bay. Grace, by contrast, was spending more time at Windemere—so much so, she told her husband, that she was feeling she needed some room for herself—a refuge where she could play the piano, read, and be alone with her thoughts. This was what led her to build another cottage across the lake, which she called Longfield Farm. Ed objected to building a second cottage, but ultimately he could not stand up to Grace. Unable to express his true feelings to his wife, he somewhat embarrassingly unburdened himself to the builder, to whom he sent a letter disavowing responsibility for the project. Marcelline took Grace's side in the dispute, claiming to understand her need to be alone, practice her piano, and be something other than "the family drudge," as Grace put it, standing at the sink and cookstove:

> It has been my purpose for 14 years ever since I purchased the farm in the face of strong opposition and much abusive language to build a little cottage on this very hill. . . . That it has been steadily thwarted up to the present time has only piled up disappointment. . . . I have gone faithfully 21 summers to the same place Windemere which was very pleasant and adequate for 8 or 9 years but after my father's death and two subsequent attacks of typhoid fever which I underwent to say nothing of other causes the place became hateful to me, so much so that I had a nervous breakdown summer after summer.[10]

But Ed, keeping to himself back in Oak Park, was convinced that Grace's need for quiet and solitude was a slight to him. Grace maintained that she had no ulterior motives. As she reportedly told Marcelline, Ed "*thinks* I want to be away from *him*. . . . That's not true."[11]

When the cottage was finished, Marcelline took Ruth Arnold's place as the family housekeeper and governess at Windemere, and Ruth moved into Longfield with Grace. Ruth Arnold is a nearly invisible figure in Hemingway biography, even though she had been virtually an adjunct member of the family since 1907.[12] Even though she was a surrogate mother to Leicester, Marcelline, and Madelaine, and virtually raised them, she is, oddly, not mentioned anywhere in their memoirs of family life. Ruth Arnold played a central role in Hemingway's upbringing, was around him for much of his youth, and in the crucial months following his return from war, she became a source of conflict, anxiety, and anger within the Hemingway family because of rumors that she and Grace were lovers. A troubled girl from a broken home, at age thirteen she was taken in by Grace, more than twenty years her senior, and invited to live in the North Highland Avenue house as a "mother's helper." Ruth was embraced by all the children, who called their nursemaid and housekeeper "Bobs" or "Bobsy." Ruth, whose letters to Grace were always addressed "Dearest Muv," lived in the house, cooked and cleaned, and was much of the time the main caregiver for the children, who grew to love her deeply. Ruth always went along on the family's annual summer visits to Windemere, where she helped Grace with domestic chores. By 1912, she had begun taking voice lessons from Grace. Clearly, she was enamored of Grace in various ways, whether emotionally, intellectually, artistically, or some combination thereof. At one point, she told Grace, "Ever since I've known you, my soul has craved for the luxurious and more beautiful things in life."[13]

Ed felt threatened by Ruth and must have perceived at least the possibility of an amorous relationship between her and his wife. At the end of that summer, when the family returned to Oak Park, Ed refused to let Ruth into the house. He fired her on the spot, and she moved away from Oak Park. Over the following several months, Ruth wrote pleadingly to Grace, asking her to find a way to allow her to rejoin the family. "No distance can separate my soul from the one I love so dearly," she told Grace.[14] Grace, trying to reassure Ed of her fidelity as wife and mother, wrote that "no one in the world can ever take my husband's place unless he abdicates it to play at petty jealousy with his wife's loyal girl friend,"[15] but Grace's language could hardly have reassured Ed, and her suggestion that he had dreamed up the whole problem undoubtedly put him again on the defensive.

Although Ed had dismissed Ruth and barred her from physical contact with any of the Hemingways, she and Grace continued to stay in touch by letter. Ruth also apparently continued to help Grace at Longfield during the summers (surreptitiously?); in one letter, she said she planned to arrive there after Ed had returned to Oak Park. After Ed's suicide in 1928, Ruth returned to live with Grace as her companion. Some years later, the two of them left Oak Park and moved to nearby River Forest.[16] Hemingway regularly sent Ruth checks to help with expenses. Although the nature of the relationship between the two women remains unknown, Hemingway may have felt somewhat embarrassed by his mother's closeness to another woman. He probably also felt obliged to take his father's side in the matter, to defend his honor, so to speak. But Hemingway also seems to have understood his mother's personality and emotional makeup—an unconventional level of insight for the time—and it is likely that he secretly approved of this kind of covert rebellion against social norms. It validated his own rebellion against bourgeois orthodoxies—not just the possibility of women having same-sex relationships, but the whole notion of a woman as married to domesticity and the care of children rather than having a professional life of her own. After all, only Hadley Richardson, the first of Hemingway's four wives, conformed to this latter-day Victorian stereotype. His other wives were all liberated working women with goals and ideals of their own—much like Grace.

Hemingway's seemingly petty public statements and private actions concerning his mother later in life—for example, forbidding her to give a magazine interview about life at home during his childhood—were probably meant to protect his masculine image against revelations that his mother may have been "different" in any way (he behaved similarly toward his son Gregory, who struggled with his sexual identity). After Grace's death in 1951, Ruth Arnold continued for a while to live in the River Forest house, and Hemingway apparently continued to send her money. Ruth remained in touch with all of the Hemingway children for the rest of their lives.

_____

Confused and worried about his parents, Hemingway chose to keep his distance that fall of 1919 and perhaps work some things out for himself. He stayed on in

Petoskey rather than return to Oak Park. He roomed at a local boarding house and tried to write some stories based on battlefield scenes and wounded-hero themes. By this time he had come around to thinking of himself as a writer and was beginning to try and start a career as an author. He wrote and revised the tales diligently and submitted them to some of the best magazines, including the *Saturday Evening Post,* but had none accepted. He did receive an encouraging note from George Horace Lorimer, the *Post*'s well-known editor, which Hemingway regarded as "a good sign," but what he was really hoping for, a better sign, he said, was "a large check."[17]

When he wasn't writing, Hemingway could be seen around Petoskey in the company of young women. One, Marjorie Bump, was a seventeen-year-old waitress whom Hemingway had gotten in the habit of waiting for when the local high school let out in the afternoons. Another was Irene Goldstein, a college girl with whom Hemingway played tennis. But the most interesting of these acquaintances, a girl named Grace Quinlan, was only fourteen years old. She regarded Hemingway as a kind of big brother, and Hemingway nicknamed Grace "Sister Luke." They took long walks together in the afternoons, and Hemingway seems to have had a brotherly affection for her, but this did not stop the neighbors in Petoskey from raising their eyebrows at the prospect of a shabby, unemployed writer escorting a girl nearly ten years his junior to local dances and other village events. Hemingway was completely proper in his interactions with these girls, but it is noteworthy that after the debacle of his affair with Agnes, a much older and more experienced woman, he should then take up with a succession of schoolgirls. He surely enjoyed their idolizing him as an older man, a war veteran who had seen vastly more of life than they. Perhaps he was also regressing imaginatively to a point in life before he'd been burdened with the fears and responsibilities of adulthood.

In December, Hemingway was invited to give a talk about his war experiences to the Ladies Aid Society at the Petoskey Public Library. In the audience was Harriet Connable, a friend of Grace's from Toronto. She and her husband, Ralph, who was the head of Woolworth stores in Canada, needed someone to stay with their invalid son, Ralph Junior, in their Toronto mansion while they vacationed in Palm Beach that winter. Harriet told her husband that Hemingway would be the perfect companion, and when Hemingway went to interview for the job, he was hired at once. Hemingway had lucked out: in addition to the perquisites of a chauffeur-driven car at his disposal, free room and board in a well-staffed home, and $50 a month plus expenses, Ralph Connable would also introduce him to people at the *Toronto Star Weekly* and perhaps land him a post there. In mid-January, Hemingway settled into the Connables' imposing mansion at 153 Lyndhurst Avenue, staying on through the spring.

Hemingway continued to write while taking care of Ralph Junior. He also met Gregory Clark, the *Star*'s features editor, and was hired as a general reporter. Hemingway wrote sixteen articles for the *Star,* on whatever topics came his way:

a profile of the mayor, an article about how to get a free shave at a barbershop, an item concerning a group of wealthy socialites who had begun a circulating art library. Hemingway's satirical tone pervades these stories, sometimes making even dull subject matter seem humorous. His sardonic attitude had been sharpened by his experiences with the military in Italy and by the disillusioning tensions he had seen in Oak Park and in his family upon his return.

In the fall, Hemingway found a writing job at a Chicago magazine called the *Cooperative Commonwealth*. Officially, the periodical was a platform for the International Cooperative Alliance, an organization founded in California in 1895 to aid and support various co-ops in the United States and abroad as a response to the growth of industrialization and urbanization. It soon became clear to Hemingway, however, that the enterprise was a scam, and that its founder, a former ad man named Harrison Parker, was a flimflam artist. The magazine was set up to solicit donations to the ICA, but when it was discovered that the money was going elsewhere, investors in the magazine sued Parker, and he was eventually convicted of fraud.[18] Hemingway needed an income, however, so he stayed with the magazine until the bitter end, in June 1921. He spent many of his evenings composing satirical rewrites of world news that he tried to sell to *Vanity Fair,* but they were never published.[19] He did manage to complete two satirical sketches, which appeared in the *New Orleans Double Dealer.* But his writing program was foundering. He needed a stability and purpose that would galvanize his ambitions to be an artist.

As had been his habit, when Hemingway settled in Chicago he roomed with a group of friends. At the center of this group, in an apartment on East Chicago Avenue, was the brother of one of his Michigan friends, Kenley Smith, and his wife, Genevieve, nicknamed "Doodles." Smith was an extraordinary person—Hemingway called him, with uncharacteristic praise, a "boy genius."[20] Y. K., as he was known, had gone to Harvard at age fourteen and worked for a Chicago advertising agency. He was well connected not just in business circles but also to writers and painters in the city. He and Doodles were liberal people; they had an open marriage in which both husband and wife had extramarital relations with mutual friends. Hemingway, antagonistic to the old-fashioned values of Oak Park, was intrigued by such behavior. One night, the Smiths gave a party, and it was there that Hemingway met the next serious love of his life, Elizabeth Hadley Richardson.[21]

Born in 1891 in St. Louis, Missouri (like Oak Park, a conservative community), Hadley had an upbringing similar to Hemingway's. She was the product of a dominant mother and a relatively passive father. James Richardson was a successful businessman who had made a fortune in pharmaceuticals but suffered a series of financial setbacks that ruined him. Fortunately, his wife, Florence, had, like Grace, a private income that offset the failure of James's business. James, however, was personally devastated by the loss. He sank quickly into depression and committed suicide when Hadley was twelve by shooting himself in the head with a pistol.

Florence was able to handle the tragedy, however, much as Grace was able to soldier on without Ed after his suicide (by the same means) in 1928. Like Grace, Florence had musical interests and was a determined woman who pushed her daughter to be an overachiever. Hadley became a talented pianist who gave concert performances in St. Louis but then had to abandon her musical career for health reasons, just as Grace had had to do because of her weak eyesight. Hadley and Hemingway had other things in common. As a girl, Hadley had fallen from a second-story window and badly injured her spine. Like Hemingway after his return from the war, Hadley had spent a long stretch of time on bed rest. Both Hemingway and Hadley had also been schooled by their mothers to be conventional but had rebelled against that way of life. Hemingway had cultivated the image of a layabout and had hung around town with young women during the past two summers in Michigan. Hadley, by her own admission, had a brief lesbian relationship with an older woman (echoing Ruth Arnold's relationship with Grace), the mother of a prep school classmate. Both Hemingway and Hadley came of age in a prohibitive sexual environment, and their sexual awakenings occurred abruptly and rather unconventionally, Hemingway's in a foreign country with a flirtatious older woman who then abandoned him.

Hadley had long reddish-gold hair and a shapely figure, although her mother had always dressed her in somewhat frumpy clothes, playing down her good looks. She was tall, athletic, and liked the outdoors, much to Hemingway's pleasure. Most important, Hadley supported Hemingway in his literary goals (unlike most of his male friends, who thought his ambitions were overblown). In April, Hemingway sent word that he had completed three chapters of a novel, and Hadley was ecstatic. She felt certain that he was going to write something "young & beautiful. Some one with the clean, muscular freshness of young things right on him at the moment of writing." She asked him if he had a typewriter. In the next letter, she predicted that she would marry him and give him a Corona. "My feeling for you," Hadley told him, "is like yours for your writing—no one can take it away."[22]

At age twenty-nine, Hadley needed to marry, or she feared she would end up an old maid. To her advantage, however, she had a trust fund of about $3,000 a year (almost $40,000 in today's money), left to her when her mother had died a few years earlier. This enabled Hadley to free herself from the constraints under which her mother had made her live, and Hemingway, who had not had much in the way of income, was surely pleased about that. Moreover, unlike Agnes, Hadley was forthright about the age issue: "Ernest," she wrote, "I never have taken an attitude of olderness to your youngerness in anything that mattered, have I? God knows I don't feel that way."[23] She then quickly discovered that Hemingway, although eight years her junior, took the controlling role in the relationship and gave Hadley a strong anchor she could trust.

In his relationships with women, Hemingway had moved from being manipulated by Agnes to assuming control of a new older woman, Hadley, and staking out the direction in which he wanted their relationship to go. As Jeffrey Meyers notes astutely, "Though much older than Hemingway, Hadley was not a substitute mother and sometimes wondered if she would not prefer him as papa."[24] In fact, during their honeymoon in Michigan a year later, Hemingway took Hadley around to visit his old girlfriends, among them Marjorie Bump, in order to show her that young girls still desired him. Hemingway held the power in the relationship; they courted long-distance, by letter, Hemingway visiting Hadley in St. Louis only once, preferring to keep her waiting for him. In a letter of 17 December 1920, Hadley openly confessed her need for Hemingway's love. She indicated that she would be tolerant of his moods and whims, even if they extended to affairs with other women: "About our being simpatica—yes dear I never did love anyone so much. I couldn't get along without you Ernest unless you had to have someone else—then that would have to be. . . . I am crazy about you and there never was such a heavenly person and I love you. . . . I am wanting the best for you and am going to do pretty nearly what you want."[25] Hemingway's dominance sometimes even made Hadley nervous. Around others, she would be fidgety and quiet, deferring to him in conversation, making suggestions but acquiescing in his ideas if they differed from hers. In one embarrassing incident at their engagement party, a distracted Hadley told the assembled guests that her fiancé had been the first American killed in Italy.

They were married in a Methodist church in Horton Bay on 3 September 1921. After a two-week stay at Windemere, they returned to live at 1239 North Dearborn Street, a dreary but inexpensive Chicago neighborhood. In early November, the *Toronto Star Weekly* gave Hemingway a permanent post as a European correspondent. This would allow the Hemingways to move abroad, where Hemingway would travel around the continent reporting on newsworthy events and dispatch his articles by cable back to Toronto.

The glamorous assignment gave Ernest the time and experience to polish his craft. It also allowed him to live in a part of the world where art and literature were valued more highly than in the United States. Finally, although his salary was modest, good fortune came the couple's way when Hadley's uncle died and left her an inheritance of $8,000. Combined with her trust fund, they would be more than comfortable, since at that time it was much cheaper to live in Europe than in America.

When it came time to choose a country as a base of operations, Hemingway immediately decided on Italy and became virtually obsessed with preparations for relocating there—buying lire, reading guidebooks, studying maps. Perhaps he was seeking a kind of restitution for what Agnes had cheated him out of. Shortly before they were due to leave the States, however, they went to a party at the Smiths' apartment and met Sherwood Anderson, the realist author of *Winesburg, Ohio* and other frank novels about American life. Anderson had been living in Paris, which he recommended to Hemingway as the center of the literary arts and the headquarters for many American writers who had fled to Europe after the war seeking change. Anderson made a convincing argument, Hemingway thought, and so he accepted the older writer's offer of letters of introduction to some of these influential people and changed his travel plans. He and Hadley would go to Paris. They would live simply and experience the avant-garde. He would give himself over to the demands of literature, with Hadley's moral and financial support. He would see the world as it really was.

4

Paris

"Paris is cold and damp but crowded, jolly, and beautiful," Hemingway wrote Howell Jenkins, a friend from his days in the ambulance corps, after he and Hadley had arrived there on 22 December 1921.[1] It had been a rough passage, Hemingway noted in letters to his family written aboard the old French SS *Leop-oldina,* and they were happy to be on dry land. When Ernest and Hadley settled in Paris, there was a lot to take in. The City of Light was home to a rich literary history abounding in legends. Here, Zola was said to have lived a life so destitute that he had to eat the sparrows that perched on his windowsill; here, Balzac reportedly hid from his creditors and the jealous husbands of his mistresses; here, Guillaume Apollinaire and Paul Verlaine drank and wrote at the Café au Départ with equal degrees of tenacity.

This, Hemingway thought, was how a writer was supposed to live. He identified with the impoverished intellectual who had chosen art over a vacuous bourgeois existence. He and Hadley had more than $3,000 a year to live on, but instead of renting comfortable quarters, they leased a dreary flat over a sawmill in a working-class district, at 74 rue du Cardinal Lemoine. It was a fourth-floor apartment in the rear of the building, with a narrow spiral staircase and a slop jar for a toilet. Hadley must have been dismayed by having to endure such discomfort; she had, after all, been raised in relative luxury. But to Hemingway, this was the stuff that hardened the writer's resolve and drove him to devote himself to his art. So Hadley acceded to her husband's wishes; she was always his most devoted supporter. Hemingway would always prefer to live in working-class areas and in ordinary, unsophisticated parts of the country. Just as he would later choose Piggott, Arkansas, and Sun Valley, Idaho, over New York and London, in Paris he chose a dark, out-of-the-way apartment on a side street rather than the chic boulevard Raspail.

The flat was located outside the boundaries of the Left Bank of the Seine, where most all of the writers and artists had settled, forming an expatriate community later known as the "Lost Generation." The hub of the Left Bank was the Latin Quarter, which got its name from the university tradition of studying and speaking in Latin, a practice that disappeared at the time of the French Revolution. Montparnasse, which lay just to the south, had developed during the eighteenth century as a center for popular entertainment, where bars, restaurants, and cabarets—which at that time were just outside the city boundaries—could serve tax-free wine.[2] That tradition survived even after the district became part of Paris in the latter half of the nineteenth century. While the area of Montmartre had been popular in bohemian circles through the 1890s, during the period immediately prior to World War I artists and poets suddenly moved to Montparnasse on the Left Bank, thereby bringing it into the limelight and attracting painters and composers as well. Even Russian political refugees such as Lenin and Trotsky became part of the intellectual community, where the social life centered around four cafés on the boulevard Montparnasse—La Coupole, Le Select, La Rotonde, and Le Dôme.

Montparnasse derived its name from a joke that students in the Latin Quarter had circulated, deriding it as a place for artistic inspiration, a pseudo Mount Parnassus, home to the Muses in Greek mythology. Hemingway appreciated the origin of the name, for he soon formed an ambivalent view of the community. His first piece for the *Star* was an acerbic send-up of the café crowd, which he mocked as a group of "bluffers and fakers": "They are nearly all loafers expending the energy that an artist puts into his creative work in talking about what they are going to do." To Hemingway, who had more drive and ambition than most major writers, such people were merely "posing as artists."[3] This could often create a stressful, competitive, even backbiting environment, as the poet Claude McKay, who lived there in the 1920s, recalled: "writers and artists plunged daggers into one another" without a second thought.[4]

But Hemingway recognized the talent there as well. When Gertrude Stein proclaimed that "Paris was where the twentieth century was," she was hardly exaggerating—Paris in the 1920s saw the greatest concentration of talent and flowering of genius of any era in literary history.[5] At its epicenter was James Joyce's *Ulysses*—at the time the most revolutionary English-language novel ever published. Extending out from Joyce's book was a wide circle that included such figures as Djuna Barnes, Samuel Beckett, Kay Boyle, John Dos Passos, Archibald MacLeish, e. e. cummings, Lawrence Durrell, Wyndham Lewis, Louis MacNeice, F. Scott Fitzgerald, Ford Madox Ford, H. D. (Hilda Doolittle), Henry Miller, Anaïs Nin, Ezra Pound, Max Eastman, Lincoln Steffens, Harold Loeb, Allen Tate, Gertrude Stein, Morley Callaghan, Jean Rhys, Donald Ogden Stewart, Evan Shipman, William Bolitho, and Edward O'Brien. Among the painters in residence were Gerald Murphy, Joan Miró, Pablo Picasso, Juan Gris, and Francis Picabia. The filmmaker Jean Cocteau, photographers such as Man Ray, sculptors such as Alexander Calder, and composers, including Erik Satie, Darius Milhaud, Francis

Poulenc, and the Americans Cole Porter, George Gershwin, Walter Piston, and Aaron Copland, all lived in Paris at one time or another during the 1920s—creating a truly international congress of creativity.

Armed with Sherwood Anderson's letters of introduction, Hemingway waded into this fount of art—an unrestrained geyser of temperamental geniuses and hapless hangers-on who were determined to be noticed and make their names live on. How Hemingway navigated these difficult waters is fascinating. Although he had little experience, Hemingway made connections quickly and easily—far outstripping many who had been there much longer. He had a talent for forming friendships naturally and for encouraging people to think of him in grander terms than his actual achievements would warrant. Hemingway established himself as one of the best of the new, up-and-coming American writers.[6]

By 1925, after only three years in Paris and having published only *Three Stories and Ten Poems,* brought out by Robert McAlmon's Contact Publishing, and the vignettes published by William Bird's small press as *in our time,* Hemingway had staked out his unique territory, successfully establishing a public image as a pure artist, connoisseur, man of the world, virile sportsman, and specimen of physical fitness. This image was so well established that it appeared in a poem by Ernest Walsh published in *This Quarter,* one of the many little magazines circulating in Paris at the time.

> *Papa soldier pugilist bullfighter*
> *Writer gourmet lionhead aesthete*
> *He's a big guy from near Chicago*
> *Where they make the shoes bigger and*
> *It's a good thing that because he ain't*
> *Got french feet Napoleon and him*
> *Wouldn't have said much together*
> *He'd have pulled Buonaparte's nose*
> *And absolutely ruined french history.*[7]

Hemingway's public image is often thought to have come about with the publication of *Death in the Afternoon,* his treatise on bullfighting, which appeared in 1932. But this image took root much earlier, and it was definitely connected to Hemingway's abilities as a writer. He somehow established the idea that a writer practiced not just the most noble of professions but was also something of an existential hero, a master craftsman with an intimate connection to life and death that no other profession shared and no layman could ever hope to understand. However he engineered this, his public persona as a masculine ideal was established well before *The Sun Also Rises, A Farewell to Arms,* and the public-image-making excursions he took to Africa and Spain in the 1930s.

Hemingway's forging of friendships in Paris is all the more remarkable given his many insecurities. Hemingway felt outclassed by the fact that so many of the expats were Ivy Leaguers and that he had not attended even a provincial university. (Hemingway's obsessive, omnivorous reading probably sprang from this feeling of intellectual inadequacy.) This is probably one reason why Hemingway worked so hard on his writing, feeling that he had to do more and prove more than others given his background. Being so hard on himself and holding himself to such high standards made him quick to pass judgment on others and to denigrate average but interesting work as substandard. His snappishness eventually evolved into a hair-trigger temper that sometimes had violent results, and it made him kick away people whom he had once regarded as friends. This was the price of his hypercompetitive nature and striving for excellence. It was also part of his credo of self-sufficiency. He wanted to do it all by himself. And despite his nearly dying at the Italian front, Hemingway also felt self-conscious about his not serving properly in the war. While others, like MacLeish, Ford, and Loeb, had been doing the work of real soldiers (e. e. cummings, too, who though also an ambulance driver had been captured and imprisoned in France), Hemingway's duty had been to dispense cigarettes and candy bars. He hated that part of his past and spent the rest of his life trying to make up for it, putting himself on or near the battlefield in Spain, China, and western Europe. Ultimately, though, his relationships with expatriates benefited Hemingway. They drove him to heights he might not have scaled otherwise. Without the alternating successes and failures he witnessed among the café crowd, without their equal parts helpfulness and hypocrisy, Hemingway would not have been spurred to write as much and as well as he did. Competition was good for him.

_____

The biggest influence on Hemingway was Gertrude Stein. Heavyset, mannish, with sensual "immigrant hair . . . cut like Joan of Arc," Stein resembled Grace Hemingway, and the young writer looked up to her as a mother figure.[8] Stein, born in Allegheny, Pennsylvania, had lived in Paris and Vienna while growing up. Her father was a railroad executive with vast holdings in real estate and streetcar lines, and she lived a privileged youth. She studied psychology at Radcliffe College under William James and then attended Johns Hopkins Medical School, intending to be a physician. But Stein soon changed her mind and moved to Paris to live with her brother Leo. She collected fine art, wrote essays, criticism, and fiction, and formed a domestic partnership with Alice B. Toklas, whom she met through her brother. Stein was truly bohemian in her disregard for appearances and her devotion to the life of the mind. Mabel Dodge Luhan, a wealthy American who moved in artistic circles in Paris and other European capitals, thought Stein was "richly attractive in her grand *ampleur*. She always seemed to like her own fat anyway and that usually helps other people to accept it. She had none of the funny embarrassment Anglo-Saxons have about flesh. She gloried in hers."[9]

Stein cut a lively and reckless figure in the city. She and Toklas—tiny, wizened, and chain smoking Sobranie Black Russians—careened down the boulevards in a big Ford they nicknamed "Auntie." A friend said of Stein's driving, "she regarded a corner as something to cut, and another car as something to pass."[10] Stein and her brother were among the early collectors of important art—work by Matisse, Picasso, and Georges Braque—and the apartment Stein shared with Toklas at 27 rue de Fleurus, near the lush Jardin du Luxembourg, was a virtual museum of modern art, showcasing the work of postimpressionist painters like Cezanne, Renoir, and Bonnard as well as examples of cubism by Matisse, Picasso, Gris, and others. Stein's writing, full of repetition and syntactical fragmentation, was a kind of cubism in prose, especially in her early book, *Tender Buttons* (1914)—for which reason it never found much of an audience. Only *The Autobiography of Alice B. Toklas* (1933), Stein's own autobiography, was a commercial success—but mostly because of its gossipy, sardonic portraits of former pupils like Hemingway.

On a Wednesday afternoon in February, Ernest and Hadley were invited to tea at Stein's flat. Stein was imperial, domineering, and blunt, but she was also accessible and generous in helping young writers. She singled out Hemingway for special mentoring. He and Hadley regularly attended the salons held in her apartment (although Hadley was treated like the other literary spouses, sent to the kitchen to be entertained by Toklas while Stein held forth to her protégés in the living room). Hemingway respected Stein, and she him. He was twenty-two; she was forty-eight. She first introduced him to the concept of bullfighting, describing it enthusiastically and piquing his curiosity about this most unusual form of blood sport. She urged him to visit Spain and see the spectacular skills of the matadors. Their friendship ripened quickly. Stein urged Hemingway to give up journalism and focus all his energy on writing fiction. "If you keep on doing newspaper work you will never see things, you will only see words and that will not do, that is of course if you intend to be a writer," she told him. Hemingway's terse, understated style owes something to Stein's similarly laconic manner of writing. Looking over some of his early writing, Stein told her student to "begin over again and concentrate."[11]

Stein was openly homosexual, as were several of the other gay and lesbian figures in the Paris coterie. In Oak Park, Hemingway had been raised to believe that same-sex unions were unnatural and therefore sinful. His father had inculcated in him a fear of the dangerous side effects and psychological associations of all types of sexual activity. The bookshelves of the house on North Highland Avenue were filled with medical textbooks containing horrific drawings of what could happen to the male genitalia when attacked by syphilis and other sexually transmitted diseases. Syphilis at the time could even be fatal, as Frederic Henry notes in *A Farewell to Arms,* when Rinaldi lets slip that he thinks he may have contracted the disease from a prostitute. Then, too, during his service in the ambulance corps in Italy, Hemingway must have been alert to the possibilities that homosexual men serving in the units might take a romantic interest in him. During his convalescence in Milan, he worried about an Englishman in the ward who used to bring him bottles of marsala.[12]

Yet Hemingway treated homosexuality with tact, deference, and open-mindedness. He appreciated that Stein and her circle did not pass moral judgment on him for writing frank and daring material, as his parents had (even when Stein objected to certain graphic scenes in "Up in Michigan," a story about a woman forced to have sex).[13] Hemingway was also genuinely curious about same-sex relationships, a fascination that would lead to his own later sexual experimentation. There were many lesbian couples in Paris at the time—Sylvia Beach and Adrienne Monnier, Djuna Barnes and Thelma Wood, Natalie Barney and Romaine Brooks, Margaret Anderson and Jane Heap, Janet Flanner and Solita Solano.[14] Stein in particular symbolized to Hemingway the powerful agent of forbidden desire—a theme that would be the centerpiece of the relationship between Jake Barnes and Brett Ashley in his first novel, *The Sun Also Rises* (1926). Although Hemingway joked to Sherwood Anderson that his friendship with Stein was like that between brothers, he also later said of her, "I always wanted to fuck her and she knew it and it was a good healthy feeling and made more sense than some of the talk."[15]

Hemingway's treatment of homosexuality in fiction could be honest and compassionate. Although his portrayal of homosexuality is fairly stereotypical in *The Sun Also Rises*, that is not always the case in other texts. "A Simple Enquiry," a story collected in *Men Without Women* (1927), concerns a military officer's homosexual interest in a servant. Rather than make unwanted advances toward the servant, however, the officer gently guides the conversation in such a way that the servant can tell him that he is not gay and suffer no punishment for it. The stories "The Sea Change" and "Mr. and Mrs. Elliot" also treat the subject. In the former, a woman is able to leave her husband for another woman, and although the husband is angered, he accepts the event as good for both of them; in the latter, both partners acknowledge their homosexual leanings and, unable to conceive a child, carry on relationships with lovers, but they remain married, content to show the world a conventional image.

Hemingway and Stein eventually fell out, however, because Hemingway could not reconcile what Stein preached about writing with what she actually wrote, which was often sloppy, disjointed, and downright unclear. Hemingway's unusually high standards for himself he also used in evaluating his friends; this is why these relationships soared but then plummeted like cannonballs from a cloudless sky, with little forewarning and almost always with acrimony and venom. Others shared Hemingway's opinion of Stein's work. The Jewish American writer Mike Gold, for example, bluntly categorized her entire body of work as "literary idiocy," and Wyndham Lewis savaged her writing as "a thick, monotonous prose-song" that expressed "her fatigue . . . and the bitter fatalism of her nature." The prose, he said, "churns and lumbers by."[16] This comment might also apply to Hemingway's view of Stein's substance as a writer, for he felt that though she wrote and wrote, she had no extensive experience to actually write about. She also, Hemingway claimed, disliked "the drudgery of revision" and "the obligation to make her writing intelligible."[17]

Unfortunately, when Hemingway fell out of friendship with someone, he felt the perverse need to demean the person. This often happened when he, as a pupil, began to outdistance one of his teachers, as in the case of both Stein and, later, Sherwood Anderson. Hemingway began to make fun of Stein as early as his 1926 parody of Anderson, *The Torrents of Spring,* where he titled one chapter "The Making and Marring of Americans." "Where were her experiments in words leading her?," Hemingway asked rhetorically (90). The following year, still smarting from Stein's rejection of him, he published a clever account of Hadley's being given the cold shoulder in an essay for the *New Yorker.* Stein retorted in 1933 that Hemingway's much vaunted originality of style was not his but hers, and that he was merely her imitator. In her *Autobiography of Alice B. Toklas,* Stein also accused Hemingway of being yellow, wounding him in perhaps the most sensitive area of all, his pride in being courageous. She even went so far as to deride his physique and physical strength, describing him as "very fragile" and jesting that "he used to get quite worn out walking from his house to ours." She also made fun of his self-professed expertise at boxing, claiming that a young boy who knew nothing of the sport had knocked Hemingway out in a matter of minutes.[18] Hemingway counterattacked, notably in *Green Hills of Africa,* where he scorned her high opinion of her own talents, and in Robert Jordan's clumsy parody of a famous Stein remark in *For Whom the Bell Tolls* (1940): "A rose is a rose is an onion . . . a stone is a stein is a rock is a boulder is a pebble" (289). Yet eventually, as with most of Hemingway's broken friendships, there were to be abject regrets and complete readjustments of memory: while he condemned her jealousy of her peers in *A Moveable Feast,* his remarks in a letter of July 1948, two years after Stein's death, revealed complicated feelings toward his former mentor. "I never counter-punched when she left herself wide open," he claimed; "I liked her better before she cut her hair and that was sort of a turning point in all sorts of things." He honestly admired and liked her sexual aspect, concluding, "I always loved her very much."[19] The loss of Stein's friendship and her attacks on Hemingway in the *Autobiography* wounded him deeply and permanently.

Sylvia Beach was another lesbian who had an important relationship with Hemingway. Born in Baltimore, Maryland, Beach was the product of a repressive Victorian home. Her grandparents had been missionaries in India, and her father the eighth of nine generations of Presbyterian ministers.[20] She had spent part of her youth in Paris, where her father was an associate pastor at an American church, and had grown up in Princeton, New Jersey, where her father became minister of a Presbyterian congregation that included one former and one future president, Grover Cleveland and Woodrow Wilson. Like the Steins, the Beach family was wealthy, and so Sylvia and her two sisters and mother traveled frequently to Europe. In midsummer of 1916, Sylvia moved from Madrid to Paris; she spent the rest of her life there.

She met Adrienne Monnier, who owned a bookstore on the Left Bank called La Maison des Amis des Livres. Encouraged by Monnier, Beach opened her own store in 1919 in a former laundry on the rue Dupuytren; two years later, Shakespeare and Company, as the venerable bookstore was called, moved to larger and busier quarters at 12 rue de l'Odéon, where it remained for the next twenty years. Both a bookstore and a lending library, Shakespeare and Company quickly became a center of activity in the growing expatriate community. In addition to selling and lending books, the store served as the sales address and principal Paris distribution point for many of the local English-language publishers and periodicals. The store remained in business until the Nazi occupation of Paris in 1941, when Beach refused to sell a German officer her personal copy of *Finnegans Wake* and chose instead to move her remaining meager stock of books upstairs to her apartment.

Beach befriended, advised, and lent books to countless expatriate writers, among them Ezra Pound and Robert McAlmon; McAlmon even used the shop as his mailing address. But Beach positively idolized Hemingway, even appearing at times to have a girlish crush on the handsome young writer. In a famous photograph of Beach and Hemingway taken outside the store, she is gazing up at him with something resembling awe; Hemingway stares straight ahead at the camera, self-confident and earnest. "No one that I ever knew was nicer to me," Hemingway wrote in *A Moveable Feast* (31).

Beach's most famous association was with James Joyce and the publication of *Ulysses.* Employing the printing services of Maurice Darantière in Dijon, Beach published the first edition under the imprint of Shakespeare and Company in 1922. The book was in constant demand among the expatriate community in Paris, and Beach's assistant was kept busy shuttling copies over to the Ritz Hotel on the Right Bank for rich Americans to smuggle back into the United States. Beach also worked tirelessly on Joyce's behalf in the fall of 1926, trying to prevent a pirated edition of the novel from running in Samuel Roth's New York–based magazine *Two Worlds.* Hemingway enlisted in her campaign and coordinated the signing of a petition, published in the 6 March 1927 issue of the *New York Herald Tribune,* to protest Roth's actions. (Soon thereafter, Roth was forced to cease publication of the book.)

Hemingway also benefited from the tutelage of Joyce, in whose writing he had quickly seen genius at work. He praised Joyce's masterwork, *Ulysses,* as "a most goddamn wonderful book."[21] In fact, Hemingway probably learned much more from Joyce's style than from Stein's, especially the Joycean technique of compressing insights into a single epiphanic moment. In this respect, many of the stories in Joyce's interconnected collection of tales *Dubliners* (1914) resemble Hemingway's coming-of-age narratives involving Nick Adams. (Joyce's "Araby," in particular, is quite similar to Hemingway's "Indian Camp" [1924].) It is often noted that Hemingway's concept of weaving together thematically related tales, as he did in *in our time,* is indebted to Sherwood Anderson's collection *Winesburg, Ohio* (1919), but it was influenced just as heavily by Joyce's *Dubliners.*[22]

Hemingway deeply respected Joyce's talent, telling a friend, "He had his problems but he could write better than anyone I knew."[23] Although Hemingway often made fun of the Irishman's frail physique, this afforded opportunities for fun and games when they went out drinking together, as they did frequently. When Joyce got drunk and challenged some stranger in a café to settle things manfully, he would simply defer to his companion, saying, "Deal with him, Hemingway! Deal with him!"[24] Nora, Joyce's wife, would greet the two men on the doorstep in the small hours of the morning after such binges and sarcastically intone, "Well, here comes James Joyce the writer, drunk again with Ernest Hemingway."[25]

Ezra Pound, a tall man with a "patchy red beard, fine eyes," and "strange haircuts,"[26] had been living in Paris for about a year before Hemingway arrived. Pound had edited T. S. Eliot's *The Waste Land* (improving the poem, it was generally agreed), and had been Joyce's most ardent champion, using his contacts in the literary world to spread word of Joyce's genius. He was also well into work on his *Cantos* and had published several volumes of influential verse. In February, Hemingway came to call on him in his ground-floor studio apartment at 70 bis rue Notre Dame des Champs, in the center of Montparnasse and only a few minutes' walk to Le Dôme and La Coupole. Hemingway observed that Pound's small, cramped flat was "as poor as Gertrude Stein's studio was rich."[27] Hemingway initially thought Pound pompous—something of a poseur. But as Pound began to open up and to read, critically but helpfully, some poems that Hemingway showed him, the younger man began to see that Pound possessed an inner fount of kindness. He was generous in the extreme. From that point on, Hemingway regarded Pound as an honest friend, saying, "He has fought his fights with a very gay grimness and his wounds heal quickly."[28] When he and Hadley visited Pound and his wife, Dorothy, about a year later in Rapallo, Italy, Hemingway gratified Pound by teaching him about the military history of the region around Orbetello: in the Middle Ages it had been a possession of the Aldobrandeschi family, who held it until the fourteenth century, when it was captured by the Sienese Republic and became a Spanish possession. Although he was horrified by Pound's pathetic attempt to play the bassoon, Hemingway discreetly held his tongue. He even taught him, at Pound's request, how to box—"with little success," according to Hemingway.[29] In this and other friendships, Hemingway took great pains to appear his own man, no acolyte or imitator of another writer—he strived to create an independent identity, but he also honestly admired his mentors' gifts.

As much as Joyce's ideas about minimalism influenced him, Hemingway also learned a great deal about economy of style from Pound. One of the primary exponents of imagism, Pound taught Hemingway, by his admission, more about "how to write and how not to write" than anyone else.[30] Pound arranged for the first six chapters of Hemingway's collection *in our time* to be published in the spring 1923 issue of the *Little Review,* edited by Margaret Anderson, and various early poems by Hemingway were reprinted in two anthologies that Pound put together, *Profile* (1923) and *Active Anthology* (1933).

Hemingway showed his affection for Pound by writing an appreciation of the poet for *This Quarter* in 1925. He pronounced Pound one of only two great

living poets, the other being Yeats. He also noted that Pound spent perhaps only
one-fifth of his time writing; the rest was given over to helping other writers,
something that Hemingway truly appreciated. "He defends them when they are
attacked, he gets them into magazines and out of jail," Hemingway wrote in the
tribute to Pound. "He loans them money. . . . And in the end a few of them refrain from knifing him at the first opportunity."[31] Years later, in 1958, when Pound
was suffering from dementia and had been arrested on charges of treason, it was
Hemingway who led the way in gaining support for him from other writers, notably Eliot, Robert Frost, and Archibald MacLeish. Hemingway was instrumental
in obtaining Pound's release from St. Elizabeth's Hospital, a psychiatric facility
in Washington, D.C., and even gave the poet $1,000 to help him out.

Hemingway's two most extensive friendships among the expatriates were
with Gerald and Sara Murphy and Scott and Zelda Fitzgerald. Both couples were
handsome, well off, and part of the avant-garde; both provided him later with
material and models for fiction; and both offered him intimate case studies for
a subject in which he was keenly interested—the corrupting power of wealth on
the artist and the dangers of the self-chosen artistic life turning into something
artificial and unworthy.

Hemingway and Fitzgerald were both products of the Midwest and of families with an overbearing mother and an ineffectual father.[32] Their relationship
was defined by a mixture of admiration and hostility. From the moment he met
Fitzgerald in the Dingo Bar in April 1925, Hemingway could see signs of looming
disaster in his new friend's life and literary career. Five years earlier, Fitzgerald
had appeared on the literary scene with *This Side of Paradise,* a coming-of-age
novel about a Princeton student and the party-mad leanings of youth in the
Jazz Age; the book made Fitzgerald an instant success. Fitzgerald would soon
introduce Hemingway to his editor, Maxwell Perkins, at Scribner's and help him
secure a publishing contract for his first novel. But his personal life was already
a mess. At their first meeting, Fitzgerald passed out from too much drink. He
then cravenly apologized to his companions—something that inspired gall in
Hemingway rather than forgiveness: he had no patience for those who could not
hold their liquor. Later, Hemingway identified Fitzgerald's alcoholism as the
choke point in his creativity: it stymied his imagination and blocked his ability
to create narrative. He thought that many of Fitzgerald's troubles with writing
were self-created and that he lacked the stamina necessary to produce consistent
good work. During Fitzgerald's long struggle with what might well have turned
out to be his masterwork, *Tender Is the Night,* Hemingway tried to encourage him
but was blunt in his advice: "you just have to *go on* when it is worst and most
[helpless]," he wrote, "there is only one thing to do with a novel and that is go
straight on through to the end of the damn thing."[33]

Hemingway also demonized Fitzgerald's wife, Zelda. He believed that she
was jealous of her husband's fame and wanted him to come to harm. "Of all
people on earth," he later admonished Fitzgerald, "you needed discipline in your

work and instead you marry someone who is jealous of your work, wants to compete with you and ruin you."[34] Zelda was openly hostile to Hemingway, once calling him "a pansy with hair on his chest."[35] Fitzgerald looked to Hemingway for advice about his personal life, going so far as to ask his friend to look at his genitals and tell him how they compared with other men's, as Zelda had told him that they were too small to give her sexual satisfaction. Hemingway told him that Zelda had made such a malicious remark because "she just wants to destroy you."[36] But Fitzgerald could not get past his self-doubt, and eventually his star fell as dramatically as Hemingway's would rise.

Likewise, Hemingway's trust in Gerald and Sara Murphy waxed and waned. Their intellectual precociousness and privileged backgrounds piqued Hemingway's curiosity, but he was uncertain about the seriousness with which they regarded art. Donald Ogden Stewart once described the couple's life as a fairy tale: "They were both rich; he was handsome; she was beautiful; they had three golden children. They loved each other, they enjoyed their own company, and they had the gift of making life enchantingly pleasurable for those who were fortunate enough to be their friends."[37] Gerald was born into an established Boston family that owned the Mark Cross Company, a maker of luxury leather goods. Sara, whose family was from Ohio, was also fabulously wealthy. Her father, Frank B. Wiborg, had made his fortune selling printing ink in Cincinnati and introduced his daughter to East Coast society by building a mansion in East Hampton, New York. The Dunes, the largest house in the area at the time, had thirty rooms and grounds that included Italianate sunken gardens, stables, a working dairy, and separate servants' quarters. Wiborg's East Hampton holdings, by one estimate, encompassed six hundred acres—a parcel that would be worth at least $1 billion today.

Sara and Gerald, who had been friends since adolescence, settled in New York when they married and began to raise a family, but Gerald had no taste for spending his life in corporate boardrooms. So they set off for Paris, with Gerald determined to be a painter. They cherished a Tolstoyan ideal of husband and wife working and living side by side. In Paris, they helped fuel the renaissance among American expatriates and eventually settled on seven acres in the south of France in a fourteen-room villa. Honoria Donnelly, the couple's youngest child, recalled that "the spot became a sort of port of call" for artists and writers—a place for an "exchange of souls and affections and ideas."[38] The Murphys named the house "Villa America." Gerald painted the sign for the entrance, breaking up the words so that it might read "vil ame" ("villa of the soul" in French) and "la rica" ("the rich one" in Spanish).

Gerald cut a striking figure. A friend described him as the sort of person who "always became a native of wherever he was,"[39] and he adopted a casual wardrobe that in subsequent years would become a kind of seaside uniform: striped sailor jersey, espadrilles, and knitted fishermen's cap. Sara was very much the striking beauty that Fitzgerald would later bring to life as Nicole Diver in *Tender Is the*

Night, her face "hard and lovely and pitiful," her bathing suit "pulled off her shoulders," her characteristic rope of pearls brilliantly white against her olive skin. Gerald and Sara created a perpetual aura of luxury, celebration, and fun.

Eventually, however, the fates seemed to conspire against them. Of their three children, two, both boys, died before reaching adulthood—one from tuberculosis and the other from meningitis. Gerald never painted again, and the couple returned with their surviving daughter to New York, where Gerald went to work managing the family businesses. After the death of his sons, Gerald said to Fitzgerald, "Only the invented part of our life—the unreal part—has had any scheme, any beauty."[40] This was the kind of comment that seemed to confirm to Hemingway his original impression of the Montparnasse crowd: people whose public lives were mostly fictions—a way of life that Hemingway scorned.

Gerald did not fit the profile that Hemingway looked for in male friends. He was neither athletic nor comfortable living the outdoor life. And although it was not widely known at the time, Gerald was bisexual, with strong homosexual leanings. Hemingway had an ironic talent for discerning sexual preferences, and early on he pegged Gerald as a homosexual. Again, his prurient interest in the intimate lives of others began to surface. (Hemingway later dramatized parts of the Murphys' life in *The Garden of Eden,* a novel that he worked on in the 1940s but that was not published until after his death.) Hemingway was drawn to Sara more intensely than his biographers have realized. As with other couples of Hemingway's acquaintance, if he did not admire the husband, he invariably became infatuated with the wife. This was the case with Pat Guthrie and Duff Twysden, as it would later be true with couples like Grant and Jane Mason. Hemingway needed women's unalloyed admiration to quell his insecurities and confirm his perception of himself as a magnetic and manly artist who lived life on his own terms.

Hemingway found Sara a sympathetic sounding board for his emotional lows. In later years, once the expatriate group had disbanded and Hemingway's infatuation with her had worn off, he often wrote to her in the manner in which a child seeks comfort and understanding from his mother. Sara would respond in the way Hemingway expected: "You are a stimulus and an ideal for your friends," she once reassured him when he worried that no one had any regard for his art. "You are generous and warm-hearted and you *know* more than anyone I can think of."[41] As was his habit, however, Hemingway later criticized the Murphys harshly in *A Moveable Feast.* Sara would later introduce him to the woman for whom he would divorce Hadley, Pauline Pfeiffer. Hiding his shame over leaving Hadley for another woman, Hemingway painted a cruel picture of the Murphys as the unnamed "rich" couple whose sybaritic lifestyle coaxed him into infidelity.

As important as these major figures were to Hemingway's nascent career, other people—less well known but usually connected to either small presses or little magazines—were just as influential. Each one published an early book of

Hemingway's that he could not have placed with a commercial press. Of the small presses, the three most influential were Contact Publishing, run by Robert McAlmon, Three Mountains Press, run by William Bird, and Black Sun Press, run by Harry and Caresse Crosby.

Hemingway's first trip to Pamplona to see the running of the bulls—the genesis of *The Sun Also Rises*—was partly subsidized by Robert McAlmon. Born to the son of a Presbyterian minister in Kansas in 1895, McAlmon married into money and arrived in Paris in 1921 with his wife, who soon left him to live with another man but settled the princely sum of $75,000 on McAlmon, who used it to underwrite a lavish lifestyle for himself and his friends. Flamboyant, alcoholic, and homosexual, McAlmon set up Contact Publishing that year. He published Hemingway's first book, *Three Stories and Ten Poems,* in August 1923, when Hemingway had been unable to place it with a mainstream publisher.

Hemingway met Bill Bird in Paris in early 1922. Bird was born in Buffalo, New York, and educated at Trinity College, Hartford. After his graduation in 1912, he joined the American ambulance service (in France), and after the war was over he came to Paris with his wife, Sally, to be a part-time correspondent for several American newspapers. Bird started Three Mountains Press—which had a relationship with McAlmon's Contact Publishing—in 1922, producing books himself by a slow process of hand printing. Its offices were at 29 quai d'Anjou, where he also lent space to Ford Madox Ford for his *translatlantic review.* Three Mountains Press published McAlmon's *Distinguished Air,* William Carlos Williams's *The Great American Novel,* Pound's *A Draft of XVI Cantos,* and Hemingway's collection *in our time.*

Harry Crosby, a Boston Brahmin by birth, was heir to one of the largest banking fortunes in New England; like Hemingway and Bird, he also served in an ambulance corps during the Great War. Like Gerald Murphy, upon returning from the war, he reluctantly went to work in the family business but rebelled by taking up with an older married woman, Polly Jacob Peabody, and creating one of Boston's most famous scandals among its blue-blooded families. They eventually married and fled the United States to take up with the bohemian crowd in Paris. They could frequently be seen in a boat on the Seine, Polly in a red bathing suit rowing her husband to work at Morgan, Harjes et Cie, the family's bank in Paris. As she rowed back home, Polly, who was well endowed, would laugh enthusiastically at catcalls and whistles from workmen lining the riverbank. She said the exercise was good for her breasts. In 1927, Harry and Polly (who had changed her name to Caresse) started the Black Sun Press, which published the Paris edition of Hemingway's satirical novel *The Torrents of Spring* in 1932.

Hemingway's well-managed relationships with these figures had a remarkable result. By the end of 1922—having been in Paris for barely twelve months—Hemingway had established a reputation as one of the best writers, even though he had yet to publish a single work of fiction. All Hemingway had published in Paris to that point were his *Star* dispatches and "A Divine Gesture," an allegorical

piece written in Chicago in 1921 that appeared in the *New Orleans Double Dealer* in
May 1922. He seems to have effected this public relations success in part through
the low-key promotion of others—he subtly promoted those who were starting
to promote him, making it seem like he was part of the in crowd without ever
having been formally invited to join the club. He forwarded to *Poetry* magazine
and the *transatlantic review* gossipy news notes about his peers. In the January
1923 issue of *Poetry*, for example, Harriet Monroe informed her readers that "a
letter from Ernest Hemingway gives us all kinds of news, in brief: that Gertrude
Stein is doing a new book while living in St. Remy in Provence this winter . . .
that James Joyce is ill and having a difficult time with his eyes; and that Padraic
Colum is likewise in Paris."[42] Hemingway carefully linked his name with those
better known than he. Yet even his early work—the experimental poems and the
vignettes in *in our time* and the satirical *Torrents of Spring*—had yet to see print.

Hemingway used a similar strategy in his journalistic networking. He seized
on every possible opportunity that covering world events could offer him. Whenever he conducted a one-on-one interview with a political figure, he always made
clear to his readers that this was a personal, exclusive report from Ernest Hemingway. In reporting on the Soviet foreign minister, for example, he would always
write, "As Chicherin said to me . . ." When he had a private interview with Maxim
Litvinov, at a heavily guarded Soviet office in Santa Margherita, he made sure to
pepper his report with "Litvinov told me" and "Litvinov said to me." Although
Hemingway cultivated the public image of someone who wanted his art to make
his reputation, he was nevertheless skilled at self-promotion and image making,
and he used these skills to great effect in Paris.

―――――

Hemingway also developed his public persona in Paris by cultivating an interest in sports—something that he had not shown much interest in previously. He
became an avid follower of, and sometimes participated in, boxing, tennis, and
bicycling. He was particularly fond of horse racing. He frequented the Enghien-
les-Bains racecourse, a short train ride from the Gare du Nord. He enjoyed the
ride because it went through an area of slums, and he enjoyed the track because
he thought it "small, petty, and larcenous," welcoming to "the outsider." He was
also an avid spectator of the six-day bicycle races at the Velodrome d'Hiver by
the Pont de Bir-Hakeim, built in 1905. Hemingway took many friends with him
to see these races, most of them unwillingly. Only Allen Tate was an aficionado,
but even he did not approach the event with the air of seriousness and as the
opportunity for learning that Hemingway did. Hemingway wanted to know every nuance and detail of each new experience that came his way. As John Dos
Passos, who would sit high up in the stands with Hemingway at the Velodrome,
recalled, "French sporting events had for me a special comical air that I enjoyed.
We would collect at the stalls and barrows of one of the narrow market streets we
both loved, a quantity of wine and cheeses and crunchy rolls, a pot of pate and
perhaps a cold chicken, and sit up in the gallery. Hem knew all the statistics and

the names and lives of the riders. His enthusiasm was catching, but he tended to make a business of it while I just liked to eat and drink and to enjoy the show."[43]

Hemingway's attraction to boxing was not as much to the violence of the sport, as one might assume, as to the elegant movement and efficient use of the body. He seems to have needed a physical release from the creative tension of writing. His mornings, spent in appraisal of his own life and experience of the world, enervated him mentally. Boxing was a physical stimulus that restored a level of energy with which he could continue to engage the world. Prizefighting at this time was also very popular, with many celebrated matches, and Hemingway loved the challenge of competition. Moreover, he began to associate it metaphorically with the literary profession—sensing his peers' vulnerabilities, challenging titles, and trying bring down those seen as the champs. In other words, it was a cerebral activity as much as a physical one. Hemingway also wrote fiction about boxing in such stories as "The Battlers," "Fifty Grand," and "The Killers."

He was fascinated by the raw brutality of the sport. A boxing match at the Pelleport Club that he attended with Hadley, Sylvia Beach, and Adrienne Monnier is a good example. Hadley was pregnant at the time, and Sylvia worried that with the intense level of spectator participation, she might be injured: "with the socking, the kicking, the yelling, and the surging back and forth, I was afraid we would be 'hemmed' in." Hemingway, unflustered, looked calmly over at Beach and explained that the blood only came "from their noses."[44]

Hemingway was strong and vigorous and had endurance—qualities that made him a good boxer. He learned how to rest his left arm, straighten his right and jab toward the face, then go to his left, then back to his right. When he connected with the nose or the jaw, he took pleasure in feeling the cartilage go squash, the blood spurt and drip, and his opponent weaken in his midsection and go down in a sprawl. He would expertly wipe away the other man's blood from his face with his glove, and, dancing on the balls of his feet, breathe slowly and wait to see if he would have to go back into action.

What we know of Hemingway's various boxing bouts is revealing, for they show much about the fragility of his ego, his inbred competitiveness, and his short temper. The best example is the Callaghan bout. One afternoon in 1929, Fitzgerald accompanied Hemingway to the American Club, where Hemingway was headed for a workout. One of his regular sparring partners was an unlikely pugilistic adversary: Morley Callaghan, a friend from his days in Toronto working for the *Star*. Callaghan, a Canadian, had studied to be a lawyer but had never gone into practice. He had moved to Paris after Hemingway established himself there, and Hemingway helped him find publishing outlets for some of his stories. Callaghan, however, was having as much success as Hemingway was, and as Hemingway's star in Paris began to rise, Callaghan began to be compared to him, which irked Hemingway to no small degree. Although Callaghan was short and pudgy, he had actually trained with professional boxers in Toronto. He had apparently never fully shown Hemingway (four inches taller and forty pounds heavier) the degree of skill he possessed in the ring, however, since their previous sessions had been subdued and merely for purposes of exercise.

Callaghan was there that afternoon, and the two men decided to get in the ring. Fitzgerald was elected timekeeper. He was given a watch and told to call "time" after three minutes, with one-minute rests between rounds. In the second round, Hemingway started to box with an aggression Callaghan had not seen before: "Ernest had become rougher, his punching a little wilder than usual. His heavy punches, if they had landed, would have stunned me." "I was wondering why I was tiring, for I hadn't been hit solidly. Then Ernest, wiping the blood from his mouth with his glove and probably made careless with exasperation and embarrassment for having Scott there came leaping in." Stepping up, Callaghan beat him to the punch. The timing must have been just right, for he caught Hemingway on the jaw, spinning him around, and down he went, sprawled out on his back. "'Oh my God!' Fitzgerald cried suddenly. 'I let the round go four minutes!'" When Hemingway got up, he said savagely, "All right, Scott, if you want to see me getting the shit knocked out of me, just say so. Only don't say you made a mistake."

Hemingway stomped off to the showers, and a legend had been born, with Callaghan the reluctant victor. That the story found its way into the New York papers is an indication of Hemingway's fame by that point, and Callaghan, out of respect for his adversary, felt he had to say something publicly so that Hemingway would not be embarrassed. As he recalled, "I wrote a lovely letter" to the *Sunday International Herald Tribune,* covering up for Hemingway, "buttering up my two friends," and "lying my head off." But it was too late. The same paper ran a cruel and wildly inaccurate story about the episode before Callaghan's letter could appear. Fitzgerald saw the story and, at Hemingway's insistence, fired off a haughty cable to Callaghan: "have seen story in herald tribune. ernest and i await your correction. scott fitzgerald." Callaghan decided that he had held his temper too long and sent Fitzgerald "a dreadful letter" that "broke our friendship forever." He regretted doing so, and the three men could never forgive one another.[45]

According to Callaghan, Fitzgerald never recovered from the incident. Hemingway never forgot it either. He frequently referred to the boxing match in letters throughout his later years. The last one reads: "Scott let the first round go thirteen minutes."[46] Things were never the same between Hemingway and Fitzgerald, probably because Hemingway's ego had taken such a licking. Each time Hemingway's physical vanity suffered a defeat, he would be forced to embark on a new existential gamble with his life. So he would naturally think of Fitzgerald's error as an act of treachery, for the result of that extra minute in the second round was a new bout of anxiety that could push his instincts onto the slippery, shifting terrain of cowardice—a nightmare of which Hemingway lived in perpetual dread.

Hemingway was hypersensitive. He could take a slight presumption and magnify it into a personal attack of hideous proportions. In Bimini in June 1936, for example, Hemingway was sportfishing and hooked a big silver marlin. At the time, the Atlantic record for marlin stood at 736 pounds. Jane Mason, with whom Hemingway was having a dalliance at the time, was in the boat, as was Arnold Gingrich, the publisher of *Esquire* magazine, and she guessed that the fish he'd caught was about 450 pounds. The fish was still on the hook, and when Mason spoke, Hemingway flinched, as if he'd been hit with a sucker punch. He turned slowly, with quiet fury, to respond to her when the line went slack. He reeled it in, lifted up the enormous hook, which bent, according to Gingrich, at an angle of "about 130 degrees," and began shaking it in Jane's face, as if he were about to claw her with it. "Four hundred fifty, huh? Look at that hook—just look at it—fourteen hundred pounds if it was an ounce." Gingrich managed to extinguish Hemingway's fury only by telling him that he had said 450 and that Jane was only echoing his comment.[47]

————

Hemingway was working hard on his fiction at this time and by November 1922 had produced a solid body of stories. He then went to Lausanne to cover the peace conference, planning for Hadley to join him later for a brief skiing vacation in the mountains. Before he left, Hemingway instructed Hadley to bring with her all of the stories he was working on so that he could continue to refine them in Switzerland. Accordingly, before she left for the train station on 2 December, Hadley carefully gathered up all the work on his writing table—both the original manuscripts and the typescripts and carbon copies—and put them in a valise to take with her. She arrived at the Gare de Lyon, found her car, and put the valise in the luggage compartment. She then went out onto the platform to buy a London paper and a bottle of water. When she returned, the valise was missing. Hadley notified the porter and together the two of them searched up and down the train to see if perhaps someone had picked it up by mistake—an unlikely possibility, since it was stowed in a clearly occupied compartment. Horrified that she had lost her husband's irreplaceable work, Hadley cried, felt faint, and even became nauseated at the thought that she would have to tell Hemingway what had happened. The following day, she arrived in Lausanne and stammered out her tearful confession.

When Hadley told him what had happened, Hemingway must have been undone not only by the loss of his work but by the terrible awareness that Hadley had treated it with such disregard. It was a turning point in their marriage and had permanent aftereffects. Hemingway determined at once to try and repair the damage if at all possible. He returned immediately to Paris and searched the apartment for anything of value that might remain—perhaps Hadley had forgotten to pack all of the stories. In the stolen suitcase, there may have been as many as eleven stories, a novel, and some poems. But his search turned up nothing but "three pencil drafts of a bum poem" which he had already scrapped.[48] Everything else was gone.

When he was certain that nothing could be recovered, Hemingway at once went into a self-protective mode, adopting the stoical position that one should never discuss casualties, never live in the past, always move forward. Many have seen the lost manuscripts incident as a kind of fortunate fall—arguing that it may actually have been better for Hemingway to start over creatively and not try to hang on and rework what he had already written. This was the view, for example, of Hemingway's third wife, Martha Gellhorn, who believed that the loss of the manuscripts was actually a gift to Hemingway—and had also spared future researchers the task of examining the writer's early, immature work. Gertrude Stein also advised him to put the loss behind him, begin afresh, and attack his fiction with a renewed sense of purpose and concentration.

But this view of the loss of Hemingway's creative work vastly underestimates its devastating effect on Hemingway. Hadley thought that he "never recovered from the pain of this irreparable loss," and Marcelline said, without exaggeration, that "it nearly killed him." In 1951, Hemingway told Charles Fenton that he would have gladly "resorted to surgery" if an operation could have erased the traumatic event from his memory.[49] His hostility toward Hadley comes through clearly in a letter to Ezra Pound, whom he told that "Hadley had made the job complete by including all carbons, duplicates, etc."[50] He did not add—he didn't have to—how stupid he considered her for doing so.

The incident sent him into a black depression from which he was not certain he could recover. He thought Hadley's mistake was nearly treasonous and—despite others' statements—he held it against her for the rest of his life. As late as 1948, while writing *Islands in the Stream,* Hemingway relived the loss of his creative work—which, since it was linked to Hadley and to their marriage, was also linked in his mind to sexuality, creativity, and fertility. When he came to write *A Farewell to Arms* a few years later, he may also have linked the traumatic incident (like the trauma of his war wound in Fossalto) to the devastating loss of the newborn child Catherine delivers in the hospital in Montreux. From this point on, Hadley's carelessness with his precious work hovered darkly in the background of the marriage and would eventually precipitate their divorce.

The loss of so much work, over which he had labored so long, was the third major episode of trauma that Hemingway had experienced in less than four years. First there had been his brush with death on the Italian front. Next came the blow of Agnes's spurning him. And now the woman he had married—and the person he had believed supported his creative work more than any other—had in one careless moment erased his work and effectively reversed the forward momentum he had established. The psychological effects of trauma can start small and grow more detrimental over time. Hemingway would not have recognized at the time the slow growth of insecurity and animosity seeded in him by these three enormously stressful events. But they would cumulatively take their emotional toll.

———

In January 1923, the thirty-one-year-old Hadley became pregnant. The couple was uncomfortable about having the baby in Paris, so in the early fall they returned to Toronto, where Hemingway started work as a staff writer for the *Star.* He missed the birth of the child, however, because the *Star* had him racing around Canada and the northern United States filing stories. Having just covered Lloyd George's tour of North America, he was on a train back to Canada with the prime minister when Hadley, after three hours of labor, delivered a baby boy at 2:00 a.m. on 10 October 1923. They named him John Hadley Nicanor Hemingway. Ever fond of nicknames, Hemingway bestowed the sobriquet "Bumby" on John, or Jack, as he came to be known as an adult, for his rambunctiousness in the womb. (The second middle name, Nicanor, came from one of Hemingway's favorite Spanish bullfighters, Nicanor Villalta.)

Toronto was dull compared to Paris—it was concrete to cobblestones; Hemingway missed the cosmopolitan environment of the smoky cafés in Montparnasse. And so, at the end of the year, he, Hadley, and the baby took a steamer back to France. Although religion would play no major role in Bumby's early life, Hemingway went along with tradition, and the boy had an ecumenical baptism at St. Luke's Episcopal Church in Paris. (His godparents were Gertrude Stein and Chink Dorman-Smith—the one Jewish, the other a lapsed Roman Catholic.) The boy had an affluent, Continental upbringing, although this brought with it some distance from his parents. Ernest and Hadley traveled with friends quite a bit—skiing, hiking, and taking in special events and festivals like those in Spain. Hemingway also traveled a lot on assignment for the *Star,* and Hadley wanted to be with him. And so, like Hemingway's other two children, with Pauline, his second wife, Bumby was left to the care of a nursemaid much of the time.

Hemingway had grown weary of the drudgery of journalism, however, and in late 1923, he resigned his post with the *Star*; by early 1924 he was a full-time self-employed fiction writer. He would never do full-time newspaper work again. His stories were now beginning to appear in the little magazines of Europe. They were collected later that year in *Three Stories and Ten Poems,* brought out by McAlmon's Contact Publishing. But both Hemingway and McAlmon knew that the author needed a larger, commercial publisher if he was to gain recognition. Sherwood Anderson again helped Hemingway by telling his own publisher, Horace Liveright, of Hemingway's work.

Liveright was one of the most original and flamboyant publishers in New York. Starting out as a bond salesman, he later began a company that manufactured toilet paper and—having a literary bent—named it Pick-Quick Papers. That business eventually collapsed, and he took a job in an advertising agency, where he met Albert Boni, who had once run a small publishing firm. With borrowed capital, Boni and Liveright joined forces and started their own publishing company; they began by reprinting British and European classics, a series they called the Modern Library. As this list took off, they used the profits to start bringing out newer, more controversial works by Theodore Dreiser, Eugene O'Neill, Hart Crane, and others.[51]

The firm quickly became one of the most avant-garde publishing houses in New York, and Liveright developed a reputation as not only a risk taker but also a world-class sybarite. He lived in the brownstone that also served as the firm's office, and it was rumored that the library contained a concealed passage leading to a secret room where many a party took place, complete with bathtub gin, cannabis, and ladies of the evening. His employees loved him—he gave them generous raises and annual bonuses, boasting that his firm was the only socialistic publisher in New York—and his authors found his indifference to public opinion a refreshing change in an industry that had typically been populated by rather fusty, prim figures who were squeamish about anything that might be thought offensive.[52] Later, however, Liveright made a series of progressively worse business decisions and fell victim to alcoholism. When he died, late in 1933, he was bankrupt and deeply in debt. Six people attended his funeral.

Liveright did well by Hemingway, however. In October 1925, he brought out a mainstream edition of Hemingway's fiction called *In Our Time: Stories by Ernest Hemingway,* intended for U.S. audiences. This edition included the vignettes from the Three Mountains Press edition *in our time,* plus fourteen full-length tales. The enthusiastic reviews of the collection transformed Hemingway from a relative unknown to an up-and-coming sensation. Fitzgerald's opinion was representative. He thought that readers would be held spellbound with "breathless unwilling interest." He allowed that the stories showed various "influences" but that they were "invariably absorbed and transmuted" by Hemingway's particular genius; he expressed amazement that Hemingway could compress a whole character into a phrase or sentence without "a single recourse to exposition." Fitzgerald concluded grandly, "Many of us who have grown weary of admonitions to 'watch this man or that' have felt a sort of renewal of excitement at these stories wherein Ernest Hemingway turns a corner into the street."[53] His promise thus seemed to be fulfilled.

In Our Time was notable for its introduction of Nick Adams, Hemingway's youthful version of himself, who vacations in northern Michigan, is taught to hunt and fish by his father, is wounded in World War I, and has ambitions of being a writer. Some of these stories—"Indian Camp," "The Doctor and the Doctor's Wife," and "The Three-Day Blow"—are among Hemingway's most famous. World War I figures in "A Very Short Story," "Soldier's Home," and, perhaps most memorably, "Big Two-Hearted River," where Hemingway's technique of omission is brilliantly evident, as the war is both the most obvious focus of the tale and the least conspicuous element of the plot. More than anything else, perhaps, what made readers take notice was the controlled tension in so many of the stories—such as "Cat in the Rain," a masterpiece of economy in which an American couple's discontent is never openly acknowledged as they converse in an Italian hotel; the wife's frustration, however, is abundantly evident in her concern for a cat outside their window who is being pelted by unceasing rain. It is virtually plotless storytelling. With uncommon precision, Hemingway is able to show us a narrative as clean and taut as a wet fishing line shimmering in the sun. The prose technique delivers the mood of the story to the reader, and the mood, in turn, conveys meaning.

Hemingway was twenty-six years old and was being lauded for depicting the world without prejudice or preconception, in a style that was unlike anything that had come before him.[54] The *New York Times* review, titled "Preludes to a Mood," is particularly instructive. The reviewer lacked tried and true literary terminology for Hemingway's prose, so he resorted to athletic metaphors: "Ernest Hemingway has a lean, pleasing tough resilience. His language is fibrous and athletic, colloquial and fresh, hard and clean; his very prose seems to have an organic being of its own. . . . His people and events emerge with miraculous suddenness. . . . The covers of his book should strain and bulge with the healthful ferment that is between them. Here is an authentic energy and propulsive force which is contained in an almost primitive isolation of images."[55]

This was indeed something completely new. By and large, nineteenth-century authors had been prone to a florid and elaborate style of writing. Hemingway, using a distinctly American vernacular, created a new style of fiction in which meaning is established through dialogue, action, and silences—a kind of fiction in which nothing crucial, or at least very little, is stated explicitly. The style would later be the victim of endless parody and imitation (and even Hemingway would imitate himself in some of his less well executed works), but for the moment, it was the clarion call of a revolution in writing.

Hemingway would several times in his later career try to define that particular style. In *Death in the Afternoon,* he wrote, "No matter how good a phrase or a simile [the writer] may have[,] if he puts it in where it is not absolutely necessary and irreplaceable he is spoiling his work for egotism. Prose is architecture, not interior decoration, and the Baroque is over. . . . If a writer of prose knows enough about what he is writing about he may omit things that he knows and the reader, if the writer is writing truly enough, will have a feeling of those things as strongly as though the writer had stated them. The dignity of movement of an ice-berg is due to only one-eighth of it being above water. A writer who omits things because he does not know them only makes hollow places in his writing" (191). On another occasion, he claimed that he did not have a "style," per se, at all. He once told his son Jack that what he had was a certain awkwardness in his writing that resulted from his deliberate and often painful attempt simply to write the truth—raw, honest emotions and precise descriptions.[56]

However one defines his writing, Hemingway was an undisputed prose innovator who did nothing less than transform the English-language novel from its baroque romanticism into a style where every word carried its weight and where the glinting edge came from polish rather than adornment. There would be irresolvable contradictions throughout his life between the man and the work. Egotistical, boorish, and downright mean-spirited behavior would alternate with uncommon kindness, compassion, and grace, but to Hemingway all that really mattered, in the end, was the writing.

Duff Twysden and
The Sun Also Rises

Nothing would get in the way of Hemingway's ambitions now. He realized that a literary career was built on momentum as much as anything else, and he needed to carry that momentum forward. A novel about bullfighting had been gestating in him since his first trip to Pamplona to see the Fiesta of San Fermín in the summer of 1923.[1] He had gone to Pamplona again in the two successive summers, and by August 1925 he had written several chapters of the book. But even before he began to write, doubts about Liveright were taking hold, and when Fitzgerald informed him that he had told his publisher, Charles Scribner's Sons, about him, Hemingway started to wish he had a more visible, prestigious publisher. It irked Hemingway that readers thought of him as a disciple of Sherwood Anderson, and Anderson was also a Liveright author. He came to feel that because people saw him as linked with Anderson, they would always hear Anderson's narrative voice in his own work, and Hemingway could not tolerate any perception that he was not unique—an original. (It was also typical of Hemingway to borrow worry, spotting something that he feared in advance, then magnifying it into a fatal flaw.) He had a three-book contract with Liveright that he wanted out of, so he hit on the unusual idea of writing a book that he was sure Liveright would not publish: a brutal parody of Sherwood Anderson. Liveright would read it and find it so offensive that he would be compelled to reject it, breaking the contract. Hemingway would then be able to get rid of both his publisher and his mentor in one book.

Hemingway's decision to use *The Torrents of Spring* to break with Horace Liveright and move to Scribner's is one of the saddest episodes in his professional life. It inaugurated a pattern in which he would kick to the curb a friend who had once helped him, in order to reap some short-term benefit. Hemingway was aware of this flaw in his personality. He later revealed to his first biographer, Charles Fenton, that he was like a lot of people who, after they have been given aid, pick a quarrel in order to get rid of their obligation.[2] This impulse sprang from Hemingway's insecurity. He had to make his mark as an individual or as nothing; he could not be beholden to anyone. As Donald Ogden Stewart put it, "The minute he began to love you, or the minute he began to have some sort of obligation to you of love or friendship or something, then is when he had to kill you. Then you were too close to something he was protecting. He, one-by-one, knocked off the best friendships he ever had."[3] Stewart, like Scott Fitzgerald, John Dos Passos, Archibald MacLeish, Morley Callaghan, Robert McAlmon, and many others, was one of those former friends who eventually became an enemy. Hemingway told Pound that when Anderson read the novel, he would never "be able to write again."[4]

Hemingway composed the slim novel of twenty-eight thousand words in one week, between November 20 and 26, taking the basic framework of Anderson's novel *Dark Laughter* as his starting point. That novel tells the story of John Stockton, who assumes a new name, Bruce Dudley, and embarks on a journey of discovery in an attempt to find meaning in life. Along the way, he falls in with various colorful characters such as "Sponge" Martin and his daughter "Bugs," runs away with his employer's wife, and tries to achieve what he perceives as the carefree happiness of southern black people, whose "dark laughter" pervades the novel. Hemingway supplemented his own version of this tale with the additional biographical details of Anderson's similar experience, in walking away from a successful career in advertising in order to write fiction—the product of too much commercial pressure in the workplace.

Hemingway's character Scripps O'Neill, his daughter "Lousy," and Yogi Johnson experience their personal crises in northern Michigan, surrounded by the sounds of Indian laughter and war whoops from the woods. Like Anderson himself, Scripps wanders down a railroad track in search of his destiny. Arriving at Petoskey, Michigan—no center of literary and cultural activity—he marries a waitress in Brown's Beanery, and the two begin to live a bohemian life. But Scripps is soon lured away by the greater literary sophistication of Mandy, another waitress at the beanery. Meanwhile, the other main character, Yogi Johnson, faces his own Andersonian crisis: it is spring, but he feels no sexual desire for a woman. After some unlikely adventures with Indian veterans of World War I, Yogi solves his sexual problem when an Indian woman dressed only in moccasins enters Brown's Beanery and awakens his lust. We last see him walking down the railroad track with his new mistress.

Hemingway showed the story around to his friends, most of whom, although they found it funny, didn't think it was worth publishing. Only Fitzgerald thought that it was a satirical masterpiece, "a nightmare of literary pretensions behind which a certain hilarious order establishes itself before the end."[5] Hemingway sent the typescript to Liveright on 7 December 1925, telling him in his cover

letter that the book was fashioned in the noble satirical tradition of Henry Fielding and that he had written it not to demean Anderson but rather to "differenti-
ate between Sherwood and myself in the eyes of the public." Disingenuously, he
suggested to Liveright that such a move would be in the publisher's best interest,
too, as "you might as well have us both under the same roof and get it coming
and going."[6] But, as Hemingway had told Pound earlier, the book was "probably
unprintable."[7]

Liveright surely saw *Torrents of Spring* for what it was, a transparent attack
on Anderson. On 30 December he cabled Hemingway, "Rejecting Torrents of
Spring. Patiently awaiting manuscript Sun Also Rises." Following up by letter,
Liveright said bluntly, "It would be in extremely rotten taste, to say nothing of
being horribly cruel, should we want to publish it."[8] Hemingway got the desired
result and at once wrote Fitzgerald, asking him to pressure Scribner's into signing him up. Ever loyal, Fitzgerald wired Perkins on 8 January that he could
have Hemingway's upcoming novel if he would agree to publish both it and
Torrents—proof, Hemingway thought, that *Torrents* was genuine and not just a
ruse for getting out of his contract with Liveright. He was not using *Torrents* as a
pretext at all, he professed, but truly cared about getting it published, advertised,
and reviewed.[9]

Hemingway traveled to New York in February 1926 to see the chief editor
at Scribner's, Maxwell Perkins. Hemingway liked the people at Scribner's from
the start: they were stable and profitable, and they would also provide an outlet
for his short stories in *Scribner's Magazine*.[10] Scribner's was one of the most distinguished publishing firms in America and something of an icon of Manhattan
society—and of the city's streetscape: their Beaux Arts–style building at Fifth
Avenue and 48th Street, designed by Ernest Flagg, housed the printing presses
in the basement, the bookstore at street level, and the sales, advertising, and
editorial offices on successive upper floors—a business model that has long since
vanished. (The site today is home to a cosmetics retailer.)

Most important, perhaps, was the role played by Max Perkins. Over the years,
Perkins has attained almost mythical status as a legendary "editor of genius," according to his first biographer, A. Scott Berg. Perkins was not just the editor of
Fitzgerald, Hemingway, Thomas Wolfe, and other titans of modern American fic-
tion; he was also their friend, confidante, moneylender, and hand-holder, and the
nursemaid to such landmark works as *The Great Gatsby, Look Homeward, Angel,* and
Hemingway's own *The Sun Also Rises* and later works. One measure of his impact
can be seen in the fact that no fewer than sixty-eight books were dedicated to him.
Perkins was born, raised, and spent most of his life in the New England of his
Puritan ancestors (he was a direct descendant of John Davenport and Theophilus
Eaton, as well as of Henry II of England). His father was a distinguished lawyer
with a Harvard education, his mother a U.S. senator's daughter, and his paternal
grandfather a preeminent art critic. Perkins attended St. Paul's School and then
graduated from Harvard in 1907 with a degree in economics. While at Harvard,

however, he had studied literature under the famous English professor Charles Townsend Copeland—credentials enough to land him a job as a reporter for the *New York Times,* from which he went on to work at Scribner's in 1910, initially as an advertising manager.

Perkins can be credited with transforming the editor's role from the nine-teenth-century image of someone concerned mainly with typefaces and proof-reading to an energizing, visionary figure who had a hand in shaping the actual elements of a story—characterization, dialogue, narrative structure, and even themes. The most famous example of this type of intervention was Perkins's work on Wolfe's first novel. It had arrived in the unsolicited "slush" pile at Scribner's as an amorphous 294,000-word manuscript that was much too long and lacked an overall design. Perkins analyzed the story, made thousands of notes, and suggested numerous cuts and changes, but he secured the author's favor by allowing him to retain the raw, coarse language of the narrative. The result was *Look Homeward, Angel,* a best seller and an eventual classic of American literature. Perkins essentially invented the role of the literary editor in the early twentieth century. He would play a critical part in the publication of Hemingway's works and in the making of his public image.

Perkins edited some of the most progressive authors of his time, writers who pushed the boundaries of what was considered good taste. Yet, ironically, as a New England blue blood, Perkins was impeccably courtly and discreet—not the type of person one would expect to bond with the likes of Hemingway. He even looked the part: he wore a felt fedora, carried a pocket watch with his Phi Beta Kappa key on the chain, and was never seen during working hours without a tie. Morley Callaghan, another Scribner's author, said that "Perkins had a talent for diplomacy in difficult human situations, and . . . a kind of nobility of spirit and a fine sense of fairness."[11] Hemingway admired Perkins's skill, modesty, and tact, but also thought him a bit of a prude. This was perhaps justified: later, when controversy arose within the firm about profanities that Hemingway had used in the manuscript of *A Farewell to Arms,* Perkins was asked to speak with Hemingway about it, a task he took on reluctantly. The editor apparently could not bring himself actually to say the vulgar words in question, so he wrote them down in a square on his desk calendar: "piss shit fuck bitch." Allegedly, the firm's president, Charles Scribner II, came into Perkins's office later that afternoon, saw the list, and said, "Why don't you take the rest of the day off, Max? You must be exhausted."

Perkins's greatest skill lay in establishing a personal rapport with his writers. This was undoubtedly what drew Hemingway to him. Perkins was also older than Hemingway by some fourteen years and very much a mentor—almost avuncular, or brotherly. He encouraged his authors to think of him in this way and guided them well. Perkins also exuded an air of trustworthiness, making his authors feel confident that he had their best interests at heart. In later years, when Hemingway was at his most volatile, he retained great confidence and trust in Perkins—no small matter given the competitiveness in the publishing industry.[12] Hemingway must have been thrilled with Perkins's offer of a $1,500 advance plus a contract for both books, with royalties of 15 percent. His career as a Scribner's author was launched, and—unlike many peers—he would remain with this house for his whole career.

————

After *The Torrents of Spring* appeared in print, Hemingway wrote a patronizing letter to Anderson defending what he'd done. He claimed that the satire was not an ad hominem attack on Anderson but a much-needed wake-up call, an opportunity for Anderson to reexamine his writing and see how it could be improved—Hemingway even presumed to tell Anderson that "when a man like yourself who can write very great things" writes something subpar, he should be told.[13] Perhaps Hemingway actually believed his own chicanery, but the notion that he had written an entire novel in order to deliver a helpful critique was patently absurd.

Anderson took the attack calmly, and in his reply to Hemingway hardly mentioned the incident, giving the impression, at least, that he was involved in many different projects and that Hemingway's novel hadn't affected him all that much. "You speak so regretfully, tenderly, of giving me a punch," Anderson wrote. "Come out of it, man. I pack a little wallop myself. I've been middle-weight champion. You seem to forget that." He also claimed that the book would help him and hurt Hemingway, adding, "You started it. I didn't."[14] Anderson's response shows his strong sense of self-possession and emotional security. Hemingway's remarks, in their defensiveness and attempt at manipulation, could not be more different.

Hemingway, in response, agreed not to "headslip" Anderson's charge that he had been snooty but to "take it on the nose." He bragged that he did not have a "glass jaw" and pointed out that when he'd decided to "sock [Anderson] on the jaw," he'd done so courageously—that is, in public.[15] In his next letter to Hemingway, Anderson opened with a bit of boxing news—the fall of Paul Berlenbach at the hands of Jack Delaney the previous evening.

But Hemingway would not leave Anderson alone. He parodied his erstwhile mentor in another story—one of his acknowledged masterpieces, "The Killers," about a prizefighter named Ole Andreson who gives himself up to death. The character in the story must be a portrait of Sherwood Anderson—once the champion of the heavyweight writing world, now past his prime—given the story's themes, the central character's attributes, and, most convincingly, the correspondence between Hemingway and Anderson leading up to the composition of the story and its later revision in manuscript. In this correspondence, both authors repeatedly invoked the image of the boxer or prizefighter as artist—a trope that Hemingway was to use repeatedly in much of his subsequent writing. Just as he saw the matador as an artist figure, he admired the boxer for the same close contact with danger and for his nimbleness and skill in protecting himself from harm. He used the same imagery in numerous comments on the writer's craft and the status of fellow authors—champs, former champs, people battling for the title—and in comparisons of book sales with purse or prize money. Anderson self-deprecatingly spoke of himself in the same terms—as a former champ who had been toppled.

"The Killers" concerns two contract hitmen who walk into a diner in a small midwestern town and lie in wait for a prizefighter who takes his meals there. The prizefighter was apparently supposed to throw a fight for the mob but did not do so. Nick Adams and two other men in the diner are held hostage by the killers, but the prizefighter does not show up. After the killers leave, Nick goes to the fighter's rooming house to tell him he is being hunted, but the man doesn't care. He is lying fully clothed on his bed and he just turns his back to Nick, faces the wall, and seemingly resigns himself to his fate, preferring not to run from his mistakes anymore.

"The Killers" strongly resembles Anderson's fiction, particularly the inter-related stories that make up his most famous book, *Winesburg, Ohio,* published in 1919. The small town in Hemingway's story, Summit, resembles Anderson's small Ohio town and has the same sense of spiritual emptiness about it. The inhabitants, likewise, carry the same air of defeat that Anderson's "grotesques" do. The main point of "The Killers" is to show the loss of Nick Adams's naïveté about evil and his realization that he must leave Summit if he is to escape its pull of futility and failure. The same is true of George Willard, the protagonist in *Winesburg, Ohio*: he too has an epiphany in which he recognizes the imperative of escape, and escape he does, as Nick does, in the closing chapter of the book. Finally, the fighter Ole Andreson could have come straight out of Anderson's "book of grotesques." He lives with a secret knowledge that he is unable to articulate. He shows Nick by example that one must step up and embrace the reality of the world or else one will end up like him, defeated. As Andreson turns his back on Nick and the world, and shifts to face the wall beside his bed, he telegraphs a crucial connection with such characters as Doc Reefy and Wing Biddlebaum in *Winesburg,* for that book repeatedly uses the motif of walls to denote symbolic barriers that have been erected between the characters and society. They are walled in, walled off, and walled out, much as Hemingway's former prizefighter has his back to the wall, figuratively speaking, in being hunted down by the contract killers. When he turns to face the wall, he signals his resignation to his fate.

But Ole Andreson is even more closely allied to Sherwood Anderson himself than to any one of his characters. Perhaps most telling are Hemingway's revisions to the story, which exists in at least three versions. In the first version, there is no mention of a fighter who is the target of assassins. Two men walk into the diner, eat and talk, and then the draft ends.[16] In the second version, the killers, Max and Al, walk into the diner, tie up the owner and the cook, and tell George, the owner, that they are going to kill "a wop" named "Dominick Nerone." There is still no mention of a boxer, and the story ends before George advises Nick to

go and warn the intended victim.[17] Hemingway revised this draft after receiving
the letter from Anderson in which he referred to himself as a "middle-weight
champion," and the revisions clearly are aimed at making Anderson the target
of the story. The name "Dominick Nerone" is changed to "Anderson"—note the
spelling—and "wop" becomes "old Swede." In the original version, the setting
is Petoskey, but Hemingway changed the town to Summit. Summit, Illinois, is
precisely halfway between Oak Park and Palos Park, where Anderson lived when
he and Hemingway became friends. Finally, the Chicago school of literature with
which Anderson is negatively associated in *The Torrents of Spring* is reinforced by
the change to an Illinois setting. Hemingway also changed the title from "The
Matadors" to the more literally grim "The Killers."[18]

Did Anderson take the smear lying down? In his remarks to Hemingway, he
conceded that his star was on the wane, but Anderson also later wrote a story
called "The Fight," which might also be read as a commentary on the *Torrents*
episode and his falling-out with Hemingway. Writing *Torrents* in order to break
with Liveright, and then following up with a direct jab at Anderson in "The Killers," was an extreme overreaction on Hemingway's part, and part of a pattern of
disproportionate reactions that characterized his personal life and public career.
Decades later, the incident was still on his mind. In 1959, he offered a backhanded
apology in a piece called "The Art of the Short Story": "I did it because I was righ-
teous, which is the worst thing you can be, and I thought he was going to pot the
way he was writing and that I could kid him out of it by showing him how awful
it was. So I wrote *The Torrents of Spring*. It was a cruel thing to do, and it didn't do
any good, and he just wrote worse and worse." Hemingway always experienced
deep regret after treating friends with such cavalier disregard. Hemingway concluded with another boxing metaphor: "I'm sorry I threw at Anderson. It was
cruel and I was a son of a bitch to do it."[19] Hemingway struggled throughout his
life to maintain friendships while remaining true to his ideal of great art. He failed
when he judged the artistic inadequacies of others too harshly, being too immature to realize that most artists—himself included—cannot sustain excellence
throughout their careers. But the damage was done. In his memoir, Anderson
wrote rather kindly of the man who had once been his pupil: "Absorption in his
ideas may have affected his capacity for friendship."[20]

———

Hemingway's third visit to Pamplona, in the midsummer of 1925, propelled
him into writing *The Sun Also Rises*. He again watched transfixed as the annual
running of the bulls and the Fiesta of San Fermín took place. Hemingway first
learned of the ritual drama of bullfighting from Gertrude Stein and Henry
"Mike" Strater, a painter he met in Paris. Stein had told him of her admiration
for one of the famous matadors, Joselito, who had been fatally gored in the ring
in May 1920. She once showed him photos of herself and Toklas at a bullfight on
a 1915 visit to Spain, and she had even written a narrative poem about another of
her heroes, the wiry matador Juan Belmonte. Hemingway was enthralled with

the concept of bullfighting. He became immediately passionate about it, could not wait to visit Spain to witness it firsthand, and continued to be absorbed in it for rest of his life.

His traumatic wounding in the Great War was still very much with him, and he had an urge to court violence and danger. As he would later write in *Death in the Afternoon,* "The only place where you could see life and death, i.e., violent death now that the wars were over, was in the bull ring and I wanted very much to go to Spain where I could study it. . . . I was trying to learn to write, commencing with the simplest things, and one of the simplest things of all and the most fundamental is violent death." The sun-drenched arena of the bullfight was where the action was. Only bullfighting could give him "the feeling of life and death that I was looking for" (2). The running of the bulls through the narrow, labyrinthine streets in the early mornings, the crowds of men and boys heaving, pushing, rushing ahead of them into the arena—the scene struck Hemingway as something that might have been painted by Goya or Velázquez. In a note he scribbled later about the Spanish bullfights he'd seen, he wrote that the experience was the only thing that gave men an appreciation of life and death.[21]

Hemingway also saw bullfighting, like boxing, as a literary metaphor, and the violence of the sport as a focal point for his mission as a writer. Writing was confrontation, an attempt to prove oneself, over and over again, and take the passivity of art out of the writer's study and into the field. To best someone was always a goal. Even the sun became a participant, a character in the drama. Hemingway was fond of quoting a Spanish proverb, "El sol es el mejor torero" (The sun is the best bullfighter), and, he added, without the sun, even the best matador was "like a man without a shadow" (21).

A group of friends accompanied Hemingway and Hadley to Spain on the July 1925 trip: Chink Dorman-Smith and a large contingent of his Paris compatriots, including McAlmon, Dos Passos (who said he was surrounded the whole time by "too many exhibitionist personalities"), Bill and Sally Bird, and Donald Ogden Stewart. After many days and nights of frolicking, feasting, and revelry, the bullfights in Pamplona came to an end. Everyone else went home, but Hemingway and Hadley followed the matadors to Valencia, Hemingway sticking to the spectacle like a leech, until his very blood coursed with it. As Dos Passos remembered, he "saturated himself to the bursting point," working on gaining the confidence of the locals.[22] Before leaving Spain, Hemingway had begun turning his experiences into fiction, starting with what he foresaw as a satirical short story about bullfighting that he provisionally titled "Cayetano Ordóñez / Niño de la Palma." He continued to work on the story in Valencia, telling Bill Smith that it was "fairly funny" and that he was skewering some of his literary friends (as he had done in *Torrents* with Anderson), specifically Ford Madox Ford, who was to be a character called "Braddocks." The earliest portions of the story in manuscript are narrated by a character called "Hem," but the names of the others are changed: Bill Smith and Don Stewart are melded into Bill Gorton. Two new acquaintances were also present; Harold Loeb first became Gerald and then Robert Cohn; Duff Twysden remained "Duff" until Hemingway began revising the first draft. She then became Lady Brett Ashley. He mentioned again to *Little Review* editor Jane Heap that he was making the book very funny and that it contained "no autobiographical 1st novel stuff."[23]

At this point, "Hem" became the journalist Jake Barnes, and Hemingway began to expand the story into a novel and to make the bullfighting aspect more a backdrop and less a central focus. The focus became Jake and his war wound, which had left him impotent: his testicles were intact, but he had lost his penis. Chink Dorman-Smith thought it was "a damn queer theme" and that there was even "something attic about it." "It would not take a great deal of effort," he told Hemingway, "to turn Pamplona [in]to Olympus and the protagonists of your tale to the Gods who were equally lax in an equally masterless and regardless of consequences manner."[24] But Hemingway was fascinated with its originality, and he completed thirty-seven loose-leaf manuscript pages in Valencia. He then began writing in the blue Cahiers notebooks he'd brought with him from Paris, and by 3 August had finished six chapters—roughly fifteen thousand words. Yet Hemingway himself was very much a part of the story. On the inside back cover of one of the notebooks, he made a rough outline of the plot, ending with "I go on down into Spain to bring Duff back. Get her letter."[25]

He changed the title to "Fiesta / A Novel" and returned to Paris on 11 August with almost eleven chapters done. On 20 August he wrote his father that he had been working "day and night" on the book and had only fifteen thousand more words until it was finished. In December, Liveright rejected *Torrents,* and Hemingway began his pursuit of Scribner's. The novel was now not a story but a "big book"—Hemingway was sensitive, and perhaps even slightly embarrassed, about his slim publications to that point, and in his letters he overestimated (and bragged about) the length of the work in progress, although when published it would turn out to be of modest length.

He completed the first draft, typed up a copy, and revised the typescript throughout the spring of 1926, promising Perkins that it would be ready for publication in the fall. In April, he sent the 330-page typescript off to a professional typist, made some more changes to the clean copy, and mailed it to Perkins on 24 April 1926. He said he would be making more changes when he received the page proofs.

The Sun Also Rises is the story of a group of American and British expatriates, based in Paris, who travel to Pamplona for the Fiesta de San Fermín, the running of the bulls, and several days of intense bullfighting. It has become known as the quintessential novel of the "Lost Generation" and a major work of the modernist movement in literature. The protagonist, Jake Barnes, is an American journalist in love with Lady Brett Ashley, but their affair remains unconsummated because of Jake's war injury, which has left him impotent. Jake remains the one constant in Brett's life as she drifts between Robert Cohn, a dilettante American novelist,

Mike Campbell, the Scottish nobleman to whom she is engaged, and a Spanish bullfighter named Pedro Romero.

The climax occurs when Cohn bursts in on a meeting that Jake has arranged between Brett and Pedro. Cohn beats up the matador, but Romero goes on to perform flawlessly in the bullfights, despite his injuries. He then leaves with Brett for Madrid. Soon, however, Jake receives a telegram from Brett asking him to come to Madrid and rescue her. It turns out that Romero is unable to tolerate Brett's unconventional ways, or so Brett tells Jake, and that she has therefore sent him packing. She intends to return to Mike Campbell and marry him. At the end of the novel, Brett and Jake resume their odd but loving relationship. Brett wants to believe that she and Jake would have been a couple if not for Jake's wound, but when she raises the question, Jake is not so sure. The last line of the novel, uttered by Jake as the two of them ride through town in a taxi, shows that he is guarded and uncertain: "Isn't it pretty to think so?"

In revising the typescript, Hemingway made several important changes. The first was to begin the novel in Paris rather than Pamplona (in medias res) and then to flash back to the events in Paris that led to the trip to Spain. Another important change was the deletion of several passages of authorial intrusion. Several times in the draft, Hemingway speaks directly to the reader in a kind of excursus on the merits of the restrained narrative method with which the author would become associated. One such passage reads, "In life people are not conscious of these special moments that novelists build their whole structures on. . . . None of the significant things are going to have any literary signs marking them. You have to figure them out by yourself."[26] Hemingway steps out of the narrative here to explain to his readers how he is writing the story (and it anticipates some of the more controversial sections of *Death in the Afternoon* and *Green Hills of Africa*—digressions in which Hemingway talks about writers and the literary profession). Hemingway probably needed to work out such strategies for himself, to talk them out, so to speak, within the actual boundaries of the text he was then creating, in order to grasp their importance fully. Later, he would excise such digressions and eventually hone a style that spoke for itself, that showed rather than told. Hemingway also experimented with point of view in the early stages of composition. He tried once in the first person, then twice in the third person, but each time he gave up after writing only a few pages.

Several scenes in particular were revised extensively: the early love scene between Jake and Brett in Paris; the conversation between Jake and the waiter in Pamplona about the man who was gored during the running of the bulls; the "corrida" scene, the day after Cohn and Romero's fistfight; and parts of the final chapter. The most notable change of all was made after the novel had been set in type. It was made on the advice of Scott Fitzgerald, who had read a carbon copy of the typescript and had urged Hemingway to cut much of the beginning of the novel and begin it with the introduction of Georgette, the prostitute—chapter 3 in the published text. Hemingway took most of his friend's advice, cutting away about 75 percent of those early pages, to the point where the published text now begins, with the opening description of Robert Cohn. Hemingway later expressed regret at losing the original opening of the novel. He made several attempts to insert sentences before introducing Cohn that captured some of the deleted material, but he eventually gave up, perhaps because, as Frederic Svoboda speculates, "by referring to the cut chapters it merely capsulizes the faults of those chapters."[27] Later, Hemingway told Max Perkins that there was "nothing in those first sixteen pages that does not come out, or is explained, or re-stated in the rest of the book—or is unnecessary to state. I think it will move much faster from the start that way."[28]

The two epigraphs to the novel can be read in light of its narrator and central character, Jake Barnes. Jake, like his creator, is a newspaper reporter based in Paris just after World War I. And, like Hemingway, Jake is wounded in action during the war and still suffers the psychic consequences of his injury. Unlike Hemingway, Jake's injury is more damaging, and it is permanent. Hemingway places Jake in a circle of expatriate Americans and Britons who are the so-called Lost Generation of the first epigraph (which Hemingway added by hand to the working typescript). The remark is attributed to Gertrude Stein, although its exact origin is uncertain. As most versions of the story go, Stein was having her car repaired somewhere in the French countryside when she struck up a conversation with the young garage mechanic who was doing the work. She is reported to have said to him, "You young people who came back from the war. You are all a lost generation." Hemingway, hearing the story from someone else, appropriated the phrase and amply enlarged its meaning by making it one of the epigraphs to the book that became, in effect, the touchstone text for an entire generation, wandering without direction, searching but never finding, out of touch with the values of their native lands but not fully connected with the values of their adopted home: living, in sum, a rootless, largely purposeless existence. Jake speaks for this point of view when he tells Cohn, "You can't get away from yourself by moving from one place to another. There's nothing to that" (11).

The other epigraph, from the Book of Ecclesiastes, applies to the Lost Generation as well. By invoking the predictability of the sun's rising every day, Hemingway was referring to the cyclical nature of existence: each day will transpire no matter what humanity does or does not do. At first glance, this seems to be a positive statement, especially when set against the pessimism of the other epigraph, about wasted life. But when set against Jake's circumstances, the sun's rising anew provides little hope for self-fulfillment, for Jake's life lacks vitality, and this causes him much emotional anguish. As much as Jake would like to steer the course of events, he cannot do so.

————

Everyone—*everyone*—appeared in Hemingway's supposedly nonautobiographical first novel—except Hadley. Why was she left out? Hemingway had begun to feel increasingly stifled by Hadley and was increasingly aware that her stolid and maternal midwestern personality did not fit in with the chic young crowd of artists and litterateurs that formed his circle. It is therefore not surprising that she was left out of the story, just as she was increasingly being pushed to the margins of Hemingway's personal life.

As Hemingway's literary fame increased, Hadley's centrality to his life decreased. Lack of money became a problem when Hadley's generous trust fund was cut by the man who managed her finances, after he made some bad investments and one of the checks she regularly received for living expenses bounced three times. Hemingway was getting tired of the frugal life he now had to live, although, at the same time, he turned down a handsome fee from one of the slick magazines. Hadley was also looking old to Hemingway, who was eight years her junior—especially after the birth of Bumby. Hadley had not lost the weight she gained during the pregnancy, and Hemingway thought she was beginning to look dowdy and unfeminine. Hadley wanted a quiet life of domestic comfort and tranquillity; the more adventurous Hemingway needed to be always on the move, visiting every sporting venue and vacation spot in Europe. Hemingway's sexual drive was also stronger than Hadley's, and he began to see her more as a mother figure than as an erotically attractive woman. She even sometimes signed her letters to him "with Mummy's love." Hemingway had had several years of exposure to the bohemian types in Paris; although initially he had thought them poseurs and fakes, he now found them sophisticated and exciting—everything that Hadley was not.[29]

Hemingway needed a vigorous woman to inspire him to write. He had lost confidence in Hadley's ability to do so when she lost his manuscripts in the Paris train station in 1922. That summer, at least in Hemingway's imagination, another woman began to take Hadley's place: Lady Duff Twysden. She was the first and most influential person to show him that the legend could be larger than the fact, and that this was the most desirable way to live. Of all of Hemingway's friends and lovers, the gulf between the person Duff had been born and the person she became was the widest. Duff was also the direct inspiration for *The Sun Also Rises*. Hemingway may or may not have had a physical affair with her, but he fell in love with her, much as he had fallen seven years earlier for Agnes von Kurowsky.

Duff Twysden was born Dorothy Smurthwaite in Yorkshire, England, on 22 May 1892. She was the daughter of a working-class father who owned a wine shop and a Scottish mother with higher social aspirations. Duff's maternal grandmother lived in the Scottish countryside, and there is some evidence of seminobility in her ancestry. There were references in Duff's childhood to minor titled families, and she was schooled in Paris in preparation for making a good marriage. Her parents divorced when she was young, and thereafter she took her mother's family name, Stirling, supposing that it sounded more elegant, apparently, than her father's surname. She spent her summers at her grandmother Stirling's home in Scotland, which was apparently grand enough to be staffed by uniformed servants. Duff, however, always stretched the truth to the snapping point, so it

is hard to separate how things actually were from how she wanted them to be.
She retailed stories of picnics in fields of heather with eligible young lords, and
of regattas and beach parties fueled by Pimm's and champagne. Like her mother
(whose dreams were not fulfilled), Duff aspired to the good life.

She had already been married twice when she arrived in Montparnasse in
the spring of 1925 with her third serious suitor, a cousin named Pat Guthrie. Duff
had originally been married to Edward Luttrell Grimston Byrom, whom she
had met during the Great War while doing work for the British Secret Service in
London. Soon after her marriage, however, Duff began seeing another man, Sir
Roger Twysden, a naval officer. Twysden was a wealthy aristocrat with a seemingly endless supply of money, and he wooed Duff with his riches. Ugly rumors
swirled around the couple: Duff was a gold digger, a commoner, and a cheat
who, Twysden's family told him, would drop him as soon as she'd run through
the family fortune. But Twysden was enchanted, and as soon as Duff was able
to divorce her husband, the two of them slipped out of London to Edinburgh,
where they were married in January 1917. Thirteen months later, Duff gave birth
to a son.

Here again, however, the fairy tale that Duff had envisioned for herself came
abruptly to an end, although how and why is an open question. The Twysden family continued to portray her as a vamp who cuckolded her husband repeatedly.
But Duff gave a much different version of events to her friends in Paris. She told
Hemingway that Twysden had terrorized her, even keeping a sword by his side
when they were in bed together. She depicted him as a volatile, alcoholic brute
who beat her whenever he liked. To escape, Duff frequently took her child with
her to her grandmother's house in Scotland. On one of these visits, Duff met
Guthrie, who lent a sympathetic ear. Soon, they too were lovers. Duff decided to
divorce Twysden, leave her child behind in Scotland, and take off with Guthrie
for Paris.

Duff was not a conventional beauty, but she was interesting-looking, intrigu-
ing, sexy. Her voice had both a lilt and a throaty huskiness to it that conveyed a
"come hither" quality to everything she said. She had a long, angular face, a high
forehead, a slender neck, and, like Lady Brett Ashley, curves "like the hull of a
racing yacht" (22). Her dress was ordinary—durable skirts and silk blouses—but
she wore her hair bobbed, in the style of the day. She exuded an effortless charm,
an insouciance, and a carelessness that one supposed went along with her impeccable pedigree. That gossip trailed her as she moved from one lover to the next
made the chase all the more thrilling, and nearly every man in Hemingway's circle
was drawn to her.

Both she and Guthrie, however, were down on their luck. They lived on
irregular charity from relatives, and their funding drifted in and out of their
bank accounts like the tide at early dawn. When they were flush, they lived at
the Ritz and ordered caviar. When they were broke, they moved to tourist hotels
and managed on absinthe and oyster crackers at the numerous cafés around the

city where the expatriate crowd gathered. Gilbert Seldes, then a reporter for the *New York Tribune,* recalled being invited to dinner at a Paris restaurant with Duff, a countess, and the countess's fiancé, a military officer. The evening progressed through several bottles of champagne; then, as Seldes recalled,

> the two women had to go to the ladies' room. That didn't surprise me. Then Captain Paterson said he had to go to the men's room. And I sat there. This is an old holdup game. I always thought I was a tough news-paperman, but this had never happened to me before. A half hour went by and the waiter handed me a bill for something like fifty dollars for all the champagne, most of which had been drunk before I arrived. I never saw any of them again. And that's how I got stuck by Duff Twysden.[30]

Hemingway was attracted to Duff for the usual reasons, but also because of her zest for life. She drank as hard as any of his male friends, and she had a calculated recklessness about her that appealed to Hemingway. They were similar in this respect. They both promoted a public image that was at odds with the emotional insecurities that actually gripped them inside. As Hemingway was fast tiring of Hadley, conditions were ripe for an affair. Initially, the naïve Hadley did not feel threatened by Duff, judging that because Duff played so sweetly with Bumby when she visited their apartment, she was somehow uninterested in mar-ried men. Duff told Hemingway that she found him sexually irresistible, and in the wild setting of the fiesta, Hemingway could hardly control himself. Hadley, understandably, became worried. "It was a very upsetting summer for me," she recalled. "I don't know why, because Ernest and I had not started to fall apart at that time. But everybody was drinking all the time, and everybody was having affairs all the time. I found it sort of upsetting. [Duff was] . . . wonderfully attrac-tive . . . , a woman of the world with no sexual inhibitions." But Duff apparently drew the line at a sexual relationship with Hemingway, claiming that she could not do it to Hadley and the baby. "You can't hurt people," she told him. Later on, Hadley was unsure. "I think it's perfectly possible [that they had an affair]," she wrote, "but I don't know it for a fact. That isn't the kind of thing a husband talks to his wife about."[31] At any rate, Hemingway's relationship with Hadley at that point changed permanently.

Among the expat group, Duff led the men who admired her a rough dance. Hemingway was hardest on her in his portrait of Lady Brett Ashley, a coolly calculating woman who uses her sexual power over men to the fullest. Readers may sympathize with Brett as a modern women seeking an identity beyond the confines of her Victorian upbringing, but she is as desperate to escape propriety, responsibilities, and money concerns as her dissolute fiancé, Mike Campbell. (In the fall of 1925, desperate for cash and aware that Hemingway was infatuated with her, she sent him a plaintive telegram—as Brett does in the novel: "Please do come at once to Jimmie's bar—real trouble. . . . S.O.S. Duff.")[32]

The one man in Hemingway's circle who succumbed completely to Duff's charms was Harold Loeb, the model for Robert Cohn in *The Sun Also Rises*. Loeb, who came from a wealthy Jewish family in New York, was the co-editor of one of the Paris magazines, *Broom*. Hemingway had met Loeb through Ford Madox Ford in the spring of 1924, and Loeb had been an asset to Hemingway—he had bought him meals, helped him get his work published, and even boxed and played tennis with him. In June, just before the trip to Pamplona, Loeb had spent two weeks alone with Duff at a resort in southern France. Hemingway found out about it, and then, learning that Duff had invited Loeb along on the trip to Spain, immediately began competing with him for her affections. Ultimately, he satirized Loeb as Cohn, a mediocre writer and an insecure, pathetic figure who is controlled by women. When *The Sun Also Rises* was published, Loeb was furious with Hemingway, who circulated the untrue rumor that Loeb had bought a gun and threatened to shoot him. If he had, it would have been for good reason. While working on the draft of the novel, Hemingway reputedly told Kitty Cannell (whom Loeb had abandoned for Duff), "I'm tearing those bastards apart. I'm putting everyone in it and that kike Loeb is the villain."[33] Faring no better in her transformation into Brett Ashley, Duff tried to pretend she didn't mind Hemingway's portrait of her. But in an interview later on, Loeb claimed that he had "heard from others that she minded quite a bit. She was quite something. Hemingway made her into a tramp. I don't think she was at all. He made her promiscuous, a drunkard, all of which I can't support. She was elegant in a way."[34]

———

The novel was published by Scribner's on 22 October 1926. The firm mounted an extensive marketing campaign for a first novel, testament probably to Perkins's faith in his new author and to Fitzgerald's ringing endorsement of him to the editor. An ad in the *New Yorker* suggested that Hemingway's star was now dramatically on the rise: "The alert reader will want to be aware of this book from the start—it will inevitably command the sharpest attention."[35] The initial reviews, however, were mixed.[36] Conrad Aiken thought the bullfighting scenes the best ones in the book but qualified his praise by noting "the magnetism" that the bullfight scenes exerted on the reader. Aiken praised the dialogue in the novel as "brilliant" but also thought that Hemingway's tutelage under Sherwood Anderson occasionally showed through: "he slips into the story something of Mr. Anderson's cumbersome and roundabout explanatory method, with its 'what I mean to say' and its 'the thing is this'"—echoes that later readers do not hear all at. Herbert Gorman praised Hemingway's impartiality toward his "deplorably febrile" characters but found the narrative "plotless" and the sentences uncomfortably cold and direct.[37]

Many reviewers were still not over the oddness of *The Torrents of Spring,* and in one review of *The Sun Also Rises,* the critic noted that Hemingway was still "in the habit of throwing pebbles at the great"—something that was "disconcerting in the present novel": "The point he seems to be making is that he is morally superior

. . . to Mr. Mencken, but it is not yet clear just why."[38] From another voice came the following: "A lot of people expected a big novel from burly young Author Hemingway. His short work [*In Our Time*] bit deeply into life. . . . Now his first novel is published and while his writing has acquired only a few affectations, his interests appear to have grown soggy with much sitting around sloppy café tables in the so-called Latin (it should be called American) quarter of Paris."[39]

A number of critics didn't seem to "get" the book: one wrote, "the reader is very much inclined to echo a remark that is one of Jake's favorites and, presumably Author Hemingway's too, 'Oh, what the hell!'" This was also the substance of Edwin Muir's comments in the *Nation and Athenaeum:* "Hemingway tells us a great deal about those people, but he tells us nothing of importance about human life." Muir did, however, think that the young author showed promise: "The Spanish scenes, Cohn's fight with the matador, the dance in the streets, the bull fight—these bring us in contact with a strong and original visual world."[40] Always the gadfly, John Dos Passos admitted that the writing was exceptional but said that he must be "growing dough-headed as a critic for not getting it"—"a cock and bull story about a lot of summer tourists getting drunk and making fools of themselves at a picturesque Iberian folk-festival." He concluded, "This is a novel of Montparnassia for Montparnassians."[41]

On the whole, however, the reviewers seemed to give Hemingway a larger-than-usual benefit of the doubt; several referred to the striking originality and power of the stories he had published in *In Our Time;* their high quality allowed these reviewers to overlook a few lapses in *The Sun Also Rises.* Over time, Hemingway's novel would consolidate his reputation as a major author. He had written it, however, during a period of intense emotional turmoil. He had begun to question his love for Hadley and had tried to initiate an affair with Duff Twysden. Rejected by Duff, he became disenchanted and turned to another woman for validation. Soon, he would fall in love with her and divorce Hadley. The Edenic atmosphere of Paris had been spoiled, and as he looked elsewhere for love and devotion, he also began to search for a new place in which to live and write afresh.

Pauline, Key West, and *A Farewell to Arms*

"An unmarried young woman becomes the temporary best friend of another young woman who is married, comes to live with the husband and wife and then unknowingly, innocently, and unrelentingly sets out to marry the husband."[1] Hemingway could have been sketching the outline of a short story when he wrote this, but he was actually describing the outline of his life in the spring of 1926, as he was finishing work on *The Sun Also Rises* and growing distant from Hadley.

Hemingway met Pauline Marie Pfeiffer in March 1925 in Paris. They were introduced by Harold Loeb's girlfriend, Kitty Cannell. Petite and small-boned, with black hair and piercing eyes, Pauline was pretty and vivacious. She had an unbridled energy that must have struck Hemingway as a strong contrast to the dispassionate, rather passive Hadley. Pauline was attracted to Hemingway immediately. The two saw each other with increasing frequency throughout 1925—perhaps sometimes even secretly, as Duff was rejecting Hemingway's advances and he needed someone toward whom to direct his passion.

Pauline had been born in Parkersburg, Iowa, on 22 July 1895. Both of her parents, Paul and Mary, were native Iowans, but they moved to St. Louis (where Hadley had been raised) in 1901. There, Pauline attended a Catholic school. Her father was not religious, but her mother, a devout Catholic, raised Pauline to follow the doctrines of the Catholic Church. Paul had a successful career in St. Louis as a commodities broker from 1900 to 1912, and moved to the family to Piggott, Arkansas, the following year, where he bought sixty thousand acres and became something of a land baron, having his fields plowed and planted (but not actually working the farm himself) and buying up neighboring properties for further development. Pauline enrolled at the Journalism School at the University of Missouri and graduated in 1918. She held a series of jobs at newspapers and magazines in Cleveland and in New York and was engaged to be married. She broke off the relationship, however, and in the early 1920s moved to Paris with her sister Virginia (Jinny), where she worked as an assistant to fashion designer Main Rousseau Bocher, editor of the French edition of *Vogue* magazine.

Pauline was closer to her uncle than to her father. Paul's brother, Gustavus, was also a man of great wealth. Gus owned a pharmaceutical company and was very generous with his money, funding many family members—including Pauline and Hemingway, when they later married. Gus had no children of his own, and so he lavished money on Pauline and doted on her, keeping a watchful eye on her suitors. When he later met Hemingway, he approved of him immediately. As Dos Passos reported, "Ernest fascinated him. Hunting, fishing, writing. He wanted to help Ernest do all the things he'd been too busy making money to do."[2]

The friendship between the two men blossomed—each genuinely liked the other. Gus would later fund most, if not all, of the important moments in Hemingway's life during his thirteen-year marriage to Pauline—a safari in Africa, a fishing boat, and an expensive house in Key West. Gus, in effect, made it possible for Hemingway to create his iconic public image; without Gus's benevolence, it is unlikely that Hemingway would have managed it. The years with Pauline were to be Hemingway's most productive ones. Gus often acted as an unpaid publicity agent for Hemingway, spreading word of his adventures to his well-placed and well-heeled friends, and passing around copies of Hemingway's books as well.

Pauline could not have been more different from Hadley. Hemingway was drawn to Pauline because of her cosmopolitan character and her freedom from family responsibilities and the obligation to earn an income. Hadley, by contrast, was beginning to seem domestic and bourgeois to him, and her dowdy looks did not help. Hadley had acquired a matronly figure; Pauline was slender and youthful-looking. Hadley had no family to speak of, whereas Pauline had abundant family support, both socially and financially. With Hadley, Hemingway had money worries; Pauline was rich. Hadley lost ground with Hemingway once his eye had turned to Duff Twysden, and even though the affair never fully blossomed, it created a permanent insecurity in Hadley that she could not shake. Pauline, on the other hand, exuded charm, self-confidence, and an appetite for life.

The three were friends initially. Hadley lived in denial of Hemingway and Pauline's mutual attraction. As Hemingway recalled it in *A Moveable Feast,* when Pauline accompanied them to Schruns, Austria, for a ski vacation at Christmas in 1925, Hadley willingly took care of Bumby while Hemingway taught Pauline how to ski. Thereafter, things got even worse for Hadley, who continued to think foolishly that her husband still loved her. When Hemingway was in Paris on his way to New York to meet with Liveright and Perkins in late January 1926, he stayed with Pauline at her apartment on the rue Picot. The affair was now in full swing. It is even possible that in the spring of that year Pauline had an abortion, or so Ruth A. Hawkins argues, reasonably enough, on the basis of new evidence in her recent book on Hemingway's marriage to Pauline.[3] Pauline even wrote Hadley that her husband "was a delight to me. I tried to see him as much as he would see me and was possible."[4] Hemingway was insecure, but Hadley somehow managed to miss this essential fact about her husband. To Hemingway's advantage, Hadley's own insecurity probably made her tolerate the arrangement, fearing that Hemingway would leave her if she forced a confrontation over Pauline. She continued to tag along on their outings, tending to Bumby while Hemingway and Pauline went off to do whatever interested them. (A revealing photograph of the three of them in Pamplona in the summer of 1926 shows Hemingway seated between his wife and his new lover, looking slightly uneasy—as if he had just let slip a lie that Hadley might check up on.) Pauline idolized Hemingway and, as many have noted, even seemed to absorb some of his writing style. In a letter to Hemingway and Hadley that July, Pauline sounded much like the wife in "Cat in the Rain": "I'm going to get a bicycle and ride in the bois. I am going to get a saddle, too. I am going to get everything I want. Please write to me. That means YOU, Hadley."[5] Hadley surely could not have missed the meaning implied in Pauline's strident remark, with what Kenneth S. Lynn calls its tone of "rich-girl certainty."[6]

Hemingway, who did not lack compassion and was angry with himself for hurting others, eventually felt terrible about the way he was treating Hadley and knew that a divorce was the only solution. "Our life is all gone to hell," he wrote to Fitzgerald in September 1926.[7] Hadley wanted to save the marriage, and Hemingway may have thought she knew best. Initially, Hadley thought that the best way to keep things from collapsing was to let Hemingway have his fun with Pauline. Eventually, she hoped, he would tire of her and come back to his wife. According to some accounts, after Hadley discovered their romance, she insisted that Hemingway and Pauline separate for a period of one hundred days in order to determine whether their passion would diminish with time. Pauline returned to her family in Arkansas; Hemingway stayed in Paris. He hated himself as a man of good intentions who was living a lie and enjoying the pleasure it brought him. Years later, he wrote that what he and Pauline did to Hadley created in him an "unbelievable" sense of "wrenching, killing unhappiness," selfishness and treachery, and a sense of "terrible remorse."[8] But the separation did not cool Hemingway's desire. "All I want is you Pfife," he wrote to her, "and oh dear god I want you so." Hemingway feared loneliness more than just about anything. He had grown up in a family of eight, and he was enmeshed in an active social circle of fellow artists in Paris; like the old man in "A Clean, Well-Lighted Place," he could not tolerate solitude. But neither did his yearning for Pauline diminish his guilt: "And I'm ashamed of this letter and I hate it."[9] Hadley made no excuses for her wayward husband. "The entire problem belongs to you two," she wrote him during this period. "I am not responsible for your future welfare—it is in your hands."[10] Hemingway continued to be wracked by guilt, and Hadley eventually relieved him of the obligation to wait out the designated hundred days. The whole episode seemed to drive home to him just how callous he had been in pursuing

Pauline to begin with. In a panicky, rambling letter to Bill Bird, Hemingway frankly confessed that divorce was inevitable, and was justified on Hadley's part: "I am a son of a bitch," he admitted.[11]

Pauline suffered, too, and additional guilt over putting her through such emotional stress seeped into Hemingway like rain through rotting wood. On 12 November, he told her how horrible he felt that her "nerves and spirit" were "broken all the time night and day" over the mess he had created. He even intimated suicide: "I'd rather die now while there is still something left of the world than to go on and have every part of it flattened out and destroyed and made hollow before I die."[12] Soon thereafter, Hadley agreed to file for divorce on grounds of incompatibility. She knew that she was making Pauline suffer and she could not abide inflicting pain on someone of whom, in spite of everything, she was genuinely fond. When Hemingway came to the apartment to collect his things, Hadley recalled, "he sat down and cried. It was the end of something. I think he was very much in love with Pauline."[13]

Hemingway married Pauline on 10 May 1927, but the marriage would prove to have its difficulties. Although he appreciated Pauline's money, he could rarely reconcile it with his devotion to his art—a conflict he later dramatized superbly in "The Snows of Kilimanjaro."[14] And although they had two sons, Pauline was often forced to choose between following Hemingway on his travels or devoting herself to her children. Perhaps learning a lesson from Hadley, who had stayed with her baby while her husband went out on adventures with another woman, Pauline always put her husband's needs above those of the children. When her first child, Patrick, was born in 1928, she left him in the care of her parents and went with Hemingway on vacation to Wyoming; similarly, when her second son, Gregory, was not yet four, Pauline gave him over to a nursemaid and followed her husband on safari in Africa. Later, additional problems would result from Pauline's background. Her devout Roman Catholic beliefs led to her support the Fascists during the Spanish Civil War, while Hemingway backed the Loyalists.

Hemingway's early biographers, probably following the lead of Hemingway himself in *A Moveable Feast,* often cast Pauline as the aggressor in the breakup of Hemingway's marriage with Hadley. But there is ample evidence that the opposite was true. Gregory's son Sean Hemingway recently brought out a new edition of that memoir, incorporating manuscript passages that were left out of the original version. In the new edition, Pauline appears in a much more positive light. The torment that Hemingway felt over loving two women at once is more evident in the restored version. "You love both and you lie and hate it," Hemingway writes, "and it destroys you and every day is more dangerous and you work harder and when you come out from your work you know what is happening is impossible, but you live day to day as in a war." In a section of the book called "Fragments"—transcriptions of Hemingway's handwritten drafts—there is an anguished reiteration of this conflict. Hemingway wrote the same statement over and over again with only minor variation, a total of eight times: "I hope

Hadley understands." The new version of the memoir also includes additional Paris sketches. One of them, "The Pilot Fish and the Rich," shows Hemingway taking more responsibility for his breakup with Hadley. While the 1964 edition casts him as Pauline's victim, he shares the blame in the new version. "For the girl to deceive her friend was a terrible thing, but it was my fault and blindness that this did not repel me," Hemingway writes in the restored text. "Having become involved in it and being in love I accepted all the blame for it myself and lived with the remorse."[15]

Hemingway was relieved when Hadley agreed to a divorce. He was so thankful, in fact, that he gave her all the royalties from *The Sun Also Rises*. It might be argued that, like Jake Barnes, he compensated for his emotional failings with financial means, but it is equally true that he was profoundly ashamed at how much he had hurt his first wife. In a moving letter, he told her that when he realized how cruel he had been to her, he "could not expect to found any basis of happiness on such continued cruelty." Therefore, assigning the profits from his first novel to her was "the only thing that I who have done so many things to hurt you can do to help you." He acknowledged that she had supported him while he was writing all his work thus far and that he "would never have written any[thing]" if not for her "loyal and self-sacrificing and always stimulating and loving" ways. He then added, on a realistic note, "and actual cash support backing"—the first time he really acknowledged that important circumstance of their life in Paris.[16] Hemingway's first wife was also, in retrospect, the best wife for him. None of his other wives, not even Mary, who was sometimes seen as "the professional Mrs. Hemingway," supported him as a writer as completely as Hadley had.

Hadley behaved with dignity during the divorce proceedings. She explained to four-year-old Bumby that his father and Pauline were in love and that nothing could be done to change that. She never criticized Hemingway for what he had done. In 1933, she married Paul Scott Mowrer, chief editorial writer for the *Chicago Daily News,* and they settled in Chicago.[17] Bumby attended a private day school there, and by all accounts Mowrer was a loving and dutiful stepfather who looked after him with the same degree of attentiveness and interest that Hemingway had. Jack later told Jeffrey Meyers that he felt fortunate to have had two fathers "who complemented each other perfectly."[18]

____

Once married, Pauline and her new husband moved into an apartment in a fashionable neighborhood near the Luxembourg Gardens—no more sawmill and slop bucket for Hemingway. The era of the expat generation, however, seemed to be waning; most of their friends had moved or returned to America. Hemingway now had bad memories of Paris and felt compelled to leave the scene of his crimes against Hadley. It was time for a fresh start. Friends had recommended Key West, Florida, an island oasis with few people and much-needed privacy. And so, in March 1928, he and Pauline sailed for Florida, arriving there in April. They found an apartment on Simonton Street and made a temporary home there.

In 1928, Key West was little more than a tropical outpost, four miles long and two miles wide and accessible only by dint of much hard traveling. U.S. Route 1, the newly opened overland highway, was missing pavement in several stretches, so one had to traverse several rickety wooden bridges before finally reaching the town of Islamorada, on Lower Matecumbe Key. From there one had to take a ferry to No Name Key—a five-hour journey—and then continue by car to Key West.

Hemingway typically needed a change of scene when he "changed" women, whether wives or lovers. Key West could not have been more different from Paris, with its cool breezes, light mists, and belle époque architecture. On the island, in contrast, heavy humidity hung perpetually over the area, with frequent wind and rain that showered as much grit and sand as water, and gales that could snap palm trees like matchsticks and send banana leaves sailing in every direction. The houses were wide and spacious and set back on deep lots; most had wraparound verandahs and hurricane shutters.

Life there was relaxed and informal. Dos Passos wrote of it, "There were a couple of drowsy hotels where train passengers on their way to Cuba or the Caribbean occasionally stopped over. Palms and pepper trees. The shady streets of unpainted frame houses had a faintly New England look."[19] Surely, one of the aspects of life on the island that appealed to Hemingway was the lax attitude toward alcohol, for he had become more than fond of the strong stuff while living in Europe—where, of course, there was no Prohibition. And, given the small town that it was, all of the residents of Key West knew one another's business—gossip was traded daily in the bars and saloons, of which there was an abundance: in fact, drinking seemed to be the main activity.

The busiest spot, later to become a mecca for tourists, was the Blind Pig, a bar owned by Joe Russell. Russell, who also ran a charter fishing business, was in part the model for both Harry Morgan in *To Have and Have Not* and Captain Freddy, the captain of the Queen Conch and owner of Freddy's bar in the same novel. Russell was a genial, droll, and often rowdy companion. Reportedly, Hemingway instantly befriended him when the barman cashed a thousand-dollar royalty check for the author when the banks refused to do so. Russell earned a living in spite of himself; he preferred to be at sea rather than stuck behind a bar, and the establishment had the disheveled air of a frontier saloon. Russell's swift running boat, the *Anita,* was used to bring rum and scotch from Cuba back to the U.S. mainland. Later, when Russell moved the establishment to the nearby corner of Greene and Duvall Streets, it was Hemingway who persuaded him to christen it Sloppy Joe's—the iconic name it still possesses. Hemingway's drink of choice was scotch and soda, although a three-hundred-pound African American bartender named Skinner sometimes persuaded him to have white rum blended with the juice of limes, grapefruits, and maraschino cherries. Hemingway grew to like the concoction, and this would also later become an iconic drink, the Papa Doble.

The area was congenial to Hemingway. Indeed, more than 70 percent of his total career output was produced while living there. He wrote much of his greatest work in Key West, beginning with *A Farewell to Arms* and continuing on through *Death in the Afternoon, Green Hills of Africa,* the stories in *Winner Take Nothing, To Have and Have Not,* much nonfiction, the screenplay for *The Spanish Earth,* and the play *The Fifth Column.* He also began *For Whom the Bell Tolls* while living there. He kept to a strict daily schedule, rising early in the morning to write for at least four hours, fishing in the afternoon, and often meeting his friends at Joe Russell's around three or later for drinks and conversation.

Hemingway did not naturally gravitate to urban centers or cities with a cosmopolitan, artistic flair. Although he began his fiction-writing career in Paris—a city synonymous with the life of the artist and bohemian culture—he had never felt completely at home among the poseurs whom he often remarked on during his time there and whom he satirized in *The Sun Also Rises.* It is true that he later painted a much more positive portrait of life there in *A Moveable Feast,* but that book, written in his declining years, was something of a wish-fulfillment fantasy, as numerous scholars have shown.[20] Mellowed by nostalgia, the book idealizes and romanticizes the City of Light and is very much at odds with the reality of his relationships with the expatriate circle. And as much as Hemingway's public persona as a gruff, stoical man of the world would eventually replace the man he really was, he was quick to associate litterateurs with phoniness. The playwright Tennessee Williams once strolled into the Floridita, the bar Hemingway frequented in Havana, and sat down for a drink with him. Williams was wearing what looked like a yachting outfit, white duck trousers, espadrilles, and a double-breasted navy blazer. Williams told Hemingway, "This reminds me of the first time I met Faulkner," and went on to suggest that he and Faulkner were soulmates of a sort. According to Williams, Faulkner was deeply depressed and could not even look at him. But they shared secrets and inner grief and communed in a way that Williams never had before with a fellow writer. Williams told Hemingway that when Faulkner finally raised his head, "his eyes were so full of sadness that I burst into tears." When Williams left the bar, Hemingway looked around at his drinking companions and muttered, "Great effort."[21]

In 1942, another peer, Somerset Maugham (whom Hemingway called "Somersault"), asked him for permission to reprint one of his stories without payment in an anthology he was preparing; Maugham told him "how it was really a work of culture and not for gain." Hemingway was innately suspicious of compliments and mistrusted Maugham's flattery ("Always you are the greatest writer in English language—you and Albert Malz. Or you've written the finest thing ever written—only one other writer [you] can be compared [to—] Sydney A. Clark"). Hemingway snidely remarked to Martha Gellhorn that Maugham's letter had a "desperate urgency like someone who had to get poison for their rosebugs whether there was any or not and the roses for all humanity."[22]

In truth, Hemingway preferred to live far from the literary crowd—in small, rustic, out-of-the-way spots: Kansas City, Petoskey, Piggott, Arkansas, northern Wyoming, Ketchum, Idaho, Havana, and Key West. He felt a particular antipathy for New York, once telling a friend, "It's a very unnatural place to live. I could never live there."[23] When hurt by Max Eastman's bad review of *Death in the Afternoon,* Hemingway referred in a letter to Perkins to "my so-called friends in N.Y."[24]

After setting up shop in Key West, Hemingway began assembling an inner circle of people with whom he could drink, fish, and gamble. One couldn't call them friends, for he had not known them long enough to establish friendships— something that Hemingway struggled to do well. It was rather as if he and they were truant boys who had banded together to plan extravagant adventures and have endless fun. The men he chose for company were not given to introspection or sharing secrets; Hemingway was rarely candid or introspective among his male friends. Women were another matter—he was very close to one female friend in particular, the actress Marlene Dietrich, and was comfortable talking to her about his personal demons. But male companionship was not to be taken seriously, and it was usually "anything goes" in these sorts of gatherings, which included shouting matches, rancor, and often physical violence. Male relationships were an important part of Hemingway's world. This was not evidence of a contempt for women, as some have suggested, or latent homosexuality, but more of a nervous negotiation of gender roles—a sign that Hemingway, and men like him, were never quite sure where they stood in the hierarchy of masculinity. In this sense, Hemingway may most closely resemble Mark Twain. Like Hemingway, Twain was a man of volcanic temperament who formed some strong and enduring friendships, but he was equally capable of turning against his friends, designating them turncoats or backstabbers and fighting them with vicious enmity.[25]

Ever fond of nicknames, Hemingway called his Key West companions "the Mob" and referred to their stomping grounds as "the St. Tropez of the poor." Chief among his new friends was Charles Thompson, whose family owned a marine hardware store nearby. Thompson, an avid fisherman, was part of a mercantile empire in the Keys: his family also owned a turtle cannery, a pineapple factory, an icehouse, and a fleet of commercial fishing boats. He was Hemingway's age and shared some of the characteristics of Hemingway's other male friends; he had been educated at St. Paul's Military Academy and had served in World War I. Like Chink Dorman-Smith, he was aristocratic in bearing and manner—and an expert marksman. (He would later accompany Hemingway and Pauline on their safari to Africa in 1933–34.) Thompson's wife, Lorine, was the assistant principal at the local high school and an omnivorous reader. Hemingway liked to visit their house, which was filled to the rafters with books.

Another friend was Eddie "Bra" Saunders, who served as Hemingway's fishing guide in the Gulf Stream and, like Joe Russell, was a model for Harry Morgan in *To Have and Have Not.* Saunders was a part-time adventurer and scalawag whose misguided explorations of the waters off Florida appealed to Hemingway's sense of romantic adventure. Saunders once told him the story of stumbling on the wreck of a boat, many fathoms underwater, through whose porthole he could see a woman with long blonde hair floating on her side. Her outstretched hand was covered in rings with precious gemstones. Saunders could not figure out how to get through the porthole to remove the jewels, so he left to see if he could get help. Before he could return to the scene, however, he learned that a crew from a Greek fishing boat had used dynamite to blow the ship out of the water and had looted it afterward. Nothing of value was left. Hemingway used this incident as the basis for the story "After the Storm," set in Key West and much different in style from his usually spare, realistic tales. Key West had this effect on him: it brought out the romantic idealist who could dream of buried treasure and an elegant, bejeweled lady who had died too young, forever reaching out to an invisible lover under the sea.

Hemingway also grew close to Jim Sullivan—"Sully" to his friends—a marine mechanic who would later help build the railroad on the Keys. Hemingway got to know Sully when he took his boat in for repairs; like Thompson, Sully had an interest in shooting and fishing. Hemingway later dedicated *Green Hills of Africa* jointly to Sullivan and Thompson, and Sullivan would be godfather to his third son, Gregory.

Both Sullivan and Saunders fit the profile of a particular sort of male friend that Hemingway was drawn to: an ordinary fellow who took pleasure in uncomplicated living and skilled but unpretentious activities, most of them involving the outdoors. But Hemingway did not break off his literary friendships during his time in Key West. In fact, he was so keen on island life that he went out of his way to share it with fellow writers and artists. Among his visitors were Dos Passos, Archibald MacLeish, Max Perkins, Henry Strater, Bill Smith, and Waldo Peirce. Predictably, some of these visits went well and others did not. Peirce, born in Bangor, Maine, was a painter Hemingway had befriended in Paris. He resembled Hemingway physically—he was large and burly—and he had also served in the American Field Service ambulance corps, on the French battlefields, from 1915 to 1917. When Peirce came to Key West in 1928, the two men went fishing, swam in the deserted navy yard, and cruised the saloons and restaurants. Peirce drew a pen-and-ink portrait of Hemingway fishing in a blue and white striped shirt that accompanied a glowing review of *A Farewell to Arms* in the *Saturday Review* and was later used on the cover of *Time* magazine in 1937.[26]

Archie MacLeish, whom Hemingway knew in Paris, also visited. MacLeish and Hemingway were quite different both in background and in their views of literature. Although MacLeish had grown up in Glencoe, a Chicago suburb similar to Oak Park, he had a pedigreed education at Yale and Harvard Law School. He had abandoned the law to become a poet, but his poetry was unexceptional, and he went on to become something of a conservative establishment figure—the Librarian of Congress in 1939 and a Harvard professor some ten years later. (In 1945, Hemingway asked a correspondent whether MacLeish could "still write anything except Patriotic.")[27] MacLeish's visit with Hemingway in Key West was similar to many episodes when Hemingway suddenly turned on his companions in abrupt, even violent, mood swings that were lingering effects of his brush with death in the war.

Hemingway took MacLeish, like all his visitors, on fishing trips, but apparently an unrecorded argument or some kind of disagreement took place while they were out on the water. A bit later in the day, Hemingway eased the boat into the shallows of a cove and told MacLeish they were getting out. Once MacLeish was ashore, Hemingway suddenly turned the boat in the other direction and raced away, leaving MacLeish stranded among the sand flies and mosquitoes.[28] When Hemingway returned to port without MacLeish, Pauline had to persuade him to go back and get him. It was typical of Hemingway to begin friendships well but soon sour on them. He feared loneliness deeply, almost morbidly, and so sought out male companionship, but he also had high standards that few of his acquaintances could ever live up to. Ironically, MacLeish had the last word on his relationship with Hemingway. After Hemingway's death, *Life* magazine asked MacLeish to write a remembrance of the author. The result was neither a glowing portrait nor a character assassination. It was an even assessment of Hemingway's fears and neuroses, and it contained one particularly astute observation about how Hemingway had lived his life. Most writers, MacLeish maintained, were observers and watchers, and translated their visual and mental notes into art. Hemingway, by contrast, was "not a watcher: he was an actor in his life. He took part."[29] By the same token, William Walton, a painter and journalist with whom Hemingway became close friends during World War II, said that his visits with Hemingway in Cuba when Martha Gellhorn was away on assignment were "very peaceful" for that reason. Hemingway's work would always go well at those times, because he "did have to have someone around" in order to be productive.[30]

This was the case with writing, too. Hemingway once told Martha when she was away on assignment, "Haveing [*sic*] to live alone and haveing [*sic*] no one to talk to . . . have been unable to avoid thinking, a thing I never practiced before except when in the hospitals. I think thinking, this . . . thinking, is probably fatal to me as a writer. The worst of Tolstoi I've found is the Thinking. I think with my nose, my hands, mouth, ears, and eyes and all acquired by them goes into a sort of mash out . . . when [I] sit at typewriter which can be ten times as true as though I had it thought out. Because when I think it out I invariably forget it."[31]

Pauline and her husband found life on the island to their liking and began to look for a permanent residence. They soon found a house on Whitehead Street. With his earnings from writing, Hemingway might just have been able to afford it, if barely, at $12,500, but that was a moot point, since Pauline's uncle Gus gave it to the couple outright as a wedding present. The house—the first that Hemingway had ever owned—was large and imposing, with a Spanish colonial look and second-floor porches fronted by ornate iron grillwork. With all the imaginable amenities, and a staff of servants to boot, Hemingway must have felt like a well-to-do Oak Parker. The house had been built in 1851 out of coral blocks (painted off-white) that had been reclaimed from the excavation of the basement by a northern manufacturer who had come south to fabricate weapons for the Confederacy. The Hemingways paid for extensive renovations to the property. Although Hemingway's earnings were high, he had his father's sense of financial worry, and he had not fully adjusted to Pauline's expensive tastes. The total cost of the house, in fact, was a fraction of what it cost—$30,000—to install a distinctive swimming pool that Pauline wanted. The pool, salty from a nearby reef, was lit from underwater by high-voltage light bulbs. The poet Elizabeth Bishop, a frequent visitor to the island, compared it to swimming "in a sort of green fire": "one's friends look like luminous frogs."[32] At a dinner party held just after the foundation had been poured, Hemingway made a big show of sticking a penny into the wet cement and then announcing, half to the pool itself and half to Pauline, "There. Now you've got every last cent."[33]

When the renovation was complete, Hemingway took the carriage house in the rear for his writing room. It was lined with bookshelves and dominated by a round wooden table. Here, he started writing *A Farewell to Arms*. He worked on a black Royal portable typewriter, sitting in a cigar-roller's chair that he found comfortable. However, there was always something monastic (and perhaps even masochistic) about Hemingway at his writing: if it didn't hurt—and that often meant physical discomfort—then it wasn't work. He often composed standing up at one of the bookcases, his pad of paper resting on its top.

―――――

In the fall of 1927, Pauline became pregnant with their first child, and the Hemingways considered going to Oak Park that summer to have the baby delivered by Ed. Hemingway's father had delivered all six of his own children and had, just that summer, begun listing obstetrics as one of his specialties. We don't know why Hemingway did not take his father up on his offer. Patrick later told an interviewer that it had always been "a touchy subject" but did not elaborate.[34] They chose Kansas City instead, near Pauline's family in Piggott.

They arrived in Kansas City on 14 June. Hemingway's distractions were many, but he was hard at work writing the first draft of *A Farewell to Arms:* "I work in the morning," he wrote Waldo Peirce, "and then have lunch then go over and watch the polo have a few drinks in the locker room while guys sit around getting dressed and smell a little sweat and bull a little then come home go swimming have supper read Zane Grey on his battles with the monsters and then go to sleep."[35] He was thinking and writing about the western front as he remembered it in the autumn of 1917. Hemingway awoke every morning to a warm and humid Kansas City. Then he sat down and summoned forth a cool autumn rain in northern Italy in 1917. He performed this mental feat in part by distilling his personal experience, but also through careful research: poring over maps, studying military history, and reading books about the war. *A Farewell to Arms* is sometimes read as almost straight autobiography, but the story actually bears little resemblance

93

――――

Pauline,

Key West,

and

A Farewell

to Arms

to Hemingway's own experiences, and he relied heavily on outside material to compensate for his lack of knowledge. Hemingway was wounded on the Piave River in July 1918, after being in Italy only a few weeks, but Frederic Henry has been in the country for some time, studying architecture in Rome. Hemingway was seized by a youthful, zealous naïveté about the conflict and yearned to take part; Henry lacks that idealistic fervor. Most important, Hemingway served in the ambulance corps for just a few weeks; Henry participates in the war from the late summer of 1915 to the early spring of 1918.

In doing his research for the book, Hemingway studied maps and histories of the Italian campaigns, almanacs, and books on related topics, perhaps, as Michael Reynolds has speculated, getting occasional research support from old friends at the *Star*. At one point, Hemingway owned more than a hundred volumes about World War I, all but seventeen of them nonfiction. Five of these books concerned the Italian front and ranged from reports on military affairs, to details about arms and ammunition, to battlefield strategy. We don't know whether Hemingway acquired these books before he began writing the novel, but they were all published before he began work on the book, so it is likely that he studied at least some of them in preparation for writing.[36] Having actually witnessed very little of the war, he relied on his reading and on recollections of the war stories of veteran friends like Dorman-Smith.

Hemingway wrote the bulk of book 3 of the novel in Kansas City, a process that drained him creatively. He told Waldo Peirce at one point that he was "all written to hell out and pooped."[37] That section details Frederic Henry's flight during the Italian retreat, following the breakthrough of Austrian and German troops at Caporetto, on the Isonzo River northwest of Venice, in late October 1917. Every step in the retreat is scrupulously accurate in its details, down to the weather, the various routes taken, and the condition of the roads: at no point in book 3, for instance, as Reynolds shows, does it rain on a day that was not actually rainy in 1917. The result of Hemingway's efforts made such convincing reading that even Italian critics who had been soldiers participating in the Caporetto retreat assumed that the author could only have written from personal experience. Of course, at the time of the historic defeat, Hemingway was just settling into his new job as a cub reporter for the *Star*.

His concentration was impressive; he got the work done no matter what the circumstances, and the circumstances were stressful—on 28 June 1928, after a seventeen-hour labor, Pauline delivered Patrick Hemingway by caesarean section. It was a difficult delivery—"Eighteen hours of labor with the thermometer at 97 then no results at all," Hemingway later reported. The baby was big: "built like a brick shit house across the shoulders," he later told Waldo Peirce. "Nothing for a guy to watch when his affections are involved." Hemingway was traumatized by the dangerous, slow, painful experience of his wife. Pauline "suffered like we know nothing about," he confided to Peirce, and she had an agonizingly slow recovery.[38] The attending physician told Pauline that she should not have any more children for at least three years, and Hemingway, as much as he wanted to try for a daughter, agreed.

Hemingway had extensive knowledge of and interest in obstetrics, and part of Pauline's experience made its way into *A Farewell to Arms,* in the painful final moments of Catherine Barkley's life as she delivers a stillborn child by caesarean and then dies of hemorrhaging. As the son of a physician, Hemingway had always known a good deal about medical treatments and patient care.

Hemingway many times thought of following in his father's footsteps and becoming a physician himself. At least the family thought he might do so. At age nine, he signed the guest book at a family dinner party as "Ernest Hemingway, MD." Ed laughed about it but was secretly pleased that his son might pursue a medical career. Attending a medical conference a few years later, Ed wrote his son, "It will only be a few years, before you and Papa will be visiting clinics together."[39] Ernest often accompanied his father on medical calls and would sometimes observe him sewing up a wound with short stitches. He was always keen to know the precise way to do something, and he probably remembered his father working under a bright light, tugging on the skin around a wound with forceps. "I do not think I could have watched them cut," Frederic Henry says in chapter 41 of *A Farewell to Arms,* "but I watched the wound closed into a high welted ridge with quick skillful-looking stitches like a cobbler's, and was glad." Hemingway also took an unusually keen, perhaps prurient, interest in other people's medical conditions. In Madrid in October 1933, for example, when a friend had to undergo emergency surgery, he told Jane Mason how he had witnessed the operation and seen three inches of intestine removed.[40]

Obstetrical complications and maternal death were common at the time. In the fall of 1918, when Hemingway had returned home after being wounded in Italy, he read all the time in the Oak Park house, "even the AMA journals from Dad's office," his sister recalled.[41] In fact, in 1918–19, the *Journal of the American Medical Association* published thirty-five full-length papers on childbirth, including one by Joseph Bolivar DeLee, one of the foremost obstetricians in Chicago at the time, on the complications and high mortality rates for women who had caesarean sections. The others addressed stillbirth, birth trauma, the use of nitrous oxide anesthesia during childbirth, and hemorrhage as a cause of maternal death.

When Hemingway was a reporter for the *Kansas City Star* in the fall of 1917, he was given the so-called shortstop run, which included Kansas City General Hospital. His first news stories of importance concerned the hospital, where he saw inefficiency and lax practices, especially among the ambulance drivers and emergency workers. His colleagues on the newspaper later recalled his fascination with medical matters. John Selby, a fellow reporter, remembered Hemingway always disappearing into "the receiving ward" or onto "the tail of an ambulance."[42] Although he did not write about obstetrical procedures, Hemingway's presence in the receiving ward and riding in the ambulances would have given him first-hand knowledge of such matters. He also wrote several medical articles for the

Toronto Star Weekly. Later, as a fiction writer, disease, illness, and injury frequently found their way into his work: the bedridden Krebs's depression in "Soldier's Home," a broken arm in "The Gambler, the Nun, and the Radio," castration and self-mutilation in "God Rest You Merry, Gentlemen," childbirth and suicide in "Indian Camp," gangrene in "The Snows of Kilimanjaro," abortion in "Hills Like White Elephants," fever in "A Day's Wait," and of course battle wounds in *A Farewell to Arms* and "In Another Country," a story also set in Italy during World War I. Health matters often weighed heavily on Hemingway's mind. He was frequently ill, accident-prone, and even something of a hypochondriac; certainly, he was capable of taking small illnesses and magnifying them into grievous maladies. Later, he would become obsessive about his vision, blood pressure, and weight.

About two weeks after Patrick's birth, the Hemingways returned to Piggott, Arkansas, where Hemingway continued to work on *A Farewell to Arms*. He was more than glad to see the Pfeiffers, because he enjoyed their company immensely. Ruth Hawkins has pointed out the family's long-unacknowledged influence on Hemingway. Paul and Mary Pfeiffer were surrogate parents to the twenty-nine-year-old author. Paul was strong and a respected community leader—unlike Ed, whom Hemingway had always thought of as ineffectual. Mary was a doting maternal presence, unlike the imperious Grace, yet was every inch Grace's intellectual equal: to Hemingway, she was the best of both worlds, a source of love and also of wisdom. Even during the rocky days of Hemingway's marriage to Pauline, Mary was infinitely patient, nonjudgmental, and kind.

Despite the nurturing environment of Piggott, Hemingway had a hard time of it with the book that summer. By 23 July, he was "no nearer finished on my fucking book than ever" and was made surly by the "bloody heat" and the "cries of Patrick." Deeply discouraged, he told Waldo Peirce, "Am about broke, made no money this year, haven't written or sold a story. Done nothing but work on this book, book probably shit."[43] Needing "tranquillity in the head and not too much heat," he journeyed to Wyoming, near Sheridan ("damned lovely country. . . . Looks like Spain"), where he met Bill Horne for a fishing vacation while also trying to finish his book. The fishing went better than the writing. Hemingway wrote Peirce that he wished he were in Valencia "with an ice cold pitcher of beer . . . instead of here trying to write to hell with novels." He had written 548 pages but felt he "could write a short story of 12 pages and feel fine and probably it would be better stuff. As it is have been in a state of suspended something or other for 3 or 4 months. . . . I wish to God Pauline would come out and I would get this book finished before she comes. Am lonely as a bastard . . . and feel like anything but work now."[44] On 18 August, with Patrick just six weeks old and being bottle-fed, Pauline joined her husband in Wyoming, leaving the boy in the care of her parents. With Pauline on site for inspiration and support, Hemingway was able to finish the first draft on 28 August, though he was not entirely confident about its quality.

The writing doubts and difficulties aside, the weeks in Wyoming were therapeutic for Hemingway. He was able to get away from the stifling summer heat of
the tropical South and revel in the wilderness—just as he had done as a boy in
Michigan. It was a "cockeyed wonderful country," he told Peirce, that reminded
him vividly of Spain. "Every time I go out and see it I wish you were here to paint
it." Hemingway could easily become absorbed in observing the natural world. In
his letters from Wyoming, there is very little about progress on his novel; most
read instead like a naturalist's logbook, full of rhapsodic descriptions of the
landscape, the wildlife, and the fishing and shooting. He wrote to Peirce of "jack
rabbits . . . as big as mules. . . . So far have shot 3 marmots (rock dogs) almost
as big as badgers, with the pistol and the head off a water snake. Of the 30 trout
caught 26 were eastern brook and 4 rainbows, I was within five of the limit at
3.30 p.m. (7 inches keep)."[45]

Wherever he went, Hemingway observed the country with a naturalist's eye.
The physical details of the world—the tastes and smells and colors—washed over
him like rain. Exploring Wyoming in July 1942, Hemingway excitedly reported the
discovery of a "harbour with high rock hills just like a norwegian Fiord" to Martha
Gellhorn, who was in Haiti at the time. "Torcazas cross the river in the evening in
a huge flight and you can shoot them from the boat. There hasn't been a shot fired
there and in the fall ducks are thick. You can't even see the entrance to the harbour
from the sea. Looks like just a wall of cliffs and then this lovely harbour and the
most beautiful river. There were huge white herons and wonderful aigrets all along
the banks and they were so tame they wouldn't even fly as you rowed past them."[46]

Even in England in 1944—a country he did not much care for—he wrote
Patrick and Gregory, "You cannot believe how beautiful the fields and the trees
are. But the country isn't broken up nor choken [sic] and you have high rolling
country and pine trees and gorse we would have to drive two thousand miles
north of home to see."[47]

The Hemingways spent the fall dashing around the United States: back to
Piggott, a visit to Oak Park, a week in Massachusetts with MacLeish, a visit with
the Fitzgeralds at the Yale-Princeton football game, then finally back to Key West
for a while. In early December, Hemingway had to travel to New York to pick up
Bumby, who had been in the care of Pauline's sister, Jinny, traveling in Europe.
Hemingway collected his son and boarded the Havana Special at Penn Station,
bound for Key West, where they would arrive in the morning. But when the train
stopped at Trenton, Hemingway was handed a telegraph from his sister Carol
in Oak Park saying that their father had died that morning. Hemingway was
dumbfounded and didn't know what to do with Bumby. Eventually, he found
a porter who was willing to look after the boy for a while and then put him on
the next train to Key West. He wired Max Perkins for some emergency cash and
took off for Oak Park by train.

When Hemingway reached the family home on 7 December, he learned that
his father had killed himself. The household, of course, was in an uproar, and

Leicester, perhaps more than anyone, was inconsolable. Leicester recalled that Hemingway "took charge" immediately. He also "took me aside and pointed out some of the realities, and his own interpretation, as soon as he had a chance." As Leicester remembered it, Hemingway told him, "At the funeral, I want no crying. You understand, kid? There will be some others who will weep, and let them. But not in our family. We're here to honor him for the kind of life he lived, and the people he taught and helped. And, if you will, really pray as hard as you can, to help get his soul out of purgatory."[48] Hemingway comforted his younger brother, telling him to ignore the petty-minded insinuations of the neighbors that Ed had disgraced himself by committing suicide. He also told him that mental illness was not well understood, and that they should try not to judge their father's feelings or his action.

Ed had made some bad real-estate investments in recent years and was depressed about the dip his portfolio had taken, although he had also suffered from painful angina, bad headaches, and exhaustion.[49] Hemingway must have felt devastated when he received the news, as he had written his father just days earlier, telling him not to worry about his financial troubles; the letter arrived at the Hemingway house minutes after the suicide. He had also visited his father only a week earlier, specifically to cheer him up. One of Carol's friends, Edith Rosenfels, who happened by the house on the day of the tragedy, was impressed by how, under horrific circumstances, Hemingway still found a way to be hospitable and kind to a stranger: "I had imagined he would be either silent and contemptuous of family and friends and Oak Park or else be loquacious and dogmatic. He was neither. He was brotherly, he was sonly, he was fatherly, he was comfortable, he was courteous."[50]

That day at about noon, Ed had come home for lunch. Leicester was at the house, having been kept out of school with a bad cold. Ed had gone into his bedroom on the second floor and, apparently without delay, taken his father's Civil War pistol, placed it just behind his right ear, and squeezed the trigger. The bullet shattered the bone of the skull and pierced the brain, killing Ed instantly. Leicester heard the shot and went down the hall to his father's room. He found him lying face up on the floor. A pool of red was spreading out beneath him. Leicester placed his hand beneath his father's head, then withdrew it quickly. It was covered in warm, sticky blood. The coroner's jury quickly returned a verdict of suicide. The family and their neighbors in Oak Park all said that Ed killed himself because of his financial troubles. But Ed had long been severely depressed. Hemingway was honest with himself about the depression that had killed his father (just as it had forced Hadley's father to take his own life, in 1903). And he understood that a violent death was acceptable, even desirable, under such circumstances. The rest of the family did not share this view.

Ed's mental instability had grown progressively worse, and his compulsive behavior had also become more extreme.[51] For example, when he and Grace were separated during her time at the lake, he wrote her every day. When, occasionally, he was unable to write, the next missive would contain profuse apologies and long-winded, unnecessary explanations. Ed had also learned some months earlier that he had diabetes and felt that he could not manage the disease. Ironically, the physician who had devoted his life to healing others could not heal himself.

In 1920, Ed wrote a letter to Grace describing his life insurance policies ("the Loyal Americans of Springfield [$1,000], the Order of Columbian Knights [$5,000], United States Life Endowment [$5,000], and Equitable Life Assurance Society [$10,000]") and giving explicit instructions in the event of his death: "Understand—the Accident Policy is for Accidental Death or blood poisoning, and the Health Policy . . . is not a life insurance. . . . All others are for death benefits. . . . Don't let your grief or sentiment come in between your good dead husband [and] the future provision of and for the necessities, and education of the darling children and your own self—Grace my darling." He even told her how to collect on the policies: "Tell one story; write it out; tell all the companies the same story. And don't tell all you know about your own affairs to every one. . . . Should there be any doubt at all as to the cause of death . . . make an autopsy and if a Coroner's Inquest is called have . . . Dr. Hoektorn [?] present in my interests for you."[52] Ed had left a similar list of instructions before he underwent hernia surgery in 1917.

At the inquest, nothing was said of possible mental illness. Grace was too overcome with grief to attend, but thirteen-year-old Leicester went with his older brother by his side. Grace spent the next several days under heavy sedation, and her family and neighbors hovered worriedly about her, praying that she would be able to cope. Hemingway eventually set up a trust fund for her living expenses—$30,000 of his own money and $20,000 given him by Uncle Gus.

Hemingway had always been drawn to suicide, but perhaps it is more accurate to say that he was fascinated by sudden, violent death—particularly the effect that it could have on a young boy. Two stories in particular comment on this theme. In the 1924 tale "Indian Camp," Dr. Adams has been called to an Indian reservation to deliver a child. The husband, in the bunk above the pregnant woman, has his face turned to the wall during her wailing, and when the delivery is over it is discovered that he has slit his throat from ear to ear. Nick Adams receives no comfort from his father when he sees a suicide firsthand. Instead, he receives a terse, pragmatic assessment of the human condition. Nick asks,

> "Why did he kill himself, Daddy?"
> "I don't know, Nick. He couldn't stand things, I guess."
> "Do many men kill themselves, Daddy?"
> "Not very many, Nick . . ."
> "Is dying hard, Daddy?"
> "No, I think it's pretty easy, Nick. It all depends." (193)

Hemingway's love for his father was also shifting and complicated. When Hemingway was young, his father persuaded him to have his tonsils removed by a friend, Dr. Wesley Peck. As Jeffrey Meyers tells the story, although it was Dr. Peck who performed the painful operation, Hemingway always held it against his father for taking out his tonsils without an anesthetic.[53] This experience is revisited in "Indian Camp," when the doctor does not sedate the woman in childbirth. When Nick asks his father to give the woman something to stop her from screaming, his father says, "No. I haven't any anaesthetic. . . . But her screams are not important. I don't hear them because they are not important" (190).

Hemingway sometimes thought his father was able to put up with his mother's imperious attitude by taking a jaded, cynical attitude toward life and death—a theme, of course, that is a hallmark of much of what the stoical Hemingway heroes face in the fiction. The clinically precise view of life and death—business as usual in a physician's eyes—may have been the best approach to an impossible domestic arrangement. Hemingway's male characters often use sex as a blunt instrument—hostility to the idea of love, the giving and receiving of pain; these themes appear over and over again, especially in the Nick Adams stories. There is the chillingly cold portrayal of a rape in "Up in Michigan," the matter-of-fact manner in which Nick breaks up with Marjorie in "The End of Something," the dismissal of women's emotional needs in "The Three-Day Blow," and Dr. Adams's cruel delivery of the news of Nick's girlfriend's infidelity over milk and blueberry pie at midnight in the family kitchen, in "Ten Indians."

An interesting treatment of medical callousness occurs in "God Rest You Merry, Gentleman," in which a distraught adolescent, in a religious frenzy, goes to a Kansas City hospital on Christmas Day asking to be castrated for his "awful lust" (492). The two physicians on call handle the boy's trouble so ineptly that the boy leaves, only to return a few hours later bleeding copiously, having tried to cut off his penis himself. An unpublished manuscript fragment features a doctor addicted to gambling who acts recklessly.[54] And a child's attitude toward death is explored in an overlooked tale, "A Day's Wait," in which a father tries to calm his son's worries about death. Schatz, a nine-year-old American boy who lives in France, develops a fever of 102 degrees. A physician diagnoses the flu and prescribes some medication. Over the next day or so, the boy's father is surprised at how depressed and fatalistic his son becomes. At one point the boy asks, "About how long will it be before I die?" (536). The father is flabbergasted and assures the boy that he isn't seriously ill. It turns out that Schatz has overheard his school friends say that you can't survive a fever of forty-four degrees. Obviously, he was bound to die from one that was 102. His relieved father explains to Schatz the misunderstanding—the French use centigrade while Americans use Fahrenheit.

The suicide of his father haunted Hemingway for the rest of his life, just as the dangerous delivery of Patrick brought home to him the fragile nexus between birth and death: after the operation, Hemingway said that Patrick was "too big" and that he'd "nearly killed his mother."[55]

When he learned the manner of Hadley's father's death, Hemingway had remarked grimly, "I'll probably go the same way."[56] Depression and suicide plagued

his family: one of Hemingway's sisters and his only brother also killed themselves;
two of his three sons received electroshock therapy for emotional distress; Gregory, his third son, had ongoing mental problems and died in jail after being arrested
for soliciting men while dressed as a transvestite; and his granddaughter Margaux,
a model and actress, died on 1 July 1996 (one day before the anniversary of her
grandfather's suicide) of what was deemed a depression-related drug overdose.
Margaux's father, Hemingway's eldest son, Jack, once said with grim humor: "My
brothers and I are determined to see just how long a Hemingway can live."[57]

Hemingway wrote *A Farewell to Arms,* like *The Sun Also Rises,* during a period of
intense emotional turmoil: the end of his first marriage, the stressful birth by caesarean section of his second son, and the suicide of his father. He thus again had
to write under difficult circumstances, but he was determined to push through,
and he did. After Ed's funeral, Hemingway hurried back to Key West to finish
his manuscript, arriving there in mid-December. He completed the book in January 1929. Always unwilling to dwell on memories and quick to bury casualties,
he asked his mother for the gun his father had used to kill himself and dropped
it into a lake to put the matter out of his mind.[58] In the introduction to a 1948
edition of *A Farewell to Arms,* Hemingway—as he was wont to do—looked back
nostalgically on the writing of the book, left out the troubling circumstances,
and idealized the process of invention and composition: every day he worked,
he said, "was something that gave a greater pleasure than any I had ever known.
Beside it nothing else mattered." That part was true: rarely did anything get in
the way of his writing. It was the one element in his life over which he felt he
had total control.

A Farewell to Arms is both a war story and a love story. It concerns the ill-fated
romance of Frederic Henry, an American serving as a lieutenant in the Italian
army ambulance corps, and Catherine Barkley, a nurse's assistant. When Henry
is wounded by a mortar shell, he is nursed back to health at the Milan hospital
where Catherine is on staff. They fall in love and Catherine becomes pregnant,
but Henry is ordered back to duty—specifically, to a post near Caporetto, where
the Italians are in frenzied retreat. Henry's ambulance gets bogged down in the
quagmire that the roadways have become, and he is very nearly shot for deser-
tion when he abandons his crew. He is forced to jump into the Piave River and
swim for Stresa, where Catherine has gone on leave. The two escape to Montreux,
Switzerland, where they spend an idyllic winter awaiting the baby's arrival. But
the baby arrives stillborn, and Catherine dies of complications resulting from the
difficult delivery.

A Farewell to Arms represents a philosophical advance over *The Sun Also Rises,*
making the two novels more than just bookends. The first novel is concerned
largely with the past, the second, with the future. Moreover, *The Sun Also Rises* is
marked by a sense of stagnation, whereas in *A Farewell to Arms* there is eventually
positive forward motion.[59] Henry changes in the course of the novel, passing

through two turning points that ultimately redirect his path in life. The first is his admission that he loves Catherine. The second, of course, is his decision to run away from the war, symbolically baptizing and cleansing himself as he swims through the current of the river to a new life, he presumes, of safety, love, family, and commitment.

The brilliance of the novel can be seen in many of its aspects, but it is essentially about people forced to cope with seismic events. In this sense, Hemingway was far more profoundly influenced in his manner and choice of subject by writers like Tolstoy, Stendhal, and Gogol than he was by Stein, Pound, and the Paris expatriates. With *A Farewell to Arms,* his writing had assumed new dimensions. His masterly prose style is also most clearly on display in this novel. (Both Hunter S. Thompson and Joan Didion said they spent months of their teenage years hunched over typewriters, transcribing the book, studying its rhythms and analyzing its syntax.)[60]

It is interesting that Hemingway chose to chronicle his experiences in reverse order at the beginning of his career as a novelist. He wrote first about his life in postwar Europe in *The Sun Also Rises,* and later about his earlier participation in World War I in *A Farewell to Arms.* He probably felt unprepared to write about his war wound and subsequent disappointment with Agnes von Kurowsky so soon after experiencing them. Like many writers, he probably reasoned—or knew intuitively—that time and distance from the real-life moment would improve the truthfulness and dramatic power of the narrative.

Study of the manuscript shows that the story unfolded in Hemingway's mind as he was writing, not beforehand. He did not know when he began the book that Frederic would flee to Switzerland with Catherine, or that he would end up standing over the dead bodies of his wife and infant son at the novel's tragic conclusion. Hemingway also evidently did not plan to partition the work into separate "books" until fairly late in the writing process. The first sign that he planned to do so appears at the top of the manuscript page for chapter 33, where the phrase "Book IV" is written. Separate leaves with the headings "Book I," "Book II," and so on are interspersed throughout the manuscript, indicating that once he came up with the idea, he went back and determined where each new section should begin. Thus much of the thematic counterpoint and structure that has made the novel so well known as an example of organic unity was discovered—or perhaps even imposed—once the narrative was well under way.[61]

The novel's conclusion is among its most famous scenes, and Hemingway labored long and hard to perfect it. He worked on the conclusion alone for ten days in the spring of 1929, between 8 and 18 May. When George Plimpton interviewed him for the *Paris Review* in the spring of 1958, he asked Hemingway how much he revised his work. "It depends," Hemingway replied. "I re-wrote the end of *Farewell to Arms,* the last page of it, thirty-nine times before I was satisfied." "Was there some technical problem there?" Plimpton asked. "What was it that had stumped you?" Hemingway answered, "Getting the words right."[62]

103

Pauline,

Key West,

and

A Farewell

to Arms

Hemingway's papers show that he was not exaggerating. Depending on how exactly one defines an ending, in the Hemingway Collection at the Kennedy Library there are between thirty-two and forty-one different "endings" of *A Farewell to Arms*. Some are in typescript, others in manuscript. Some run to only a paragraph or two; others are several pages in length. They all presuppose Catherine's death in some way, but they also vary widely with respect to which thematic strands they pick up from earlier portions of the narrative. The ending on which Hemingway worked most diligently was one in which Henry awakens on the morning after Catherine's death and struggles to assimilate what has happened. He experiences a delayed response, and his recognition of the enormity of the event is triggered by his seeing "the electric light still on in the daylight by the head of the bed." Then, Henry says, "I knew what it was that had happened and [that] it was all gone now and that it would not be that way any more"—a double illumination, one might say. This fragment ends on a deeply pessimistic note.

Scott Fitzgerald read the manuscript, compiling ten handwritten pages of suggestions, which he dutifully sent to Hemingway, among them advice on where to end the book. Fitzgerald suggested that Hemingway end the book at chapter 34, with one of its most memorable passages: "The world breaks everyone and afterward many are strong at the broken places. But those that will not break it kills. It kills the very good and the very gentle and the very brave impartially. If you are none of these you can be sure that it will kill you too but there will be no special hurry." Scrawled at the bottom of Fitzgerald's ten-page letter in Hemingway's hand is his three-word reaction—"Kiss my ass"—leaving no doubt of his dismissal of Fitzgerald's suggestions.

Hemingway's reaction, however, did not do justice to Fitzgerald's idea. In a letter to Hemingway of 1 June 1934 concerning his own novel *Tender Is the Night,* Fitzgerald described his own sense of an ending, invoking Joseph Conrad's claim that the greatness of a novel lies in its lingering aftereffect on the reader rather than its ability to be boiled down to an "old-fashioned Alger book summary." Fitzgerald's method of accomplishing this was to stop after a "burst of eloquence"; Hemingway's approach, in contrast, was "to take a reader up to a high emotional pitch but then let him down or ease him off." "You convinced me," Fitzgerald later said, conceding that the ending Hemingway chose to publish was the best one.[63]

Before its publication in book form in September 1929, the story had been serialized in *Scribner's Magazine* in six installments, beginning in May, and the serial version ended differently. The serial ending, often called the "funeral" ending, comments on the choices that a writer must make in determining which parts of a story to tell. Henry comments on how he has told his story and how he might have told it differently: he could have described meeting the undertaker, for instance, and what is involved in burying someone in a foreign country, but he concludes that "in writing you have a certain choice that you do not have in life."

The raw language of *A Farewell to Arms* was a cause of some concern to Hemingway's publishers, especially as the book was slated to appear first in the magazine, a family-oriented periodical. Hemingway had received a princely $16,000 for the serial rights to the book, an unusually large amount at the time (approximately $200,000 in today's money.) He therefore was willing to go along with some necessary cutting and softening of the text. Dashes or ellipses would indicate where potentially offending words and phrases had been removed from the serial version. When the proofs of the first installment were sent to Hemingway, Robert Bridges, the magazine's editor, pointed out that even the dashes might be inappropriate in the high school classrooms that used the magazine as ancillary reading. Hemingway made no reply, but when he saw the proofs of the second installment, he realized that Bridges (or someone) had made two substantial cuts, one of six lines and the other of ten, and blew up at Perkins, writing that he would rather return the money than have someone other than himself edit the text. He noted that his prose style consisted chiefly of omission, so he should be the one doing the omitting. Perkins wrote back to tell him that no further changes would be necessary.

In June, however, the book galleys arrived, and dashes had been inserted in place of such words as "fuck," "balls," and "cocksucker." Hemingway told Perkins that Erich Maria Remarque's *All Quiet on the Western Front*—a best seller in England and Germany—contained the very same words and was about to published in the United States. But Hemingway did not want his book to be suppressed, either, so he grudgingly went along with the expurgation once more. As it turned out, however, the book in its serial form was banned in Boston—the first time the city's police had prohibited a whole issue of a magazine (as opposed to a book). Controversy, of course, sells titles, and Hemingway's novel would end up benefiting greatly from the publicity. But Perkins set that possibility against the equally strong likelihood that legal action might be taken against the firm if it printed the vulgarities in the book version. He told Hemingway that there was "considerable anxiety for fear of the federal authorities being stirred up," and so Hemingway once again acceded to the censorship. "I understand," he told Perkins, "about the words you cannot print—if you cannot print them—and I never expected you could print the one word (C-S) that you cannot." Dashes were therefore substituted for the coarse language. When the British edition of the novel was published, it was even more heavily expurgated. Sometimes the American dashes were retained; in other places, a more anemic version of the original muscular word was substituted—for example, "It's finished" for "It's fucked."[64]

A Farewell to Arms was published on 27 September 1929 in a first printing of 31,050 copies. Another printing of ten thousand copies was ordered at the time of publication, and a week later another ten thousand copies were printed. After seven printings, the total number of copies produced was 101,675. By 12 November, Perkins was reporting to Hemingway that the book had sold forty-five thousand copies: "Everything seems right. . . . [the novel] has been the best seller in all the lists." The previous week, the stock market had crashed, ushering in what would

105

Pauline,

Key West,

and

A Farewell

to Arms

become the Great Depression, but Perkins correctly predicted that the economic crisis would not affect sales of "so outstanding a book as 'A Farewell.'"[65] By the end of the year, sales stood at sixty thousand copies, and Hemingway had his first best seller. He earned royalties of 15 percent on the first twenty-five thousand hardcover copies sold, and 20 percent on all copies sold thereafter. Although Hemingway thought the firm was not doing enough to promote the book and was critical of the dust jacket design, he eventually conceded that sales were "certainly damned fine" and apologized to Perkins for his alarmist reaction to the Wall Street slump and how it might affect his book. Since then, *A Farewell to Arms,* like all of Hemingway's major novels, has never gone out of print.

Reviews were, to say the least, enthusiastic; barely a dissenting voice was heard anywhere in the country. Such eminent critics as Clifton Fadiman and Malcolm Cowley gave it rave notices. In the *Richmond Times-Dispatch,* James Aswell, aware that he was offering "extravagant praise," was sufficiently emboldened to write, "If before I die I have three more literary experiences as sharp and exciting and terrible as the one I have just been through, I shall know it has been a good world."[66] The reviewers almost unanimously singled out what would become the two most famous scenes—the retreat from Caporetto and the agonized-over conclusion. Henry Seidel Canby, in fact, thought that the retreat scene was based on personal experience, so accurate was its description.[67] Dos Passos said it was "a magnificent novel because the writer felt every minute the satisfaction of working ably with his material and his tools and continually pushing the work to the limit of effort."[68] Hemingway must have been irritated when one critic, however, Burton Rascoe, brought up the "Anderson influence" again: interviewed by Edmund Wilson, Rascoe referred to Hemingway's "prose experiments, showing the influence of both Ring Lardner and Sherwood Anderson, with here and there a sentence or a paragraph of genuine power."[69]

Some reviewers brought up the censorship episode, most of them using it as a way to note that times had changed and that a writer as advanced as Hemingway, as Harry Hansen said in the *New York World,* could "no more be banned than he can be ignored."[70] Most reviewers were taken by the love story, comparing it to *Romeo and Juliet* or *Tristan and Iseult* in its poignancy. Commentators saw all the elements of great epic fiction: love and war, beauty and loss. A few writers took offense at the brutality of the novel, the chief detractor being the novelist and critic Robert Herrick. In a *Bookman* review titled "What Is Dirt?" Herrick argued that while official censorship was to be deplored, publishers and authors should censor themselves, and he regretted that Hemingway or Scribner's had not done so with this book. Herrick objected to indelicate descriptions of vomiting and Frederic and Catherine's clandestine lovemaking, which he described as "another lustful indulgence. . . . It has no significance, no more than what goes on in a brothel, hardly more than the copulation of animals." Herrick took the old-fashioned position that such things certainly happen, especially during wartime, but that the novelist did not need to describe them in explicit detail.

The lone voice in a chorus of praise, Herrick predicted that the novel would go down in history as nothing more than "dirty" or "just unpleasant garbage."[71]

Hemingway's friends were just as complimentary as the reviewers. MacLeish gushed, "you have mastered the self-imposed problems of your technique. There was a time when I wondered whether the restrained & tense understatement of your prose would not limit you to a certain kind of material. Now no one can wonder that. The world of this book is a complete world, a world of emotion as well as of feeling. . . . I send you my complete praise & my profound respect. You become in one book the great novelist of our time."[72] Hemingway was pleased, to say the least, and allowed himself in a letter to Perkins some unrestrained excitement. "In spite of having written the bloody book and having worked over it so much that I am completely unable to read it," he said, when he read the glowing reviews, "I wanted to go right out and buy one."[73]

Spain and
Death in the Afternoon

The stratospheric success of *A Farewell to Arms* brought Hemingway to the pinnacle of his career. He was now firmly established as a professional author and a public figure. When he went to New York in early 1930 for a brief meeting with Max Perkins, he found that he was the talk of the town. Newspapers wanted to interview him. Advertisements for his new novel were everywhere, and a deal for a stage adaptation was being negotiated with the playwright Laurence Stallings. A film version was produced, starring Gary Cooper and Helen Hayes, and although Hemingway did not like the movie very much, the sale of the rights brought in $24,000 and introduced him to Cooper, with whom he became lifelong friends. The Modern Library paid $3,000 to republish *The Sun Also Rises* in March.

That month was also the time of the "grand venture to the Dry Tortugas."[1] Among visitors to Key West that spring were the novelist Josephine Herbst and her husband, John Herrmann, who were later joined by Max Perkins and Mike Strater, Hemingway's painter friend from Paris, who was also an avid deep-sea fisherman. The Dry Tortugas, a small group of islands located at the end of the Florida Keys, some seventy nautical miles out to sea, were renowned for their fishing; some of the islets were little more than sandbars just barely breaking the surface of the water. When the four men reached Garden Key, the second-largest island in the chain, a storm blew in, and they had to take shelter in a shed near Fort Jefferson—a massive coastal fortress said to be the largest masonry structure in the Americas. The trip thus turned out to be an all-male adventure of mishaps—like something conceived by Tom Sawyer and his hapless followers. Back in Key West, Herbst and Pauline were plainly worried. Herbst wrote Katherine Anne Porter, "It is over 2 weeks and a northwest wind has been blowing so hard they can't make the passage back. I laughed my head off when they went, taking 24 cans of spaghetti and 12 of beans for a 4 day trip but I guess they knew what they were about."[2] The crew finally made it home after more than two weeks.

Hemingway was not very visible in print during the year 1930. His stories appeared in four different anthologies that year, but he published only one new story and one article. The story was "Wine of Wyoming," a Prohibition tale based on a trip he had made to that state in 1928—a local-color story that appeared in *Scribner's Magazine* in August and was later reprinted in the 1933 collection *Winner Take Nothing.* Hemingway later told Perkins that the tale was "nothing but straight reporting of what [I] heard and saw when was finishing A Farewell to Arms out in Sheridan and Big Horn."[3] He may also have begun "A Sea Change" at this time, about the breakup of a married couple when the wife informs the husband that she is having a lesbian affair.

Restlessness, preoccupations, and distractions seemed to obscure his artistic vision at this time. Vestiges of trauma from previous years still clung to him, like clouds surrounding the peak of a giant mountain. This was due in part to Hemingway's chronic depression and in part to his constant need to overcompensate, to get the jump on his peers, to keep the competition more than several lengths behind him. His father's suicide had hit Hemingway hard. More than a year after the event, he still grieved and could not banish his father's tragedy from his mind. In addition, looking over his shoulder at writers who he felt were trying to overtake him, Hemingway began to think about the next type of book he would write. He came to feel that he had to make a dramatic gesture. He wanted it to be a book like no other, in several tenses, with several points of view, and with several voices. Publishing such a discursive—perhaps even anomalous—type of book had its risks, of course, but Hemingway was nothing if not a risk taker. He seemed determined to make the world see him not merely as a fiction writer but equally as a man of letters. He wanted to show stylistic versatility, and to convey something of his scholarly side as well: the master of a discipline who passes along his knowledge to the world.

These were the circumstances that gave rise to his next book, a treatise on the art of the bullfight called *Death in the Afternoon.* The book is many things—a spectator's guide to the sport, an examination of Spanish culture, a meditation on life and death, and an aesthetic manifesto of sorts in which Hemingway aired his ideas about authorship and, perhaps predictably, got in some jabs at competitors. But *Death in the Afternoon* can best be understood as a passionate rumination on a recurring theme: the tragedy of violent death. It is a treatise on bullfighting and a paean to the rituals of Spain, but it is ultimately an anatomy of violence and a profound meditation on mortality. Its creation was spurred by the violence Hemingway had witnessed in his life and, more specifically, by his father's violent death. The matadors in the book are not heroes who courageously face down death so much as they are playmates of mortality, juking the bulls and the horses along as if tempting death with enticements to carry them off in an instant. For Hemingway, violence almost always led to death, which was his particular obsession. He thought about death, his son Gregory once said, "from an extraordinarily young age," and "his favorite saying was 'your one and only life.'"[4] In Italy during World War I, before Hemingway was wounded, he met an Italian soldier who struck him as too old to engage in combat. Yet the man told him, "I am not too old to die." In most of Hemingway's work, death is abrupt and savage.

As early as 1925, Hemingway had told Max Perkins that he wanted someday to "have a sort of Doughty's *Arabia Deserta* of the Bull Ring," a "very big book" that would introduce American readers to tauromachy but also to Spanish culture in general, for he had grown to love Spain deeply and saw it as the last good country.[5] It had escaped the ravages of World War I, it was not yet industrialized, and, most important to Hemingway, it valued ritual and ceremony as necessities of a life lived truly. The bullfight symbolized this perfectly in its orderliness and discipline. Unlike ultramodernized and industrialized Paris, Spain was a place of simple and solemn truths, tied to the land and not to the machine.

At this time, Spain was in a period of transition. King Alfonso XIII had been deposed, and in late 1931 the republic had been established under Niceto Alcalá-Zamora, a lawyer and career politician who had been active in the Liberal Party. This was the beginning of the "chaotic and critical" five-year period leading up to the Spanish Civil War.[6] Hemingway foresaw the precarious political state into which Spain—and Europe as a whole—was slipping. Indeed, he foresaw much more brutality to come, and he believed that artists needed to show how violence could be transmuted into grace. "The truly great killer must have a sense of honor and a sense of glory far beyond that of the ordinary bullfighter," Hemingway observed. "In other words he must be a simpler man." For a country to love bull-fights, Hemingway believed, "the people must have an interest in death" (184). *Death in the Afternoon* could be a Baedeker guide to the Spanish countryside in 1932, so tactile are the geographical and cultural contours that Hemingway draws—the rocky terrain, the aged leather of the wineskins, the country folk in their black smocks and striped gray trousers. The crowds are portrayed realistically, without metaphor or abstraction and unmasked by mustaches and berets. Thus the beauty of Spain, the elegant violence of the bullfight, and the precise and dignified manner of those who accept death gracefully all come together to form the thrust of the book.

Hemingway had followed bullfighting enthusiastically from 1923 to 1931, missing only the 1928 and 1930 seasons (because of Patrick's birth and the writing of *Death in the Afternoon*). He had written about bullfighting in 1927, when the *Boulevardier* published his article about a matador, "The Real Spaniard," in addition to a lengthy short story, "The Undefeated," and *The Sun Also Rises,* all of which drew upon his considerable knowledge of the *corrida de toros.* Hemingway had also published an article in the *Toronto Star Weekly* that had explained the bullfight to an English-speaking audience. And in March 1930 he had published "Bullfighting, Sport, and Industry" in *Fortune* magazine.

He began planning *Death in the Afternoon* in the humid early months of 1930 in Key West. Perkins's visit that spring enabled him to try out his ideas on an objective listener, and he began writing sometime in March. By 20 May he had written seventy-four pages, he told Mike Strater.[7] He then began making plans to escape the tropical heat and flee to the high country of the west, Wyoming and Montana, where he could work in a different environment—a different stimulus to his creativity, he felt, would be needed for this very different type of book. Before leaving Key West, however, he enlisted the help of Gus Pfeiffer, who had a contact in Barcelona who procured for Hemingway the books and periodicals on bullfighting that he needed to study.[8]

Leaving Patrick in the care of his grandparents in Piggott, Arkansas, Hemingway, Pauline, and Bumby headed west, arriving at Lawrence Nordquist's L-Bar-T Ranch outside Cooke City, Montana, in mid-July. The ranch was situated sixty-eight hundred feet above the floodplain of the Clarks Fork of the Yellowstone River, sheltered by Squaw Peak, which rose to ten thousand feet behind it, and the Beartooth Mountains, at eleven thousand feet, across the river. Hemingway followed a regular routine of writing in the morning, fishing on the river in the afternoon, and food and conversation with the other guests around the huge open-hearth fireplace in the evening. Pauline and Bumby returned to Piggott after a month, but Hemingway stayed on through the rest of the summer and fall, writing, hunting, and fishing.

By 28 September he had completed approximately two hundred pages of a first draft. His progress, however, was halted twice. In August, his horse bolted while he was riding through the pine woods and his arms and leg were lacerated. The left side of his face received a nasty gash that took six stitches to close up and seemingly forever to heal. He was laid up for several days. At the end of October, his work again skidded to a halt when he had to be hospitalized for almost two months after an automobile accident. John Dos Passos had come to visit in late October, and on the last day of the month he, Hemingway, and Floyd Allington, a friend from Red Cloud, Nebraska, left Cooke City for Billings on a camping and fishing trip. On the evening of 1 November, twenty-two miles outside Billings, Hemingway was driving along, his night vision impaired by his weak eyesight, when the headlights of an oncoming car distracted him and he swerved to the right. The car ended up in a ditch, and the group had to be rescued by a passing motorist. Dos Passos and Allington emerged unscathed, but Hemingway was badly hurt. He was taken to St. Vincent's Hospital in Billings, where an X-ray showed that he had an oblique fracture of his right arm just above the elbow. He was in excruciating pain and was given morphine. A surgeon bound the bones with kangaroo tendon and then sewed up the nine-inch incision. Hemingway's arm was immobilized for three weeks. He lay in the hospital worrying about his writing arm, as he had worried in Milan some twelve years earlier about whether he would lose his leg. Pauline came to stay with him and found him "depressed from the pain and worry." He could not sleep with the gnawing pain from the fracture. Being a doctor's son, Hemingway was apt to imagine the worst, having seen some pretty frightening medical situations as a boy.

His fears were not unfounded. Hemingway eventually had to undergo three operations before the arm was properly set. Confined in Billings for seven weeks, he entered a black depression. He wondered if his legendary bad luck and propensity for accidents was cosmic retribution for past sins. He wrote Perkins:

> Since I started this book have had compound fracture of index finger—
> bad general smash up in [a] bear hunt—14 stitches in face inside and
> out—hole in leg [from being thrown by the horse]—then that right arm—
> muscular spiral paralysis—3 fingers in right hand broken—16 stitches in
> left wrist and hand. Eyes went haywire . . . [wearing] glasses now. Can't
> do more than about 4 hours before they go bad.

"Alone with the pain in the night of the fifth week without sleeping," he said, summing up his troubles. Somewhat superstitious, Hemingway may even have subconsciously brought on some of these incidents and ailments, still feeling guilty for what he had done to Hadley, for his father's suicide, and for leaving the infant Patrick in order to write his new book. (People in the throes of depression often have a series of mishaps and accidents.) This may have been the beginning of a pattern of guilt-induced setbacks that got in the way of his writing and even stalled him out creatively in the 1940s, when he wrote almost no fiction at all. He also felt that he had not paid adequate attention to Pauline and worried about whether she still loved him. Part of that angst was assuaged when Pauline came to Billings, but for those weeks in the hospital, Hemingway was definitely not himself. He grew a full beard and never wore anything other than his hospital gown. He battled insomnia and his nerves grew brittle. Archibald MacLeish was sufficiently worried that he came to sit with him for two days, at great expense and difficult travel circumstances. Hemingway, in the grip of pain and depression, accused MacLeish of coming only to see a greater writer die.[9] When he eventually was released, he and Pauline left for Piggott, to spend Christmas there with her family, and then returned for their fourth winter in Key West in January 1931. But the pain in his elbow would not go away, and he had no feeling in his wrist; he had to undergo physical therapy for another six months before things returned to normal.

The spring of that year was consumed with supervising renovations on the Whitehead Street house, which Gus Pfeiffer, Hemingway's financial guardian angel, had purchased for them. The local paper, the *Key West Citizen,* made hay of the fact that the famous writer ("whose summer home" was "his chateau near Paris, France") had put down roots in the place where they had spent several winters. "They like the climate here so well and enjoy fishing so much," the

Citizen proclaimed, "that they have decided to invest in a residence. The place they have acquired is conceded to be one of the most ideally located homesites in the city. With but little improvement of the large lawn and substantial building, the premises will become one of the most beautiful spots in Key West." The paper went on to give the amount of the property taxes and the cost of repairs.[10] Hemingway was fully involved in approving and supervising the renovations to the house, working on an almost daily basis with plumbers, electricians, and carpenters and thus further lengthening the amount of time it was taking him to finish a draft of the bullfighting book. Pauline became pregnant in February, and the Hemingways began preparing for another child, which Hemingway hoped would be a girl.

In the late spring of 1931, Pauline, Hemingway, and Patrick sailed for Europe. He went on to Spain for an intensive research tour while Pauline and Patrick stayed behind in Paris, though she joined him in Spain later in the summer. Hemingway made more notes and continued to work on a draft of the book. There was plenty of good material, for Spain was in turmoil. Monarchists supporting King Alfonso had taken to the streets rioting and looting. Civilians had been killed, and a general strike was under way. Hemingway told Waldo Peirce that he hoped he could get to Madrid "before they set up the guillotine in the Plaza Mayor."[11] The capital was under martial law, and supporters of the king were fast losing public support. Even as steadfast a supporter of monarchy as the Catholic Church was backpedaling in response to the cries for a republic. The primate of Spain, Cardinal Segura, fled the city for Rome.

The street violence competed for attention with the new season of corridas, which began on 24 May. Hemingway saw Nicanor Villalta (after whom his son Bumby had been named) perform at the Corrida de Abono, and he went to Aranjuez to scout out Domingo Ortega, who was being touted as the next great star of the bullring. Hemingway could have been a Spaniard, so immersed was he in following the culture of the fights, learning about the rising stars, and keeping track of all the technical statistics associated with the season. He also met up with Sidney Franklin, whom he had met in Spain in 1929. Franklin, born Sidney Frumpkin in Brooklyn in 1903, had studied bullfighting for many years in Mexico before making his debut in Spain as a matador himself. Hemingway described him in *Death in the Afternoon* as "a better, more scientific, more intelligent and more finished matador than all but about six of the full matadors in Spain today" (387). Franklin was badly wounded at one point when a bull gored him, and he nearly bled to death. (He had to have three inches of intestine removed in a complicated operation; Hemingway observed the procedure and then stayed with Franklin while he recovered from the surgery.) Later, Franklin would become something of an expert on bullfights, even hosting American television shows about the sport and penning a best-selling autobiography, *Bullfighter from Brooklyn*.

In early August, Hemingway returned to Paris to collect Bumby, who had come to visit and to see his first bullfight in Pamplona. The boy was in thrall to "the place where the young lads with the swords place the capes,"[12] but, like his father, had no patience for ineptitude—or so it seemed, as he followed suit behind the rowdy Pamplona crowd who booed his namesake, Nicanor Villalta, during his performance. All the while, Hemingway was amassing a mountain of data for his book. He had collected more than one hundred photographs and annotated them in detail. He had also completed an eighty-page glossary of bullfighting terminology that was, in addition, a kind of vade mecum of Spanish customs and culture, filled with comments on Spanish insults, shellfish, wine, crime, and beer, as well as numerous stories about the history and lore of the sport, unsubstantiated and probably apocryphal. He returned to Paris to revise and enlarge the first eighteen chapters of the manuscript. Two more, he calculated, were needed before the book would be complete.

With Pauline now seven months pregnant and undoubtedly worried about another difficult birth, the Hemingways left Paris to return to Key West on the *Ile de France*. The following month, they went to Kansas City to be near the research hospital there (and to have Pauline's obstetrician, Don Carlos Guffey, close by), taking temporary lodgings at the Riviera Apartments. On 12 November, Pauline gave birth to Hemingway's third son, Gregory Hancock Hemingway (named "for any of numerous Popes, for Gregorian chant, and for Greg Clark of Toronto," Hemingway said),[13] again by caesarean section. The birth was so difficult that the doctor told Pauline it would not be safe to become pregnant again. Pauline had to remain in the hospital for weeks; her wound was not healed until Thanksgiving, and during this time Hemingway lived alone, visiting her daily and working on his bullfighting book. Almost exactly one year earlier, it had been he in the hospital bed (in Billings) and she sitting in the bedside chair. He could not have failed to acknowledge the reversal of fortune; after twelve months, his handwriting was still crooked from the automobile accident. And although Hemingway was certainly happy to have a healthy wife and child, he was disappointed that he had yet another son. "I want a girl very much," he wrote Peirce, "but don't know how to go about it."[14] Hemingway would never have a daughter, only sons, but he would soon fall into the habit of calling younger women whom he doted on and mentored (and sometimes became infatuated with) "Daughter."

Hemingway continued work on the bullfight book while Pauline remained confined to the Kansas City hospital. As usual, the words emerged fluidly at times, like water from a spigot; at other times, they came haltingly, in spurts of great effort. He told Perkins that the last parts were so well written that the difficulties were bearable.[15] "My bloody book is finished except for one piece of translation in the appendix," he wrote Guy Hickok on 12 December 1931. "Am getting Mss copied in Key West and sending it to Scribner's. To be out in the fall."[16] Hemingway was elated: "Really maybe best one yet," he wrote. And to Archibald MacLeish he said, "Believe made the god damn miracle we have to always make happen at the end happen again."[17]

When Hemingway finished the book that December, however, it did not look much like what he had originally envisioned. As he continued to study bullfighting (eventually witnessing the death of some fifteen hundred bulls), the project grew. Hemingway had originally intended a sort of picture book with a brief accompanying narrative. But as he did his research, the writing swelled. In addition to more than eighty pictures, *Death in the Afternoon* in published form contained 278 pages of text, the eighty-page glossary of terms, and three appendices. This was not the lean type of book that Hemingway had written in earlier years; it was encyclopedic by comparison. After the initial elation of completing it, Hemingway seems to have had sober second thoughts about the thoroughness of his longest book yet. The final line reads, "My God, you could not get in all the bootblacks; nor all the fine girls passing; nor all the whores; nor all of us ourselves as we were then." The slippery nature of observation and memory would present him with an aesthetic dilemma for most of his remaining years. Much work, he came to feel, was left unfinished, and when memories were lost or distorted, the truth could never be complete. It is notable that after so much effort with *Death in the Afternoon,* Hemingway still felt that he had not put it all down—that he still had failed to capture either the essence or the entirety of his beloved Spain.

Hemingway gave the manuscript to Dos Passos, and his friend wrote back in February 1932 with the equivalent of a standing ovation. So excessive was Dos Passos's praise that some of his comments beggar belief. Calling it "the best thing [that] can be done on the subject" and "hellishly good," Dos Passos averred that he "kept having the feeling I was reading a classic in the Bohn library like Rabelais or Harvey's Circulation of the Blood." Yet he also argued that it "would be a shame to leave in any unnecessary tripe," and questioned whether some of the material was appropriate, especially the material about writing and literature: "Dont [*sic*] you think that's all secrets of the profession—like plaster of paris in a glove and oughtn't to be spilt to the vulgar?" he asked, using an argument that might resonate with Hemingway—the cabalistic character of the divine art of authorship.[18]

But Hemingway would not budge on the "excess" material. He justified it to Max Perkins, saying that he had "put all that stuff in so that anyone buying the book for no matter what reason would get their money's worth." "All that story, dialogue, etc. is thrown in extra," he told Perkins. "The book is worth anybody's 3.50 who has 3.50 as a straight book on bull fighting," he argued, adding that this made it a better value for the money—a contention that seems to convey some uncertainty about the market for his book.[19] In writing *Death in the Afternoon,* Hemingway was experimenting with yet another style—a third style that was distinct from his jocose, satirical voice and his terse, elliptical one. The new style gathered momentum as the details piled up, and seemed almost to crush the reader with the accretive effect of all that material. It reads more like something that Theodore Dreiser would have written than Ernest Hemingway.

He was taking an enormous risk in publishing so unorthodox a book, knowing that it might fail and thus damage his reputation.

The cheerleading Perkins had loved the deep detail from the start. "The book piles upon you wonderfully," he had written Hemingway earlier that year, "and becomes to one reading it—who at first thinks bull fighting only a very small matter—immensely important."[20] Ultimately, however, Hemingway deleted a great deal of the philosophizing (perhaps on the advice of Max Perkins, or maybe heeding Dos Passos after all), but he also inserted what had already been published as a stand-alone story, "A Natural History of the Dead," in the second half of chapter 12, to highlight the analogy between bullfighting and war. Like the opening pages of "A Way You'll Never Be," "A Natural History of the Dead" is full of battlefields littered with bloated corpses and men assaulted by bullets, shells, gas, and disease. From these scenes of naturalistic observation, Hemingway moves to a confrontation between an officer who wants to shoot a dying man whose life cannot be saved and a physician who wants to try to save it anyway. Hemingway seems to suggest that brutality involves both the living and the dead: the doctor throws iodine in the officer's eyes in order to subdue him so that he can attempt to operate on the fallen soldier.

Hemingway also made late changes in the dialogue between the narrator of *Death in the Afternoon* and his interlocutor, the Old Lady (possibly a stand-in for Gertrude Stein), moderating some of the frankness of these conversations about art and life. But the largest cuts occurred in the final two chapters, where Hemingway shifts his focus from the arena to the salon—that is, from bullfighting to writing. The last two galley proofs of chapter 20 discriminate among the local colorist, the commercial artist, and the writer who creates rather than describes. These passages, Robert Trogdon argues, reveal that Hemingway was determined "to set the trend in literature and not merely to pander to the public's desires."[21] For whatever reason—commercial pressure, personal doubts—the entire section was omitted from the published version.

Once the book was complete, Hemingway was intent on playing a role in marketing it. Perkins floated the ideas of publishing parts of the book in *Scribner's Magazine* and allowing the Book of the Month Club to offer it as a main selection. Hemingway, however, did not like the idea of cutting up the chapters and publishing sections of the book in a piecemeal fashion. The chapters needed to be digested whole, as it were, as that was the way he had fashioned them. (Hemingway also wanted more money than the magazine was willing to pay.) He also opposed the idea of the Book of the Month Club selling the volume because he felt that its sales would cut into the Scribner's sales and that Scribner's, which was trying to keep costs low during the Depression, would not make as great an effort to sell the book if the Book of the Month Club was also selling it by subscription. Perkins agreed on that point, and the idea came to naught.

From the start, too, Perkins had worried about the physical format of the book, because the pictures took up so much space. Here again, cost was a factor.

He explained to Hemingway on 2 February that the book needed to be big enough to "give the pictures a real show," but at the same time he made clear that the publisher did not want to "put too high a price on it in such days as these." Perkins soon resolved the issue of page size, but by April he had decided that the original plan to intersperse the photographs with the text was unrealistic in terms of cost. Perkins wanted the book to be priced no higher than $3.50, which would mean including only sixteen full-page illustrations. Hemingway was furious. He wrote Perkins that the photos were intended to convey to readers what he could not fully express in words—an unusual statement from so fastidious a writer. He complained that he had damaged his eyesight that summer looking at negatives, choosing the best ones for the book. He would agree to drop the color frontispiece, but not the photos, at least a hundred of which were necessary to tell the whole story. Eventually, editor and author agreed that sixty-four photographs would be reproduced by offset (as opposed to halftone) and would be grouped in a gallery in the middle of the volume. Perkins said that this would keep the reader from being distracted from the text, but in truth it was a cheaper way to include so many photos; when published, the book contained eighty-one photographs. Hemingway conceded in a telegram two days later that the idea seemed a "very intelligent and excellent solution."[22]

Ultimately, however, despite Perkins's praise and encouragement, Hemingway's book had already been more or less orphaned by Scribner's through weak advertising strategies, a predictable American lack of interest in bullfighting, and, most of all, the Depression. The 1930s saw the rise of proletarian literature in America—fiction and nonfiction that drove an argument against the wealthy capitalist class and championed the workingman. It was an era in which writers were thought to be duty bound to use literature for purposes of raising social awareness, heightening class consciousness, and democratizing the world to erase inequalities. Because Hemingway chose to write a different sort of book, the feeling among the literati was that he was thumbing his nose at them, implying that he was in a class by himself. Certainly, Hemingway was aware of the growth of his standing as a public figure, and he clearly used *Death in the Afternoon* to enhance the mythic persona he was creating, but the truth is that he wrote the book not primarily for reasons of ego but for the challenge of stretching himself imaginatively and stylistically.

———

As it turned out, most of the critics seem to have understood Hemingway's intentions. When the book was published on 23 September 1932 (in a sizable first printing of 10,300 copies), the reviews were more favorable than might have been expected, considering the arcane nature of the subject. Laurence Stallings saw *Death in the Afternoon* as a celebration of one of the most "manly" of arts, and Ben Ray Redman, praising the book in the *Saturday Review of Literature,* spoke for those who already knew something of the bullfight. H. L. Mencken called it "an extraordinarily fine piece of expository writing," although he felt that if

Hemingway had cut "the interludes behind the barn," it would have been even better.[23]

Those who liked Hemingway's latest effort, however, warned that others would treat it with less respect. The *New York Times Book Review* and *Bookman* gave it mixed reviews, suggesting that, given its subject matter, the book was successful, but regretting that its style was not as impressive as the graceful prose Hemingway employed in his stories and novels. Perhaps the best representation of this opinion was a long essay by Malcolm Cowley in the *New Republic*. While Cowley respected the author's skill and pronounced the book "a Baedeker of bulls, an admirable volume," he went on to criticize the "cruelty" and "bravado" inherent in the work. Cowley also found the style less effective than that of *A Farewell to Arms*.

Other reviews were less sympathetic. The *New Yorker* pronounced the book an act of professional suicide by a heretofore-successful novelist. The magazine's critic, Robert Coates, wrote in dismay, "I have never seen a bullfight, and though I have no idea what my reactions to one might be, I am sure at least of this: that I'd a thousand times rather see one than be told about it, even by one so skilled . . . as Mr. Hemingway undeniably is." Many critics slammed Hemingway's change from writer to actual character in one of his own works, taking issue with his blustery tone, particularly in passages in which he criticized other writers. This undoubtedly accelerated the dissemination of the "Papa" persona that would grow over the remaining thirty years of his life. Granville Hicks, reviewing the book in the *Nation,* saw Hemingway's putting "as much of himself as possible into his book" as a strength rather than a weakness, calculating that he ranked "so high among contemporary novelists [that] more people will read the book because they are interested in Hemingway than will read it because they are interested in bullfighting." That, Hicks said, was his only basis for "going on to [even] talk about the author."[24]

Such reviews emphasized the author's personality and saw the book as an index to the growth of his public image. Herschel Brickell thought it was "full of the vigor and forthrightness of the author's personality" and "the essence of Hemingway."[25] The publication of the book speaks directly to the measure of fame that Hemingway had acquired, and to his considerable impact on popular consciousness. Myths about Hemingway were by now circulating as common-place biographical facts—that he had Indian blood, for instance, or that he associated with gangsters. Hemingway's public relations capital became the coin of the realm. Thus, before *Death in the Afternoon* appeared, the bullfight was of little or no interest to much of the world outside Spain. After the book was published, it became a topic of great interest—first as a curiosity, but eventually as an element of popular culture the world over. Hemingway helped bullfighting become respectable and worthy of serious attention; before *Death in the Afternoon,* it had been regarded at best as unpleasant, at worst a mark of savagery. Hemingway's book is still the most widely discussed and quoted text on tauromachy. Just as important, people who have never seen a bullfight understand the event as a metaphor for the cheating of death, the importance of proper form, the arrival of the "moment of truth" when the matador is exposed to the bull's horns and the animal is killed.

The book also endeared Hemingway to the Spanish people. Reaction to the book in Spain was overwhelmingly positive. Four reviews of *Death in the Afternoon* appeared in the Spanish press in 1933. Two were by writers on bullfighting, the prolific Tomás Orts-Ramos, who wrote under the name Uno al Sesgo, and Rafael Hernández, Hemingway's friend and bullfight critic for the popular Madrid daily *La Libertad*. A third was by Lino Novás Calvo, the novelist, translator, and essayist, whose review appeared in the prestigious *Revista de Occidente,* a magazine dedicated to literature and ideas. The fourth, a brief, unsigned column, appeared on the literary pages of one of the most influential Madrid dailies of the early 1930s, *El Sol.* These writers all praised the book as an introduction to the bullfight and endorsed Hemingway's competence as an aficionado. As Nancy Bredendick concludes, the Spanish reception of the book stands in stark contrast to academic writers' clichés regarding the book's formlessness, length, and detail. "While some see Hemingway's interest in bullfighting as darkly atavistic or hopelessly romantic," Bredendick notes, "and others see it as cynically exploitative and sensationalistic," the Spanish critics saw his interest as primarily aesthetic and "utterly sincere."[26]

Hemingway's reputation in the United States was assailed by an infamously injurious review that came from the pen of the writer and political activist Max Eastman. The review, which appeared in the 7 June 1933 issue of the *New Republic,* was titled "Bull in the Afternoon." Eastman opened with some innocuous generalizations but then went straight for the throat, calling the book mere "juvenile romantic sentimentalizing over a rather lamentable practice of the culture of Spain." He challenged Hemingway's argument that the spectacle was a tragedy, insisting that it was merely a case of men torturing and killing dumb animals. Moving from the book to its author, Eastman suggested that Hemingway's defense of the bullfight showed his insecurity about his own masculinity, which had caused Hemingway to adopt a "literary style of wearing false hair on the chest."

Hemingway's reaction to Eastman's ad hominem attack is curious. In a letter to Perkins, Hemingway revealed not so much anger as emotional hurt—his feelings were raw and vulnerable, and he gave Perkins to understand that Eastman had wounded him emotionally. Given to melodramatic, theatrical responses to such incidents, Hemingway wailed, "I am tempted never to publish another damned thing. The swine aren't worth writing for. I swear to Christ they're not. Every phase of the whole racket is so disgusting that it makes you feel like vomiting."[27] Hemingway was hypersensitive to criticism, and harsh criticism could even make him physically ill. In similar episodes involving reviews, he often used words like "vomit" and "just sick" in bemoaning his misfortune at the hands of critics. His tough exterior truly belied a sensitive soul within, fragile on many levels.

Hemingway wounded others, but he could be wounded very easily himself. A case in point is his reaction to negative reviews of *Winner Take Nothing,* his second story collection, which appeared in 1933. He protested to Perkins that the critics were wrong: "A fool like [Henry Seidel] Canby thinks I'm a reporter. I'm a reporter and an imaginative writer. And I can still imagine plenty and there will be stories to write As They Happened as long as I live. . . . I cant write better stories than some that I have written—What [Clifton] Fadiman asks for—because you cant write any better stories than those—and nobody else can—But every once in a long while I can write one as good—And all the time I can write better stories than anybody else writing."[28]

Hemingway could also hold a grudge. In August 1937, five years after the publication of *Death in the Afternoon,* he was in New York, and one afternoon he called in at Scribner's to see Max Perkins. As it happened, Max Eastman was there, too, and when Hemingway walked into his editor's office and saw a sworn enemy, matters quickly deteriorated. According to Perkins, Hemingway threw an open book at Eastman, and Eastman rushed him. Hemingway later told a reporter, "We were just fooling around, in a way. But when I looked at him and I thought about [his review] I got sore. I tried to get him to read to me, in person, some of the stuff he had written about me. He wouldn't do it. So that's when I socked him with the book." Characteristically, Hemingway then backpedaled. "I didn't really sock him," he said. Eastman was standing by the window, he said, and "if I had I might have knocked him through that window and out into Fifth Avenue. That would be fine, wouldn't it? That would have got me in wrong with my boss, and he might have had me arrested. So, though I was sore, I just slapped him. That knocked him down. He fell back there on the window seat." At the end of the interview, Hemingway added, "Here's a statement. If Mr. Eastman takes his prowess seriously—if he has not, as it seems, gone in for fiction—then let him waive all medical rights and legal claims to damages, and I'll put up $1,000 for any charity he favors or for himself. Then we'll go into a room and he can read his book to me—the part of his book about me. Well, the best man unlocks the door."[29]

Eastman's version of events was, of course, different. It ended with "Ernest on his back, both shoulders touching the floor, and me on top of him." "It is true that I neglected the excellent opportunity to hit him," Eastman told a newspaper reporter, "but I am afraid the real reason for that is that my mama brought me up not to do such naughty things. As for his offer of $1,000 if I will lock myself in a room with him 'with all medical rights and legal claims waived,' I think if I accepted it the chances are about fifty-fifty that you would find me caressingly carved up in little cubes and stowed in the ice chest. And my price for that is more than $1,000. I did not call Ernest a big bully. I called him a lunatic."[30] An editorial the following day in the *New York Times* printed the rumor that there was going to be a rematch. If so, the writer opined, it "really ought to be staged in Carnegie Hall for the benefit of the Nobel Peace Fund or something." No rematch, however, ever took place.

Hemingway's pugnacity and reputation for brawling had by now reached legendary levels, going all the way back to his bout with Morley Callaghan in Paris
in 1929. The year before the fracas with Eastman, Hemingway had been involved
in a well-publicized fistfight with the poet Wallace Stevens in Key West, although
they later made up and became friends. Hemingway was mercurial and quick to
challenge even the smallest slight. Thin-skinned and defensive, he simply could
not accept that others did not regard him as the greatest living American writer.
In a letter to Sara Murphy describing the fight with Stevens, Hemingway said,
"I don't know anybody [who] needed to be hit worse than Mr. S. . . . I think he
is really one of those mirror fighters who swells his muscles and practices lethal
punches in the bathroom while he hates his betters."[31] This was unfair—and it was
not the first time, or the last, that Hemingway projected his own image onto one
of his antagonists.

———

Hemingway's pugnacious public image was the opposite of the warm and compassionate side that he showed to his family—especially his children. As a family man, Hemingway was considerably gentler, kinder, and more accepting of
people's flaws. Having been effectively orphaned by his own father's suicide,
Hemingway was determined that his own children should have a strong paternal
role model. Perhaps Hemingway overplayed this role, but it is to his credit that
he saw this as one of his life's goals. It is true that his sons felt enormous pressure
to live up to his high expectations, but Hemingway was a concerned and devoted
father. His bibliographer Louis Cohn reported that when he and his wife once
visited the Hemingways at a New York hotel, they watched Hemingway help
Patrick go to the bathroom and then sang him a French lullaby at bedtime. On
another occasion, his eldest son, Jack, was being bullied by a housemaid in Key
West, who apparently went around with a giant land crab held in the folds of her
apron. She would use the crab to scare the boys into obedience. The maid was
dismissed when Hemingway learned of her cruelty.

Hemingway wanted the best for his boys. This was particularly true with his
third son, Gregory. Gregory would experience profound trauma and psychological challenges later in life; much of this has been blamed on his father, but
Hemingway usually did his best to help his son. Nicknamed "Gigi" (pronounced
with hard g's), the boy did not get much attention from Pauline and was perhaps
therefore the most mischievous of Hemingway's three sons. Gigi once coated a
pair of his father's cats with green paint, but even then, Hemingway could not
bring himself to discipline him. He was tolerant and did not lose his temper. He
did not allow any of his boys to push him over the edge, as he did with his peers
and competitors. Pauline left most decisions regarding the boys to her husband.

Hemingway tried hard to be the ideal father. One friend recalled that he sang
the boys to sleep, stayed up all night when they were sick, and even lied to a maid
who turned in one of the boys for some transgression that Hemingway felt was
not severe enough to warrant punishment; he told the woman he had spanked

the boy, although in fact he had only gone into another room, closed the door, and slapped his own thigh loudly, simulating a beating.[32]

Often capable of great empathy, Hemingway was deeply concerned when he saw others in pain. The most poignant example of this, perhaps, was his distress over the eventually fatal illness of Gerald and Sara Murphy's son Patrick. On 5 April 1933, he sent Patrick, confined in a Manhattan hospital where he had been for some time, a kind letter full of encouragement and support. He tried to take the boy's mind off his dire circumstances by describing a fishing expedition he was about to make.[33] In January 1937, when the boy was dying, Hemingway drove from Manhattan to the Murphys' home in Saranac Lake to visit him. The sight of the young man lying in bed, in obvious pain, made Hemingway cry, and he had to rush out of the room.

In his memoir, *Papa,* Gregory recorded that his mother admitted her maternal shortcomings. "Gig," she once told him, "I just don't have much of what's called a maternal instinct, I guess. I can't *stand* horrid little children until they are five or six—[and] they're still pretty awful then." As a result, Gregory and his brothers were frequently left alone while their parents took extended trips—Gregory, for example, was only about three and a half years old when the Hemingways took their twelve-week African safari in 1933–34. Gregory and Patrick were raised largely by an older German woman named Ada Stern, who served as nurse, governess, and nanny. Instead of snuggling with and being cared for by Pauline, Gregory was bathed by Ada and slept in her bed with her. Gregory asserted that his mother "left my rearing entirely to Ada, an odd sort of Prussian governess, who had never married in her youth, which by the time we met was far behind her. . . . Any infraction of her innumerable rules would cause her to fly into a screaming fit. . . . She would pack her bags and go hobbling down the stairs with me clinging to her skirts, screaming, 'Ada, don't leave me, please don't leave me!'" He later described her as a "pretty monstrous woman" and, more interesting, soon understood that she was a lesbian who apparently entertained lovers in the Hemingway house while the boys' parents were away.[34] The situation reminds one of the Hemingway children being left in the care of Ruth Arnold, although in that era Arnold's sexual proclivities—whatever they were—would not have interested Hemingway or his siblings. The emotional difficulties that Gregory experienced later in life, especially those involving his sexuality, must have had some of their origin in his childhood.

Although Hemingway tried to devote equal attention to all three of his children, Gregory often felt that Patrick was favored. One taunting event may bear witness to this—when Patrick concocted a spray bomb of powders (mosquito repellents, toothache remedies, and talc) and lobbed it at his brother, whose eyes were irritated by the mixture; Gigi cried uncontrollably from the burning sensation in his eyes. Hemingway found out about it and confronted Patrick, who bravely confessed to the deed. According to Gregory, however, Hemingway seemed pleased that Patrick had not only admitted culpability but described how he had thrown himself into the "attack" with gusto, fiercely assailing his opponent. This incident shows how, as the boys grew older, Hemingway became more aware of them as people rather than offspring. Hemingway did not shy away from—or necessarily find anything wrong with—violent fighting tactics or displays of brawn.

Perhaps because Gregory knew that his father had wanted a girl instead of another boy, he tried over-hard to please him. Strong, stocky, and keenly intelligent, the dark-eyed boy in many ways resembled his father, who once said that Greg had "the biggest dark side in the family, except me." Father and son shared a similar steely determination, and by age eleven, Greg was showing signs of the same athletic gifts his father possessed. He loved fishing. In *Islands in the Stream,* Schatz's face is described as "lighting instantly" when his father asks him about a fly he is tying (50). Gregory was also a champion marksman who shot as if guided by radar. He had good instincts and was careful in the field; he never took a shot out of range or tried to hit a bird who swooped too close. Greg also won many shooting tournaments, which made Hemingway swell with pride. When Hemingway entered his son in the Cuban pigeon-shooting championship tournament, Greg defeated more than 140 contestants, including some of the best wing shots in the world, to tie for top honors.

But if there was triumph, there was also tumult. As a student at prep school in Connecticut, Greg was instructed to write an original story for English class. Wanting to please his father, he resorted to copying a tale already published, by no less august an author than Ivan Turgenev (ironically, the author of *Fathers and Sons*). The teacher spotted the plagiarism, confronted Gregory, and contacted Hemingway, who barely spoke to the boy for weeks afterward. (Hemingway wrote a story about the plagiarism incident titled "I Guess Everything Reminds You of Something," which was published after his death.) Years later, when Greg was a young medical student living in Los Angeles, they quarreled almost irreparably. As his boys became men, the aging Hemingway took on younger wives and lovers. He then competed with his sons—in at least some small sense—on a sexual level, comparing his exploits and liaisons with attractive young women to their amorous relationships.

The boys clearly wanted to please their father, and Hemingway would lavish high praise on their accomplishments. But he also criticized their deficiencies severely when they did not live up to his high expectations. In 1936 he wrote to Pauline's mother, Mary Pfeiffer, "It is only this last year that I have gotten any sort of understanding or feeling about how anyone can feel about their children or what they can mean to them. . . . I was never a great child lover but these kids are really good company and are very funny and I think (though may be prejudiced) very smart."[35]

Hemingway liked to be around youth. He liked the way his sons and other young men looked up to him as a teacher and role model. He had many disciples, among them Arnold Samuelson, a would-be writer who helped out as a part-time crewman on Hemingway's boat, the *Pilar,* in 1934. Another was Walter Houk, who worked in Havana in the late 1940s and ended up marrying Hemingway's secretary. This was also true of Hemingway's relationship with younger women. Honoria Donnelly, the daughter of Gerald and Sara Murphy, recalled years later moments when Hemingway showed her how to perfect a certain skill, like cleaning a fish: "He was very gentle and had a quality that somehow made you want to please him; you wanted to do well in front of him."[36]

Hemingway's relationship with his mother was also far less fractious than has been depicted. While it is true that he said some vicious things about her, he also cared for her financially after Ed's death, as we have seen, even though Grace often hectored him for not writing to her frequently enough. In 1932, she wrote him from Oak Park, "I won't bother you with any more letters after this as it will take you some time to answer the past six that I have written you." Irritated, Hemingway responded that he was uncomfortable replying to someone who adopted such a high moral tone, but he refrained from further criticism. Hemingway and his mother were almost exactly alike in manner and personality: competitive, self-absorbed, unwilling to suffer slackers or poseurs, and intensely ambitious. He never publicly acknowledged the similarities, but one cannot help but assume that he recognized them and thought about them frequently.

For all that has been written about Hemingway's relationship with his own father and how it influenced the themes and topics of his fiction and his relationship with his sons, maternal figures also had a deep and lasting influence on Hemingway's life. With the single exception of Hadley Richardson, Hemingway was attracted to women who were far from motherly—Pauline, Jane Mason, Martha, and Mary. Hemingway was famous for giving people nicknames, and his array here is complex and fascinating. Pauline (a feminized form of a male name) became, ironically, Poor Old Mama ("P.O.M.") in *Green Hills of Africa*. Martha (an unambiguously female name) became "Marty," more properly a man's name. Mary was always referred to as "Miss Mary." For companions on outdoor adventures, in drinking, and in conversation, he chose stalwart, capable male friends. But for women to whom he could draw close and enjoy a true, intimate friendship, he tended to gravitate toward motherly types. He became very close, for instance, to the mothers of two of his wives, Mary Pfeiffer and Edna Gellhorn. He also took great comfort in the companionship of Adriana Ivancich's mother. Indeed, he spent almost as much time with her as he did with his young ingenue. Hemingway sometimes seems to have understood the needs of these older, "domestic" women more than those of his younger wives, with their varied interests and desires.

Hemingway ran into conflict often with his wives, but little has been written about his long-standing rift with his younger sister Carol. Carol visited Hemingway in Key West while a student at Rollins College in Winter Park, Florida, in 1930–32. Hemingway encouraged her in the study of French and creative writing, tutored her in different subjects, and sent her lists of books he thought she should read. Carol fell in love with a classmate at Rollins, John Gardner, in 1932, and after a few months Gardner asked her to marry him. When she told her brother, he was angry and forbade her to marry Gardner. When she pushed back, he threatened to cut her off completely—sounding very much like his mother—and said he would never see or speak with her again if she went through with the marriage. Carol married Gardner the following year, during a semester at the University of Vienna, and Hemingway made good on his threat, in spite of Carol's many attempts over the years to contact him and her many peace offerings, all of which he spurned.[37]

The opposition to his sister's marriage was irrational and may have signaled the beginning of some kind of breakdown in mental connections (perhaps an early sign of the paranoia that would plague Hemingway later). He called Gardner "priggish" and "an inverted boy scout"—comments without any tangible basis. They amounted, in effect, to fantasies or fabrications—ideas that literally came out of nowhere. Hemingway may have seen Gardner as a threat to his close relationship with his sister. He may not have wanted anything to obstruct her adulation of him and thus responded like a jilted lover. Hemingway's hypersensitivity is clearly in evidence here: the smallest slight or threat could produce disproportionate consequences.

Almost inevitably, Hemingway's relationship with Pauline also began to run aground. In 1931, Gregory had been delivered by caesarean section, as Patrick had in 1928. Both were difficult births, and the doctor told Pauline that it would be dangerous to have any more children. Hemingway would now never be able to have the daughter he longed for, at least not with Pauline. Moreover, Pauline was an observant Roman Catholic and balked at using birth control. Hemingway grew convinced that this rigid orthodoxy had extinguished the flame of their passion and caused his sexual dissatisfaction. A rift developed in their marriage, which would end in divorce a few years later, and became an excuse for Hemingway again to indulge his wandering eye, just as he had when he left Hadley for Pauline.

FIG. 1

The Hemingway home at 439 North Highland Avenue. Photographer unknown. Papers of Ernest Hemingway, Photograph Collection, John F. Kennedy Presidential Library and Museum, Boston.

FIG. 2

The Hemingway family in 1905:
from left, Marcelline, Madelaine
("Sunny"), Ed, Grace, Ursula, and
Ernest. Younger brother Leicester
was born in 1915. Photographer unknown. Papers of Ernest Hemingway, Photograph Collection, John
F. Kennedy Presidential Library
and Museum, Boston.

FIG. 3
opposite

In his Red Cross uniform. As an
ambulance driver, Hemingway was
given the Italian rank of *sottotenente,*
or second lieutenant. Photographer unknown. Papers of Ernest
Hemingway, Photograph Collection, John F. Kennedy Presidential
Library and Museum, Boston.

Gino-Fish
Chicago.

FIG. 4   "Ag" and "The Kid." Recovering from his injuries in Milan with Agnes von Kurowsky, the first great love of Hemingway's life. Photographer unknown. Papers of Ernest Hemingway, Photograph Collection, John F. Kennedy Presidential Library and Museum, Boston.

FIG. 5   On the slopes in Schruns, Austria, 1926, with Hadley and John Hadley Nicanor Hemingway, known as "Bumby." Photographer unknown. Papers of Ernest Hemingway, Photograph Collection, John F. Kennedy Presidential Library and Museum, Boston.

FIG. 6   Gertrude Stein with Bumby, her godson, in Paris, 1924. Photographer unknown. Papers of Ernest Hemingway, Photograph Collection, John F. Kennedy Presidential Library and Museum, Boston.

FIG. 7   First time in Pamplona, summer 1923. Photographer unknown. Papers of Ernest Hemingway, Photograph Collection, John F. Kennedy Presidential Library and Museum, Boston.

FIG. 8   Pauline, striking a sensuous pose in Key West. Photographer unknown. Papers of Ernest Hemingway, Photograph Collection, John F. Kennedy Presidential Library and Museum, Boston.

FIG. 9   The Whitehead Street house in Key West, given to Hemingway and Pauline by the beneficent Uncle Gus. Photographer unknown. Papers of Ernest Hemingway, Photograph Collection, John F. Kennedy Presidential Library and Museum, Boston.

FIG. 10

With "Sloppy Joe" Russell (the model for Harry Morgan in *To Have and Have Not*) and Russell's boat, the *Anita;* it was often used to bring rum and scotch from Cuba back to the mainland. Photographer unknown. Papers of Ernest Hemingway, Photograph Collection, John F. Kennedy Presidential Library and Museum, Boston.

FIG. 11

Jane Mason with Carlos Gutierrez, the first mate of the *Pilar*. Photographer unknown. Papers of Ernest Hemingway, Photograph Collection, John F. Kennedy Presidential Library and Museum, Boston.

FIG. 12 Hemingway's first safari in Africa, 1933–34. It lasted only twelve weeks, but it left him entranced by the continent for the rest of his life. Photographer unknown. Papers of Ernest Hemingway, Photograph Collection, John F. Kennedy Presidential Library and Museum, Boston.

FIG. 13
opposite Martha Gellhorn at about age thirty. In Hemingway's imagination, Gellhorn was connected with the romance of the Spanish Civil War. Photographer unknown. Papers of Ernest Hemingway, Photograph Collection, John F. Kennedy Presidential Library and Museum, Boston.

FIG. 14 The last great cause in the last good country: with Basque separatists in Spain, 1937. Photographer unknown. Papers of Ernest Hemingway, Photograph Collection, John F. Kennedy Presidential Library and Museum, Boston.

FIG. 15
Hemingway and Gellhorn in China during the Second Sino-Japanese War, ca. 1941. Photographer unknown. Papers of Ernest Hemingway, Photograph Collection, John F. Kennedy Presidential Library and Museum, Boston.

FIG. 16
Hemingway's press identification card in World War II. Photographer unknown. Papers of Ernest Hemingway, Photograph Collection, John F. Kennedy Presidential Library and Museum, Boston.

FIG. 17

By the roadside somewhere in France, summer 1944. Photographer unknown. Papers of Ernest Hemingway, Photograph Collection, John F. Kennedy Presidential Library and Museum, Boston.

FIG. 18

Father and sons, Cuba, 1945. From left, Patrick, Jack, and Greg. Photographer unknown. Papers of Ernest Hemingway, Photograph Collection, John F. Kennedy Presidential Library and Museum, Boston.

FIG. 19 Hemingway with Adriana Ivancich, the inspiration for Renata in *Across the River and into the Trees*: "She had pale, almost olive colored skin, a profile that could break your, or anyone else's heart." Photographer unknown. Papers of Ernest Hemingway, Photograph Collection, John F. Kennedy Presidential Library and Museum, Boston.

Report from Africa:

HEMINGWAY, WIFE KILLED IN AIR CRASH

—Story on Page 2—

'NO SIGN OF LIFE' AT WRECK . . .

Mrs. Mary Hemingway, fourth wife of Pulitzer Prize winning author Ernest Hemingway, is believed to have perished with him in the crash of a charter plane in the East African jungle where they had been on safari. At right, one of the best . . . with a leopard he shot several weeks ago. *(Other Photos, Page 2)*

FIG. 20

One of many newspaper stories falsely reporting Hemingway's death after the second plane crash, in central Uganda. Hemingway collected the clippings in two scrapbooks and read over them obsessively. Photographer unknown. Photo from The Mirror Pix Photo Archives, courtesy of Papers of Ernest Hemingway, Photograph Collection, John F. Kennedy Presidential Library and Museum, Boston.

FIG. 21

With the famed bullfighter Antonio Ordóñez: "He is spooked sometimes in the night the way we all are and prefers to sleep in the daytime . . . but he loves his work truly." Photographer unknown. Papers of Ernest Hemingway, Photograph Collection, John F. Kennedy Presidential Library and Museum, Boston.

FIG. 22

Hemingway in Spain, 1959. Photo:
Mary Hemingway. Papers of Ernest
Hemingway, Photograph Collec-
tion, John F. Kennedy Presidential
Library and Museum, Boston.

FIG. 23

Finis: Hemingway's burial in
Ketchum, Idaho, 5 July 1961. Photo:
Francis Miller. Slade Paul Collec-
tion / Getty Images.

Jane Mason
and Africa

While still married to Pauline, Hemingway began a dalliance with Jane Kendall Mason, a twenty-two-year-old woman he had met on the ocean liner *Ile de France* in the fall of 1931 as he and Pauline were returning from Spain. Jane, a curvaceous blond, was ten years Hemingway's junior (and fourteen years younger than Pauline). With Pauline unable to bear more children, Hemingway probably saw Jane as a future wife. She was married, but he persuaded himself that she could easily divorce her husband, take up with him, and have a family. Although their relationship was on again, off again, it lasted from the spring of 1932 through 1936—a good four years. And although he treated Jane badly at times, as he did nearly every woman with whom he got involved, Hemingway cared for her deeply, felt injured when their relationship failed, and did much to help her after they parted ways.

Jane was as much an ally to Hemingway as anything else—someone he could run off and play with, outside the boundaries of his marriage to Pauline. Jane was feminine but could also be one of the boys. Tall and lean, with blue eyes, a soft complexion, and long, thin, tapered fingers, she had an innocent image that made her irresistibly attractive to Hemingway, and she played it up for all it was worth. Like Pauline, Jane could be pretentious and sound affected. While on vacation, she wrote to a friend, "There is something about this place which forces even the most robust and gutsy to dash about in whispers. . . . I have taken the gun of my sister-in-law, as a French grammar might put it, and have tried to shoot skeet. . . . As for the writing I have done one piece which may, or may not, turn into something which could double for a portion of tepid hash with an underdone egg."[1] She had done some modeling for print advertisements, most famously in an ad purveying Pond's Beauty Cream. She was good at fishing, shooting, and waterskiing, but also at needlework, writing, music, and sculpture. She could hold her liquor and hold her own in drinking with men—straight gin with a champagne chaser was her beverage of choice. Mario Menocal Jr., a friend of Hemingway's at this time, said he "had never known a woman so perfectly at home in the almost exclusive company of men and who insisted on being treated by them as 'one of the boys.'"[2] Yet Jane was no mere pretty face. Hemingway was attracted to her because she was a woman of many accomplishments and possessed a great intellect. They discovered that they were soul mates in many ways.

Like Hemingway, Jane could be accident-prone and was often unwell. It is no exaggeration to say that at one point or another she broke nearly every bone in her body.[3] She wrote Hemingway once, after a car accident, that her life had been one long succession of operations and hospital stays, though she was only in her early twenties. Describing one hospital confinement, she wrote Hemingway, "Today the X-Ray man arrived, bearing in tow the apparatus with which to photograph my beautiful spinal cord. I always said I would turn out to be the backbone of the nation."[4] But her bright, bantering manner masked deep unhappiness. Jane was depressive and felt unfulfilled. She never made a success of any of her pursuits or interests, and she was self-conscious about it. At one point, she made up an ironic inscription for her tombstone: "Talents too many, not enough of any."[5]

Jane was born in Syracuse, New York, in 1910—like Pauline, she came from a moneyed family. Her mother, who divorced when Jane was just a child, was a singer. She remarried, and Jane was brought up in Tuxedo Park, a wealthy suburb of New York City, in an enormous mansion that could have belonged to some European royal family; it had more than a score of rooms, a lily pond, a teahouse, and a private orchard. Like the American princess that she was, Jane attended Briarcliff School, was educated in Europe, and had at least two debuts in Washington, D.C. She married Grant Mason, a stolid, more or less uninteresting son of a very wealthy WASP family. Mason had been educated at St. Paul's School in New Hampshire and at Yale and had co-founded Pan American Airways, which established its first office in Key West. The Masons moved to Jaimanitas, Cuba, a lavish estate set among several tropical gardens about thirty miles outside Havana. Here, their social world became legendary, a page out of a handbook on the luxe life that could have been written by the Fitzgeralds or the Murphys. Parties were frequent and were fueled by an endless supply of alcohol. The Masons were childless, Jane being infertile, but they adopted two young English boys (Hemingway was godfather to the elder one, Antony) and raised them as their own. Most of the time, however, the boys were given over to the care of an English governess and grew up not knowing their parents very well at all.

Grant Mason was even and likable, but Jane was temperamentally attracted to adventure and risk, hence her pursuit of Hemingway. After their relationship began, Hemingway would take his boat over to Havana and put up at the Hotel Ambos Mundos. He told his son Jack that when Jane came to visit him there, she would scale the outside of the building, creep along a two-and-a-half-foot-wide ledge, and climb in through his window. Although this may have been a fantasy, it took life in Hemingway's imagination and settled into his consciousness, not just as an alluring image of Jane as risk taker, but as an excuse to cuckold a husband who was not worthy of someone with such a thirst for life. Hemingway was contemptuous of any man who, as he said in "The Short Happy Life of Francis Macomber," couldn't "keep his wife where she belongs." "All women married to a bad husband," he wrote to Archibald MacLeish, "are bad luck to themselves and their friends."[6] Hemingway later satirized Mason in *To Have and Have Not* as Tommy Bradley, the vapid, unlikable playboy of the yachting set. Jane appears in the novel as his wife, Helene, who cheats on her husband with impunity.[7] Hemingway would also later use Jane as the model for Margot Macomber, and Jane herself, inspired by Hemingway's safari, would make her own trip to Africa to camp and hunt with Bror von Blixen-Finecke, the former husband of novelist Isak Dinesen and himself the partial model for the white hunter Wilson in the same story.

Like all of Hemingway's friends, male or female, Ernest also became Jane's instructor—in this case, he taught her about marlin fishing in Cuba. Just as Hadley had stayed behind with Bumby while Hemingway went skiing with Pauline in Austria, Pauline now stayed behind with the children in Key West while Hemingway went to Cuba to fish with Jane. Under Hemingway's tutelage, Jane became much better at knowing her surroundings—something Hemingway always admired. When he was away from Key West once, she wrote him a long letter detailing a fishing expedition in the Caribbean. He later complimented her on her account, calling it a "masterly and exhaustive treatise on fish and fauna" and comparing it to a Kipling poem.[8]

Jane's impetuous behavior could be dangerous. She did not quite have a death wish, but she certainly tempted fate. One of the couple's favorite games was to drive at high speeds in Jane's roadster on the narrow, curving roads outside Havana, where collision was a real threat. It was a primitive form of chicken, but instead of speeding toward an oncoming car, they simply took turns pressing the accelerator closer and closer to the floor in an attempt to force the passenger to lose his or her nerve and tell the driver to slow down. One afternoon in May 1932, on a road near Havana, Jane was driving a large Packard with Antony in the backseat, along with Hemingway's sons Patrick and Bumby. A "large speedful monster of a bus" came toward them from the opposite direction, meandered out of its lane, and forced Jane's car "off the highway so that we catapulted over a fine precipice and landed on our top," which crumbled under the weight of the big car.[9] The automobile rolled over on its side and down an embankment, finally coming to rest with its roof on the ground and its chassis in the air, wheels spinning. Fortunately, Jane had the presence of mind to turn off the ignition, or the car might have exploded. The doors of the car were jammed, but someone had left a window open just enough to allow them all to crawl through to safety.

Bumby helped the other two children out of the car, but Jane suffered a serious spinal injury. The incident lodged itself in Hemingway's fatalistic imagination, and, like other accidents that showed up in his fiction, reappeared in *Islands in the Stream* years later, when Thomas Hudson receives word via telegram that his two sons and their mother have been killed in a motor accident near Biarritz. After the accident, Hemingway was almost sick with concern about Jane's recovery. "I can't imagine anything worse," he wrote her. "You've had worse torture than the bloody martyrs. . . . Poor old poor old Jane."[10]

Like Hemingway after his brush with death in World War I, Jane became deeply depressed. She may have tried to kill herself. One afternoon, she jumped off the second-story balcony of her house in Jaimanitas, breaking her back. Down the middle of her back was a seven-and-a-half-inch scar; another scar marred her leg where the bone graft was taken to repair her fractured vertebrae. She would undergo further back surgeries in the coming years and be treated for depression by a psychoanalyst. Hemingway was the first to see her at the Anglo-American hospital in Havana after the apparent suicide attempt. He examined the X-rays and talked with the doctor about her injuries. They were severe enough that her husband sent her to New York to receive special treatment at a hospital there. Months of physical therapy followed. When she returned from New York, Hemingway wrote her, "I feel so terribly damned bad about them having to operate on your back that I can't write you, but . . . here goes."[11] Jane's husband, Grant, by contrast, wrote off the incident as a stunt designed to gain his sympathy—one of her many "changeable fits of elation and depression"—a description that could also have fit Hemingway.[12] Indeed, Jane and Hemingway were nearly identical in their emotional makeup.

Hemingway's letters to Jane are romantic and solicitous. Hemingway sounds like he is trying to keep up a brave front while feeling miserable from missing her. In one, he said he wished he could "write very funny letters full of splendid cracks," but instead simply found himself hoping she was safe and happy.[13] He shared with her his worry about how the critics perceived him, even confiding that one negative review of a recent work had upset him so much that it made him vomit. In another letter, he spoke of his deep hurt when a reviewer claimed that Hemingway was only in it for the money. Another reviewer claimed that he wrote because he was sexually impotent.[14] Hemingway seems to have held nothing back from Jane. He obviously felt that he could confide in her in ways that he could not with Pauline.

Ironically, it was a matter of confidence that precipitated their breakup. Jane's depression had become so severe that she went into the care of a prominent psychiatrist, Dr. Lawrence Kubie. In addition to his medical expertise, Kubie had literary aspirations, and at some point in his treatment of Jane, he came into contact with Henry Seidel Canby, the editor of the *Saturday Review of Literature*. Canby was intrigued by Kubie's psychoanalytic theories as applied to authors and works of literature, and he commissioned the psychiatrist to write

psychoanalytic profiles of Erskine Caldwell, William Faulkner, and Hemingway.
Although there is no definitive evidence, it is impossible not to think that Kubie
used the information gathered from Jane's sessions to fuel his speculation about
Hemingway, which he then submitted to Canby for publication. As it turned
out, Canby could not bring himself to print the piece about Hemingway, but the
author learned about Kubie's manuscript and regarded it as an act of treachery
on Jane's part, although the break would not come until later on.[15]

A little later, Grant Mason received an appointment to the Civil Aeronautics
Board, and the Masons left Cuba to live in Washington, D.C. One year later, they
divorced. Jane's life continued to be unhappy. She struggled with depression and
alcoholism for much of her life and married three more times, the last in 1955,
to Arnold Gingrich, the *Esquire* editor who had met Jane through Hemingway
when Gingrich visited him in Key West. After suffering a severe stroke, she died
in 1981.

Pauline knew what she faced in her rival, Jane, and decided that the best way
to keep her husband was to take him away from areas where he might get into
trouble. She therefore prevailed upon her munificent uncle Gus to finance an
African safari, something Hemingway had wanted to do for a long time. The two
set off in August 1933 with their Key West friend, Charles Thompson, leaving their
children in the care of Ada Stern.

Hemingway had been fascinated with Africa since he was a small boy reading
Theodore Roosevelt's accounts of big-game hunting there, especially his 1909–10
Smithsonian expedition, recounted in the best-selling *African Game Trails* (1910),
published by Scribner's. Like Roosevelt, Hemingway had learned as a child all
about flora and fauna and the geology and topography of land. He had found
and collected specimens to bring home and study further, and was encouraged to
use the scientific method to describe what he had collected with as much accuracy
as possible. Africa was also a topic Hemingway encountered while working as
a reporter for the *Toronto Star Weekly*. The first book that Hemingway reviewed
as a professional writer was René Maran's novel *Batouala,* which addressed the
repression of human rights in central Africa under French rule. Hemingway enjoyed Maran's picture of "a native village seen by the big-white eyes, felt by the
pink palms, and the broad, flat, naked feet of the African native himself."[16] In the
book that he would later write about his safari, *Green Hills of Africa,* he recorded
what he saw with precision and authenticity.

African settings had been used in British fiction virtually since the origins of
the novel form, but American writers of the eighteenth and nineteenth centuries
rarely set their works in Africa. There had been slave narratives, such as the one
by Olaudah Equiano (1789), and various propaganda novels that argued against
abolition, such as Sarah J. Hale's *Liberia; or, Mr. Peyton's Experiments* (1853). But
the only modern fiction writers of note who had set works in Africa were Edgar
Rice Burroughs and H. Rider Haggard. Burroughs, creator of *Tarzan of the Apes,*

and Haggard, author of *King Solomon's Mines,* both saw Africa as an Edenic land-scape. Hemingway rejected the Africa of utopian fantasy and followed Joseph Conrad in using it as an arena of conflict and challenge for his characters. Africa, with its rugged landscape and difficult climate, was an unindustrialized continent that offered the perfect testing ground for change. Hemingway wanted to get there before Western civilization steamrolled over it.

After the publication of Hemingway's safari book and his stories set in Africa, the continent began to become a tourist destination, not just for the idle rich who wanted to go on safari but for people of ordinary means who were eager to experience the exoticism and raw beauty that he had written about. Hemingway popularized Africa in the world's imagination, just as he had done with Spain and bullfighting in *Death in the Afternoon.* And, as with sportfishing, the Hemingway association was also good for business. The clothing outfitters Ker and Downey experienced a huge rise in profits because of Hemingway's books. Today there is a luxury tour company purveying "journeys of distinction" called "Hemingways Expeditions." Hollywood, as ever following the trends, began to make numerous films based in Africa or other exotic locales, like *Mogambo, Nor the Moon by Night,* and *King Solomon's Mines.* More than any other writer, Hemingway established Africa in the American consciousness.[17]

The Hemingways and Thompson arrived in Mombasa, Kenya, on 22 November 1933. Hemingway kitted himself out to look the part of an intrepid explorer, with a wide-brimmed Stetson and a khaki jacket with rolled-up sleeves, epaulets, and plenty of bellows pockets into which he stuffed as many bullets as would fit. (In photographs from the trip, he looks almost like a walking munitions dump.) Mombasa in the 1930s was a busy port city. The roads were clogged with slow-moving trucks belching smoke and splattering mud from the frequent and often-violent downpours. Humidity hung in the air like the fronds of the mango trees that lined the thoroughfares. Yet it had its loveliness as well. Karen Blixen, who wrote under the pen name Isak Dinesen, described it in *Out of Africa* as "all built from coral-rock, in pretty shades of buff, rose, and ochre," like "a picture of paradise painted by a small child. . . . The air is salt . . . the breeze brings in every day fresh supplies of brine from the East, and the soil itself is salted so that very little grass grows, and the ground is bare like a dancing-floor."[18]

The trio spent the weekend in Mombasa and then caught the train for the journey inland to Nairobi. The completion of the Uganda Railway in 1901 had provided easier access to the interior highlands of British East Africa (now Ke-nya), where large game, especially elephants, lions, Cape buffalo, and rhinoc-eroses were plentiful. Rattling through the dust, the train passed all manner of wildlife, easily visible through the large windows. In the distance was the square, snow-topped peak of Mount Kilimanjaro, shrouded in clouds. They were headed for Machakos, a Kenyan town two and a half hours by car from Nairobi, to meet up with their safari guide, Philip Hope Percival, a successful farmer and a storied white hunter. Hemingway would immortalize him as Pop in *Green Hills of Africa* and as Robert Wilson in "The Short Happy Life of Francis Macomber." Hemingway could not have been more fortunate in his choice of guide, for Percival had the same kind of intense affinity with safari that Hemingway admired among the aficionados who understood the importance of the bullfight. Hemingway took an instant liking to Percival (as did Pauline), and they became lifelong friends. They corresponded until just a few months before Hemingway's death in 1961.

Born in Somerset, England, Percival had attended boarding school and then worked briefly as a journalist. He had married his childhood sweetheart, Vivien Smith Spark, in 1909; it was she who managed their isolated Potha Hill Farm, an ostrich farm, in Limuru during Percival's long absences from home when on safari. When Teddy Roosevelt made his famous 1909 hunting trip through Africa with another famous white hunter, R. J. Cunninghame, as his guide, he advised Percival that the farm would be more profitable if he converted it to raise cattle; Percival took the former president's advice and became a successful cattle baron. During World War I, Percival worked for British intelligence, resuming hunting on his return to Africa. He quickly built his business into a world-renowned enterprise, and his client list soon read like the photo captions in a high society magazine: Gary Cooper, the Vanderbilts, George Eastman of Eastman Kodak, Baron Rothschild, and dozens more.[19]

Like his peers, Percival was a romantic, colorful figure from a privileged English background who embraced a life of risk and adventure—the very type of man Hemingway admired. Like Chink Dorman-Smith, Percival had the qualities of unstudied masculinity that Hemingway respected, and, also like Dorman-Smith, he came from an upper-crust background that bred a calm, no-nonsense approach to life that typified many a character in Hemingway's fiction. In *Green Hills of Africa,* Poor Old Mama ("P.O.M.," that is, Pauline) rhapsodizes over Percival as an ideal man: "brave, gentle, comic, never losing his temper, never bragging, never complaining except in a joke, tolerant, understanding, intelligent, drinking a little too much as a good man should, and, to her eyes, very handsome" (64). Roosevelt described Percival in *African Game Trails* as rugged, handsome, and highly skilled, a "tall, sinewy man, a fine rider and shot. . . . He wore merely a helmet, a flannel shirt, short breeches or trunks, and puttees and boots, leaving the knee entirely bare."[20] Denis Zaphiro, who hunted with Hemingway and Percival during the second African safari, in 1953–54, called Percival "perhaps the greatest hunter living" at the time: "Unspoiled reputation. Always chosen when the best hunter was needed. Father to us all."[21]

In Machakos, the group had to wait several days, until 20 December, for Percival to return from a hunting trip. While waiting, they practiced their shooting on the Kapiti Plain, targeting guinea fowl and gazelle. Hemingway also met and befriended Alfred Vanderbilt, who was staying at the farm until his own guide returned. This was Bror von Blixen-Finecke, whose estranged wife, Karen Blixen (Isak Dinesen), would later write *Out of Africa.* Hemingway seems to have been of two minds about Blixen. In print, Hemingway had nothing but praise for him, commending him for his impeccable form. In an article for *Esquire,* Hemingway wrote that Bror Blixen could "mask [his] phenomenal skill under a pose of nervous incapacity which serves as an effective insulation and cover" for the "truly great pride in the reserve of deadliness" that he lived by. And "Blix, who can shoot partridges flying with a .450 No. 2 Express rifle will say, 'I use the hair trigger because my hand is always shaking so, what?' Or stopping a charging rhino at ten yards, remarking apologetically to his client who happened to have his rifle already started back to camp by the gun bearer, 'I could not let him come forever, what?'"[22] Privately, however, Hemingway thought far more highly of Percival. He told Charles Cadwalader, the director of the Academy of Natural Sciences in Philadelphia (who would join Hemingway in Cuba the following year to conduct ichthyological research on board the *Pilar*), that there was "sort of a lobby that revolves around Blix (Blix has nothing to do with it) that tries to cry down Philip as a hunter in order to build up Blix as a super-hunter. Blix is a super-hunter all right but the idea that no one hunts in Africa that doesn't hunt with Blix is a lot of kosher pickles."[23]

While in Nairobi, Hemingway also came to know Beryl Markham, Bror Blixen's aerial game scout. Dramatically attractive, with a long face and a steel-cut profile, Markham was an Englishwoman who had lived in Africa most of her life, hunting barefoot with the Nandi, scouting elephants in the wild. She had dabbled in horse breeding and racing for a while, then picked up flying at a time when many people had never seen a plane. In 1936 she became the first woman to make a solo transatlantic flight from east to west, setting off from England in a tiny turquoise and silver Vega Gull monoplane. She flew for more than twenty-one hours and survived a crash landing in a bog on a tiny island off the coast of Nova Scotia. Hemingway did not know Markham well, although at least one of her biographers speculates that Hemingway made sexual advances toward her, which she rejected.[24] In a letter to Max Perkins, Hemingway called her "very unpleasant." But apart from that brief aside, the letter praised Markham's writing skills to the skies, and would later play a role in enlarging Markham's reputation. Upon its original appearance in 1942, her account of life in colonial Kenya, *West with the Night,* made an initial splash but was quickly forgotten and went out of print. When the book was reissued in 1983, however, some remarks from Hemingway's letter to Perkins accompanied the publicity materials and were quoted liberally on the dust jacket. Hemingway had told Perkins, "she has written so well, and marvelously well, that I was completely ashamed of myself as a writer. I felt that I was simply a carpenter with words, picking up whatever was furnished on the job and nailing them together and sometimes making an okay pig pen. But this girl . . . can write rings around all of us who consider ourselves as writers."[25] High praise, indeed, and compelling testimony to Hemingway's generosity to fellow writers who he felt had made the cut. The remark also shows that Hemingway was obviously not afraid of strong-willed, ambitious women. *West with the Night* sold well upon its reissue and is now something of a cult classic.

When Percival arrived, the party left Machakos for the Tanganyika border, arriving the next day at Namanga. They then went on to another settlement, Arusha, before finally reaching the Rift Valley the next day and moving up toward Lake Manyara and the Ngorongoro game reserve. Here, they came upon their main hunting area, the Serengeti Plain, west and southeast of the present-day Tarangire National Park. The first person to chart this area had been Stewart Edward White, an American hunter, who had set out from Nairobi in 1913. Pushing south, he later wrote, "We walked for miles over burnt-out country. . . . Then I saw the green trees of the river, walked two miles more and found myself in paradise."[26] The Serengeti ecosystem is one of the oldest on earth, with a vegetative climate and fauna makeup that has been essentially unchanged for two million years. The Maasai, who had grazed their cattle on its vast grassy plains for millennia, called it "the place where the land moves on forever." The region is perhaps most famous for its migration of more than a million wildebeest and about two hundred thousand zebras, who flow south from the northern hills to the plains for the short rains every October and November, and then swirl west and north after the long rains in April, May, and June. Today, the region attracts nearly a hundred thousand tourists a year. But it was still relatively unknown when Hemingway arrived in 1933.

By the end of December, Hemingway's life on safari had settled into a comfortable rhythm. He and his companions would rise early, eat, and then move out in the coolness of the morning to stalk their quarry. He recalled in *Green Hills of Africa*, "I would lie in the fallen leaves and watch the kudu feed out and never fire a shot unless I saw a better head than this one in back, and instead of trailing that sable bull, gut-shot to hell, all day, I'd lie behind a rock and watch them on the hillside and see them long enough so they belonged to me forever" (282). Around noon, when the heat became oppressive, they would return to camp for lunch and then read and nap until late afternoon, when they would venture out again in search of prey. In the evening, it was supper, conversation, and alcohol-inspired revelry before bed.

Hemingway was not a spectacular shot, but he could brag in one of his *Esquire* letters that he had done a more than creditable job: "good heads of Eland, Waterbuck, Grant Robertsi and other gazelles," he reported in precise language. "A fine roan antelope, two big leopard, and excellent, if not record, impalla [*sic*]; also the limit all around on cheetah."[27] The hyenas were a source of both derision and amusement. The group brought down thirty-five, but Hemingway wished he had had the ammunition to kill a hundred more. The animal was clearly a bottom-feeder to Hemingway, who described it as a "hermaphroditic, self-eating devourer of the dead, [and a] trailer of calving cows" (38). All in all, he ended up bagging three lions, a buffalo, and twenty-seven other animals, but Thompson was the better shot, bringing down more animals than his travel companion. When Thompson killed a rhino whose horn was much larger than Hemingway's, the writer became unbalanced, almost physically sick. "We all spoke like people who were about to become seasick on a boat, or people who had suffered some heavy financial loss" (84). Hemingway was displeased that he had not won the "contest," as he perceived it. He could be intensely hard on himself; everything played out like a game, and there was never any ambiguity about who had won and who had lost. Thompson was relatively ignorant of Hemingway's competitive streak and so was surprised when Hemingway did not compliment him on his hunting prowess. But Hemingway recorded his displeasure in *Green Hills of Africa,* in a passage where Pauline tries to restrain her husband: "Papa," she says, "please try to act like a human being. Poor Karl. You're making him feel dreadfully" (86).[28] Hemingway described the incident realistically, making no excuses for his competitive nature: "We had tried, in all the shoot, never to be competitive. . . . I knew I could outshoot him and I could always outwalk him, and, steadily, he got trophies that made mine dwarfs in comparison." Percival's assessment was blunt: "We have very primitive emotions," he said (293).

The safari was interrupted in mid-January 1934 when Hemingway contracted amoebic dysentery. It was a frightening experience. One day, while visiting the Ngorongoro crater, he began to bleed. At first, he thought it was just diarrhea, but he soon began having almost continuous bowel movements and, even more ghastly, three inches of his large intestine came out of his body. He had to wash the prolapsed organ with soap and water and stick it back inside himself. Soon, he could no longer even rise from the camp bed, and Percival's assistant radioed for a private plane to collect him. He was evacuated to Nairobi, flying high over the mountaintop of Kilimanjaro (an experience later depicted in "The Snows of Kilimanjaro"), treated, and put up at the New Stanley Hotel to recuperate.

> Alone with the pain in the fifth week of not sleeping I thought suddenly of how a bull elk must feel if you break a shoulder and he gets away and in that night I lay and felt it all, the whole thing as though it would happen from the shock of the bullet to the end of the business and, being a little out of my head, thought perhaps what I was going through was a punishment for all hunters. Then, getting well, I decided if it was a punishment I had paid it and at least I knew what I was doing. I did nothing that had not been done to me. (148)

Hemingway was given regular injections of emetine, an anti-amoebic drug that caused prolonged vomiting, and spent the days in bed writing another article for *Esquire* and answering his mail. He recovered quickly, however, and was back in Tanganyika a week later.

The safari was completed on 20 February. Hemingway and his party spent a few days fishing at the mouth of the Tana River, and then on 28 February departed Africa on board the MS *Gripsholm.* The ship docked at Villefranche on 18 March, and from there the Hemingways took a train to Paris, where they stayed nine days. They returned to New York on the *Ile de France* (where they made the acquaintance of film star Marlene Dietrich, with whom Hemingway would become lifelong friends). Docking there on 2 April, Hemingway made a trip to the Wheeler Shipyard in Brooklyn and placed an order for his own fishing boat (which he would name *Pilar*), paying for it partly with his earnings from the *Esquire* articles.

——

Two years later, in 1936, Hemingway used the experience of safari as the basis for one of his finest stories, "The Short Happy Life of Francis Macomber." The story concerns a wealthy man who is emasculated by his wife and is cowardly in the face of danger. He redeems himself when he faces almost certain death with moral courage. In a tragic twist at the end, he dies, but he does so, Hemingway makes clear, in affirmation of his own self-worth.

Hemingway based the narrative in part on a story that Philip Percival had told him one evening around the campfire about an English couple who had gone on safari with a British army officer, the expedition ending in the husband's death under suspicious circumstances. The English couple were Audley and Ethel Blyth, wealthy aristocrats who in March 1908 met Colonel John Henry Patterson, an engineer working in Nairobi. Patterson's superiors allowed him to take the Blyths along with him. Patterson was a womanizer who had little trouble seducing Mrs. Blyth. The pair made no secret of their adultery, causing Mr. Blyth great shame. One night a pistol shot was heard in the camp, and it was discovered that Mr. Blyth had shot himself in the head—apparently a suicide, whether from depression or the destabilizing effects of delirium and fever, contracted in the wild. Before an official investigation could be undertaken, Patterson apparently ordered the body and all of Blyth's clothes and other effects burned. He and Mrs. Blyth then returned to Nairobi.

There was enough suspicion surrounding Blyth's death to provoke the colonial governor of the East Africa Protectorate, one Lt. Colonel Sir J. Hayes Sadler, to start an inquiry almost one year later, in February 1909. Testimony was taken from the gun bearers and other Africans in the camp that night that confirmed the affair between Patterson and Mrs. Blyth but stopped just short of implicating either one in the death of Mr. Blyth. Even if Patterson was not legally liable for Blyth's death, however, he was morally liable. Knowing this, he resigned his commission, although the official word put out by the colonial secretary, Lord Crew, was that Patterson had resigned for health reasons. Patterson was in fine enough health to write an account of the event in November of that year, in a book titled *In the Grip of the Nyika,* which gives a crude description of his dalliance with Ethel Blyth and of Audley Blyth's death.[29]

Hemingway's story shares many similarities with this incident. Like Audley Blyth, Francis Macomber is emasculated by his predatory, adulterous wife. The white hunting guide is shamelessly two-faced and deceitful, bullying and belittling Macomber for being a cuckold. It is also unclear whether Macomber's death is intentional or accidental. The Patterson affair was good enough material to be transformed into fiction, but Hemingway saw more provocative possibilities in making the wife rather than the white hunter the presumably culpable party in her husband's death. As he does so often, Hemingway links sex and violence in the story. Margot and Wilson brutalize Macomber with a kind of psychological bullying. Macomber finally gets his chance to bring down a buffalo but only wounds the animal. He must then continue to fire until he finishes the job. It is then that Margot shoots him in the back of the head as he moves in to finish off the buffalo. Critics have written extensively about whether Margot intends to kill her husband or whether the shooting is accidental. The consensus is that her action is deliberate; by murdering her husband, Margot steals Macomber's power and authority and puts herself in control. Shooting and sex culminate in a violent eruption of power.

"The Snows of Kilimanjaro," Hemingway's second African story, was published in *Esquire* in 1936. It is an ominous tale in which a writer on the brink of death looks back ruefully on all the things he failed to write about. He blames his wealthy wife for corrupting him with money and a life of comfort and ease. The story poignantly explores Hemingway's awareness of what he had become—how the public image had overtaken the artist devoted to his calling.

In the story, Harry Walden, a successful novelist, lies immobile in an African camp where he is on safari, dying from gangrene in an untreated cut in his leg. Isolated, Harry and his wife, Helen, must wait for some time until a rescue plane can come and take Harry for medical treatment. Neither knows whether the plane will arrive in time to save his life.

Illness, not violence, is the ironic focus of the story: a minor, accidental scratch from a thornbush in the wild becomes potentially fatal. Harry gets the scratch taking a photograph, not hunting—he is holding a camera rather than a rifle. Hemingway understood the irony of successfully avoiding the dangers that come with big-game hunting, only to be felled by a minor threat. Hemingway probably saw a good many of his father's patients being treated for gangrene from farming accidents, camping mishaps, and the like. Gangrene is also a metaphor: Harry rots, literally, from the inside out, and he cannot conceal the source of his debility: the smell of putrefaction assails him and Helen as they sit helplessly in the camp, watching time tick away.

At the end of the story, Harry falls asleep and dreams that the rescue plane has arrived and he is being flown out of the camp. In the air, the plane passes over Kilimanjaro, and Harry recalls the Maasai saying, printed as an epigraph to the story, about the leopard who lies frozen on a plateau, never reaching the summit. Hemingway uses the mountain and the leopard as symbols of aspiration: like the leopard, Harry never makes it to the top, and he regrets that he will die without scaling the heights, in spite of having the talent to do so.

Unlike "Macomber," this story consists almost entirely of interior monologue, with little narrative action. Most everything takes place in Harry's mind. He thinks about the stories that he has never written, and the reader witnesses scenes from his life, rendered in italicized extracts: a Turkish attack during World War I, skiing on Alpine snow "as smooth . . . as cake frosting and as light as powder" (154), consorting with prostitutes in Constantinople. The most plangent memory is of his life as a young writer with his first wife in Paris. This was the first time that Hemingway used his Paris experiences in a creative work—reminiscences that would eventually culminate in his posthumously published memoir, *A Moveable Feast*. In contrast to the moneyed life that Harry now leads, with its attendant tensions and anxieties, his life in Paris was one of happy poverty, symbolized by the crooked streets and ramshackle flats in his neighborhood: "There was never another part of Paris that he loved like that, the sprawling trees, the old white plastered houses painted brown below, the long green of the autobus in that round square, the purple flower dye upon the paving. . . . And in that poverty, and in that quarter across the street from a Boucherie Chevaline and a wine co-operative he had written the start of all he was to do" (168).

The memory makes one realize how long after the fact Hemingway held the guilt of forsaking Hadley in his heart and mind—now almost ten years. It might even be said that he compared the trauma associated with betraying his first wife to the long, slow, painful death that Harry faces in the story. Lost happiness and disabling nostalgia plague Harry at the end of his life. Like the writer that he is, he tries to stave off death by "writing" about it in his head, knowing that the more he writes, the longer he will live, and that coming to the end of the story will mean death. Perversely, for Hemingway, this meant that the more he continued to write about the loss of Eden in Paris, the harder it was to rid himself of the guilt and shame with which he associated it.

Hemingway got the idea for "The Snows of Kilimanjaro" in April 1934, when he was invited to tea in New York by a female admirer who offered to underwrite his expenses for a second safari. Hemingway declined, fearing that another extended trip would curtail his literary productivity, and he imagined what might happen should he, or someone like him, accept the woman's offer. The story is a frank self-assessment by Hemingway—a facing up to his anxieties about death, corruption, and the debilitating effects of money and women. (The writer's first name, Harry, and last name, Walden, may allude to Henry David Thoreau and his gospel of simplicity and being true to oneself.) Hemingway had begun to worry about his career. He had published no novel since *A Farewell to Arms* in 1929—only, when it came to book-length works, nonfiction. A novel, Hemingway was wont to say, is a championship bout, and the nonfiction simply did not get as much notice. Hemingway's battle with amoebic dysentery figures in the story as well. Although he was in no danger of dying, his natural anxieties must have brought the fear to his mind, especially as he flew over Mount Kilimanjaro in the plane that took him to the hospital in Nairobi.

He knew that the public image had in some ways overtaken the writer in him, and although his marriage to Pauline, as he described it in *Green Hills,* was dear and tender (unlike Harry's marriage to the "rich bitch," Helen), he worried that enjoying her family's wealth made him a bought man. It was often Hemingway's cruel habit to slap down people who shared his faults, criticizing them for traits and behavior of which he himself was guilty. Hemingway does this to Scott Fitzgerald in "The Snows of Kilimanjaro" when Harry refers to a fellow writer named Julian and "his romantic awe of [the rich] and how he had started a story once that began, 'The very rich are different from you and me.' And how someone had said to Julian, Yes, they have more money" (170). The story to which Harry refers is Fitzgerald's "The Rich Boy." In the *Esquire* printing of "Snows," Hemingway actually used the name Scott instead of Julian. Fitzgerald protested to Max Perkins and told Hemingway to lay off him in print. Hemingway was thus persuaded to change the character's name to Julian for the story's printing in *The First Forty-Nine Stories,* but the line from "The Rich Boy" was unaltered.

Hemingway thought that Fitzgerald had been destroyed by his desire for a life of soft living and the pleasures of celebrity. Yet these same things plagued Hemingway. It was almost as if Hemingway thought that he could inoculate himself from this fate by writing about it—or could even invalidate the reality of what was happening. Fiction was truth telling, but it was also an attempt at wish-fulfillment. In a revealing contrast, it was actually Fitzgerald who was confronting his flaws head on at this time. The same year that "The Snows of Kilimanjaro" appeared, *Esquire* was also serializing Fitzgerald's series of essays about his moral and artistic failures, later collected as *The Crack-Up.* Hemingway thought that this was little more than public whining, and he reacted negatively to the book. There is something more, probably: Hemingway himself by this point had long been battling chronic depression. He had earlier confessed to John Dos Passos just how deep and debilitating the illness was: "I felt that gigantic bloody emptiness and nothingness like couldn't fuck, fight write and was all for death."[30] Hemingway did not want to be reminded of his own struggles to keep the darkness at bay.

———

Green Hills of Africa began as a short story that Hemingway started writing while on safari. He wanted it to be "a damned fine story" and to appear at the end of his upcoming collection, *The First Forty-Nine Stories.* He also considered publishing it, along with the *Esquire* articles, in a different collection. Perkins argued strenuously that it should be published "by itself" since it would "detract" from the story collection to "add anything else to the same volume. It does not make it more desirable, but less so."[31] Hemingway agreed, especially as the story "kept going on and on," until by November 1934 it was about seventy-four thousand words, much too long for a story or even a novella. Hemingway cut it heavily but still doubted that he could remove more than three or four thousand words and accomplish his goal. As with *Death in the Afternoon,* he had fallen in love with his subject, a feeling that comes through in many passages of the published version. Near the end of the narrative, for example, he frankly confesses,

All I wanted to do now was get back to Africa. We had not left it, yet, but when I would wake in the night I would lie, listening, homesick for it already. . . . I loved the country so that I was happy as you are after you have been with a woman that you really love, when, empty, you feel it welling up again and there it is and you can never have it all and yet what there is, now, you can have, and you want more and more, to have, and be, and live in, to possess now again for always, for that long, sudden-ended always. . . . If you have loved some woman and some country you are very fortunate, and if you die afterwards it makes no difference. (72–73)

Hemingway justified the length of the story along much the same lines that he had *Death in the Afternoon.* He told Perkins that "one thing" he had learned "this last year is how to make a story move." He pointed out that the book had "plenty of dialogue and action" as well as "plenty of excitement," and that although it was "a hell of a good book" by itself, he wanted "to get out a book of super value for the money." He also responded to claims that he had given up writing novels for this type of book. He was planning next to issue either a story collection or an essay collection: "I want to follow with a novel that will knock them cold. But I am not in a hurry about it—And can always publish both books first—I'd even write another novel and let this one wait. There is no hurry on anything that is any good."[32]

Hemingway kept at the book upon his return to Key West in April 1934, writing up the events of the final month of the trip and, as he had with *Death in the Afternoon,* incorporating commentary about literature and authorship. In negotiations over the sale of the book to Scribner's, Max Perkins found Hemingway "touchy as hell." Hemingway may have been more anxious about the reception of this book than any previous ones, as he was determined to use it to answer those critics who had been putting him down so harshly in recent years. He completed the first draft of what he referred to as "the long bitch" in November 1934.[33]

Green Hills of Africa appeared as a serial in *Scribner's Magazine* from May to September 1935. Hemingway corrected proofs in the late summer and early fall of that year, and the book was published by Scribner's in November 1935 in a first printing of 10,550 copies. Sales of the book, however, fell flat. Only twelve thousand copies sold between October 1935 and October 1937. Reviews were mixed: Hemingway did not get the attention he wanted for his running commentary about art and life, and his detractors seem not to have risen to the bait he had dangled before them in his belligerent remarks about the literary establishment.

To some degree, as Robert W. Trogdon speculates, the Scribner's marketing department had hurt sales by advertising the book as a travel memoir about hunting adventures, similar to Roosevelt's *African Game Trails* (which Scribner's had also published). Hemingway clearly saw the book as an imaginative work, but he also told Perkins, "Don't advertise the book as a novel. It is neither a novel nor a travel book. It is a book that you can sell as well as Fleming's first book with the additional advantage of haveing [*sic*] a known name to it if you handle it right. If you cant [*sic*] get anybody to figure out what sort of book to call it will try to help you out."[34] The book's hybrid form made it something of a puzzle, but only because nothing like it had yet appeared. *Green Hills of Africa* is an early entry in a genre that would not become popular until the 1960s: the nonfiction novel, examples of which include such books as Norman Mailer's *Armies of the Night* and Truman Capote's *In Cold Blood*. Hemingway structured the volume in four sections: "Pursuit and Conversation," "Pursuit Remembered," "Pursuit and Failure," and "Pursuit as Happiness." The story told in these four segments is one of successful hunts for lion, buffalo, and rhino, and a long and only partially successful hunt for a trophy kudu. In "Pursuit and Conversation," Hemingway writes of his life as a writer. He does this principally by introducing a sort of straw man, an Austrian emigrant named Kandisky, who is pleased to find that Hemingway the big-game hunter is also Hemingway the writer, whose work he has read. Kandisky provides the perfect foil for the Hemingway persona, asking him about his own work and about other American writers.

Hemingway obliges the Austrian by furnishing his opinions on writers living and dead. Emerson, Hawthorne, and Whittier, Hemingway tells Kandisky, all made the mistake of thinking that previous classics (by English authors) could furnish a model for their own potential classics, and therefore failed to produce great works. Melville did some good writing but employed too much "rhetoric" for Hemingway's taste. Similarly, Poe was technically proficient, but his work was "dead." Thoreau had potential, but Hemingway had not been able to read him because he was too "literary" for a naturalist. Henry James, Stephen Crane, and Mark Twain were the good American writers, according to Hemingway. Twain, in particular, provided the model for all later American fiction writers in *Huckleberry Finn* (20–22).

The other foil is Poor Old Mama, or P.O.M., as her name is abbreviated. Pauline Pfeiffer Hemingway was perhaps the best critic of any of Hemingway's four wives. In the book, her literary counterpart makes occasional judgments on writing, all highly favorable to Hemingway; her presence also allows Hemingway to avoid attacking other writers or praising his own work directly by putting the words into his wife's mouth. The best example of this technique is P.O.M.'s treatment of Gertrude Stein. Stein, Hemingway's mentor in the early days of his career, had recently attacked Hemingway in her *Autobiography of Alice B. Toklas* (1933), partly by putting words into the mouth of her long-time companion Toklas. Now Hemingway responded in kind. When Hemingway recalls sadly how little he was repaid for helping Stein find a publisher, Poor Old Mama responds that Stein is jealous and malicious. Hemingway is then able to be generous. Stein was a good writer and a nice person when he first knew her, he tells his wife, but she was corrupted by her ambition.

The book is very revealing of Hemingway's inner demons. "Hemingway" the character criticizes Hemingway the person for nearly spoiling the pleasure of a once-in-a-lifetime adventure with his childish desire to show that he is a greater hunter and a better shot than his close friend "Karl" (Charles Thompson), and for allowing his bitterness toward the innocent and apologetic Karl to poison their friendship. More darkly, the book expresses Hemingway's fear of betraying his talent and becoming corrupted. In a famous passage, he indicts America for destroying its writers, both commercially and critically: "Our writers when they have made some money increase their standard of living and they are caught. They have to write to keep up their establishments, their wives, and so on, and they write slop. . . . Or else they read the critics" (23). Speaking of Fitzgerald and Sherwood Anderson, he concludes, "At present we have two good writers who cannot write because they have lost confidence through reading critics" (23). The critics have become "lice who crawl on literature" (109).

Unsurprisingly, few of those "lice" supported Hemingway in their reviews of the book. Edmund Wilson, who had consistently championed Hemingway in the past, wrote in a retrospective piece a few years later that *Green Hills* "must be the only book ever written which makes Africa and its animals seem dull." Bernard DeVoto reacted negatively to Hemingway's nasty swipes at other writers and the literary establishment. In the *New Masses,* Granville Hicks invited Hemingway to "let himself look squarely at the contemporary American scene" and stop indulging himself with books where the focus was more on him than on his subject. Hemingway should be not writing about Spain or Africa, Hicks contended, but about his own land and its attendant economic problems and social inequities.[35]

Hemingway grew increasingly frustrated with his critics in these years. He did not think they understood his experimentation with style and subject. He intensely disliked their acting like they "owned" him—telling him what to write, calling the shots in his career. This doubtless made the contrarian Hemingway feel even more strongly that he should continue to strike out in new fictional directions, whether they were thought to be escapist, narcissistic, or anything else. Yet Hemingway was not tone deaf to the realities of Depression-era America or to the realpolitik of global affairs. He was actually highly attuned to them. In fact, he would soon insert himself into one of the more urgent political crises of the early twentieth century, the war in Spain. But he would write about it on his own schedule, and in his own way. Art, he believed, should not be made to order.

9

Martha Gellhorn and the Spanish Civil War

After the publication of *Green Hills of Africa,* a new woman entered Hemingway's life: Martha Gellhorn. Hemingway met Gellhorn in Key West on a December afternoon in 1936. She, her mother, and her brother had been vacationing in Miami, but they had grown tired of it and had driven out to the Keys looking for something less humdrum and less crowded with tourists. The family wandered into Sloppy Joe's and found Hemingway on his perch at the bar. Martha and her mother, Edna, recognized the author and went over to talk to him. He was immediately struck by the twenty-eight-year-old Martha, for she was a beauty. Like Jane Mason, she was tall and languid, with "distracting legs," blond hair, and blue eyes. And, like Pauline, she was amusing, glib, and full of self-confidence, speaking in a "low, husky, eastern-seaboard-accented voice" that was alluring and sensuous.[1]

Martha had much in common with Hemingway's family and with his other wives. Her father, a native Austrian, had been, like Hemingway's father, an obstetrician. He was also a faculty member at Washington University Medical Center in St. Louis—the hometown of both Hadley and Pauline. Like Hadley, Martha had lost her father when she was quite young and had been raised by her mother. Both women had also attended Bryn Mawr. Martha had something in common with Pauline as well. Both women had been trained as journalists and had worked briefly for *Vogue* magazine in Paris. Martha, however, was thirteen years younger than Pauline and already had risen rapidly in her profession. Her youth, in fact, belied all that she had done and seen. Martha had been in love with a Frenchman, Baron Bertrand de Jouvenel, a handsome journalist with whom she had lived. Her professional work included newspaper articles and pieces for the *New Republic,* written from her base on the Left Bank. She had also published two books: a mostly autobiographical novel, *What Mad Pursuit,* and a collection of stories, *The Trouble I've Seen,* based on her experiences working for the Federal Emergency Relief Administration, one of President Roosevelt's recently created agencies; it carried a preface by H. G. Wells and was reviewed favorably in many major outlets, including the *Spectator,* where Graham Greene praised her "hard and clear" stories for being "quite amazingly unfeminine," noting, in a sexist manner, that she had "none of the female vices of unbalanced pity or factitious violence."[2]

Through the FERA administrator, Harry Hopkins, Gellhorn had met and become close friends with Eleanor Roosevelt, who encouraged her to work for social justice. Gellhorn's work with FERA galvanized her social conscience. She wrote passionate articles exposing the crushing poverty in the Dust Bowl region of the country. She lobbied strenuously for assistance for the poor. And later, as civil war loomed in Spain, it was Gellhorn who turned Mrs. Roosevelt away from her isolationist views and toward the Loyalist cause. She would also profoundly influence Hemingway, whose love for Spain would reach new heights as Martha told him of the dangers posed by the rise of fascism. If not for Martha, Hemingway might not have signed on to report on the war in Spain and to go on to lobby extensively for the Loyalists. Martha became the woman whom Hemingway imaginatively connected with the romance of the Spanish war, just as he had earlier connected Agnes von Kurowsky with the youthful adventure of World War I.

That day in Sloppy Joe's, the afternoon faded into evening, and over the ritual Papa Dobles, Gellhorn succumbed to the Hemingway charm. When Hemingway did not show up for dinner at Whitehead Street, Pauline sent Charles Thompson to fetch him. Thompson found him at the bar, but Hemingway was so deep in conversation with Gellhorn that Thompson couldn't persuade him to leave. He had to return to report to Pauline, with some embarrassment, that Hemingway was still at the bar "talking to a blonde in a little black dress."[3]

As strong-minded and independent as Gellhorn was, she was starstruck by the older Hemingway. In the early days of their quickly ripening romance, she was the student and Hemingway the master teacher. Hemingway showed her how to shoot and fish and gave her history lessons in the rituals of Spanish bullfights (just as he had taught Hadley to ski and Pauline to hunt). She was enthralled by his storytelling ability and his travels. Eventually, her mother and brother left Key West to return home, but Martha stayed on at the Colonial Hotel on Duval Street, with Hemingway showing her around the island and swimming with her in his backyard pool. She was so often at Whitehead Street that she once told Pauline (perhaps disingenuously) that she felt like an adjunct member of the family. (This reminds one of the similar way in which Pauline had inveigled her way into Hemingway's life by calling frequently at Hemingway and Hadley's Paris apartment and accompanying them on ski trips in Europe.) Very quickly, too, Hemingway took her into his confidence, giving her the manuscript of the new novel he was then working on, *To Have and Have Not,* to read and comment on. Full of fire, Hemingway told her marvelous stories of the revolution in Cuba, which fueled her imagination and made her want to write more. Like Hemingway, her eye was always on conflict. She recognized that the Spanish war could provide great material for art, and she was eager to get involved, despite the danger. "If there is a war," she presciently confided to Mrs. Roosevelt, "then all the things most of us do won't matter any more."[4]

Gossips in Key West quickly began to whisper that the two were more than just friends, and Pauline, who knew that her marriage to Hemingway was precarious, was disheartened but also realistic. She had survived the threat from Jane Mason, but it looked as though she could do nothing to stop the powerful attraction between her husband and Gellhorn. She was also honest enough to admit to herself that she had acted just like Gellhorn during Hemingway's marriage to Hadley Richardson. Hemingway, for his part, felt the usual intense guilt and self-loathing at cheating on Pauline, just as he had felt in hurting Hadley. Archibald MacLeish confirmed this when he wrote of Hemingway's passion for Pauline: "how he ever broke through so strong a feeling, I have never understood."[5] When he later divorced Martha in an angry breakup that left him both bitter and bereft, it might well have been because he still felt bad about cheating on Pauline. Hemingway never let himself forget or escape the consequences when he did anything that smacked of disloyalty.

Martha left Key West by car on 10 January, and Hemingway flew north to meet her in Miami. They had supper together, then took the same train as far as Jacksonville. Hemingway went on to New York to transact some business there; Martha returned to St. Louis for a visit. In February, Hemingway would set out on the first of four trips to Spain over a period of two years. Martha would be there with him for much of that time—reporting, writing, and enjoying his company. As he had in the beginning with Pauline, Hemingway tried to be discreet in his relationship with Martha, but by the time they began spending so much time together in Spain, it was difficult for Hemingway to ignore the powerful attraction.

During their affair, Martha drew inspiration for her own writing from Hemingway, and she began to produce more work owing to his company: stories, articles, and the beginnings of a new novel flowed from her pen at an impressive pace. Hemingway later claimed that he taught Gellhorn how to write—an apparent untruth, since she already had two books to her credit when they met. Hemingway may, however, have helped make Gellhorn a better writer, or at least a more Hemingwayesque writer. Reviewers of her later work often made this point. But those comments may have been based as much on assumption as on evidence. By that point, too, Hemingway's trademark style had become so well known that it was already influencing masses of contemporary writers; indeed, it would have been difficult, starting in the 1930s, to *avoid* writing like Hemingway. The epigraph of her first novel, *What Mad Pursuit,* was taken from *A Farewell to*

Arms: "Nothing ever happens to the brave." Gellhorn's novel tells the story of three young women who try to do meaningful work in a world that does not take them seriously. It is remarkably similar to *The Sun Also Rises,* if that novel had been narrated from a female point of view. Both novels employ similar themes of impotence and independence. The difference resides in the matrix of gender. In Gellhorn's novel, the characters are "lost" because of gender inequality. They seek to be treated the same way that men are and to have the same experiences that men do, but are thwarted.[6]

The idea for *Liana* (1944), Gellhorn's second novel, which was published after their marriage had effectively ended, was suggested to her by Hemingway, who urged her to write a novel about Cuba. Hemingway was actively by Gellhorn's side in the writing of this book, although his input seems to have been editorial and suggestive rather than collaborative. He would copyedit Martha's manuscript pages each night as she finished them and offer ideas about the direction of the plot. Hemingway also arranged for Max Perkins to put the book on the Scribner's list, although Perkins insisted that he took *Liana* on its own merits and not because its author was Mrs. Ernest Hemingway.[7] *The Wine of Astonishment* (1948), also written after her divorce from Hemingway, is in some ways a parody of her former husband's work. Of all of Gellhorn's work, this book contains the most Hemingway tropes, phrases, words, and characterizations. By sarcastically replicating Hemingway's trademark elements, Gellhorn may have been attempting to do what Hemingway did in writing *The Torrents of Spring*: kill off a literary mentor through parody.

After their divorce, it irked Gellhorn considerably that people thought she owed her success as an author to Hemingway. As the years went on, she grew to resent him more and more, frustrated at always living in Hemingway's shadow. This resentment came to the fore in the 1950s, when the first academic critics and biographers began to become interested in Hemingway. Scholars and researchers would contact Gellhorn, but only because they wanted to find out something about Hemingway, and she eventually refused to grant interviews. (Later, she softened and began to grant such requests, on the condition that Hemingway not be mentioned during the interview.) "I was a writer before I met him and I was a writer after I divorced him," she said. "I refuse to be a footnote to someone else's life."[8] Nonetheless, Gellhorn was inevitably overshadowed by Hemingway, almost until her death in 1998 at the age of eighty-nine. When one Hemingway scholar, Sandra Spanier, wrote her in 1990 to say she thought the time was ripe for a revival of interest in her work, Gellhorn was cynical: "Dear girl, people are always 'rediscovering' me, you'd be amazed. Everybody does it and nothing works; I am never going to be a great saleable property. . . . I always said I was going to wait for posthumous fame and glory, [which] suits me fine."[9]

____

Hemingway and Gellhorn had been seeing each other, off and on, for almost a year when Scribner's published *To Have and Have Not* in October 1937. After an eight-year stretch without a novel, Hemingway returned to the form with a book that spoke to social injustice and the class struggle. His last major fictional work had been *A Farewell to Arms,* which had appeared to enthusiastic reviews in 1929. In the interval, Hemingway had occupied himself in writing *Death in the Afternoon* and *Green Hills of Africa.* As we have seen, however, these books had met with a good bit of critical disapproval, reviewers feeling that Hemingway had abandoned his artistic strengths in favor of lesser aesthetic forms. Many, too, thought that Hemingway was writing only to further the public persona that he had helped create for himself, and that he was no longer devoting himself to high art.

Hemingway was well aware of the drop in his literary approval ratings, and he wanted badly to restore himself to favor with the literary establishment, but he had to do it on his own terms. He was also under enormous pressure at the time to produce a novel that would address social and economic injustice in the United States. The 1930s were the decade of fallout from the Great Depression. The literary consensus was that art should serve social ends, as many writers, such as Dos Passos and Steinbeck, were doing. It should expose inequities, right wrongs, increase social awareness, and, ultimately, do something to try to offset the economic imbalance in society. The literary Left was enormously powerful at this time, and the opinions of critics like Alfred Kazin and Granville Hicks could make or break a writer.

Hemingway, however, had always been indifferent to the social significance of art, ambivalent about politics, and opposed to doing anything "fashionable." In *Green Hills of Africa,* he wrote:

> A country, finally, erodes and the dust blows away, the people all die and none of them were of any importance permanently, except those who practiced the arts, and these now wish to cease their work because it is too lonely, too hard to do, and is not fashionable. A thousand years makes economics silly and a work of art endures forever, but it is very difficult to do and now it is not fashionable. People do not want to do it any more because they will be out of fashion and the lice who crawl on literature will not praise them. (109)

He thus ended up writing a novel that would satisfy his critics but would also have a hidden edge. In *To Have and Have Not,* Hemingway may seem to be endorsing proletarian goals, but much of the novel can also be read as a satire, or even a subversion, of that very subject.[10]

The protagonist of the novel is Harry Morgan, the captain of a charter-fishing boat in Key West. Hemingway named the character after the sixteenth-century buccaneer Sir Henry Morgan, who sailed the same Gulf Stream waters around which the novel is set. The book is divided into three parts, "Spring," "Fall," and "Winter." In each part, Morgan's fortunes decline. First, he is cheated by a wealthy sportfisherman, a misfortune that leads him to agree to smuggle illegal Chinese immigrants into the United States. In part 2, Harry loses an arm when he is shot trying to outrun a U.S. customs patrol. In part 3, he dies while ferrying a group of Cuban revolutionaries from Key West to Cuba. Harry is a burly, hard-shelled "conch" who prides himself on being an individualist. He makes his own way and answers to no one as he struggles to support himself and his three daughters.

Part 3 of the novel introduces a second major character, Richard Gordon, a left-wing novelist whose books all concern the trampling of the underclasses by the capitalist elite, and whom Hemingway portrays in an unfavorable light. Gordon was based on John Dos Passos, whose proletarian sympathies were widely known at the time. (Hemingway also acknowledges Dos Passos in the novel by employing a cinematic technique that at times reminds one of the "Camera Eye" sections of Dos Passos's *U.S.A.* trilogy.) Gordon is Harry Morgan's antithesis, a weak-willed figure with no innate writing talent. (In addition to being a man who writes proletarian novels, he could be a character in a proletarian novel himself.) He struggles to complete a novel in progress, and when he cannot, he goes to a bar and is made fun of by a wharf rat who tells him that his books are meaningless. He is further humiliated by his wife, who has suffered from his numerous extramarital affairs. Hemingway uses Gordon as a foil to Morgan (notice the similarity of their names), preferring Harry's raw honesty to Gordon's pretentious artificiality.

Morgan is not a traditional laborer or proletarian but an individualist who is out for himself. He has no use for social organizations; he is basically unprincipled in what he does to get by; and he acts like a capitalist in his methods and aims. Hemingway shows great sympathy for Harry's courage in the face of danger, even if what he does is not wholly ethical. Harry's much-quoted credo, "a man alone ain't got no bloody fucking chance" (225), is not necessarily an endorsement of the collective; it can just as easily be read as an assertion of individualism. A man out on his own is a minority, Hemingway is saying, in the age of the mass. He admires Harry because he asserts his uniqueness in an era of joiners. The title of the novel, which concerns the "haves and have-nots" of American society, is ambiguous. Hemingway endorses neither those who have nor those who have not—although Harry and his lower-class friends do have a spirit and vitality that Gordon, for instance, and the owners of the fancy yachts lack.

As he had in *Death in the Afternoon* and *Green Hills of Africa,* Hemingway experimented liberally with form in *To Have and Have Not.* The tripartite structure allowed him to vary the novel's point of view. Part 1 consists of Morgan's first-person narration. Hemingway writes in the third person in part 2. Part 3, the longest of the three sections, shifts narrative perspective several times. The novel closes with an extended interior monologue by Harry's wife, Marie, a passage reminiscent of Molly Bloom's soliloquy in *Ulysses* that may be something of an homage to James Joyce, whom Hemingway admired deeply.

Hemingway composed the novel in a somewhat disjointed manner. He worked on the book intermittently from 1933 to 1937, and not until near the end did he think of it as a novel. His intention was to publish a book of short stories. Part 1 appeared in *Cosmopolitan* in April 1934—three years before the book appeared—under the title "One Trip Across." Part 2 was published in *Esquire* in February 1936 as "The Tradesman's Return." By April 1936 Hemingway had completed three other long stories ("The Snows of Kilimanjaro," "The Capital of the World," and "The Short Happy Life of Francis Macomber"). His initial intention may have been to include these in a collection of stories. Perkins liked the idea and even suggested another possibility; the new stories could be combined with Hemingway's *Esquire* essays. But Hemingway was "not very hot about mixing in articles and stories," feeling that it would give critics "the opportunity to dismiss it all." He didn't think it would "be a good idea to take a book of the best short stories I've done and get it damned as a hybred [*sic*] book and cursed by all that N.Y. outfit that foam at the mouthe [*sic*] at the mention of fishing or shooting or the idea that I ever have any fun or any right to have any fun. . . . They don't read books; just look for a damning point or a praising point and that must be economic. They can't tell literature from shit."[11] Hemingway, in other words, did not want a reprise of the reviews of his previous nonfiction books. Perkins conceded the point, and plans were kept on course for a story collection.

In late June 1936, however, Arnold Gingrich visited Hemingway in Key West and told him he was "crazy" not to work the two Key West–Havana narratives into a full-length novel. Eventually, Hemingway agreed, and wrote Perkins, "with luck it is a good book," and said that he had decided "to go on and finish that now" in Wyoming, where he was bound.[12] Perkins again agreed with Hemingway's decision, wiring him on 20 July, "delighted by your change of plan for book." Hemingway spent the rest of the year finishing the novel, alerting Perkins on 26 September that the end was in view: "Have about 55,000 some words done." He added, "It has gone very well lately. . . . When finish this book hope to go to Spain if all not over there. Will leave the completed Mss. in a vault so you will be covered on it. I can go over it again when I come back. In case anything should happen to me you would always be covered financially. . . . Hope to finish my first draft this month i.e. October. If I go to Spain will see you in N.Y. on way through."[13]

With such good news about his progress, Perkins hoped the novel could appear in the spring. But Hemingway did not finish the novel in October. Things had gone south for his fiction writing, probably because he was distracted by travel to and from Spain. On 2 December, he wrote Perkins from Havana (where he had gone on a fact-checking trip), "I wish this son of a bitching novel finished. About yesterday I was ready to end it and call it vol one of a trilogy. I know now why the boys write Trilogies."[14] On 2 January 1937, Hemingway, with great relief, was finally able to wire Perkins, "finished book today." He could now turn his attention exclusively to Spain, where much of his imagination had been all along, anyway, and eleven days later he signed a contract with the North American News Alliance to cover the Spanish Civil War.

But the writing he had done to finish *To Have and Have Not* lacked organic unity. Rather than start afresh, Hemingway used what he had already written as the starting point for a longer narrative, tacking on a final section that was only artificially connected to the preceding parts. The manuscripts for the book also show that he did very little revising—uncharacteristic for so methodical a writer as Hemingway.[15] He was definitely doing a rush job, for he pinched out small episodes in the story during brief stays in Key West, working on the novel between trips to Spain to monitor and write about the conflict there. At this time, Hemingway's mind was probably most on the war in Spain, not on his work in progress. He may have had trouble focusing on both the revolution abroad and the fictional narrative at once.

Hemingway claimed in a letter to Max Perkins that he meant to contrast two places—Key West and Havana—but Key West is symbolically the more important of the two.[16] *To Have and Have Not* is the only novel Hemingway wrote that is set in America, but just barely. Key West is one of the most remote of all locales, a village perched on the very tip of the southernmost land mass in the United States—an isolated island that at the time had as much in common culturally with its Caribbean neighbors as with the upper peninsula and points north. Key West is thus like Harry, who is out on his own, receiving support from no one, struggling to maintain self-sufficiency in the face of great odds.

The novel received mixed reviews, with the balance, as Robert W. Trogdon notes, "tilted toward those reviewers who did not like the book."[17] Writing in *Newsweek,* Sinclair Lewis found the book dull and unoriginal. Louis Kronenberger, in the *Nation,* thought that Hemingway should not have published the book, as it reflected badly on his craft. In the British periodical *Now & Then,* V. S. Pritchett approved of the book because of its apparent left-leaning politics: it was "very lively," and Hemingway had shown the new literary-political dilemma "in a new and interesting phase." *Time* magazine put the author on the cover of its 18 October issue and declared that Harry Morgan was Hemingway's greatest character yet. George Stevens, on the other hand, called the book Hemingway's weakest. "I remember less about 'To Have and Have Not' after two weeks," he wrote, "than about 'A Farewell to Arms' after eight years or 'The Sun Also Rises' after eleven."[18]

The view of Hemingway at this point in his career was perhaps best summed up by Bernard DeVoto in a *Saturday Review* piece titled "Tiger, Tiger!" DeVoto said, without much tact, that Hemingway's characters lacked psychological complexity. They had become mere "physiological systems organized around abdomen, super-renal glands, and genitals"—"sacs of basic instinct." DeVoto chastised Hemingway for being consumed by his idea of what constitutes humankind: "He has grown . . . increasingly belligerent about personalities more complex than those he creates, about ideas, about every kind of experience that is not localized in or near the viscera."[19] DeVoto loudly made clear that *To Have and Have Not* was not the endorsement of leftist politics that the literary establishment had expected from Hemingway.[20]

Hemingway's public response to these sour reviews of his novel was predictably angry, but he may have privately taken some ironic comfort in the knowledge that he had said, and then proved, that he was not the kind of writer who could produce on demand fashionable novels of political commitment. The book's poor showing may have just gone to prove his contention that advancing social theories was not the job of great literature. Great art, as he had shown in *The Sun Also Rises* and *A Farewell to Arms* (and would later show in *For Whom the Bell Tolls*), conveyed an emotional response to the universal condition of human suffering, not to economic injustice or the artificial notion that humankind must band together in awkward political solidarity. Such literature was contrived, Hemingway thought, and he was quick to put the experience behind him and turn his full attention to the war in Spain.

———

When Spain collapsed in civil conflict in 1936, it became almost inevitable that Hemingway would write about it, so closely had he always kept abreast of developments in that country. The war, moreover, turned out to be a rich mine of material for Hemingway, and he wrote prolifically during this period. The war produced not only one of his greatest novels, *For Whom the Bell Tolls,* but also a screenplay, *The Spanish Earth,* a play, *The Fifth Column,* several speeches and articles promoting the Loyalist cause, and much front-line reportage.

The war began in July 1936 when a right-wing military uprising, beginning in Spanish Morocco and led by General Francisco Franco, tried to oust the legitimately elected left-leaning Republican government, called the Popular Front. Franco's Nationalists, as the name suggests, feared that their country had been fragmented by the various separatist movements that had ruled parts of Spain for many years, and they wanted to reunify the country under a central dictatorial authority. Their leaders were generally affluent and conservative and had monarchist leanings; most were of the wealthy landowning class and were strongly pro-Catholic. The Republicans thought the church had long been corrupt and was too readily collaborative with Franco's forces. As Stanley G. Payne puts it, "The special privileges . . . enjoyed by the Church" made it a "target for the left. . . . The Church was blamed for the ills of contemporary Spanish society."[21]

To turn back the Nationalists, a confederation of people loyal to the Spanish Republic—the so-called Loyalists or Republicans—was organized; chief among them were the International Brigades, electoral alliances formed among various left-wing and centrist parties. The brigades comprised a miscellany of people with different political viewpoints and from different nations who were united in their opposition to fascism in general and to Franco in particular. But at their core were the Spanish people, those with democratic ideals and egalitarian principles, many of them from the lowest socioeconomic classes, including peasants who worked the land. These people were the ones most passionately committed to the cause, the ones whose zeal compelled them to commit the tragic acts of fighting and killing their own countrymen who opposed them on the other side.

The Spanish Civil War instantly became one of the great fabled revolutions—a war that attracted writers, artists, and Western intellectuals of many backgrounds, among them George Orwell, André Malraux, and W. H. Auden, who thought he would "probably be a bloody bad soldier" but asked, "how can I speak to/ for them without becoming one?"[22] (Auden volunteered for the ambulance corps but ended up working in propaganda broadcasting instead.) The British poet John Cornford, who served with a machine gun unit of the Commune de Paris Battalion, part of the 11th International Brigade, and who fought in the defense of Madrid through November and December 1936, gave his life for the Republic one day after his twenty-first birthday. The great Spanish poet Federico Garcia Lorca, a native of Granada, was arrested by Nationalist militia for his outspoken leftist views and killed; his body was never found. Another poet, the Englishman Laurence E. A. "Laurie" Lee, looking back on what eventually were recognized as long odds against the Loyalists, wrote, "I believe we shared something else, unique to us at that time—the chance to make one grand and uncomplicated gesture of personal sacrifice and faith, which might never occur again. . . . It was the last time in this century that a generation had such an opportunity before the fog of nationalism and mass-slaughter closed in. Few of us yet knew that we had come to a war of antique muskets and jamming machine-guns, to be led by brave but bewildered amateurs. But for the moment there were no half-truths and hesitations, we had found a new freedom, almost a new morality, and discovered a new Satan—fascism."[23]

Hemingway's commitment to the Loyalists was not quite as deep-seated as that of others, but he was earnest in support of the cause. Among other things, his involvement reveals Martha Gellhorn's political influence on him. His support for the Spanish Republicans also brought out many of his best qualities, inspiring him to boost morale and secure aid in whatever form he could, even when it put him in harm's way, as it often did. In addition, his involvement in the war intensified and complicated his already awkward relationship with the Left. When Hemingway made known his support for the Loyalists in Spain, critics who had been castigating him for spending his artistic energy on what they saw as frivolous topics suddenly welcomed him as a convert. (As he later put it, "I had to go to Spain before you goddamned liberal bastards knew I was on your side!")[24] But Hemingway's perception of the war was more complex than that. He was not a joiner, and most failed to understand that his opposition to the juggernaut of fascism was not the same thing as supporting communism.[25]

Hemingway made his first of several trips to Spain during the conflict in early 1937. On 13 January he signed on as a correspondent for the North American Newspaper Alliance. By 27 February he had arrived in France with Sidney Franklin and Evan Shipman, one of his closest friends since the time in Paris in the 1920s. (Shipman sometimes lived in Hemingway's house in Key West and even tutored Bumby in French; Hemingway remained close to Shipman until the latter's death in 1957.) On 14 March, Hemingway arrived at the Spanish border, and that month five dispatches for the newspaper alliance appeared under Hemingway's byline in U.S. newspapers. In Madrid, he made the Hotel Florida his base of operations. Gellhorn, as the correspondent for *Collier's* magazine, arrived soon thereafter. The city had just come under siege. Gelhorn remembered Madrid as cold, enormous, and pitch black—a battlefield waiting in the dark. Disaster swung aimlessly all over the city, like a compass needle: "You could only wait. . . . You waited for the shelling to start, and for it to end, and for it to start again," she wrote.[26]

Gellhorn, despite her impeccable credentials and strong track record, had never covered a war before. For that reason, it is sometimes thought that she was simply there to accompany Hemingway. But although she did not know the other reporters, as Hemingway did, and although she was expected to defer to them all, she blazed her own path and filed a series of reports that are stunning in their insight, intensity, and precision. Like any good reporter, she stayed in the background of her stories and let the danger of the moment speak for itself—as in this excerpt from "The Third Winter" (1938): "In Barcelona, it was perfect bombing weather. The cafés along the Ramblas were crowded. There was nothing much to drink; a sweet fizzy poison called orangeade and a horrible liquid supposed to be sherry. There was, of course, nothing to eat. Everyone was out enjoying the cold afternoon sunlight. No bombers had come over for at least two hours."[27]

Hemingway, by contrast, put much of himself into his reporting (as he had done when he was a European correspondent for the *Toronto Star Weekly*) and thus sacrificed realistic detail. Gellhorn had a masterly command of the detail but also compassion for her subject. She visited the front when she could, but she was drawn more often into shops and factories, homes and hospitals. The climactic scene of "The Third Winter"—set in a ward of wounded, sick, and hungry children—provides unforgettable images of what Gellhorn called "the face of war." She once said that she had never known any male reporters who even went near the hospitals. "But I was a great frequenter of [them]," she recalled, "because that's where you see what war really costs."[28]

That summer, the fighting escalated, and in July a series of coordinated rebellions gave Franco's forces control of nearly half the country within four days. Initially, the Spanish government refused to acknowledge the seriousness of the uprising and delayed arming the civilian population until it was almost too late. Worse, without help from other large industrialized nations, the Republican cause was severely handicapped. The United States pursued a policy of isolation. Great Britain dithered, taking the view that such disorder was appropriate in a county that had fallen into the hands of communists and anarchists. George Orwell described the situation in *Homage to Catalonia,* one of the best books to emerge from the war: in one district, amid alleyways where the hammer and sickle had been scrawled on the walls, and café windows proclaimed the triumph of collectivism, he observed militiamen being given "what was comically called 'instruction'" in preparation for fighting at the front by people who knew next to nothing of battle tactics.[29] It was as if a violin maker had been called in to fix a tank engine.

The Loyalists' situation worsened dramatically when Germany and Italy answered Franco's appeal for assistance. Italy sent twelve bombers immediately. Hitler, seeing an excellent opportunity for pilots and reconnaissance personnel to gain experience flying and fighting in wartime conditions, sent torpedo boats and fighter planes. In September, the city of Toledo fell to the Nationalists, and on 1 October, Franco—the youngest general ever to serve in the Spanish army—was named head of state. Martial law was declared, and in the first weeks of Franco's reign, truckloads of political suspects, many of them "red oppressors," were taken to the outskirts of towns and killed—some twenty thousand by most estimates.

In October, the first airstrikes on Madrid began, and a grim battle for the heart of Spain got under way. Nationalist armies approached from the northwest and southwest, and by the middle of the month they controlled every town within fifteen miles of the capital. The Popular Front soldiers showed immense bravery and courage, but they were undisciplined and untrained—many did not know how to dig trenches or even how to take cover. The losses mounted, and soon the eyes of the world turned to Madrid: would it fall to Franco? In the city, workers rallied around Dolores Ibárruri, the popular leader of the working class, who urged her fellow Madrileños to resist at all costs: fight with any weapon, she cried, pour boiling water on the traitors. *No pasarán* (They shall not pass!) was the rallying cry that rang through the city, which became a fortress for more than ten days as the battle raged. The people resisted, even as, by mid-November, some two thousand missiles were falling on the city center every day, and there were no air-raid shelters in which to seek safety. German bombers blackened the skies, a dozen at a time. But the Nationalists could not break the steel will of the ill-armed Madrileños: children helped build barricades and women stood arm in arm to face the advancing army. The Fascists were repulsed, and for a time Franco's movement lost some of its momentum. Still, the war was far from over.

At the Hotel Florida in the center of Madrid, Hemingway and Gellhorn had a close view of the battles. The conditions were horrible. Their room had no hot water, many of the windows in the building had been blown out by the intense shelling, and, as Gellhorn said, "you could walk to the war": the front was only seventeen blocks away. Hemingway showed great physical courage in these days. George Seldes, a foreign correspondent for the *Chicago Tribune* and the *New York Post,* recalled that Hemingway's

daily or almost daily visits to the wrecked building in no man's land he used as an observation post were an exhibition of courage. From there he could see both the Loyalists as well as the Franco trenches opposite. My wife and I each went to the front-line trenches *once.* But Hem and Herbert Matthews [a *New York Times* reporter] climbed out into no man's land almost every day and lay on their stomachs on the floor near a smashed second-floor window to watch the fighting. And Franco shelled everything, including this hideout.[30]

The courage came from Hemingway's fatalism. Whether you ran ahead or hung back, he believed, didn't matter if your time had come.

Moreover, he called the conflict in Spain a "bad" war because nobody was right. All that mattered to him was that human suffering be relieved. To bomb a hospital in Toledo or detonate a hand grenade in a working-class district of Madrid was neither Christian nor humane, and he wondered why the church had not sided with the oppressed. He felt great empathy for the suffering of the Madrileños. Hemingway learned of the work of Dr. Norman Bethune, a thoracic surgeon at Sacré-Coeur Hospital in Montreal, who had perfected a way to store refrigerated blood so that the wounded could be given transfusions from mobile blood banks. Hemingway sought out hypodermic needles that could be delivered to Bethune's unit, so desperate were they for the needed supplies to help save lives.

Hemingway and Gellhorn combed through the city on some days and on others drove out into the surrounding countryside to report on conditions. Swerving around vehicles, sounding the horn, and shouting their way past civilians, they plowed over gutted country roads in a Ford station wagon that was so poorly camouflaged you could see it from almost a mile away. On one trip north to Guadalajara, they were able to gauge the mixed emotions of optimism and resignation that seemed always to hang over the Loyalist forces. Franco's army was under heavy siege; it had dug in and was temporarily trapped. The Republican soldiers laughed, smoked, and sunbathed as Hemingway and Gellhorn moved among them. But in the hospital, where they helped deliver blood and supplies, "desperately tired" men stank of "ether and sweat." A doctor cleansed a wound that looked to Gellhorn like eroded soil, "ridged and jagged and eaten in."[31] Over time, they drove thousands of miles across the country, often writing for twenty-four-hour stretches. They were often painfully cold and rarely got a square meal.

The scene back at the Hotel Florida was another story. Swarms of foreign correspondents gathered to share food, stories, and comfort, and Hemingway was in his element. He was easily the most famous person there, and it was he who kept spirits up and, in his calm, even manner, assumed the air of a veteran who had seen everything and knew the score. It was like a hurricane party, with revelers inoculated against the fear outside by liberal consumption of wine and spirits. Every evening around eleven, they would gather in the sitting room in the suite of Sefton Delmer, a British journalist, and stay up late drinking and talking. When it got hot, Delmer would open the windows and put Beethoven's Fifth Symphony on the gramophone, its thunderous chords echoing through the night air to the accompaniment of artillery explosions.

Claud Cockburn, a correspondent for the *British Daily Worker,* recalled that Hemingway could "talk in a very military way and . . . sound very convincing." One day, he was explaining to several others how it would be impossible for a shell to hit the hotel, when a shell actually "whooshed" through the room above them and the ceiling collapsed. Cockburn, "pale as marble," stood stock still, "holding a coffeepot in his hands as if it were a votive offering."[32] Yet Hemingway, unperturbed, continued calmly on, giving the distinct impression that "this episode had actually, in an obscure way, confirmed instead of upset his theory."[33] A little later, however, Hemingway suggested that events might have shifted and that it might be time to come up with a new theory.

Hemingway and Gellhorn were there to witness the worst atrocity of the war, on 26 April 1937. At 4:15 in the afternoon, German planes swooped in low over the Basque town of Guernica, dropping bombs and grenades and strafing the ground. People running down the dirt roads were cut to shreds, and buildings were razed by heavy bombs. Wave after wave of explosives rocked the town for more than two and a half hours, reducing Guernica to rubble. In all, 1,654 people died; almost nine hundred more were wounded. Then the more awful truth became known: the town had no strategic military value. Germany had used it merely as target practice, as an opportunity for their pilots and gunners to try out the incendiary methods they would use later, in World War II.

Soon, more than two-thirds of Spain was under Nationalist control. The Republicans were outnumbered, especially with the support Franco received from Germany and Italy. New recruits became harder to find, as volunteers who returned home told stories of battlefield executions and other horrors. On 15 December 1937, the Republicans pushed back, choosing the remote and mountainous town of Teruel, in the east, to make a stand. Again, however, they were ill prepared. They began the offensive without artillery or aerial preparation. Most of the battles were fought on the streets, and it was eighteen degrees below zero. Machinery froze; men were felled by frostbite. More than ten thousand Republican soldiers died.

Hemingway was in the country for the last great battle of the war: the siege of the Ebro delta, from 24 July to 26 November 1938. The Republicans had chosen the site to try to restore communications with central Spain, but the struggle to break Franco's stranglehold was futile. Ten thousand pounds of bombs rained down on the Republican army every day for three weeks, and Ebro proved to be the final campaign for the International Brigades. Hemingway was the last to cross the river and leave the lost ground behind. The Republican cause lay buried in the mud, mixed with the blood of its defenders.

Its demise was hastened by Britain's withdrawal of its forces in September and by the general appeasement of Hitler by France and Great Britain, which effectively destroyed Republican morale by removing any hope of an antifascist alliance with Western powers. Eight days before the new year, Franco launched a major offensive against Republicans in Catalonia. Then, on 14 January 1939, Tarragona fell, followed in quick succession by Barcelona, two weeks later, and Girona on 5 February. On 27 February, the United Kingdom and France recognized the Franco regime. Only a few strongholds in Madrid remained, but these were quickly quashed. Franco marched triumphantly into Madrid on 28 March 1939, and within a week the war was over. The cost was high: thirty-three thousand Nationalist soldiers and thirty thousand Republican soldiers killed. Franco went on to hold the reins of power in Spain for more than thirty-five years, and the people's dreams of democratic egalitarianism were shattered as the iron gates of wealth and power clanged shut.

Hemingway was forever changed by the Spanish war, just as he had been by World War I. In Italy, the change had been personal. In Spain, a much greater sense of loss and change overcame him as he shook his fist in anger at the Fascists, vowing revenge; the war had changed a whole country and, with it, Hemingway's idea of Spain as a utopian haven. The list of casualties in his life grew longer, and a melancholy resignation about the prospects for human progress began to set in.

———

Hemingway supported the Loyalist cause wholeheartedly and did much on its behalf. He wrote and narrated a film, *The Spanish Earth,* and arranged for its showing; he produced a play, *The Fifth Column,* which ran on Broadway; and he gave a fiery speech at the second convention of the League of American Writers, a Popular Front organization, in New York on 4 June 1937. "Really good writers are always rewarded under almost any existing system of government that they can tolerate," Hemingway said. "There is only one form of government that cannot produce good writers and that system is fascism. For fascism is a lie told by bullies." "A writer who will not lie cannot live or work under fascism," he declared.[34]

The speech on 4 June at Carnegie Hall drew a crowd of more than thirty-five hundred people. Archibald MacLeish chaired the session. Not being a Communist Party member, he was a bit confused as to why he had been chosen, except that as an editor of *Fortune* he represented "the other side"; he could also produce Hemingway, which was what the organizers wanted.[35] Outside the packed auditorium, more than a thousand people (most of whom had probably shown up to hear Hemingway) were turned away. The Murphys were there, as were Dawn Powell, Vincent Sheean, and Van Wyck Brooks. MacLeish read telegrams of support from the likes of Thomas Mann and Albert Einstein. Donald Ogden Stewart spoke first, followed by Earl Browder, secretary of the Communist Party of the United States. Then the "dark serious burning-eyed" Joris Ivens, the Dutch filmmaker with whom Hemingway had been working on *The Spanish Earth,* showed a rough version of the film and urged the audience to join the cause.[36] Hemingway took the rostrum at 10:30 p.m. and delivered his address, capping off his characterization of the Fascists as agents of evil and persecutors of the innocent with the statement, "Every time they are beaten in the field, they salvage that strange thing they call their honor by murdering civilians." The speech was very well received. Paul Romaine, a prominent bookseller who for years had been urging Hemingway to become more political, claimed that it was "magnificent, as if everyone had taken him into their arms, truly a companion . . . in the fight against fascism." "How could this fight be lost," Romaine wrote, "with Hemingway on our side?"[37] Gellhorn spoke the following afternoon, but, as would become the pattern, her remarks were mostly forgotten in the wake of Hemingway's star turn.

Hemingway's most extensive artistic participation in the war effort was his collaboration with Ivens on *The Spanish Earth*. The project is interesting for both the way it helped the cause in Spain and the way in which it furthered Hemingway's development as a writer. Ivens was a staunch supporter of communism; in fact, he had toured U.S. college campuses in the 1930s showing documentaries supporting the communist system. The most famous of these was Helen van Dongen's *Spain in Flames*. But that film, which was mainly a compilation of newsreel footage showing Franco's atrocities, had limited success in demonstrating the war's impact on the lives of poor Spanish peasants.

The Spanish Earth, by contrast, was sophisticated and polished, and its reach extended much further. The theme of the film was that the peasants had established their right to work the land by democratic means. The threat of a military takeover and the institution of absentee landlords, who took the land away from them by force, spurred them to fight: "We fight," the film says at one point, "for the right to irrigate and cultivate this Spanish earth which the nobles kept idle for their own amusement." Ivens had initially been working with John Dos Passos on the film, but in April 1937 Dos Passos learned of the killing of José Robles, a Spanish academic who generally supported the Republicans but ran afoul of the Communists as they became increasingly involved in the Loyalist cause. Robles was shot as an alleged Francoist spy. Dos Passos, sickened over the incident, no longer wished to participate in Ivens's project and suggested that Hemingway take his place. (The event marked the beginning of Dos Passos's gradual turn to the political Right.)[38]

Joris Ivens had been born into a wealthy family in the Netherlands and had developed an interest in film through exposure to his father's photography business. His early work was highly experimental and featured impressive cinematography, but it was not until he went to the Soviet Union in 1929 that he found his métier: propagandistic political documentaries. His film about the new industrial Soviet city of Magnitogorsk, *Song of Heroes,* premiered in 1931, followed two years later by *Borinage,* a pro-communist documentary about life in a coal-mining region.[39]

Hemingway and Ivens had met that spring of 1937 in Paris, when Hemingway arranged to deliver some money he had raised for the film in America. The two men hit it off immediately, establishing an easy rapport. Hemingway tried to convince Ivens that he knew all about the costs of war, telling him the story of his injury in Italy. Ivens understood Hemingway's point of view, but he later wrote that the author "knew Spain in peace, but not in war. In Paris he could see things from a distance, but I knew that once we were there things would be different." Ivens was also impressed by the sheer physical bulk of his new comrade: "a kind of big boy scout who imposed himself by his physique and his manner of expressing himself. . . . He was a very physical man who knew how to control himself and never showed his fear."[40]

They produced the film with little funding (Archibald MacLeish and Lillian Hellman made large financial contributions), and Hemingway proved to be immensely useful. He acted as translator, military advisor, scout, and even stevedore, lugging the heavy film camera and other equipment from place to place, ever mindful that these objects were precious cargo and that if anything happened to the camera, the project was finished. The heat was oppressive as they filmed the assaults on Madrid from the mountains, jogging up and down the rough terrain, sweat rolling down their faces. In the Morata de Tajuña area, studded with olive trees, they fell in behind the infantry and filmed the tanks as they "moved like ships up the steep hills and deployed into action."[41] Hemingway acted like the commanding officer of the film regiment, barking orders and making cutting remarks if he thought someone was not pulling his weight. He wanted always to be exceptional, first in everything, and his competitive nature was everywhere on display.

However, when it came to writing and narrating the script, according to Ivens, Hemingway retracted his hard shell and became the perfect willing and humble student, open to any and all instruction. Hemingway had never written for film before—in 1937, it was still an emerging art form—and in his first draft he made the usual beginner's mistake of telling too much, writing more narration than there was room for in the fifty-minute time frame. When Ivens returned the script to him, covered with red ink, Hemingway was for a moment incensed: "You God-damned Dutchman. How dare you correct my text?" he retorted, but he quickly backed down, for he saw that there was far too much talk. He needed to let the images speak for themselves, and to tailor his words to reinforce the pictures on the screen. "Don't write about what you see," Ivens instructed him. "Don't repeat the image."[42] Hemingway agreed, and took another stab at the script. Always a quick learner, he avoided all the mistakes of the first draft and succeeded in producing a narration that married the words and pictures perfectly.

Hemingway also narrated the film. Orson Welles had been tapped for this job, but when Lillian Hellman and Fredric March, two of Ivens's supporters, heard the finished product, they thought Welles's voice was too polished for the ragged, grassroots character of the film. They wanted something more human, and they turned to Hemingway to read his own words. At first, he demurred. "No, no, I can't," he said, somewhat fearfully. "I don't have the proper training in breathing"—a flimsy excuse, perhaps, to cover up his nervousness at being asked to perform in an area in which he had no expertise.[43] A. E. Hotchner, Hemingway's close associate in the 1950s, believed that the microphone was one of Hemingway's deadliest enemies.[44] Hotchner had a hard time getting Hemingway to say anything that was to be recorded, and he took to carrying a small, transistorized device called a Midgetape in his pocket, to get unguarded conversations on record. Hearing Hemingway speak is always a mild surprise. His voice was thin and reedy, with a flat midwestern accent that never sounded quite full or commanding enough to match his burly physique and huge public presence. In the case of *The Spanish Earth,* however, its humanness and unprepossessing nature matched the feeling of the film perfectly. It gave the film an added dimension—a sensibility that no other voice would have been able to convey as well.

The film was well received and proved to be an effective fund-raiser for the Loyalist cause. Its most famous showing came on 8 July 1937 at the Roosevelt White House, an event that Hemingway and—to some controversy—Ivens attended. (One newspaper story carried the headline "Communist Director Invades White House.") The Roosevelts were impressed by the film but thought it could have been even more propagandistic. The film was shown a few days later at the Los Angeles home of actor Fredric March; Hemingway spoke at this event, which raised more than $17,000 for the purchase of ambulances for the resistance. Although the film was never commercially distributed, it got a lot of attention, in large part due to Hemingway's writing and narration. One reviewer wrote, "Much of the carrying power in understatement should be credit to Ernest Hemingway's commentary. . . . [With his] feeling for the people of Spain which comes from the heart, the combination of experience and intuition directing your attention quietly to the mortal truth you might well have missed in the frame, there could hardly be a better choice."[45] The film, which officially premiered at the Fifty-Fifth Street Playhouse in New York on 22 August 1937, has since become a classic.

Hemingway's play about the Spanish war, *The Fifth Column,* was written at the Hotel Florida during the siege of Madrid in the fall of 1937. The term "fifth column" was reportedly coined by a Nationalist general, Emilio Mola y Vidal, who declared in a radio address that a cadre of his supporters was working within Madrid to overthrow the Loyalist regime while four columns of regular soldiers were marching toward the city. The term thus came to be used to describe a group of secret sympathizers or supporters of an enemy working within the borders or defense lines of a country or government. *The Fifth Column* tells the story of an American war correspondent named Philip Rawlings, a man much like Hemingway, who is covering the conflict while based at the Hotel Florida in Madrid. Four columns of Franco's army are advancing on the city, and to combat the threat, Rawlings—a Loyalist supporter—becomes a counterspy for the Republican army. The conflict in the play arises when Rawlings has to choose between running off with a pretty American girl, Dorothy Bridges, with whom he has fallen in love, or staying in the city helping to try to repel the Nationalist forces.

The story is an improbable melodrama, but it sheds revealing light on the relationship between Hemingway and Gellhorn. Philip is depicted as one might expect—as a physically imposing presence and man of action. Dorothy idolizes Philip, who emotionally abuses her even as he admires her good looks. "Don't be a bored Vassar bitch," he says, echoing Harry's opinion of Jig in "The Snows of Kilimanjaro" (3). He demands Dorothy's subservience, and she readily complies. In the character of Dorothy, Hemingway had clearly created another wish-fulfillment version of his current love interest. To many friends, it was astonishing that the two got married at all, considering, as his friend William Walton put it, his "having put into the play the hostility that he had."[46] Martha was anything but compliant, and her fierce independence was what eventually soured Hemingway on her. But her marrying him despite his portrayal of her in the play shows his strong influence on her emotions. Perhaps, too, she felt early on, like most of Hemingway's women, that she could change him.

Finding a producer for the play proved to be a challenge; it finally opened on Broadway on 6 March 1940 but closed after only eighty-seven performances. Scribner's later published a special edition of 1,174 copies, and Hemingway included it in *The Fifth Column and the First Forty-Nine Stories* (1938), a compilation of his three story collections to date plus four uncollected tales. That volume received good reviews; the critics praised the stories but considered the play political propaganda, not fiction. Many also found the play weak dramatically.

The Spanish Earth, Hemingway's speeches and fund-raising activities, and *The Fifth Column* were the most visible testaments to his commitment to the Loyalist cause during his forays in and out of Spain in wartime. After the Fascist victory, Hemingway withdrew from Spain and did not return for many years. But he still held Latin and Hispanic culture dear, and he would write about the war one more time in *For Whom the Bell Tolls,* a best seller that would return him to fine form in the novel-writing game.

Cuba and
For Whom the Bell Tolls

Hemingway returned from Spain in December 1938 to begin work on his next novel. Three months later, though still married, he officially left Pauline and moved to Cuba. Martha had found them a crumbling nineteenth-century farm-house to rent in the village of San Francisco de Paula, in the hills above Havana. Called Finca Vigía (Lookout Farm), its fifteen acres were planted with lush flower and vegetable gardens. It was quiet and remote. Hemingway and Martha set up house there, while Pauline began divorce proceedings back in Key West.

Hemingway had first visited Cuba in 1928, while living in Key West with Pauline. He had taken the four-hour boat trip back and forth to fish there many times since then and was thoroughly familiar with the exotic, lizard-shaped island. Key West and Cuba were tied closely together at the time, both economically and culturally. There was much intermarrying between Americans and Cubans, and Key West residents routinely took the ferry to Havana for the nightlife and shopping.[1] Hemingway liked the Latin culture, the informality, and the solitude. In fact, he had some form of contact with Cuba for more than thirty years—two-thirds of his creative life—and he lived there full-time for more than twenty years. Cuba thus had a much greater impact on his creativity than any location in Europe or the United States.

In 1939, Cuba was far from the oppressive political environment that it came to be later in the twentieth century. It was ruled by Fulgencio Batista, who had come to power in 1933. Batista at the time was a colonel who masterminded a soldiers' revolt against the dictator Gerardo Machado. When a provisional government was put in place, Batista, who turned out to be more cunning than his superiors presumed—overthrew the president and took charge of the country himself. Batista seemed benign at first, but he turned out to be as controlling as

Machado had been. He held on to power until the end of 1958, when Fidel Castro took control.

Havana was a hedonist's playground. Every imaginable vice could be freely indulged there—a far cry from repressive, pious Oak Park. Brothels were abundant, liquor was cheap, and for a mere $1.25 one go could go to the Shanghai Theater and see a nude cabaret revue, with—as Graham Greene described it—"the bluest of blue films in the intervals." (When the films bored him, Greene went in search of "a little cocaine" and found that "nothing [could] be easier" to obtain.)[2] There is no evidence that Hemingway participated in such amusements, but he doubtless enjoyed the liberating thrill of being able to do whatever he wanted to, away from his associates in Key West, and away from Pauline as well. He also associated Cuba with his four-year affair with Jane Mason—another corrective to any lingering midwestern Protestantism that Hemingway may have carried with him to Cuba in a hangover of guilt over leaving Pauline.

In fact, Hemingway's first abode was the scene of his former crime: room number 511 of the Hotel Ambos Mundos, where he had conducted his affair with Jane Mason. Then as now, the name of the hotel was the perfect metaphor for Hemingway's modus operandi: "both worlds." Just as he had experienced the frisson of pleasure sleeping with Jane while married to Pauline, he now had escaped from Pauline and into a completely different environment where he was free to be with Martha.

His room, in the northeast corner of the hotel, looked out over the entrance to the harbor, across the chockablock rooftops of the old city and east to the fishing town of Casablanca. Hemingway said that he always slept with his feet pointed toward the east so that the sun shining on his face in the morning would wake him. "If you do not choose to get up," he would write about this ritual, "you can turn around the other way in the bed or roll over, . . . [but] that will not help for long because the sun will be getting stronger and the only thing to do is close the shutter."[3] He would rise early in the morning, shower, pull on an old pair of Bermuda shorts, Basque slippers, and whatever shirt was at hand, and walk down Obispo Street through a cornucopia of smells that was stronger than a shot of rum: tobacco, roasted coffee beans, and the dust billowing out the tops of burlap sacks filled with flour. At a corner café he would have breakfast and read the morning paper. If he chose to fish instead of write that day, he could look up at the Cuban flag waving high over Morro Castle and check the wind direction to see if conditions were favorable for chasing marlin.

He liked the somewhat shoddy city. No one recognized him there, the Latin ambience was reminiscent of Spain, and many Loyalist refugees had fled there during the war. As he had in Key West, Hemingway settled on a regular watering hole, the Floridita, at the corner of Obispo Street and Monserrate, in the old quarter of Havana, a large, popular place that could have been the set for Rick's Café in the movie *Casablanca*. Fans spun slowly on the ceilings, prostitutes scouted prey, and con men kept their eyes peeled for a soft touch.

As he had in Key West, Hemingway began assembling a group of cronies to drink with, fish with, and serve as an audience for his stories. These packs of acquaintances followed Hemingway around with slavish devotion—"like a crowd of Cuban zombies who think he is Hernán Cortés," Katy Dos Passos recalled; basically insecure, Hemingway needed a band of admirers to bolster his self-confidence.[4] He found many of them in Cuba. But these friends benefited from Hemingway's closeness with them as well. Ever generous, he was quick to help them in need, give them things they expressed a desire for, and teach them skills like shooting and sportfishing. One acquaintance later recalled that Hemingway had an invigorating effect on people, that he "always enhanced life for his friends."[5] Indeed, Hemingway had an infectious enthusiasm for so much. When he found that he liked something, he became an evangelist for it, working ceaselessly to convert everyone else to his newfound interest.

One such friend was Mario "Mayito" Menocal Jr., whose father had been a general in the Cuban army and president of the country from 1913 to 1921. Menocal had thus grown up in a comfortably well-off family. He had been educated in the United States at the Lawrenceville School, and for many years ran a dairy farm, and then a sugar mill, on the family estate. Hemingway had met Menocal in Bimini in 1935. In Cuba, Menocal was a frequent visitor to Finca Vigía. He came for the books—the enormous number of volumes in Hemingway's private library. Hemingway would lend him whatever he wanted to read, and he would often suggest authors and titles to Menocal as well. Later, as their friendship blossomed, Hemingway would go fishing on Menocal's large yacht, the *Delicias*. When Hemingway went on his second African safari in 1953–54, Menocal came along for part of the trip. Each man regarded the other as a surrogate brother, and Hemingway was saddened when Menocal had to leave Cuba during the Castro revolution.

Another intimate was Menocal's cousin, Elicio Arguelles, who owned a jai alai fronton in Havana where Hemingway went to play, bet, drink, and talk away the nights with his Basque friends.[6] Arguelles greatly admired Hemingway, especially his physical strength. When Hemingway took up sportfishing, Arguelles liked to come along to watch the author wrestle marlin and other fighting fish up onto the deck. He thought Hemingway epitomized the man of the world, the man who loved life. "I have never known a man who enjoyed life more," he recalled. "He did everything to the fullest." Leicester Hemingway—who, curiously, did not visit his brother much once he'd moved from Key West to Cuba—observed that Hemingway always needed to have someone around to serve as a "spiritual kid brother," someone to show off for and someone to teach.[7] In Key West, Arnold Samuelson had briefly filled this role; in Cuba, some years later, the part would be played by Walter Houk. Most people found Hemingway's company genuinely invigorating. "Things became more enjoyable when done with him or looked at through his eyes," Menocal recalled. "He managed to imbue the most trivial sporting activity with his own sense of the challenging and the dramatic."[8] The vitality, perhaps, masked an inner depression, invisible to those around him.

Hemingway probably would have been happy staying in the Ambos Mundos indefinitely, but Martha wanted more space and domestic comfort. She could not abide the bachelor's sloppiness he fell into whenever he was on his own. Martha was always orderly, pressed, and neat; Hemingway would often wear the same shirt two days in a row, and he wouldn't bother to knock the fish scales off his arms when he came in from a day on the water. So Martha went in search of better lodgings and found Finca Vigía, which they rented for $100 a month until December 1940, when Hemingway purchased it with the earnings from *For Whom the Bell Tolls*. To reach the property, one drove through miles of hillside squalor—"four hundred years of dust, the nose-snot of children, cracked palm fronds, [and] the shuffle of untreated syphilis," as Hemingway described it in *Islands in the Stream* (241)—but upon reaching the house, a veritable paradise awaited. One drove up a driveway lined with mango trees to a big limestone villa set off by banana trees, bougainvillea vines, and dark green shrubs. Surrounded by a tropical garden, the secluded property provided plenty of room for writing, reading, and listening to music—one of Hemingway's favorite after-dinner pastimes. The villa also stood high on a hill, providing Hemingway with much needed privacy.

Inside, it looked like a house built of books—floor to ceiling books, more than eight thousand of them. There were cookbooks, novels, and other works of fiction, history, and music. The heads of big-horned mammals—safari trophies—stared blankly from the walls in almost every room. The living room, nearly fifty feet long, with a high ceiling and gleaming white walls, set off Hemingway's small but choice collection of paintings (including a Miró, two by Juan Gris, a Klee, a Braque, and five André Massons). In one large corner of the living room stood a six-foot-high rack filled with dozens of magazines and newspapers from the States, London, and Paris. Casual piles of books littered windowsills and tables and spilled a trail into two large rooms adjacent—a library and a bedroom study. The library contained nearly two thousand volumes carefully divided into history, military subjects, biography, geography, natural history, some fiction, and a large collection of maps; the bedroom study held about nine hundred volumes, mostly military manuals and textbooks, history and geography books in Spanish, and sports volumes. Hemingway described the house simply as "a good place to work because it is out of town and on a hill so that it is cool at night. I wake up when the sun rises and go to work and when I finish I get a swim and have a drink and read the . . . papers."[9] The atmosphere proved conducive to writing, for here he was able to reconstruct the tumultuous events of the Spanish Civil War and produce a best-selling novel.

———

Hemingway began writing *For Whom the Bell Tolls* in late February or early March 1939, only a few months after his return from Spain. "Great writing comes out of a sense of injustice," Hemingway once said, and he wanted to move quickly while the heroic struggles of the Spanish people were still fresh in his mind.[10] He had waited more than ten years to write of his experience in the Great War; this time, he knew that another, larger war was soon to come and felt he could not wait to write about Spain. *For Whom the Bell Tolls* is his longest and most ambitious work. He later told Robert van Gelder of the *New York Times* that he was determined that the novel "had to be all right" or he would have felt that he had to get out of the business of writing books, "because my last job," he said, "*To Have and Have Not,* was not so good."[11] Mindful of his critics, Hemingway undertook to write nothing less than a *War and Peace* set amid a different conflict, a book both noble and epic.

On 25 March 1939, Hemingway wrote Max Perkins that he had started on another story that he actually "had no intention of writing for a very long time" but had found that he enjoyed the work and had piled up fifteen thousand words before he knew it. The ever-superstitious Hemingway then told Perkins that he was going to press on with the book, but that he would not show it to his editor for fear of jinxing his progress. Hemingway was confident; he even compared his work on the story to how he had felt while writing *A Farewell to Arms*—he knew exactly where the story was headed and how he would present it.[12] Perkins replied on 18 April that he was glad that the book was going so well, sending his encouragement in a direct but light-handed way. Hemingway told Perkins on 10 May that he was averaging between seven hundred and a thousand words a day, and that he felt he could do even more but was holding back so as not to rush the writing—pacing himself, as it were, for what he envisioned as a long haul. On 30 May he reported that he was up to page 213 of the manuscript. Both Perkins and Charles Scribner responded to his progress updates, politely praising his forward motion and saying little else. Hoping for a blockbuster to redeem the relatively weak performance of *To Have and Have Not,* both editor and publisher seem not to have tried to learn anything specific about the story but were instead simply pleased that Hemingway had thrown himself into it so completely.

Hemingway estimated that he was about two-thirds of the way through the first draft on 10 July, when he wrote Perkins that he had completed fourteen chapters, totaling 342 manuscript pages. In reality, Hemingway still had quite a way to go; he had actually completed only about one-third of the eventual book. He worked steadily on the novel until late August, when he took off on a trip west, dropping Martha in St. Louis to visit her mother. Hemingway drove on to Cody, Wyoming, where he was joined by his sons. In September, he and Martha moved in as guests of the lodge at Sun Valley, Idaho.

On 27 October, Hemingway finally gave his editor something concrete to go on. Having written more than ninety thousand words, he told Perkins, "This is a novel and it is also from the inside. How it really was. All the things that people with party obligations could never write and what most of them could never know or, if they knew, allow themselves to think. Have two wonderful women (Spanish) in it so far. Maybe more later. It will either be about fifteen or twenty thousand words longer or else fifty thousand words longer. There is a part about Madrid I don't know whether to write or not. I think I will."[13] Keeping up the momentum, he had written 474 typewritten pages by mid-November. He had a moment's doubt at this point about whether it would take him too long to complete the novel and whether he should offer up a collection of stories as a substitute until the longer book was finished. Perkins, envisioning a publication date of late spring for the new novel, warned him off the story collection, and Hemingway took his advice. He told Perkins that he was "in the stretch of the book."[14]

At the end of the year, he had packed his belongings for the permanent move to Cuba. He did not think he could realistically work in Key West with his marriage to Pauline effectively over. Perkins may or may not have known of Hemingway's marital strife, but he reassured Hemingway that he could perform great "feats of concentration," as evidenced by all the work he had done so far. "I am sure it will be a great book," Perkins concluded.[15] In early 1940, Hemingway sent Perkins some sample pages but stipulated that he not show them to the "ideology boys"—that is, the leftist critics—and indicated that he had found a way to handle obscene language in the dialogue.[16]

The search for a title for the new book began in earnest in early February. "Want a big one," Hemingway told Perkins. "I don't have to worry about over-titling this one. She'll carry quite a lot." As for the sample pages, Perkins responded with more praise and patience, assuring him that he should not worry about how long it was taking him to complete the book, although he did suggest a little later that it would be good to have the title by 22 April, as he wanted it to put in a press release, to build interest for fall publication. By 20 April 1940, Hemingway had completed thirty-five chapters and had chosen an epigraph from John Donne's *Meditations*; he wired Perkins that the title of the book was to be *For Whom the Bell Tolls* and that he planned to dedicate it to Martha.

Work continued through the summer. By July, Hemingway had reached the point near the end of the narrative where the wounded Jordan feels his consciousness seeping out of him and sights the Nationalist soldier below him through his rifle's scope. Perkins encouraged Hemingway to add on to this by way of conclusion. When Perkins sold the novel to the Book of the Month Club (the first Hemingway work to appear therein), he said that the final chapters were "written, but not yet to the complete satisfaction of the author." Hemingway, however, had actually not even outlined such chapters. A typed noted that was pasted into the proof copy that went to the Book of the Month Club reads:

> Two short chapters, amounting to 1,500 words in all, will bring the book to a conclusion. In the first of these Karkov and Golz meet after the failure of the attack, and in driving back from the front they talk together about it, and about Robert's message and his success in blowing up the bridge. In the second, Andres and Gomez motorcycle back to the outpost and then Andres makes his way over the ground he covered before, and eventually reaches the abandoned camp, sees the ruined bridge, and knows all that has happened there.

These chapters are written, but not yet to the complete satisfaction of the author. He wished to wait until after reading the proof up to this point before perfecting the end. editor[17]

Hemingway soon decided, however, that the book was better off without this material, perhaps remembering his several failed endings to *A Farewell to Arms*—also discarded—in which he tried to tell readers what happened to the survivors after the war. He finished sometime in mid-July and went to New York to hand deliver the last part of the novel to Perkins, who read it with Hemingway peering over his shoulder.

Hemingway worked like the devil correcting proofs of the book. He later told an interviewer that when Scribner's sent him the first galleys in August, he "spent ninety hours on the proofs . . . without once leaving the . . . room."[18] In reading the proofs, Hemingway became worried that the typeface was too small and indistinct, and he hoped that this wouldn't harm sales. He shared this concern with Perkins, who assured him that if necessary he would have the whole book reprinted. But there was no need—the book was a best seller, and the movie rights, which his agent Donald Friede sold to Paramount, fetched $100,000. (After this novel, more income came from movies than from books.) Final corrections were made in early September. Hemingway finished on 16 September and sent Charles Scribner a wire concluding, "that's all may commence firing." The book was slated for publication on 21 October 1940.

——

The story of *For Whom the Bell Tolls* unfolds in the span of roughly sixty-eight hours in the hills outside Madrid, where guerrilla bands are plotting action against Franco's troops. The date is May 1937; the story begins at midday on a Saturday and ends sometime Tuesday morning. Its protagonist, Robert Jordan, is perhaps Hemingway's most complex creation. A university professor from Montana, he takes a leave of absence when war breaks out in Spain and joins the Loyalist cause. He is both similar to and different from Frederic Henry in *A Farewell to Arms*. Both Henry and Jordan are accidental (or at least nonprofessional) soldiers. Both fall in love with a woman caught up in the war, yet Jordan cares about things outside his immediate circle; Henry's only concerns are for himself and Catherine. Unlike Henry, Jordan takes up arms for ideological rather than personal reasons. Jordan seems to be idealistic about the Republican cause, yet he is also a rugged individualist who often professes no interest in politics—a follow-up to Harry Morgan's idea of "a man alone."

An academic protagonist was an unusual choice for Hemingway. Although Jordan's profession does not figure prominently in the book, it is odd that Hemingway would look positively on a professor, since in many respects he was anti-intellectual, or at least anti-academic. In the 1950s, when English professors began to write scholarly articles on his work and research his life, he professed disdain for what he saw as their narrow, pedantic view of literature. Perhaps, in

For Whom the Bell Tolls, he wanted to show how someone with no apparent connection to violence and war could become a man of action when circumstances required it.

The action of the novel follows Jordan from the beginning, when he is behind enemy lines plotting to blow up a bridge, through a series of meditations and flashbacks, to the closing scene in which the bridge explodes. The narrative pacing is superb; the story has a strong sense of urgency because Hemingway chose to compress events into a short time span. Readers know from General Golz's deadline, delivered to Jordan at the outset, that Tuesday morning will bring a close to the action. *For Whom the Bell Tolls* is the tightest of Hemingway's novels in a structural sense, even though it is much longer than his previous novels.

The book is organized into forty-three chapters of varying length. Short and long chapters are staggered throughout the book, creating an effect of mounting tension that will culminate in the explosion of the bridge. The events of Saturday occupy seven chapters and a total of seventy pages. Sunday unfolds over the course of twelve chapters and 190 pages; Monday occupies more chapters (sixteen) but fewer pages (120), the faster pace building tension and suspense as we approach the climactic event. Tuesday morning is presented in five long chapters totaling ninety pages. The final, crucial three to four hours of the action are drawn out, duplicating the prolonged intensification of Jordan's anxiety as he approaches the end of his mission. The effect is a sense of life slipping away and of the need to pack in as much as possible in the precious time remaining.

Like *A Farewell to Arms, For Whom the Bell Tolls* is both cyclical in structure and based on a series of dichotomies. It opens and closes with the same scene in the forest: Jordan lying on his stomach on a carpet of pine needles, sighting his target and waiting for the bridge to blow. Hemingway thus brings events full circle (an effect that would have been lost had he taken Perkins's advice and added two final chapters). Throughout the novel, Hemingway alternates and juxtaposes scenes and concepts. At the end of the story, for example, the rush of Andrés trying to get through to Golz is set against the countdown to the blowing of the bridge. The action behind the lines is set against the scene at the front. Similarly, scenes of intense violence and destruction alternate with scenes of love, often presented as memories. Pilar is the historian of the novel; it is she who tells the most memorable tales from times past, as when the town was taken by the Fascists, or of when she lived with the bullfighter "in the old days." In much the same fashion, Anselmo narrates the scenes of peasant life. Maria has the most distinctive, because most horrifying, memory to relate—how the Fascists killed her parents and then raped her.

An unusual feature of the novel is how the writing calls attention to itself. This style shows Hemingway continuing to experiment with narrative form; it is nothing like his early prose, in which he sought to make the language transparent and let the ideas present themselves. By contrast, in *For Whom the Bell Tolls,* he tried to create a formal style of speaking and narrating, which sounds odd to the modern ear. Rhetorical flourishes abound—almost biblical in their style and cadence—and the Spanish characters speak a vernacular Spanish that Hemingway must have thought sounded more authentic than Castilian Spanish. The style was both admired and criticized. Native Spanish speakers who reviewed the book took Hemingway to task for his rhetorical experiments, saying that he did not understand the language or had falsified it for dramatic effect. To be sure, the *thee*s and *thou*s seem stilted at first, and some readers may continue to be put off as they move through the book. But, to Hemingway's credit, the manner in which the Spanish characters speak seems to lend them not just a formality but also a dignity and solemnity, thus dignifying and elevating his subject.

Hemingway was not as successful in his decision to replace coarse or lewd language with words like "obscenity," "unprintable," and "unnamable." This was obviously his jab at the censors and his statement of independence from the still-puritanical restrictions of American publishing. But a sentence like "I obscenity in the milk of thy unprintable" calls attention to the language and gets in the way of the idea being evoked. It comes perilously close to being silly self-parody. Why wouldn't Hemingway simply use the profanity?

As his career advanced, Hemingway was generally allowed greater latitude in the matter of using profanity or obscenity in his work. In *A Farewell to Arms*, he had been forced to accept dashes in place of expletives. In *Death in the Afternoon*, Scribner's had allowed him a bit more freedom, printing "F—k" in "A Natural History of the Dead" (143–44) (although when that story appeared in *Winner Take Nothing* the following year, it appeared as "F—" [151–53]). In Harry Morgan's death speech in *To Have and Have Not*, Hemingway was allowed to spell out the word for the first time: "No matter how a man alone ain't got no bloody fucking chance" (225). The novel was the first Scribner's title in which this expletive was printed; no doubt, the importance of the speech convinced Perkins that the word should be rendered intact. But Hemingway and Perkins did not discuss vulgar language in *For Whom the Bell Tolls*, because there were no strong expletives in English in any version of the novel.

The manuscript of *For Whom the Bell Tolls* reveals that Hemingway used no profane words during its composition. The first draft indicates that he was still unsure about how to present the offensive language in his story. Often, in the manuscript, when one of his characters utters a profane word or phrase, he uses the vague term "obscenity." Later, in the revision stage, he substituted a more specific word. For example, in chapter 9 he changed "obscenity" to words such as "besmirch" and "vileness." Also, in chapter 25, "obscenity thyself" was changed to "defile thyself."[19] Hemingway seems to have gone to great lengths to get around the obscenity issue: using the Spanish translation for the English profanity, for example, or even a phonetic alteration of a profane word—for example, replacing "fuck" with "frig" or "muck."[20] He might have made these changes in order to avoid a confrontation with his publisher; after the serialized version of *A Farewell to Arms* was banned in Boston, Scribner's was wary of controversy. Of course, the publisher had allowed Hemingway to say what he meant in Morgan's speech at the close of *To Have and Have Not*.

A better explanation emerges when Hemingway's marriage, finances, and publishing plans for the novel are considered.[21] The composition of *For Whom the Bell Tolls* coincided with the end of his marriage to Pauline and his developing relationship with Martha, whom he would marry on 21 November 1940. In order to gain freedom from Pauline, Hemingway had to produce a best seller, a work that would generate enough income to replace the subsidies he had been receiving from her wealthy family, which he would lose after a divorce. He may simply have decided that a book without profanity would stand a better chance of climbing onto the best-seller list.

Money was an important consideration. Although the 1930s were Hemingway's most prolific decade as a writer, his books had not earned him much income. Between 1930 and 1938, Scribner's published or reissued six of his books: *In Our Time, Death in the Afternoon, Winner Take Nothing, Green Hills of Africa, To Have and Have Not,* and *The Fifth Column and the First Forty-Nine Stories*. In addition, he was writing articles for the magazines *Fortune, Esquire,* and *Ken,* as well as for the North American Newspaper Alliance, and publishing short stories in *Esquire, Scribner's Magazine,* and *Cosmopolitan*. But, as Robert W. Trogdon has shown, this prolific output did not translate into much money. Compared to *A Farewell to Arms,* none of the books of the 1930s sold well. From 1930 to 1938, Scribner's printed only 4,275 copies of *In Our Time*; 22,780 copies of *Death in the Afternoon*; 20,300 copies of *Winner Take Nothing*; 12,532 copies of *Green Hills of Africa*; 41,085 copies of *To Have and Have Not*; and 15,100 copies of *The Fifth Column and the First Forty-Nine Stories*. The combined total was 116,072 copies—a mere 14,397 more than all the printings of *A Farewell to Arms*. Moreover, many of these copies were unsold, and an author is paid a reduced royalty on remaindered copies. Sales of his work to magazines brought in additional income, of course, but except for the *Esquire* "Letters," Hemingway's sales to periodicals were sporadic at best.

The type of story also merits consideration. In *For Whom the Bell Tolls,* Hemingway created a narrative that has all the hallmarks of an adventure yarn—a type of story that he knew would please his readers and attract a wide audience. He begins with a scene that could be a credible opening for a James Bond thriller: the lone operative on a top-secret mission, behind enemy lines, with only meager supplies, a flask of what may be the last drop of absinthe in Spain, and a determination to get the job done. He must use his guile and his wits to carry out a dangerous, perhaps even impossible, mission. Robert Jordan is a romanticized figure; he is not meant to be realistic but rather a kind of fantasy of the devoted warrior. Hemingway understood that readers would gravitate to such a fast-paced and compelling tale.[22]

The book was also popular because it confirmed what nearly everyone believed would be the shape of conflicts to come. *For Whom the Bells Tolls* depicts the conflict in Spain as an event of global significance. Hemingway presents the fate of the peasants as tied to the fate not just of Spain but of Europe and democracy. If the Fascists won in Spain, Hemingway believed, then Hitler and Mussolini would have free rein to set about conquering other territories and vanquishing their enemies in a quest for domination. And that, of course, is precisely what happened. People reading the book in 1940, then, were likely to give an extra measure of gravity to Jordan's idealistic quest to stop fascism before it could take root. There is no reading experience quite so pleasurable as one in which one's predictions about the course of world events are confirmed by a famous person.

Robert Jordan is less well informed than his creator: he is still learning about politics, his political thinking is rather naïve, and his polemical statements are a bit windy. He likes to go to Russian headquarters at the Gaylord Hotel to listen to Karkov and the other leaders because he feels that he can learn from them. He says that he has placed himself "under the Communist discipline for the duration of the war" because the Communists have the "soundest and the sanest" program for prosecuting the war. Later, however, Hemingway shows the reader how the Communists treat André Marty, a Frenchman who became a powerful figure in the Communist sector. Marty indiscriminately had people executed but was protected by Communist leaders.

Hemingway knew of the Russian crimes committed during the Spanish conflict. Of all the novels, stories, plays, and other fictional treatments of the Spanish Civil War, *For Whom the Bell Tolls* comes closest to presenting a balanced view of the complicated pressures and tensions that informed both sides in the conflict. The more he wrote about the war, the more mature his view of it became. *The Spanish Earth,* his journalism, and *The Fifth Column* support the Republican defenders, but late short stories such as "Under the Ridge" express his disillusionment with both sides in the battle.

In the novel, there is as much violence on the Republican as on the Fascist side. The Loyalists are not all noble, merciful, and altruistic. In one memorable passage, Pablo, the leader of a band of guerrillas who are Republican sympathizers, tells all the townsmen to form a line leading to the edge of a cliff, arms them with clubs, rakes, and other makeshift weapons, and makes the Fascists run down the line. The men beat them as they fall off the cliff. Hemingway is also careful to avoid stereotyping the Fascists as evil monsters. Lieutenant Berrendo, for example, the Fascist whom Jordan is preparing to shoot at the end of the novel, is a decent human being who abhors the atrocities he must commit as part of the Fascist cause.

Hemingway's view of humanity here is closely aligned with the sentiments expressed by Harry Morgan in *To Have and Have Not.* Jordan's view of man, like Morgan's, is that man's loyalties are to himself. In *For Whom the Bell Tolls*, the Spanish are not only capable of great betrayal but also demonstrate a selfish, even slavish, attachment to their own towns, their own families, their own people, their own small bands of fighters. Jordan knows that he will have to work with unpredictable, unreliable people who cannot necessarily be trusted, but he has to do his best with what is available. Jordan, like Hemingway, is honest about the war. Hemingway did not sugarcoat human nature; he created flawed human characters.

Scribner's published *For Whom the Bell Tolls* on 21 October 1940. Among mainstream reviewers, the novel fared well. Edmund Wilson hailed it as a sign of the return of Ernest Hemingway the serious artist. Although Wilson's *New Republic* review noted some weaknesses, chiefly in the novel's structure, on the whole Wilson saw the book as an artistic advance on Hemingway's part. Henry Seidel Canby, Clifton Fadiman, Howard Mumford Jones, Malcom Cowley, and other major critical voices joined Wilson in praising the book.[23]

Leftist critics, for the most part, thought that Hemingway had redeemed himself politically and that the work restored him to the highest level of American writers. Some writers on the left, however, thought he had betrayed the Loyalist cause by showing the Russian leaders committing atrocities just as terrible as those committed by the Nationalists. Reviewing *For Whom the Bell Tolls* for the *New Masses,* Alvah Bessie accused Hemingway of having no "depth of understanding" in treating the political complexities of the Spanish Civil War, and of lacking appreciation of the inherent goodness of the Spanish people and the dedication of their Communist allies. Further, Bessie saw the love story as cheapening a book that could have been profound, aiming instead to appeal to readers of a popular women's magazine.[24] Similarly, writing in *Partisan Review,* Dwight Macdonald called Robert Jordan a "monster" whose political naïveté mirrored that of his creator.[25]

———

Like *A Farewell to Arms, For Whom the Bell Tolls* had been written during a period of intense stress and inner turmoil. Hemingway realized that he needed to make a clean break with Pauline. They had kept up the pretense of a stable marriage for a long time, and both seemed to be in denial: the letters they exchanged when Pauline left for an extended tour of Europe in the summer of 1939, just before the separation, are emotionally flat, preserving a false veneer of normalcy. To Hemingway, everything was "fine"; he hoped that Pauline would have a "swell time." She told him not to worry, to "be well." Hemingway had fallen for Martha, but it was not necessarily true that he no longer loved Pauline—we see him replaying, essentially, the emotional dynamic of his falling for Pauline and leaving Hadley. And, as in the earlier betrayal of Hadley, he felt intense guilt in leaving Pauline for Martha. In the immediate aftermath of the separation, although he characteristically tried to blame Pauline for the failure of the marriage, he soon lost heart and dropped that shameful lie, owning up to the ugly truth: that he was to blame, that he was a fool.

When he moved from Key West to San Francisco de Paula, he had his assistant, Toby Bruce, pack up most of his personal belongings (including some manuscripts and correspondence) and store them in the back room of Sloppy Joe's bar. (There they remained until August 1961, when his fourth wife, Mary, whom he was to wed in 1946, went back to Florida and Cuba to retrieve their belongings after Hemingway's death.)[26] Pauline and Hemingway tried to hide their marital troubles from Patrick and Gregory, but as the latter wrote in his memoir, things eventually devolved into the usual shouting and door slamming—the typical "'amicable divorce,'" as he noted wryly.[27] Hemingway did not contest Pauline's taking custody of the boys, feeling that they needed their mother's presence more than his, and that he, anyway, was often away for long periods of time—a fact that had contributed to the estrangement in the first place.

After her divorce from Hemingway, Pauline, at age forty-four, tried to make a life for herself in a variety of ways. For a short time, she opened a knitting shop in Key West with Lorine Thompson, but that venture collapsed quickly. She reportedly had several dalliances with naval officers in the area. But she eventually found companionship—and romantic love—with another woman, the poet Elizabeth Bishop, who bought a house on Whitehead Street in 1938 and became a part-time resident there the following year. Pauline would have several other lesbian relationships in the years to come.[28] She was gracious to Hemingway and his family after the split, even writing to Grace Hemingway that no single party was to blame, and that she would always think of Grace as her mother and the rest of the Hemingway clan as her family. The heart of another was a dark forest, Pauline believed. She observed to Grace that people could only do what they could and that, "really considering what they have to contend with in this world, it is amazing that they do as well as they do."[29]

Hemingway was contrite after leaving Pauline for Martha. In an unpublished fragment titled "The Monument," he agreed with Pauline that he had been foolish for taking up with Martha.[30] Just as he had promised Hadley whatever she wanted when he asked for a divorce, so too, when Pauline threatened that if he divorced her she would take "everything he had," he reportedly replied, "If you let me divorce you, you can have everything I've got."[31] In a letter to Maxwell Perkins three years later, Hemingway also made this insightful comment: "The first great gift for a man is to be healthy and the second, maybe greater, is to fall [in] with healthy women. . . . But start with a sick woman and see where you get. . . . Take as good a woman as Pauline—a hell of a wonderful woman—and once she turns mean. Although, of course, it is your own actions that turn her mean. Mine I mean."[32] Hemingway had a strong sense of honor, which—ironically and unfortunately—he often violated.

Eventually, Hemingway settled into life at Finca Vigía with Marty. Changing wives, he had to change habitats, just as he had done when fleeing Paris with Pauline. (Even when Hemingway returned to Paris from his various expeditions to Spain in the late 1930s, he stayed on the "other" side of the Seine: the Left Bank dredged up too many memories, too many ghosts from the past.) Exhausted after writing *For Whom the Bell Tolls* and depleted after the tumult of packing up his things in the Key West house, putting them in storage, and taking up a new life in Cuba with Marty, Hemingway had little desire to write. To assuage his oppressive feelings of guilt, Hemingway diverted himself not by writing but by sportfishing, which became more important to him than ever, and he spent more and more time on the water. When he returned to writing fiction in the second half of the 1940s, these adventures became an integral part of his work.

Hemingway's interest in sportfishing began when he met Carlos Gutierrez in the Dry Tortugas off Key West. Gutierrez, a Cuban, told Hemingway about the great marlin that could be caught in the Gulf Stream. As Hemingway grew older, his appetites grew larger. Fishing for trout in cold mountain streams was no longer sporting enough; bigger game awaited. To pursue marlin, however, Hemingway needed a craft with a long cruising range and sleeping accommodations for himself and a crew for overnight expeditions. He found such a boat in the *Pilar,* which he purchased for $7,500 in May 1934, mostly with the income from his *Esquire* pieces. Gutierrez was hired as first mate, but he was later lured away by someone else while Hemingway was in Spain reporting on the civil war. Hemingway replaced Gutierrez with Gregorio Fuentes, who would later be one of the models for the character Santiago in *The Old Man and the Sea.*

The *Pilar* was a beautiful boat.[33] Commissioned from the Wheeler Shipyards in New York, she sported a varnished mahogany cockpit, a black hull, and a green roof. The boat was thirty-eight feet long and could do sixteen knots with its two engines, of seventy-five and forty horsepower, respectively. Later, Hemingway added a flying bridge with controls, making the craft a complete sportfishing machine. The *Pilar* served Hemingway well, as he plied the waters for sport and, later, conducted reconnaissance missions for the U.S. government during World War II, trying to lure German subs to the surface. He and Fuentes made a pact that the boat was never to sail again once either man died. Fuentes kept his promise and donated the boat to the Finca Vigía museum, where it sat untouched for many years. Recently, the Cuban government granted the museum funds to start its restoration.

Hemingway took deep-sea fishing—as he took everything else—very seriously. He was careful to learn the proper techniques, to seek the advice of experts skilled in the sport, and to discover the best spots for the biggest catch. The long, dark silver body of the marlin enticed him the most, with its wide pectoral fins spread out like a bird's wings. Four fishing lines, like long whips, trailed the *Pilar* when Hemingway went cruising. Teasers zigzagged off the bow, churning the water into a white foam. Seated in the fighting chair, Hemingway would wait patiently until he felt a strike. Then he would lock the gear and jerk the heavy rod back, hard and fast. He savored the feeling of the powerful fish pulling on the line.

When Hemingway bought the *Pilar,* the fishing and boating industries were in a time of transition in the United States, and Hemingway can be at least partly credited with changing the public face of both activities. Before Hemingway popularized sportfishing, the idea of recreational activity on the water was largely associated with playboys and other wealthy layabouts with money to burn.

Hemingway changed that, beginning with such works as *To Have and Have Not,* in which sportfishing began to be portrayed as a physical and spiritual challenge, like earlier Hemingway interests—bullfighting, fly-fishing, and big-game shooting. Hemingway became as closely associated with boating and fishing as he did with these other activities. His picture appeared frequently in such magazines as *Life* and *Look* in the context of fishing. When he made the cover of *Time* magazine in 1937, his face was encircled by a black marlin, and when Cuba issued postage stamps in 1999 commemorating the centennial of his birth, in the background was a leaping sailfish. After World War II, when fiberglass boats became affordable, deep-sea fishing came within reach of ordinary people, not just the yachting crowd, many of whom wanted to be like Hemingway.

Hemingway was also an innovator who took a holistic approach to the sport. He early on adopted tackle outrigger lines, which could handle baitfish up to ten pounds in weight. He perfected his craft by listening to both native fishermen and top ichthyologists, with whom he shared observations. He was the first person ever to bring a giant tuna onto Bimini's docks undamaged by sharks, a feat he accomplished by boating the fish before it tired and could be ripped into by predators. This took skill, a sense of timing, and sheer strength, and thereafter the technique was called "Hemingwaying" a fish. Thus Hemingway helped to lead Americans onto the waters, just as he had led them into the wild.

He taught his two younger sons to fish as well, and after the breakup with Pauline, when the boys had to be ferried back and forth to visit their father in Cuba, he tried very hard to exert a good influence on them, to play a meaningful role in their lives, and to make strong and lasting connections with them. Jack would join them when he could, creating at least a temporary picture of a united family. Life with the boys at Finca Vigía was usually without conflict. Hemingway talked to his sons, played with them, listened to their adolescent problems. Marty was also a good listener. She had the advantage of not being their mother, so she was all fun and games, without the worry and discipline that Pauline would convey. Jack, now just entering his twenties, had something of a crush on Martha, who was, after all, youthful, glamorous, and full of energy—as well as a great raconteur, with terrific stories about what she'd seen on the battlefield.

When Martha was traveling abroad on assignment, Hemingway was able to devote almost his entire day—minus the hours spent writing—to sole charge of the boys, whom he playfully called the childies. Characteristically, he had to find something to blame on Martha, but his assessment of his fathering skills is interesting. "I think what I am probably learning about now is Childies. You always write about them so well and so poignantly and don't give a goddamn about them. Maybe you get it all in the writing. I can't write about them or anyway never have much and love them like hell and [am] beginning to understand them a little. Anyway, I have answered every question they could think up all summer."[34] He wrote Patrick and Greg in Key West often, asking them about their schoolwork and their friends and, as divorced fathers do, weaving into the letter encouragement to buck up until he could see them again, and holding out enticements of what they would do on the next visit or vacation. In one letter, Hemingway sounds about as genial and fatherly as one can get, when he dangles an adventure to Wyoming in front of them. He writes, "Now here comes the good news. Here is the surprise. O.K. Guess. We are all going to the ranch. Yes sir. To the ranch."[35]

In these years, Hemingway often connected with his children through sports—namely, fishing, shooting, and baseball. Greg was good at both shooting and baseball, and Hemingway was proud of his son's skills. In a letter to Martha, he described a tournament in which Greg took all the prizes: "You would have been proud of our Giggy. . . . Giggy killed every sort of correo that could come out; low ones; drivers to the right, to the left, high screamers and two slanting incomers. He killed twelve straight and was one of only four straights. He hit his thirteenth, which was an absolutely impossible bird (but he had killed eight impossibles) with both barrels and it died outside."[36] Hemingway encouraged the boys to play with the village children by setting up a baseball team ("The Gigi All-Stars"). They held regular games and practices during visits. "All your pals ask after you nearly every day and they are getting to play ball quite well," he wrote Gregory. "The honroners and Ernesto are really fielding very well. I bought them a bat for $2 and they have fielding practice every afternoon. We will have some swell ball games when you come over for Christmas."[37]

The boys grew to love the cats that inhabited the property, too. Hemingway was apparently amused when young Patrick wanted to "educate" the cats on the ways of fishing and the sea. Patrick drew up a mock certificate titled "Boat Cat Licence [sic]," with a photograph of one of the cats pasted in the lower left-hand corner. Opposite that, Hemingway wrote a declaration that read: "Having passed the standerd [sic] tests _____ is fit to practice Boat Catery in Caribbean Waters / (signed) Jose Gato / Inspector."[38]

So many accounts of Hemingway emphasize his self-absorption and his cruel treatment of his wives, lovers, and peers. Although he would have some difficulties with his sons as he grew older and mentally unwell, he was a tender and solicitous parent during their adolescence, and, as with most things, he worked hard at trying to perfect his skills as a father.

China and World War II

Hemingway and Martha were married in Cheyenne, Wyoming, on 21 November 1940, and Hemingway entered a fallow period in his writing career. Between 1940 and 1945, Hemingway wrote no fiction at all. The only literary project he undertook was an introduction to *Men at War,* an anthology brought out by Crown Publishers in October 1942. He was exhausted by the work that had gone into *For Whom the Bell Tolls,* and he feared, irrationally, that he would never be able to do so well again. As late as August 1942 he was telling Martha, "I suppose if you are a writer you're a writer till you die or it dies. But sometimes I think I've been writing a long time and do you know it honestly I am still tired from Bell Tolls book. It seems ridiculous but it is so."[1]

Hemingway did, however, keep up the journalistic work. In early 1941 Martha got a contract from *Collier's* to cover the Second Sino-Japanese War, which had been going on since 1937 and was now seen as a harbinger of events that might lead the United States into war with Japan. Hemingway had been following developments there with some interest. His uncle Willoughby had been a medical missionary in the northern province of Shanxi, and Hemingway remembered the fantastic stories with which Willoughby had regaled him and his siblings on visits to their summer cottage on Walloon Lake: Willoughby had once removed his own appendix on horseback; he had met the Dalai Lama; he even made up the tall tale that the word "Hemingway" meant "Hunter of Wolves" in Chinese. Thus Hemingway had something of a romantic attachment to China. But he also did not want to be upstaged by Martha, so he negotiated a similar deal for himself with the liberal New York newspaper *PM.*

Hemingway also did intelligence-gathering work during this trip. In late January at the Lombardy Hotel in New York, just before sailing, Hemingway

178

‾‾‾‾

Ernest

Hemingway

A NEW

LIFE

received a telephone call from Harry Dexter White, the director of monetary research for the Treasury Department, who had learned of his upcoming trip and wanted to get his view of the Sino-Japanese conflict. The Departments of State and Defense were closely monitoring the situation in Asia, but Treasury was also involved because the U.S. government was financing the global resistance to the Axis powers, and the Japanese had recently formed an alliance with Nazi Germany and Fascist Italy. White was more than just the director of monetary research; he was, in truth, as Peter Moreira puts it, Treasury Secretary Henry Morgenthau's "assistant secretary in everything except title."[2] He asked Hemingway to gather information on the relationship between the Communists and Kuomintang, and on the transportation situation on the Irrawaddy River in China and along the Burma Road—in effect, to spy on the Chinese for the federal government. Hemingway's newspaper assignment would be a perfect cover, and he agreed. He would end up loving counterespionage work, and this assignment would give him the credentials to approach the government again in 1942 to do counterespionage work in the Caribbean.[3]

The war had begun in July 1937 when the Japanese claimed that they were fired on by Chinese troops at the Marco Polo Bridge near Beijing. Using this as an excuse, the Japanese launched a full-scale invasion of China using recently conquered Manchuria as a launching base for their army. The Japanese came up against little organized resistance and, in November, China's most important port—Shanghai—fell, followed shortly thereafter by Nanjing (Nanking) in December. The Japanese army ransacked Nanjing, murdering as many as a quarter-million people as they went.[4] Chiang Kai-shek, the Kuomintang leader, had to establish a new capital in Chongqing (known to Westerners at the time as Chungking). Still the Japanese pressed on, and within five months one million Chinese were under Japanese control. The Japanese had captured all of the major cities in China by the end of 1937, along with all of China's major communication systems. After this initial success, the Japanese did not advance much farther into China—the interior of the country contained little of strategic importance, and the relatively small Japanese army worried that it would not have the resources to stretch itself out over so vast a country. But by 1941, when Hemingway and Gellhorn arrived in China, there were two million Japanese soldiers there.

After a stop in Los Angeles, where Hemingway consulted with the producing studio about the film version of *For Whom the Bell Tolls,* he and Martha set out for China on the *Matsonia.* The crossing was rough, and when they arrived for a layover in Honolulu, Hemingway grew truculent, spitting out rude responses to people who approached him at a reception given in his honor; he told Martha he was going to "cool" the next son of a bitch who touched him. Fortunately, the stay was brief, and they flew from the island via Guam to Hong Kong, arriving in late February. They spent a month in the Peninsula Hotel in Kowloon and in a country hotel on the far side of the island at Repulse Bay. Hemingway liked Hong Kong much more than he had Honolulu; soon he was drinking, shooting, and going to the racetrack to lay bets. As always, he acquired a group of follow-ers who were content to sit and listen to him tell stories, which he gloried in. As Martha later wrote, Hemingway "was seen laughing with waiters and rickshaw coolies and street vendors, all parties evidently enjoying each other. He loved Chinese food and would return from feasts with his Chinese crook-type friends swearing they'd been served by geisha girls, and describe the menu until I begged him to stop, due to queasiness. . . . He felt that the Hongkong Chinese, given to gambling, rice wine, and firecrackers, had great savoir vivre."⁵ Martha herself quickly tired of Hemingway's self-indulgent performances and *pronunciamentos* about living well and would walk away brusquely when things got out of hand. Hemingway, seeing her disgust, would sarcastically inform his listeners after she had disappeared that she was going to take the pulse of the nation.

Soon, however, just as they had in Spain, he and Martha forgot their argu-ments and headed for the action. On 24 March they made for Naxiong, flying over Japanese lines in a freight plane with no cabin pressure, sloped floors, and canvas chairs—another rough crossing with an even more perilous landing: since the Japanese were continually bombing the airstrips, the runways had to be relo-cated frequently, and the pilots, who lacked the use of instrumentation, were never quite sure where they were going to touch down until they were almost at ground level. They landed safely, however, at Naxiong and drove all day on roads that were rivers of mud to the headquarters of the seventh of eight war zones. From there, Hemingway visited a Kuomintang unit in the Guangdong Province (formerly Can-ton) while Martha stayed behind, ill from the food, the water, or both. He ate, slept, and went on patrols with the soldiers in order to get an idea of their lives during wartime. He spent a month at the front, going everywhere with the troops. He traveled down the river by sampan, on horseback, and on foot. There was one twelve-day stretch when it rained so frequently that he never had dry clothes.

Whereas Hemingway enjoyed the adventure and felt like he was back in Spain during the war, the usually self-possessed Martha was distinctly irritated and uncomfortable. Martha was very fastidious—she liked everything kept clean and orderly and may even have been something of a germophobe (an unusual trait in a reporter sent to cover war-torn nations). Hemingway complained that she kept the Finca looking like a hospital, while he, as we have seen, often wore the same clothes two days in a row, his bedroom always spilling over with books, magazines, pencils, and sheaves of manuscript. (He did much of his reading and writing in bed.) Thus China's environment did not bother Hemingway, but it was torture for Martha. Opium dens and brothels dominated the city streets. Peo-ple treated the roads and sidewalks like rubbish piles. Almost everyone Martha passed by seemed to have malaria or tuberculosis or leprosy, the whole country a veritable pit of sepsis. She felt claustrophobic and manic and later referred to the squalor she saw on the trip as appalling.⁶

The couple spent forty-three hours on a boat back to Shaoguan and twenty-five hours on a four-hundred-mile trip to Kweilin; they then traveled to remote

Chongqing, almost eight hundred miles from Hong Kong, on a Douglas DC-3, the only passengers in a cabin full of banknotes being shipped across the country. In Chongqing—a dirty, shapeless city of cement buildings and poor shacks that served as the country's wartime capital—they met with Kuomintang leader Chiang Kai-shek, who told Hemingway that he feared the Communists more than he feared the Japanese. They then had a secret meeting with the Communist leader Chou En-lai (Zhou Enlai), who was a friend of Joris Ivens. Hemingway described Chou En-lai as "a man of enormous charm and great intelligence who keeps in close touch with all the Embassies and does a fine job of selling the Communist standpoint on anything that comes up to almost everyone in Chungking who comes into contact with him."[7]

While Martha remained in Chongqing, sick in bed with another stomach virus, Hemingway set out alone, flying north to Chengdu to visit the Chinese military academy, where he met with officers and cadets. The inquisitive writer peppered his hosts with questions about armaments, maneuvers, and strategies. Hemingway then returned to Chongqing, and together he and Martha journeyed by car and train to Yangon (then known as Rangoon), where they spent a sweltering week in late April, just before the monsoons. Perhaps from the strains of so full a schedule, Hemingway collapsed and was overcome with depression, forcing a rest of several days at the hotel. Martha then went on to Singapore and Jakarta; Hemingway flew back to Hong Kong on what turned out to be another unsettling journey on a plane full of "chinescoes and a crippled missionary with a busted back."[8] After a week in Hong Kong, he took off for Manila for nine days, his last stop before flying to New York, and thence home to Finca Vigía.

Upon returning, Hemingway wrote Henry Morgenthau a six-page single-spaced letter presenting his views on China and the relationship between the Kuomintang and the Soviet Union. Hemingway was thorough and precise; one and a half pages contained a transcript of statements that Chou En-lai had made to him over dinner that seemed to contain useful information. In the end, Hemingway predicted correctly that after the war, China would fall to the Communists.[9]

———

Japan attacked Pearl Harbor on 7 December 1941, and the United States joined World War II. In June, Hemingway had published seven news stories in *PM* on conditions in China, but beyond that he seems not to have been writing much. His experience in China, however, had whetted his appetite for more espionage work, and he saw an opening in the ongoing conflict to offer his services to the war effort. On various fishing expeditions, Hemingway thought he had found evidence of submarine refueling stations in the Caribbean, and in the summer of 1942, he approached the American government and volunteered as a lookout for the German U-boats that were known to be trolling the waters off Havana. He recruited some other friends to help him and formed, in essence, an amateur spy network.

Hemingway's project, which Martha gave the derisive nickname "The Crook Factory," has come to be seen as frivolous and unimportant. (Martha thought that Hemingway had only volunteered so that he could get fuel vouchers for the *Pilar* and go fishing on the pretext of patrolling the sea.) But this view of Hemingway's activities does not acknowledge the full range of his involvement. It also ignores what he and his colleagues actually accomplished and, perhaps most important, ironically, how the episode began a disenchantment between Hemingway and the federal government that resulted in his later being targeted by the FBI and other agencies as a possible subversive.

Hemingway contacted the U.S. ambassador to Cuba, Spruille Braden, in April 1942 and proposed using the *Pilar* as a decoy to draw U-boats to the surface. The threats posed by German U-boats were considerable. Two months earlier, in a coordinated attack, U-boats had destroyed seven oil tankers at the entrance to Lake Maracaibo, a passage for Venezuelan crude oil on its way to the refinery at Aruba, which produced roughly seven million barrels of gasoline, aviation fuel, and lubricants a month to support the British war effort.[10] Also in February, nineteen ships had been sunk by U-boats in the Caribbean, nineteen more in March, eleven in April, and thirty-eight in May. By the end of November 1942, 263 ships lay at the bottom of the sea. Hemingway was right to see the possible dangers.

Hemingway found a sympathetic contact in Braden, a career diplomat who had served as the U.S. ambassador to Colombia before taking up the sensitive post in Cuba in the spring of 1942, soon after America entered the war. He was a fierce anticommunist who considered Hemingway a patriot and thought him more than capable of doing a good job with the mission. In his memoir, Braden also noted the large Spanish contingent in Cuba—more than three hundred thousand people, of whom at least fifteen to thirty thousand were "violent Falangists" (i.e., Francoists). "These Spaniards," he said at the time, "have got to be watched."[11] Braden gave the go-ahead for Hemingway's secret mission.

Hemingway began in June with a crew of six. The plan was that the *Pilar*, outfitted as a fishing vessel, would be spotted by the submarines, who would order her to pull alongside and be boarded. Two men were stationed in the *Pilar*'s bow with submachine guns and two in the stern with hand grenades. Also on board was "The Bomb," a huge improvised explosive device. Gregory, then twelve years old, remembered it as "shaped like a coffin, with handles on each end." Once parallel with the enemy, the crew of the *Pilar* was to cast off the tarps and fishing nets that were covering her considerable hidden armament and open fire on the sub. Two men would heave "The Bomb" into the open hatch of the conning tower, and the sub would be destroyed. ("What if The Bomb misses?" Marty asked. "Don't you think I know the realities of war?" Hemingway fired back.)[12] The American embassy in Havana took Hemingway's efforts seriously and followed up on all the reports he sent in.

Ironically, the seriousness with which the FBI took Hemingway's activities was the beginning of the trouble with that agency that would plague Hemingway

for the rest of his life. Most of Hemingway's crew were Spanish refugees from
Franco's revolution, Loyalists who had sought safety in Cuba; Hemingway knew
some of them from his pro-Republican activities in Spain during the civil war.
That these friends were regarded as pro-communist alerted the FBI to Hemingway's activity, and in October 1942 J. Edgar Hoover ordered that a file be opened
on the author and that he be surveilled in Cuba. Braden and the other diplomats
to whom Hemingway reported knew none of this; Hoover installed his own agent
in Havana, Raymond Leddy, to keep tabs on Hemingway. Leddy reported to
Hoover via memoranda that confirmed Hoover's suspicions about Hemingway.

In Washington, Hoover's surveillance of Hemingway was coordinated
through one D. M. Ladd. An internal memorandum from Ladd to Hoover is
one of the initial documents in a 122-page file on Hemingway that is now in the
National Archives. Hemingway, Ladd wrote, "joined in attacking the bureau
early in 1940," apparently comparing the FBI to the Gestapo. Ladd also noted
that Hemingway was connected with "certain individuals . . . charged with vio-
lation of federal statutes in connection with their participation in Spanish Civil
War activities." Hemingway had signed a declaration, along with many others,
criticizing the FBI's arrest of these people in Detroit. Hoover responded that
Hemingway was the "last man," in his view, to be used in an operation like the
one being proposed: "His judgment is not of the best, and if his sobriety is the
same that it was some years ago, that is certainly questionable." He concluded
that Hemingway "has no particular love for the FBI and would no doubt embark
on a campaign of vilification" if he knew he was being watched.[13]

Of even greater concern to the FBI was the fact that Gustavo Durán, the
skilled commander of Loyalist forces during the Spanish Civil War, was part of
Hemingway's U-boat operation. Hemingway had met Durán in Paris in 1929 and
was drawn to him instantly. He fit the profile of the type of male acquaintance
that attracted Hemingway: he was skilled, courageous, worldly, and successful
in battle. Hemingway used Durán's participation in the attack on Segovia during the Spanish Civil War as inspiration in *For Whom the Bell Tolls*. In the novel,
Robert Jordan thinks of Durán's achievements on the night before battle—the
greatest tribute that Hemingway could pay to a friend.

Durán was something of a prodigy. After graduating from a Jesuit school,
he trained at a business college in Madrid and then at a music conservatory. He
did compulsory military service and then lived in Paris from 1928 to 1934, where
he studied music, worked as a pianist, composed ballet scores, and tutored the
children of the violinist Yehudi Menuhin. He was both soldier and scholar and
counted other artists among his friends, notably André Malraux, who used Durán
as the model for the character Manuel in his novel *Man's Hope*. When the civil war
began, Durán was called up as a reservist. He quickly ascended through the ranks,
demonstrating his abilities as a confident and inspiring leader. He commanded
a battalion in August 1936, a brigade in January 1937, and a division in July 1937,
and was promoted to the rank of colonel, in command of the Twentieth Army

Corps, in November. When the Loyalist cause collapsed, Durán barely made it out of the country alive, fleeing to Marseilles and then to London, where he met his future wife, married, and moved to the United States in May 1940.

The FBI regarded Durán as a threat to national security. In a memorandum from D. M. Ladd to Hoover, Ladd noted that Durán had been a member of the Youth Socialist League at the beginning of the Spanish Civil War and became a member of the Communist Party in December 1936. Ladd made two recommendations for dealing with Durán, in two long paragraphs, but they have been redacted. It is clear, nonetheless, that Hemingway's association with Durán cast suspicion on him as far as Hoover and the FBI were concerned.[14]

Out on the water, Hemingway and his crew were not exactly spotting targets right and left, but the threat was certainly real, and their presence as a lookout did aid the government. Moreover, before beginning the operation, Hemingway stipulated that should any crew members, excepting himself, be killed or captured by the Germans, they would be considered casualties of war and be indemnified so that the government would be responsible for compensating their families for service to their country.

There was some activity. Once, a lone U-boat was spotted, but it quickly turned north and sped away. Two days later the embassy called Hemingway to say that the sub had been spotted again by several tankers near the mouth of the Mississippi River in New Orleans. On 9 December 1942, Hemingway reported that he had seen a German submarine make contact with a Spanish steamer, the *Marques de Comillas*, off the Cuban coast. On another occasion, Hemingway learned that Germans had surfaced off Cayo Coco and had robbed some fishermen there. He sent Gregorio Fuentes out on a skiff, hoping to draw them again, but no Germans appeared.

Hemingway also became interested in rumors of a new type of technology that used oxygen rather than carbon-based fuel to power submarines. He felt that if the supply of this new type of fuel could be monitored, it might crack the German sub capability. He investigated the supply chain of oxygen and oxygen tanks in Cuba, but either the technology did not actually exist or the threat was deemed not to be critical. In any case, Hemingway made regular reports to the government about all that he learned.

In Braden's opinion, Hemingway "built up an excellent organization and did an A-One job." He thought Hemingway's contribution so worthwhile that he recommended that Hemingway be given a medal for his service, though the idea went nowhere.[15] Eventually, the network disbanded. In April 1943, FBI operatives took up permanent posts in Cuba and did the work that Hemingway had originally envisioned, expanding the U.S. base of intelligence in that country. Soon thereafter, the navy eliminated the U-boat threat altogether. It can be argued, however, Hemingway's contributions to the war effort were more dangerous, more complex, and more useful than is sometimes thought.

Just as Hemingway had problems maintaining his literary productivity after the success of *For Whom the Bell Tolls,* he began having marital problems with Martha almost immediately after they wed. His best times with Martha had been in Spain during the war. Hemingway had associated romantic liaisons with warfare ever since his adventurous days on the Italian front in World War I. But once he and Martha had settled into a domestic routine at the Finca, there was not much to attract him or keep him interested.

In Hemingway's mind, like the clichéd refrain of many an old song, women were often to blame for his troubles. His mother refused to pay for his college education and drove his father to suicide. Hadley lost his manuscripts. Pauline broke up his marriage to Hadley; then Jinny, Hemingway later came to believe, broke up his marriage to Pauline by telling her of his affair with Martha Gellhorn.[16] Marty posed an altogether different problem. She became too competitive for Hemingway, bruising his ego by often writing more and better than he and getting choice journalistic assignments. Hemingway, probably feeling more lonely than upstaged, would haul out the tired argument that a woman's place was at home with her husband. Thus when Martha went to Europe to cover World War II, Hemingway assailed her with telegrams accusing her of abandoning her domestic obligations: "are you a war correspondent or my wife in bed?"[17] Hemingway also wrote petulant letters to Edna, Martha's mother, saying that her daughter "evidently thinks a wife has no duties at all of any kind to her husband; neither to ever be with him and help him so he, also, can write; neither to take any responsability [*sic*] or share in takeing [*sic*] care of common property, nor to help with any of our common interests. Actually I am very fed up on it. Very."[18]

Martha stood up to Hemingway, with the result that they fought almost constantly. Stories of the Hemingways' explosive arguments began to take on epic proportions. Carlos Baker reports two incidents in particular at the end of 1942. The first occurred when they were out to dinner and Hemingway scolded her in public for being stingy with Christmas presents for the staff at the Finca. He drove off in a rage, leaving her at the restaurant. Out on another occasion, she insisted on driving because he was drunk. He slapped her with the back of his hand. She slid behind the wheel and proceeded to drive, but then deliberately ran the car through a ditch and into a tree, leaving Hemingway dazed and inebriated in the passenger seat as she strode home. Gregory told Michael Reynolds that when Hemingway and Martha were having difficulties, Hemingway's drinking became unrestrained. He went on benders, spending night after night sitting at the bar at the Floridita. Because he was driven by a house servant, he never had to worry about finding his way home.[19]

Two such competitive egos were inevitably bound to clash. Hemingway was always ashamed of his bad behavior, and after these hateful confrontations, both parties felt a good deal of regret. Hemingway wrote Martha poignant letters asking for forgiveness and chastising himself for the hurt he had caused. When one

of their cats died just after he and Martha had quarreled, Hemingway wrote a
sad and moving apology.

> I love you and . . . I know how dreadful it is for you about our dear
> Woolsi. All last night I could not sleep one bit for thinking about her.
> But worse than her about how bad for you. I loved her as much as you
> did but I had loved F. Puss and the Sudbury Coal cat but she was like
> your child. I feel so terribly to have been bad so that I cannot help you
> now in Woolsi's death. All I can say is that I will try all my life each day
> and each night to be good and to help you. I had tried very hard to be
> a better man and better friend and husband and I think I was maybe
> some better for quite a long time. Now I am starting all over but that
> doesn't bring back our Wools.[20]

They quarreled and made up, quarreled and made up, but the periods of respite
were very short.

Hemingway's slovenliness also repelled Martha, who was like a cat in her
mania for cleanliness. This conflict added another variable to the tension between
them. After coming home from fishing all afternoon, and sometimes part of the
night, Hemingway would rarely change his bloody, fish-scale-spattered clothes.
He must have stunk, yet he would sit down to dinner as if nothing was wrong.
Martha was a smart dresser and would be kitted out in stylish clothes, while her
husband across the table could have been mistaken for a bum on the dole.

Another strain on their marriage was that Martha never understood Hemingway's fear of being alone. Wherever Hemingway lived, he assembled groups
to keep him company, and wherever he traveled, there was sure to be a band
of followers—watching the bullfights in Spain, fishing on the *Pilar,* hunting in
Wyoming. Martha, by contrast, often craved solitude, especially as the Finca
was usually bustling with assorted guests and sporting companions. Martha's
solution to this hubbub was to get away, to travel on some journalistic assignment. She disliked the slow pace of tropical life and also felt bad about living
in luxury—with servants, tennis courts, a swimming pool—while the rest of the
world suffered under the strains of war. Her social conscience was troubled by
the soft life at Finca Vigía, and this became the source of another conflict between
husband and wife: what was Hemingway doing for the war effort?

In truth, Hemingway's lassitude and temporary loss of drive had been developing even before the end of the Spanish war. In December 1937, as an enraged
Pauline shouted at him when he showed up belatedly in snowy Paris after fighting with Loyalist troops outside Teruel, he began suffering from an alcohol-
related liver disorder, and a physician put him on regular doses of Chophytol
and Drainochol, drugs that help the kidneys and liver eliminate toxins. He was
depressed because he feared losing Pauline and knew that she was morally right
to lash out at him. Yet he pined endlessly for Martha. The three years of working

on *For Whom the Bell Tolls* drained him mentally and physically. It is little wonder that he could not spur himself to write in the years that followed.

The marital problems, although they were only one aspect of Hemingway's distraught emotional profile at this time, continued. Martha missed her husband when she was away but felt claustrophobic at home. She wanted to continue her career in journalism, and Hemingway resented her long absences from the Finca. Martha spent the early part of their relationship covering the war in Finland (November 1939–January 1940). She then tried to remain in residence at the Finca, but the two quickly slid back into a pattern of obsessive quarreling. Martha later told Bernice Kert, "I was not received with loving tender care. . . . Ernest began at once to rave at me, the word is not too strong. He woke me when I was trying to sleep to bully, snarl, mock—my crime really was to have been at war when he had not, but that was not how he put it. I was supposedly insane, I only wanted excitement and danger, I had no responsibility to anyone, I was selfish beyond belief."[21] After a painful period in which she could not adjust to being housebound, she took off again, and she spent the remainder of their marriage somewhere else—reporting for *Collier's* in the Caribbean (1942), and then covering the war in Europe (1943 45). In fact, when they decided to part ways in November 1944, it was on foreign soil—in France, where Hemingway too was reporting on the war. When the marriage ended, Hemingway told Sara Murphy that he needed "a wife in bed and not in the most widely circulated magazines."[22]

Although, as we have seen, Martha did not want being Ernest Hemingway's wife to overshadow her career, there was some ambivalence here. Martha always resented it when people referred to her as Mrs. Hemingway, and she was careful to publish under her own name, but she must have felt a certain measure of pride by association with her husband, because when she wrote on Finca Vigía letterhead, she always typed "Mrs. Ernest Hemingway" at the top of the page and signed the letters "Martha Hemingway," or sometimes "M. G. Hemingway." Oddly, these were mostly letters to friends and acquaintances, not to anyone she was trying to curry favor with or impress. Longing for each other when they were apart, but seemingly unable to get along when they were together, Martha felt she had no choice but to abscond.

Hemingway's alcoholism became a serious problem in their marriage as well. Hemingway's tremendously strong constitution enabled him to drink vast amounts without passing out or becoming too impaired to function. But that did not mitigate the impact of such heavy consumption on his health. His brother claimed that in the late 1930s in Key West, Hemingway was drinking about seventeen scotch and sodas a day. In Cuba, he sometimes took a bottle of champagne to bed and emptied it before falling asleep. In Europe during World War II, according to Buck Lanham, Hemingway was "a massive drinker. Bottle at bedtime, drank all day."[23] Bored, unable to write much, his wife away on assignment, Hemingway had little to do but drink and fish.

Things soon got so bad that Martha began to strike back at Hemingway's criticisms in her fiction. She published several stories that concerned aspects of their marriage. In one, a wealthy husband and a very beautiful wife exploit each other's assets. In another, a husband having an affair asserts his own selfish needs above those of his family. The third and most bitter of the stories concerns a novelist who is unable to write, becomes deeply depressed, and turns to alcohol. These stories also imply that Hemingway and Martha were sexually incompatible. Martha claimed that Hemingway could not satisfy her sexually; Hemingway said that his wife was unresponsive. Hemingway also wanted to have a child with Martha—a daughter—but she did not want anything to impede her writing and traveling. In her second marriage, to *Time* magazine editor T. S. Matthews, she did adopt a son, Sandy, although their relationship was never very close.

———

As the war in Europe ground on, Hemingway also had the safety of his oldest son, Jack, on his mind. Jack had taken classes at both the University of Montana and Dartmouth College but had not graduated. After the attack on Pearl Harbor, he enlisted in the army and served briefly in a military police detachment in North Africa. Then, with some help from his influential family, he entered the Office of Strategic Services as a captain. His first mission was to parachute into occupied France to assist the French Resistance, where he was very nearly captured by a German patrol only hours after landing. Late in October 1944, while helping a French partisan infiltrate an enemy position, Jack was taken prisoner by a German unit and spent six months at Moosberg Prison Camp before being released, much to his father's relief. The French government awarded Jack the Croix de Guerre for his heroism, making Hemingway immensely proud.[24]

Hemingway had been monitoring the events in Europe carefully as he watched fascism sweep across the continent. Indeed, he spent much of his time tracking these developments and acquired an impressive command of the latest war news. Hemingway began to consider himself such an expert on the war, in fact, that he told Martha that he should keep a diary of his predictions of how the war would unfold, suggesting that this could be of help to foreign policy experts and future historians.[25] Martha turned a deaf ear to his bragging and told him that if he really wanted to make himself useful, he should go to Europe and cover the battles. In November 1943, Martha got a commission from *Collier's* and left for London as a correspondent. Hemingway remained behind, mired in lassitude and drink. Martha's father, Paul, died in Piggott on 26 January of the following year, adding further to her sense of unease. She flew back to Cuba in mid-March, only to endure more conflict and argument with Hemingway.

In April 1944, probably not wanting to be upstaged by his wife, Hemingway too got a contract with *Collier's* to cover the war, effectively demoting Martha. Each magazine was permitted to have only one correspondent at the front. Hemingway was the marquee writer, so naturally the magazine made him the chief, and Martha, by default, became his subordinate. This must have infuriated her, but she seems initially to have borne it with grace. She even got Hemingway a priority seat on a flight to London, on 17 May 1944, by pulling strings with the British embassy in Washington. But Hemingway did not try to get her a seat, too, responding that "they only fly men."[26] Afterward, it took Martha two weeks to get to England herself on a freighter loaded with dynamite. Relations between them worsened further when Hemingway arrived in London in May and took a room at the Dorchester Hotel. He made the acquaintance of Mary Welsh Monks, a *Time* magazine reporter, and would soon begin an affair with her. Martha wrote her friend Hortense Flexner, on 17 May, "As far as I'm concerned it is all over, it will never work between us."[27]

Hemingway's bad luck struck again a week after arriving in London. He went to a party given by Robert Capa, the photographer, in Belgrave Square. While Hemingway was being driven home, during a blackout, his driver hit a water tank in Lowndes Square. Hemingway was thrown against the windshield and concussed. Blood streamed down his face and a ringing began in his ears that lasted a month. He was taken to the emergency room at St. George's Hospital. The gash on his scalp was sewn up with more than fifty stitches. (The spectacular crash attracted enough attention that one London paper reported Hemingway dead.) Three days later, Martha finally arrived in Liverpool and, hearing of the accident, rushed to London to be by her husband's bedside. When she arrived at the hospital, she found him surrounded by friends and champagne bottles, not looking ill in the least. By the end of the visit, Martha had told him that she never wanted to see him again.

In fact, Hemingway was seriously injured and no one knew it. The physician on duty did not deem the head injury serious enough to warrant reopening the gash to drain what turned out to be undiagnosed hemorrhaging. But given what we now know about Hemingway's subsequent illnesses, injuries, and generally poor health, the doctor's decision was almost certainly the wrong one. The head injury created the first of a persisting series of health problems with which Hemingway would contend for the rest of his life. Martha's dismissal of the seriousness of his condition angered Hemingway. "I am sick of her Prima-Donna-ism," he wrote to Patrick, and he told Buck Lanham that he had "torn up [his] tickets on her."[28]

Mercurial and bristling with resentments of various sorts, Hemingway also found himself in a city that he had never spent much time in and did not much like. His view of the British began in mild bemusement at their airs and customs and evened out over the course of his life into benign indifference. But he could also be caustic and dismissive of the British people.

Hemingway's ancestors were English on both sides. As a boy, he had loved listening to his grandfather Hall's stories of English history, and had loved reading English authors, from Rudyard Kipling to the suspense writer Marie Belloc Lowndes. Later, he came to respect the British painter and writer Richard Ford as the figure he thought best understood the Spanish and wrote the most insightfully about Spain. Many of Hemingway's close male friends were British—Chink Dorman-Smith, Philip Percival, and Charles Sweeny, to name a few. In Paris, he had been enamored of the Englishwoman Duff Twysden. The British characters in his fiction are generally depicted in a positive light—Catherine Barkley, Robert Wilson, Pop in *Green Hills of Africa,* the sportsman Wilson-Harris in *The Sun Also Rises,* and even the manipulative Lady Brett Ashley, whom Jake Barnes cannot help but love. Moreover, Hemingway many times mentioned the heroic RAF pilots in his reports from the front lines during World War II, admiring them for their courage and humility.

But Hemingway was never as well received by British readers as he was at home. Although he won high praise from such authors as Arnold Bennett and D. H. Lawrence, the literary establishment there thought that his style was precocious, his talent thin, and his public demeanor overbearing. Hemingway, in turn, disliked English authors' preoccupation with social status and class distinctions. He quarreled and then fell out with Ford Madox Ford and Wyndham Lewis over just these sorts of issues. In *A Moveable Feast,* he characterized Ford, "breathing heavily" and "holding himself as upright as an ambulatory," as condescending to writers just starting out, and when Ford cut such a person dead while sitting with Hemingway at a sidewalk café, Hemingway felt bad for the victim of Ford's scorn (75). He remembered Wyndham Lewis as dressing and acting so pretentiously around other artists that it was "embarrassing" to look at him in his studied "pre-war uniform." Hemingway said it made Lewis look like a character out of *La Bohème* (76–77). And he felt that his British publisher, Jonathan Cape, had never completely done right by him. Hemingway believed that Cape had not invested enough in the marketing and advertising of his books and that, because Hemingway was American, he had always put less effort into promoting him than he had his list of English authors.

Britain's colonial presence around the world also struck Hemingway as callous and misguided. In Hong Kong, Hemingway had told an interviewer that the moral environment in the city was very low, because the British refused to acknowledge that prostitution was a problem. Their class consciousness led them to see only the "beautiful girls from all parts of China" and not the "50,000 prostitutes in Hong Kong . . . swarming over the streets at night."[29] In *Under Kilimanjaro,* Hemingway lambastes a certain "G.C." (for "Gin-Crazed"), the British game warden for the Kajiado District of what was then British Kenya. The man had bungled a promising career in one British protectorate, only to move to another one. "He was intolerant of fools," Hemingway says, "and of the British white trash that sometimes come out to the colonies posing as civil servants. There were many of these and they must be good at their specialties or they would not have been graduated from the dreary educational institutions which produce them" (169).

Hemingway thought the English government had been cowardly in refusing to oppose Hitler and Mussolini during the Spanish Civil War. Their appeasement he later called "Coitus Britannicus / referring to her allies: F—cked from the back with withdrawal." In a devastating assessment of the British in a letter to Perkins in 1940, Hemingway called them "a degenerate people" whose politics was "suicidal." He called the British volunteers in the International Brigades "absolute scum": "After the Jarama fight they deserted by whole companies; they were cowards, malingerers, liars and phonies and fairies. They were absolutely paniced [*sic*] by the tanks and their officers, when they were brave, were so stupid that their stupidity was absolutely murderous." He allowed that there were some "fine" exceptions, but in general he felt that the "bums and clochards of Lyons that Herriot shipped to Spain to get rid of . . . were twenty times better soldiers than the English."30

Hemingway often contrasted the British unfavorably with the Spanish, whom he consistently admired. In *Death in the Afternoon,* he applauds the Spanish for their outlook on death: they "do not spend their lives avoiding the thought of it and hoping it does not exist only to discover it when they come to die." They "know death is the unescapable reality, the one thing any man may be sure of." Hemingway had no truck with anyone who would try euphemistically to joke about death or avoid considering it because it was merely "unpleasant." He mocked the English-descended Henry Wadsworth Longfellow for his line "Life is real! Life is earnest! / And the grave is not its goal." Hemingway, tongue in cheek, asks, "And where did they bury him?" (264).

———

While in London, Hemingway was briefly reunited with his kid brother, Leicester, who was in the army as part of a documentary film unit that included Irwin Shaw and William Saroyan. Leicester, born in 1915, was sixteen years younger than Hemingway. Like many a person with a famous older sibling, Leicester spent most of his life in Hemingway's shadow and trying his best to be like his brother. His career, however, was erratic. From 1935 to 1940, he worked as a journalist for daily newspapers in Chicago, Philadelphia, and New York. He then entered the army and served in France and Germany. At various times, Leicester was a boat builder and a charter-fishing captain in the Caribbean. At one point, he even managed a jai alai fronton in Miami. Over the course of his life, he published six books, including a novel and a memoir, none of them as successful as his older brother's works. "He found it a challenge to live up to the image, to the greatness of the name," John Hemingway, one of Gregory's sons, once said in an interview.31

Leicester's physical resemblance to Hemingway was remarkable—so much so that people might have mistaken one for the other. He had the same burly build and rugged demeanor, tending to portliness in his older years. In photographs taken at Hemingway's funeral, Leicester looks even more the double. His thinning salt-and-pepper hair is swept back over his head and he is wearing round wire-rimmed spectacles, just as Hemingway did. Later, he grew a beard, and the doppelganger effect became downright eerie.

Whenever Leicester tried to emulate his brother (whom, for obscure reasons, he called "Baron"), the self-absorbed Hemingway was apparently unaware that Leicester was pulling the same kinds of stunts that he himself had pulled. For example, Leicester once wrote their mother that he had fought with a boa constrictor on some unnamed misadventure. Hemingway replied to him, "Will you please stop this kind of crap before you give the old woman a heart attack?"[32] Hemingway apparently failed to see that he was prone to the same kind of self-aggrandizing myth making, or perhaps he thought that only he was entitled to such behavior.

Leicester's greatest attempt to mimic his brother came when he published his only novel, *The Sound of the Trumpet,* in 1953. This war-based narrative follows the exploits of a Hemingway stand-in, Rando Graham (sometimes called Grahamstein), who is a war correspondent in Europe and a fiction writer. Graham's activities in Europe closely follow those of Hemingway. The novel garnered only mild praise, however. *Time* magazine called it "a series of dramatically unrelated clichés which add up to a minor war document disguised as a novel. What Leicester Hemingway chiefly demonstrates is the importance of being Ernest."[33] Learning of the review, Hemingway tried to help heal Leicester's bruised ego. "It was the most unjust and dirty review that I have ever read," he wrote his brother.[34] He even considered sending an angry letter to the editor of the magazine, but did not do so.

Perhaps unsurprisingly, Leicester's only success came after his brother's death. In the late 1950s, Leicester had begun work on a family memoir, which he showed to Ernest in 1959, asking for his brother's blessing. But Hemingway refused, even threatening legal action if Leicester proceeded without his permission. One year after Hemingway's death, in 1962, *My Brother, Ernest Hemingway* appeared to positive notices and was briefly a best seller, since the degree of public curiosity about Hemingway was probably then at its peak. The book was serialized in *Playboy* magazine, was translated into eleven languages, and became a notable book on the *New York Times* 1962 summer reading list. In the photo on the dust jacket, Leicester seems dressed and posed to look like Ernest—hunched over his typewriter, fingers at the ready, gaze intently focused on the page before him.

Thereafter, Leicester developed into an eccentric with odd habits and manias. With the profits from the book, he indulged one of his most bizarre interests, founding a micro-nation in the Caribbean that he called "New Atlantis," after the incomplete utopian novel by Sir Francis Bacon. Leicester believed in the existence of the mythical underwater kingdom; he claimed to have seen part of it from the window of an airplane over the Caribbean Sea. Leicester's new "country" had a brief existence on an eight-by-thirty-foot bamboo raft anchored in the waters off Jamaica. It was later washed away in a storm—a wasted effort.

Leicester never got over his older brother's unwillingness to bestow his approval. His first wife thought that this was what blighted his achievements. "I wanted Les to be his own person," she said, but he never really was. Jack

Hemingway, in the appendix to a 1982 commemorative edition of Leicester's memoir, noted, "He was a fine writer who was forced into the ring too early against a tough pro and made to suffer the inevitable comparisons. He and his brother came out of the same nest and both had fine qualities as human beings. Somewhere along the line, success and other things killed a lot of the finest qualities in Papa. Leicester remained unspoiled." Leicester recognized his brother's need for uncritical admiration, and he tried to fulfill it. He observed in his memoir that "if the kid brother could show a little worshipful awe, that was a distinct aid in the relationship."[35] But Hemingway apparently did not want Les to fill that role. Instead, he went through a succession of acquaintances whom he thought of as surrogate sons or younger brothers— A. E. Hotchner, Gianfranco Ivancich, Arnold Samuelson, and Walter Houk, among others. When Leicester contracted type 2 diabetes in 1982 and was told by doctors that both of his legs might have to be amputated, he borrowed a .22 caliber handgun from a Miami Beach neighbor and, like his father and brother, killed himself with a shot to the head. He lived only five years longer than Hemingway had, dying at age sixty-seven, another suicide.

Hemingway had come to the war in Europe at just the right time. Beginning his assignment for *Collier's* in late May 1944, he was there for the days that led up to the largest, most important, and most secretive event of the entire war, the Allied landings on the beaches at Normandy. On the morning of 5 June, Hemingway moved out with the troops onboard the transport ship *Dorothea L. Dix*. The following day, the boat crossed the English Channel and headed for Omaha Beach. Hemingway was allowed to get in one of the LCVPs (landing craft, vehicle, and personnel boats) that pushed off the ship toward the beach. He did not, however, wade ashore himself. Regulations required that he stay put in the LCVP and watch the action unfold through his binoculars. Hemingway followed orders and wrote his report from the relative safety of the LCVP. But you wouldn't know it from his lead article, "Voyage to Victory," in the 22 July issue of *Collier's*. Hemingway made it sound as though he had splashed ashore with the soldiers, and maybe even taken part in the battle, too.

Gellhorn, lacking the credentials to get aboard the troop ship, finagled her way onto a hospital transport in the D-Day fleet. She also made it to Normandy—but one day late, on 7 June. This turned out to work in Gellhorn's favor, however, because the hospital ship was allowed to send personnel ashore. Gellhorn pretended to be a nurse's aide, and she waded ashore with her "colleagues" to carry the wounded back to the transport on stretchers. She therefore got to see the carnage on the beach firsthand, whereas Hemingway had to be content with what he could make out from the LCVP and the deck of the *Dorothea L. Dix*. Ironically, Gellhorn's report on D-Day appeared in the same 22 July issue of *Collier's* that Hemingway's did. The battle for control of the beachhead may have been over, but the personal battle offshore was in full swing. Later, Gellhorn wrote a congratulatory note to Hemingway, saying that she was happy that

he had gotten to see the battle, but also telling him with triumph that she had
managed to actually get to the beach. She then proceeded across Europe on her
own, steering clear of any U.S. officer above the rank of captain. "I had no food
rations," she said. "I ate only what was given to me by ordinary soldiers. And as
a result, I saw the war from a truer angle, through the eyes of the infantrymen
who finally won it."[36]

Hemingway continued to report on the war. In France in mid-July, he met
Colonel Charles Trueman Lanham, known to his friends as Buck. The First Battalion, 22nd Infantry Regiment, which Lanham commanded, was pushing toward
Paris when Hemingway fell in with it. Lanham, a graduate of West Point, was lean
and gray and somewhat small of stature. He was an amateur poet and writer as
well as a combat soldier, the very combination that Hemingway found desirable
in a male friend. He later became something of a guardian of Hemingway's reputation, working closely with Carlos Baker, Hemingway's first biographer. Lanham
drew up a chronology of the World War II experience for Baker's use (now part
of Baker's papers at Princeton University), and Baker submitted drafts of sections
of his biography to Lanham, on which Lanham made comments and suggestions.
Lanham loved the honor of having an esteemed academic pay so much attention to him and validate the importance of his relationship with Hemingway.[37]
Hemingway idealized his friend to almost heroic proportions, creating an ideal
combat comrade with whom to share his adventures. After the Allied victory in
France, Lanham was promoted to general, attacked Cologne, and met the Soviet
army at the Moldau River. When the war ended, he served in occupied Austria
and Czechoslovakia and also became a model for Colonel Richard Cantwell, the
protagonist of *Across the River and into the Trees*.

Lanham was in charge when Hemingway pulled one of his most audacious
stunts of the war. As they drove toward Paris, Hemingway orchestrated a controversial effort to gather military intelligence in the village of Rambouillet, twenty-
three miles southwest of Paris. He armed himself and brought along a small band
of French irregulars. The Maquis, or French Resistance fighters, accepted his
leadership without question and called him "Le Grand Capitaine" and sometimes
"Le Chef." A correspondent was not supposed to lead troops, but Hemingway
claimed that the soldiers "placed themselves under my command."[38]

Hemingway's lieutenants included his driver, Archie Pelkey, a man with
"bright red hair, six years of regular Army, four words of French, [and] a missing
front tooth."[39] Also with him was Irving Krieger, a young officer Hemingway
had talked into rushing ahead of the regular army, establishing a base of operations, and gathering intelligence. "He wanted to keep on going to Paris," Krieger
recalled. "I told him what I had done could be explained but to go farther and
jeopardize my soldiers more would require further interrogation." Later, Krieger
was embarrassed that he had been pushed into the escapade by Hemingway. "The
only reason I got out there," he said, "was due to Ernest Hemingway's aggres-
siveness in his desire to get a story and get to Paris first."[40]

After the retreating Germans had evacuated, Hemingway and the soldiers held the town. They established headquarters at the Hotel du Grand Veneur, raised the American flag, took prisoners, and got valuable information about enemy defenses on the road to Paris. David Bruce, then a colonel in the Office of Strategic Services and later American ambassador to Germany, explained:

> Ernest's bedroom was the nerve center of these operations. There, in his shirt sleeves, he gave audience to intelligence couriers, to refugees from Paris, to deserters from the German Army, to local officials, and to all comers. A fierce looking F. F. I. [French Forces of the Interior—i.e., a Resistance fighter] with a machine gun at the ready stood guard at the door. Within, Ernest, looking like a jolly, dark Bacchus, dispensed the high, low and middle justice in English, French and broken German. His language was strong, salty, and emphatic.[41]

Hemingway wanted to keep going. When Irwin Shaw rolled in to Rambouillet, Hemingway tried to talk him into commandeering a motorcycle. "Let's look for Germans and draw fire," Hemingway suggested. Since the Germans were already retreating, Shaw didn't see any point in doing this and refused to go along. He told Hemingway that it would be foolish and dangerous, and Hemingway relented.

As they strode into Paris on 25 August, Hemingway began to devise some of the self-aggrandizing legends that would later become famous, as he set about personally "liberating" the Ritz Hotel. The few Germans left behind in the city offered little resistance. They were cloistered behind drawn shutters and hunkered down in the dark, "like nuns in the path of warfare," as David Bruce put it. Conditions were bad. There was not enough fuel in the city to power the electric plants, so blackouts were common. Food and candles were also in short supply, but hard liquor and wine were abundantly available. A corner of the Ritz dining room had been converted into an army mess, and the American troops would eat breakfast there with various distinguished people staying in the hotel, including some of the royal family of Holland.[42]

Hemingway, predictably, also bragged about the extent of his combat experience. He later claimed to have killed many Germans, and certainly he killed some, but he probably took credit for more than he actually did. As his friend William Walton put it, "It was a dream picture he had of what a war correspondent would do. But then a war correspondent who was much better than the military themselves, and could take over. He thought if he had the chance, he could take command. He rather thought that he was taking command." Hemingway went so far as to compare himself to André Malraux, who had flown combat missions, led more than fifteen hundred Maquis in the Dordogne region of southwestern France, escaped from a POW camp at Sens, and taken part in several major military operations. Hemingway could claim no such achievements, but his intentions were good and the troops liked him, which counted for a lot. As Walton put it, "to me some of the good periods of his life . . . were in the war, because he had an outlet for his desire to fight and in a sense, led the life of a soldier and he got great satisfaction from this. And it spilled over into the rest of his life. He was nicer to people and gentler. His attitude toward GI fighters was very avuncular and attractive and they liked him. They sensed it."[43]

In late August, Hemingway got word from Lanham that his regiment was fighting at Landrecies. Hemingway hastened there to rejoin the 22nd and saw some fighting, but his activities were cut short after four weeks, when he was summoned by the inspector-general of the U.S. Third Army to a judicial investigation at Nancy on 6 October 1944.

Word of his adventures at Rambouillet had leaked out (perhaps from other war correspondents with whom he was competing), and military authorities were alarmed by allegations that he had carried a weapon and engaged in combat. At the hearing, ironically, Hemingway for once had to downplay rather than exaggerate his military accomplishments in order to avoid being court-martialed. He later gave a disingenuous account of his actions to a newspaper reporter. On 23 June 1951, Hemingway wrote to C. L. Sulzberger of the *New York Times,* "I had a certain amount of knowledge about guerrilla warfare and irregular tactics as well as a grounding in more formal war and I was willing and happy to work for or be of use to anybody who would give me anything to do within my capabilities." Hemingway was eventually exonerated when Colonel Bruce said he had given him written permission to carry a gun; Lanham also vouched for his bravery.

Once the inquiry was concluded, Hemingway rushed back to Lanham's 22nd Infantry in time to witness the Germans' last stand in Hürtgen Forest, between Aachen and Bonn. The conditions there were miserable. The sun was rarely visible, snow was melting everywhere, dripping from the trees in the darkness, and every road became a quagmire of mud and dead bodies. Each night, the temperature dropped below freezing. The foot soldiers had built their own improvised shelters—"doggy huts," they called them—slapped together with pieces of tin, cardboard, and bricks, with a stovepipe poking lopsidedly out the top. Two or three men lived in each shack.

The ferocious and costly battle raged from 15 November to 4 December, and twenty-four thousand American lives were lost. The mass carnage must have reminded Hemingway of the high number of casualties in the Great War. It stuck with him, for descriptions of the fierce fighting later found their way into Richard Cantwell's memories of battle in *Across the River and into the Trees.* Hemingway was well liked by the servicemen, and he acted bravely during the battle. Hemingway and William Walton lived in a captured woodcutter's hut that made Walton think of Hansel and Gretel. Every morning, as he and Hemingway started their rounds, "GIs would rise up out of their doggy huts. They'd see Ernest and call out, 'Hi, Ernest,' or 'Hi, Papa' after he got to be well known. And he just loved it. He really did."[44]

Hemingway put himself at risk almost as much as the regular soldiers did. In Villedieu-les-Poêles in Normandy, he had thrown grenades into a cellar where Nazi troops were hiding. On 22 November, armed with a machine gun, he killed some Germans when they attacked Lanham's outpost in the Hürtgenwald. Another incident occurred that is not so widely known. William Walton recalled one chilly, gray December morning when it was so overcast that they considered themselves fairly safe from attack by German aircraft. Walton thus got Archie Pelkey to drive him and Hemingway out to check on the dugouts and command posts. They came to a straight stretch of road, unusual in those parts, with deep ditches on either side. About half a mile down this stretch of road, Hemingway suddenly threw back his head and appeared to hear something. He screamed at Pelkey to slam on the brakes. They skidded to a stop and Hemingway yelled, "Oh, God, jump!" The three men hurled themselves down the embankment into the ditch just in time to hear a heavy, lumbering aircraft roaring close overhead and spraying the jeep with bullets, though they never saw the plane through the thick cloud cover. "Ernest, how the hell did you recognize that sound?" Walton asked. Hemingway pulled on his flask, wiped his mouth, and responded, "Spain! The last time I heard it was during the war. I'll bet the Krauts are down to their last aircraft. They've sent out an old crate like that to see what damage they can do. They probably know the division is going to pull out and were patrolling the road." They made no move to get back in the jeep, calculating that the plane would make another pass. It did, strafing the vehicle with more bullets, and then roared over the tops of the tall, dark trees and, presumably, on to its next target. The three men made it back to camp safely, glad for the cover of the forest.[45]

Hemingway was honored for his participation in World War II in a small ceremony in June 1947 at the U.S. embassy in Cuba. The army awarded him the Bronze Star, a medal given for "heroic or meritorious achievement or service, not involving participation in aerial flight, in connection with military operations against an armed enemy." Hemingway was praised for having circulated "freely under fire in combat areas in order to obtain an accurate picture of conditions. Through his talent of expression, Mr. Hemingway enabled readers to obtain a vivid picture of the difficulties and triumphs of the front-line soldier and his organization in combat."[46]

———

The most serious consequence of Hemingway's participation in World War II was that he was dangerously concussed on two occasions. The damage caused by the concussions was probably exacerbated by subsequent accidents and injuries. His injuries, accidents, and illnesses almost certainly account for his unusually seething hatred for Martha after they decided to part ways, and they probably also account, at least in part, for his creative struggles in the latter half of the 1940s.

Just three months after his car accident in London in 1944, with headaches still bothering him, Hemingway was traveling with the 22nd Infantry when he commandeered a German motorcycle and sidecar and struck off on his own as

Lanham's unit was mopping up German resistance at Villedieu-les-Poêles. Some
Allied soldiers later spotted Hemingway on the outskirts of Saint-Pois, lying flat
in a ditch as German tracer bullets whizzed above his combat helmet. The motorcycle lay upended in the middle of the road; a mortar shell from an antitank
gun had landed about ten feet in front of it as Hemingway was making his way
down the road. Hemingway lay pinned down in this position, his head roaring,
for an excruciating two hours, as the Germans sprayed machine gun fire above
him and the dirt from the ditch splattered up into his face. He was badly hurt
by the accident. For several weeks afterward, he had double vision and pound-
ing headaches. The accident also seems to have affected his mental alertness. At
least one acquaintance said that Hemingway was speaking slowly and slurring
his words, even writing backward in a loopy script.

In December, Hemingway caught pneumonia from traveling with the infantry in cold, damp weather. The infection was so bad that he coughed up blood
in his room at the Ritz Hotel, where he'd gone to recuperate. When he returned
to Paris early the next year, the headaches returned as well. When he arrived in
Cuba in mid-March 1945, the headaches were still bothering him, his speech had
slowed, and he was experiencing some short-term memory loss. In June, after
spending about a month with Mary Welsh Monks at the Finca, he was driving
her to the airport when he lost control of his car and had a terrible wreck. Mary's
face was cut badly. Hemingway injured his head again and broke four ribs.

Hemingway had begun talking with Martha about a divorce, and they finally agreed to part ways in the fall; the divorce was final by 21 December 1945.
Hemingway's sometimes atrocious behavior toward Martha may in part have
been the result of his injuries. She thought that his mental health was in serious
question—that he had grown "progressively more insane every year."[47] She also
believed that Hemingway was an inveterate liar and could not be trusted.

But Hemingway was even more bitter than she, because in contrast to his first
two marriages, in which he had hurt his wives, this time his wife had hurt him.
This filled him with a dull misery, like the gnawing pain of a rotten tooth. And,
as always when he was injured, he lashed out like a wounded animal and tried to
inflict equal pain in return. Hemingway felt that Martha's better qualities—her
beauty, her political knowledge, and her writing ability—were outweighed by her
arrogance, her snobbery, and her unwillingness to stay by his side and encourage
his work. He came to feel that marrying Marty had been the biggest mistake of
his life, and he could blame no one but himself for his stupidity.

Mary, Adriana, and
Across the River and into the Trees

While still married to Martha in the spring of 1944, Hemingway had started an affair with Mary Welsh Monks. Despite the failure of three marriages, he still believed that he was better off with a wife—that marriage brought out his good qualities and encouraged sobriety, devotion, and good behavior. It also staved off Hemingway's greatest fear, which was loneliness. Mary, who became Hemingway's fourth wife in March 1946, was with him during the years of his greatest fame, as the winner of the Nobel Prize for Literature, but also of his rapid deterioration, as mental and physical illness drove him to become increasingly mercurial and, eventually, abusive to her and to his friends. Of his four wives, Mary was also the one who most readily gave up her independence and became, in most people's minds, a professional "Mrs. Hemingway."

Hemingway and Mary were introduced by the novelist Irwin Shaw one spring afternoon at the White Tower restaurant in London. At the time, Shaw was having an affair with Mary, who was married to an Australian journalist named Noel Monks. A reporter herself, Mary had joined the *Time* magazine bureau in London in 1940; one of her colleagues there was William Walton. Mary was a flirtatious type. In her autobiography, she recalled that on the day she met Hemingway, she was wearing a tight white sweater with no brassiere, as if defying standards of propriety. Taking note of how she was dressed, Shaw told her, "Wait till you see how many people will drop by our table during this lunch." As if on cue, Hemingway walked up a few minutes later and said to Shaw, "Introduce me to your friend."[1]

Born in 1908, the same year as Martha Gellhorn, Mary was Martha's physical opposite. Whereas Martha was tall and long-boned, Mary was petite and small-boned, almost diminutive, even pixie-like. She always reminded people of Mary

Martin, the popular stage actress who immortalized the role of Peter Pan. Mary was energetic and hardworking, competitive, flirtatious, and, like Martha, did not let the fact that she was a woman in a man's world (journalism) stop her from taking on big assignments and pushing for advantages in pay, opportunities, and perquisites. Like Hemingway, she came from humble origins and had been raised in a conservative environment against which she later rebelled.

Mary was an only child born into a plainspoken farm family in rural Walker, Minnesota, a tiny outpost in the northern part of the state. The family soon moved to Bemidji, a somewhat more developed town, but her opportunities were still limited. Her father, Tom, was a logger who supplemented his income by taking tourists on jaunts down the Mississippi River on a steamboat called the *Northland*. She loved her father very much and grew up wanting to be like him; she naturally adapted herself to the masculine environment that he created. "Maybe," she later wrote, "it was not so much that he treated me like a boy, but rather like a human being, who could do anything and try anything."[2] Her mother was a Christian Scientist who, like Grace Hemingway, felt that she had married down. Both parents, however, believed in the value of hard work. Mary's mother encouraged her to find her own way, and not to let being a woman stop her from doing what she wanted. Like Hemingway's parents, Mary's mother and father were not particularly compatible, but they too soldiered on for the sake of their child. Mary later remarked that this was her parents' most sterling quality—that they stayed together and made the marriage work, even in the face of painful emotional difficulties. Mary herself would do much the same thing when Hemingway's abuse became extreme. She took the emotional blows and stuck it out.

Mary entered Northwestern University in the fall of 1926 and majored in journalism. She earned her own way through school, picking up part-time jobs in restaurants and offices to pay her tuition and living expenses. At one point she fell in with a group of classmates, all of them as money-starved as she was, with whom she moved into a house—a kind of unofficial commune where everyone pitched in to keep their stomachs filled. Mary became romantically involved with another journalism student in the house, Lawrence Cook, and married him. The partnership did not last quite two years, however, because Mary dropped out of school to support her husband, working for a while on a trade magazine for florists, while he refused to find adequate work himself. Mary learned a lot about journalism from her on-the-job training, and a lot about marriage, which convinced her that hers was not working, and so the two quietly divorced.

On her own again, Mary moved to Chicago and went to work for a syndicate that specialized in sweatshop journalism—throwaway weeklies that offered no opportunity for "real" writing (an experience similar to Hemingway's youthful stint in Chicago at the *Cooperative Commonwealth*). Her experience, however, enabled her to land a job with the *Chicago Daily News* as a society reporter. Although she yearned for the crime beat or for city hall assignments, she knew that she was lucky to break in at all, so she worked hard at producing good work.

199

Mary,
Adriana, and
*Across the
River and into
the Trees*

(Coincidentally, the managing editor of the newspaper was Paul Mowrer, Hadley's second husband, and one of the other reporters on staff was Hemingway's brother, Leicester.)

Eventually, the paper sent her to England, where she worked her way into favor with the owner of the *Daily Express* in London. By July 1937, Mary had such plum assignments as an article on the disappearance of Amelia Earhart over the South Pacific. In the summer of 1938, she married Noel Monks, but they, too, were incompatible. Mary liked the high life; Monks, as she described him in her autobiography, was conservative and abstemious. When Mary began seeing Hemingway in London in the spring of 1944, she had already decided to divorce Monks.

The independent-minded Mary decided to marry Hemingway when she could not get Irwin Shaw to propose to her. One afternoon in the bar of the Ritz, after many months of trying to get Shaw to take the hint, she finally blurted out, "Irwin, are you going to marry me?" Shaw responded, "No, whatever made you think that!" "All right then," she replied, "I think I'll marry Ernest." Later that week over lunch, Hemingway told Mary that he was going to visit her room later that evening. Part of her hoped that he would not show up, but when he did, she was thrilled. Hemingway promptly unfolded himself on one of the two twin beds in the hotel room. They talked for several hours, and when Hemingway stood up to leave, he said, "I don't know you, Mary, but I want to marry you." Mary assumed he was drunk, but he was not. As he left the room, he turned back to her and said, "This war may keep us apart. Just please remember I want to marry you."[3]

Mary was well suited to be Hemingway's wife. Although she had once written in her journal that she "never liked anyone because he was titled or socially important, or rich, or famous," she was nevertheless acutely conscious of Hemingway's star power. Like Martha Gellhorn, Mary played the role of a celebrity's wife when it suited her. Sam Boal, another friend, recalled that once, on a cruise, he noticed that when she met "a new person on the ship and she was building up to the moment they'd want to know who she was, she'd take out her calling card—Mrs. Ernest Hemingway!"[4]

Like Hemingway, Mary could rough it uncomplainingly when she had to. Having lived through the Blitz in London, when nightly German bombers dropped tons of high explosives on the city and fires leapt from rooftop to rooftop, she developed a hard-shell resiliency and an indifference to trauma. In one aerial raid, all the windows in her apartment were blown in, but she calmly packed her remaining possessions and moved to another flat nearby. She was always the one racing out into the blackout for a cab.

Hemingway was at ease in Mary's company. She placed no demands on him, as Martha had done, and enjoyed sex as much as he did—also apparently unlike Martha. In London that spring, they strolled the city and lunched at West End pubs and restaurants. The champagne flowed freely, and there was always interesting conversation in the circles that gathered around Hemingway in his room at the Dorchester. She later met him in Paris after he and the Resistance

201

Mary,

Adriana, and

Across the

River and into

the Trees

fighters arrived there after the German retreat. He introduced her to Picasso at his studio and showed her where Stein and Toklas lived on rue de Fleurus. Later, when Hemingway went off with Buck Lanham, he bombarded Mary with love letters: "I am just happy and purring like an old jungle beast because I love you and you love me. . . . We will fight . . . against loneliness, chickenshit, death . . . and many other worthless things—and in favour of you sitting up straight in bed lovelier than any figure head on the finest, tallest ship. . . . Dearest Mary. . . . Please love me very much and always take care of me Small Friend the way Small Friends take care of Big Friends. . . . Oh Mary darling I love you very much."[5] Hemingway was a romantic at heart, and though he could be cruel, he was also capable of extreme tenderness. He wanted and needed to be loved, and he wanted to return that person's love in kind. But his psychic imbalances and the manic, self-destructive behavior to which they often led prevented him from sustaining a loving attitude toward most people.

In Cuba, they enjoyed each other's company. They cooked out, packed picnic lunches, and went to the shooting club. As was his habit, Hemingway invented a nickname for Mary, "Pickle" (the first of several), and they fished and swam in the cool waters of the Gulf Stream. Mary immediately endeared herself to Hemingway when, on her first trip on the *Pilar,* she landed a white marlin. "Now, here's a woman I could love forever," Hemingway reportedly said to Gregorio Fuentes.[6] "Every way I thought things would be good for her they are," Hemingway told Buck Lanham. "And she is so damned good to me and for me that you [*sic*] there's nothing you can write about it. Am as inarticulate about it as about a battle. . . . If you were ever lonesome all your life and loved the sea too and were always lonesome on it you can imagine what is like to be with somebody that really loves it."[7] With Mary there, Hemingway did not fear loneliness.

By the end of 1944, with the clarity that comes from closing the door on a failed marriage, Mary had asked Noel Monks for a divorce. By the spring of the following year, she was en route to Havana to visit Hemingway at the Finca, and they were married in Havana on 14 March 1946. Hemingway vowed to take good care of Mary, and he also provided for her aging parents. Each month, Hemingway sent them money to supplement their small savings—an admirable gesture of commitment. "My only ambition," Hemingway wrote Tom Welsh, "is to make her a good husband . . . and if you need a son around for any purposes ever please remember you have one."[8]

_____

After a long period of dormancy, Hemingway finally began to write fiction again in the fall of 1945. The next several years would prove to be a period of great productivity for him, but also of great creative anguish, because although he was writing steadily, he was never able to bring much of this work to completion or even to a point of revision that satisfied him. All of this work, however—*Islands in the Stream, The Garden of Eden, True at First Light,* and *Under Kilimanjaro*—was eventually published by Scribner's after his death.

In late September 1945, Buck Lanham and his wife came to the Finca for two weeks. Perhaps spurred by Lanham's visit, Hemingway began composing, with manic intensity, a new novel of great scope, which he referred to as a book about warfare on "land, sea, and air." Rose Marie Burwell, in her groundbreaking study of Hemingway's posthumous work, refers to this urtext as "four schizophrenic fictional structures" that would eventually be separated and published individually. Two were published in Hemingway's lifetime (*Across the River and into the Trees* [1950] and *The Old Man and the Sea* [1952]), and two appeared after his death (*Islands in the Stream* [1970] and *The Garden of Eden* [1986]). *Islands* was the "sea" part; *Across the River* was the "land" part; and the "air" part was never written.

Over the years, the narrative cells that made up this manuscript multiplied and metastasized, outgrowing all boundaries. Later on, two other unpublished books, the narrative of his African safari (published in two versions as *True at First Light* [1999] and *Under Kilimanjaro* [2005]) and his memoir of the Paris years (also published in two versions as *A Moveable Feast* [1964, 2009]), would grow out of the same thematic concerns that were on his mind as he began *Islands in the Stream* and *The Garden of Eden* in the fall of 1945.[9] All of these narratives attempt to present a vision of the artist in the twentieth century—especially the writer's struggle to sustain creativity, whether alone or in an intimate relationship. And they are all marked by stylistic experimentation.[10]

Hemingway put in the longest sustained stint of work on what would be published as *Islands in the Stream* at the Finca and in Sun Valley, Idaho, between October 1945 and the late spring of 1948. He told Max Perkins in March 1947 that he had been working "steadily and well," "re-writing from the beginning" the earliest part and other parts where he thought he had not gotten it right. He estimated that the manuscript would run to about 907 pages and predicted that "a lot of it will take very little re-writing."[11] But just three months later, Perkins was dead from a heart attack—a sudden turn of events that jarred Hemingway from his iron concentration on the book and put him at loose ends for most of the rest of the summer. In addition, his middle son, Patrick, sustained an undiagnosed concussion while playing with his brother, Gregory. Hemingway had to care for Patrick for sixty-four days straight, putting him, he reckoned, two months behind on the book.

He resumed work on the novel in the early fall of 1947, and when he went to Idaho the following month, he could report that things were going well, the "change of climate" acting "as a super-charger." By the end of April 1948, he could tick off for Buck Lanham an itemized daily word count that sounded encouraging—an average, perhaps, of 750 words per day for that month—but with the added proviso, "Hope it isn't all shit."[12]

As if in a self-fulfilling prophecy, Hemingway began two months later to feel that two narratives were colliding with each other in the manuscript. He therefore laid *Islands* aside and began working on *The Garden of Eden* as a separate book. He abandoned both narratives in 1949 to start a story that would become *Across*

203

_____

Mary,

Adriana, and

Across the

River and into

the Trees

the River and into the Trees. He then took up *Islands* again in April 1950 for a brief period in which he was simultaneously rewriting *Across the River,* then revising the galleys of that novel, and also composing a provisional ending for *The Garden of Eden.* From March through mid-May 1951, Hemingway pressed on with *Islands,* and then began revisions in the summer.

In August he reported to Bill Walton that it was such a tough job that he did not think he could get away to join him in Mexico for a trip the two had planned: "There is over 1200 pages of this re-write to do and since you left, working hard I have only done about 200 and never worked harder."[13] Hemingway was still hard at it in the fall, when he asked Marlene Dietrich if she would be willing to read what became section III, "The Sea Chase" ("At Sea" in published form). "It is very quiet and simple and there is no picture in it," he told Dietrich. "But I have tried for something past where I have ever been able to go and I would love it if you would read it. You mustn't show it to anybody though and remember it is an uncorrected copy that Mary made. . . . It would be wonderful if you [would] read it, wonderful for me I mean, because I get tired, when I am writing like this, to read and can not write and only drink myself to death on Ballantine's Ale."[14] He continued revising and cutting the manuscript until 24 December, when he pronounced *Islands* finished.

Divided into three sections, the novel tells the story of a painter named Thomas Hudson who lives on the island of Bimini, where Hemingway spent the summers of 1935 and 1936, and part of the summer of 1937. Part I, "Bimini," which Hemingway described as an "Idyll . . . destroyed by violence,"[15] concerns Hudson, his friend the writer Roger Davis, and Hudson's three sons (modeled on Hemingway's own sons), two of whom are killed with their mother in an automobile accident (similar to the accident that had occurred in 1933, when Gregory and Patrick were riding with Jane Mason). The focus of this part of the story is the contrasting portraits of two artists, Hudson and Davis. Hudson has a private income from oil leases in Montana, and is thus free to paint whatever he likes, without regard for whether the paintings sell. Davis, by contrast, is a very talented writer who must lower himself by churning out slick entertainments that will keep the wolf from the door. At the end of the section, however, Davis, inspired by Hudson, goes out west to try to produce the kind of art that he will be proud of.

Part II finds Hudson as a kind of unofficial agent for the U.S. military during World War II, hunting German U-boats in the Gulf Stream. In this section of the novel, however, Hudson and his crew are between missions. Part II also introduces one of Hudson's ex-wives and describes the death of his third and youngest son, who is killed flying an RAF mission in Europe. Part III describes the submarine hunt referred to in part II. Hudson and his crew track down the crew of a sunken U-boat and engage them in a vicious firefight that leaves Hudson dead.

The editing of the published novel, which appeared in 1970, was largely the work of Hemingway's authorized biographer, Carlos Baker, although Baker never acknowledged his role in the project. Instead, Scribner's printed a brief preface by Mary Hemingway in which said that she and Charles Scribner Jr. "worked together in preparing" the book "for publication from Ernest's original manuscripts." Although Mary claimed that they did nothing more than correct spelling and punctuation and make a few deletions, scholarship has shown that many changes were made in part III, "At Sea," including the restoration of cuts that Hemingway had made in the original manuscripts and the conflation of several chapters.[16] An early title for the 1945 urtext was "The Islands and the Stream," which Mary Hemingway and Scribner changed to *Islands in the Stream.*

The reviews were mixed at best, most reviewers reading the book merely as unreflective autobiography and balking at the narrative's disjointedness and somewhat discursive style. This reaction against the "typical" Hemingway style of terse, staccato prose and subtle understatement, trademarked and honed to perfection in the 1920s, recalls critics' browbeating of Hemingway in the 1930s, when he began to try out different modes of expression in *Green Hills of Africa* and *To Have and Have Not.* The movement toward a more interior style can be seen in the depiction of Robert Jordan in *For Whom the Bell Tolls,* Hemingway's most psychological novel. The streams of loose syntax, the words that deliver blunt emotion—these were first steps toward a more postmodernist style. Hemingway continued writing in this vein in the urtext and in the works that followed it. It may even be that the more expansive style ("something past where I have ever been able to go") was due to Hemingway's change of locale—his fleeing the constricted environment of Paris, with its unhappy personal memories and his belief that France had been used up in his imagination, for the wide vistas and flat, open spaces of Key West and Cuba. Knowing that reviewers did not appreciate this new style, Hemingway must have felt unsure of himself in continuing to use it. Perhaps one reason that he could never finish the novel was his uncertainty about how successfully he had employed the new writing technique.

Uncertainty came to define his working days during this period. He would race ahead with an idea, flesh it out on paper, then pull back and begin again in an altogether different direction. False starts and missteps became the pattern of his writing, and virtually nothing got finished. Hemingway began to feel himself a failure, perhaps compounding his failures as a four-time husband and his sense of unworthiness as the often absent father of three boys. The other narrative that emerged in fits and starts from the 1945 manuscript would become *The Garden of Eden.* Rose Marie Burwell has argued convincingly that traces of the lineage of *The Garden of Eden* can be seen in various parts of the *Islands* manuscript, which is not surprising given that Hemingway originally intended one narrative unit. *The Garden of Eden* is about a writer, David Bourne, and his new wife, Catherine, who honeymoon in the south of France. Catherine becomes jealous of her husband's creativity and tries initially to distract him, then eventually to sabotage David's work through a series of increasingly bizarre means. First, she entices him into a series of sexual games that involve gender reversal and other forms of sexual experimentation; then she befriends another woman, Marita, and suggests a ménage à trois. Finally, unable to dissuade David from writing his book (about his boyhood adventures with his father in Africa), she burns his manuscripts and runs off, leaving David with the impression that she is going to commit suicide. In the end, David takes up with Marita and, with her help, is able to reconstruct much of what Catherine destroyed. The intermingling of artistic and personal/sexual identity is a core theme of both *Islands in the Stream* and *The Garden of Eden*.[17]

Three of Hemingway's four wives seem to have a presence in the story. Catherine is almost certainly modeled on Mary. Like the character, Mary had short blonde hair, often dressed in tight-fitting sweaters, and—apparently—worked at perfecting the full-body tan. Moreover, Mary wrote in her diaries of her desire for sexual role-playing in bed, and Hemingway was happy to play along. In a letter to his wife from this period, Hemingway remarks that he will be "Mary's Catherine."[18]

Pauline and Mary, ironically, became good friends in the spring and summer of 1947. Pauline made several trips from Key West to the Finca to help care for Patrick and to advise Mary on the construction of a four-story white tower she was having built behind the main house. The first floor contained a bath and a workshop, the second became a lair for the more than fifty cats that Hemingway had adopted (and developed a strange obsession with), the third comprised mostly storage, and at the top, with a magnificent view of the city, was Hemingway's writing room. Pauline's interactions with Mary presaged the development of the character of Marita (a conflation of Pauline and Mary, though the name also suggests Martha Gellhorn). At this point, the composition of *The Garden of Eden* was at least informally under way, but it was dropped again in the fall of 1948 when the Hemingways went to Italy. (There, Hemingway met Adriana Ivancich, and by early the next year he had started a new narrative about duck hunting near Venice, which became the frame for *Across the River and into the Trees,* published in 1950.)

Still, nothing progressed very quickly or very far. Hemingway endured terrible headaches because of his earlier concussions and other ailments. He worked with painful slowness, but also with an iron-jawed determination to keep producing. He wrote mostly in longhand, frequently while standing at a bookcase; occasionally, he would use the typewriter ("when trying to keep up with dialogue"). Over these years, he carefully logged each day's work. Except for occasional spurts when he was engaged in relatively unimportant efforts, his daily output ran to between four hundred and seven hundred words. Mary remembers very few occasions when it topped a thousand words. He did not find writing quick or easy. "I always hurt some," he remarked.[19] He disliked the fourth-floor study, finding it "far too quiet"; the loneliness it produced in him acted like a depressant, making him feel alone in a dark room. Loneliness constricted his heart, his capacity for love, and it crippled his writing ability. One day he went up to the tower

205

Mary,

Adriana, and

Across the

River and into

the Trees

to write and spent fifteen minutes trying in vain to make a phrase. Defeated, he came downstairs and never again used that room for working. The tower turned out to be a folly.

————

Hemingway's morbid fear of loneliness was exacerbated when a number of close friends died. Scott Fitzgerald had a fatal heart attack, brought on by alcoholism, in 1940. The following year James Joyce died, also of conditions made worse by a lifetime of heavy drinking. In 1946 Gertrude Stein passed away, and Ezra Pound was incarcerated in a mental hospital. In 1947, Katy Dos Passos was killed in a car accident. Even more emotionally difficult for him to accept was the death of his mother, Grace Hall Hemingway, on 29 June 1951.

At times, there were sunnier skies. In July 1946, at age thirty-eight, Mary found herself pregnant. Hemingway was delighted with this second chance for a long-awaited daughter. But in August, on their way to vacation in Sun Valley, Idaho, Mary awoke one morning in a motel in Casper, Wyoming, with a searing pain in her abdomen. Hemingway called an ambulance, and Mary was rushed to the hospital. The emergency room doctor diagnosed an ectopic pregnancy. One of Mary's fallopian tubes had ruptured as she slept, and she was hemorrhaging badly. An intern was the only physician on duty; the resident surgeon was away on a fishing trip and could not get to the hospital until late that evening. The nurses began to administer plasma and fluids, and Mary was stable until she was being prepared for surgery, when her veins suddenly collapsed. The intern did not know what to do and told Hemingway it was hopeless. Mary would not be able to withstand the shock of an operation; he should tell her good-bye.

Hemingway refused to accept the doctor's prognosis. He put on rubber gloves and got a nurse to find a vein and make an incision; Mary needed plasma again. The nurse inserted the needle, but then the plasma would not flow. Hemingway cleared the IV line "by milking the tube down and raising and tilting" it until the plasma was flowing. By the end of the first pint, he later wrote Buck Lanham, "she was comeing [sic] back enough so that [I] insisted that they operate. . . . Now today is feeling fine. . . . They removed the ruptured tube and the other tube and all other organs are intact and OK." "But Buck," he continued, "it was the closest one I've ever seen. Dr. had given her up—and taken off his gloves. Certainly shows never pays to quit."[20] Although Mary lost the fetus, Hemingway's quick and decisive actions saved her life. She was now forever indebted to him, and nothing he could do to her, however cruel, would shake her faith and trust in him.

The superstitious Hemingway was also bothered by disturbing omens that he interpreted as presaging more loss. Eight months after Mary's health crisis, both Gregory and Patrick were injured in the car accident with Pauline. Greg cut his knee and Patrick complained of a headache, but the doctors said that he had not suffered a concussion and shrugged it off as nothing serious. Some days later, he became feverish, and during the night turned violent and irrational. Intracranial bleeding had resulted from an undiagnosed concussion. Hemingway slept on a mattress outside his son's door until the danger had passed, and when Patrick refused to eat, Hemingway administered rectal feedings. He nursed his son back to health, although it took Patrick more than three months to recover fully. Both incidents soured Hemingway on the authority of physicians. Coming to believe that they did not always know best, Hemingway tried in his later years to treat himself for his physical and mental ailments, with disastrous results. These episodes also turned his depressive mood even blacker.

207
____

Mary,
Adriana, and
*Across the
River and into
the Trees*

In the late 1940s, perhaps to assuage the depression and anxiety caused by these losses and near losses, and perhaps also because his literary labors were bearing little fruit, Hemingway reinvigorated his campaign to become the best-known living writer. He undertook something of a concurrent "career," furthering his public image through nonliterary or only partly literary activities. This involved writing reviews and prefaces and forewords for other writers' books, but also public letters, press statements, blurbs, and even endorsements for such companies as Pan American Airways, Ballantine Ale, and the Parker Pen Company. "Ernest Hemingway says: Each generation of Americans needs to re-discover Europe," read the banner for the Pan Am ad. A picture of the author, looking preternaturally healthy and strong, appeared on one side of the ad, with the caption "Pan-American and I are old friends." To the right is a larger photo of an ancient European bridge over a river at low tide, with the battlements of an old castle in the background alongside the spires and minarets of a cathedral.

Hemingway also burnished his celebrity status by associating with the actors who played "Hemingway men" in the film versions of his stories: Humphrey Bogart in *To Have and Have Not,* Gregory Peck in *The Snows of Kilimanjaro,* and, especially, Gary Cooper in *For Whom the Bell Tolls.* Hemingway and Cooper shared a twenty-year friendship based on many common interests and similarities in personality. Both shared a passion for hunting and sports and decorated their houses with trophies. Both had hunted big game in Africa. And both were pursued by ambitious women. Early on, Hemingway told a friend, "if you made up a character like Coop, nobody would believe it. He's just too good to be true."[21] Hemingway's tough-guy persona was shaped in part by the millions of people who saw these actors performing onscreen.

Hemingway allowed interviewers and photographers to visit him at the Finca and take pictures of him fishing, boxing, and shooting, further bolstering the myth. Interestingly, Hemingway managed to link these activities with literature. If other writers had gone on safari or taken up boxing or spent countless hours watching bullfights, they would have been rebuked for neglecting their writing. (In fact, Hemingway rebuked some of them himself in certain book reviews.) Yet somehow Hemingway made it seem that everything he did—whether writing at his desk or piloting the *Pilar*—was for the enrichment of American literature.

____

Unable to move forward with his writing projects, Hemingway also began to retreat into the past. It had been his habit throughout his writing life to live elsewhere in his imagination. While in northern Italy, he wrote of the trout streams of upper Michigan in the Nick Adams stories. In his cold-water flat in Paris, he portrayed small-town America. In the scorching heat of Kansas City, he depicted the front in World War I Italy. Even while touring Spain in the late 1940s, he described the natural beauty of Cuba in an article for *Holiday* magazine. It was probably inevitable, then, that he would return to Italy, where he had experienced the great turning point in his life. In September 1948, Hemingway took Mary to revisit the site of his wounding in World War I: Fossalta, on the Piave River.

Arriving in Venice, they stayed at the five-hundred-year-old Gritti Palace, a fashionable luxury hotel across from the Church of Santa Maria della Salute, built in the seventeenth century as an offering for deliverance from the plague. Mary toured the sights, sometimes with a reluctant Hemingway, though he was delighted to be in the beautiful ancient city. He also enjoyed socializing with the Venetian aristocracy who patronized the Gritti Palace. He and Mary also spent time at Cortina d'Ampezzo, where Hemingway had gone skiing with Hadley in 1923.

At Cortina, Hemingway met Count Federico Kechler, a well-known sportsman from one of Venice's oldest families. Kechler in turn introduced Hemingway to Baron Nanyuki Franchetti, a famous hunter and great aficionado of duck shooting in the northern lagoons. Early in December, Franchetti invited Hemingway to a weekend hunt at his estate near Latisana. Hemingway intensely loved the "vallee"—the Italian word for what was essentially a country estate or park filled with rivers and streams, and he accepted immediately (Mary had gone off alone to visit friends at Fiesole). A few days later, he was being driven to the Franchetti lodge. On the way, he and his new friends were to stop at San Michele to pick up a young woman who was joining them for the weekend—Adriana Ivancich, whose family home was near the Franchetti estate. Ivancich was waiting in the rain at the crossroads outside town. When the car slowed, she slid into the backseat and was surprised to see a rather large, broad-shouldered man in the passenger seat up front. Kechler turned to her and said, "By the way, do you know Ernest, Ernest Hemingway, the writer?" Hemingway raised his flask, offered her a drink, and made a toast to the effect that she was a great sport for waiting for them in such nasty weather. He knew that the Americans had bombed her house during the war and said, "I hope you'll forgive us." "It is not the fault of anybody," Adriana replied. "War is war." Hemingway took a liking to her immediately.

The day continued gray and miserable—it poured rain throughout the hunt—but the young woman was beautiful. When the party returned to the main house that evening, Hemingway took stock of the nineteen-year-old Adriana and her aristocratic features—her long, aquiline nose, high forehead, and beautiful face, with its swanlike contours. Her eyes were a lively shade of green, giving her an intensely curious gaze, and her hair was a rich, long black. It looked lustrous in spite of the pouring rain. Ever the gallant, Hemingway took out his comb, broke it in two, and gave half to Adriana.

Hemingway stayed in contact with her, inviting her to lunch at Harry's Bar, and, a while later, to dinner at the Gritti Palace with her brother Gianfranco and with Mary. Thirty years her senior, Hemingway became infatuated with Adriana, a fact that did not escape Mary's notice; she wrote in her diary that Adriana and her husband "were busily launching a flirtation."[22] The flirtation quickly escalated in Hemingway's mind; his feelings were aroused by the eagerness and attentiveness of someone so much younger than he, and the fantasy that he could have her took hold of him like an obsession.

Adriana always maintained that their relationship was like that of a teacher to a student, or a father to a daughter—in other words, that they were not lovers. She told Bernice Kert that "he was a much older man, even though there was something of the big child about him. At times I even felt the desire to protect him against himself. But 30 years was for me a lifetime. I never thought of being in love with him. I appreciated his kindnesses and his attention. We were friends. I learned much from him."[23] Hemingway's numerous physical debilities might actually have prevented intimacy. In fact, given his illnesses and other limitations at this point in his life, Hemingway may even have been impotent. But attracting the attention of so famous a person as Hemingway was the most important event in Adriana's life.

With her attention firing his imagination, Hemingway began to think about a story about duck hunting that he had begun on the island of Torcello. This eventually became the framing narrative for the novel *Across the River and into the Trees,* the story of Colonel Richard Cantwell, an army officer who is dying of heart disease, and his affair with a young Italian girl, Renata, who tells him of her family's tragic history at the hands of the Fascists. The attraction between the two characters is powerful and erotic—and clearly a wish-fulfillment fantasy on Hemingway's part: "she had pale almost olive colored skin, a profile that could break your, or anyone else's heart" (80). "The colonel kissed her and felt her wonderful, long, young, lithe and properly built body against his own body, which was hard and good, but beat-up, and as he kissed her he thought of nothing" (109).

For Hemingway, the attraction was not just physical. Hemingway showed Adriana his own emotional vulnerability as they sat on the balcony of the Gritti Palace one night and looked out on the landscape. Hemingway confided his fears and anxieties, his worries and concerns. Tears rolled down his cheeks as he allegedly told Adriana, "I love you in my heart and I cannot do anything about it." Adriana knew that Hemingway "was terribly serious" from the tone of his voice, and she felt paralyzed. "It was like waiting for an avalanche, an avalanche that would break from the mountain at any moment." "I know what you need to be happy," Hemingway said. "I will live to make you happy." But then his voice changed: "I would ask you to marry me, if I didn't know that you would say no."[24] Eventually, the Hemingways returned to Cuba, but once home, Hemingway

209

Mary,

Adriana, and

Across the

River and into

the Trees

wrote a steady stream of letters to Adriana, and Mary wondered when his passion for her would cool.

Hemingway worked steadily on *Across the River* through the summer and early fall, finishing it on a return trip to Europe at the end of the year. He was usually very disciplined about his work. Even after a riotous late night, he was almost always up at six o'clock in the morning, standing at a tall bureau, where he wrote either by hand or on a typewriter. A clipboard stood to one side and on the other was a large piece of cardboard on which he had marked the dates in one column and the number of words generated per day in the column beside it.

The plot of his new novel was simple. Richard Cantwell is dying of a heart ailment and does not have long to live. He travels to Italy to revisit the sites where he felt most alive—the cities and battlefields in which he served during the two world wars. He goes to Venice for a weekend of duck hunting, feasting, and drinking on an aristocrat's estate, where he meets his friend's nineteen-year-old daughter, Renata, who tells him her family's tragic history. As he leaves the estate in his staff car, Cantwell succumbs to his heart condition and dies. Interwoven throughout the story of the three days on the estate are Cantwell's memories—defending the Piave River, the breakthrough in Normandy, the taking of Paris, and the bloody battle for the Hürtgen Forest.

The character of Cantwell was based mostly on Buck Lanham and partially, as Jeffrey Meyers theorizes, on Chink Dorman-Smith, Hemingway's World War I comrade. Cantwell, following orders, throws his brigade into an impossible battle in France, loses an appalling number of men, and is reduced in rank to colonel when the military politicians need a scapegoat. Although he stays in the army, Cantwell becomes embittered toward most of the leading Allied generals: he criticizes Eisenhower, Patton, Philippe Leclerc, and Montgomery, as he tells Renata the story of his World War II experiences. Such commanders subjected him to friendly fire; what the enemy was unable to do, his own compatriots accomplished.

Dorman-Smith had had a similar experience. In 1947, Hemingway was reading *Operation Victory,* by Francis de Guingand, which revealed that Dorman-Smith had been demoted by Field Marshal Montgomery, commander of the British Eighth Army. Dorman-Smith had designed battle plans that Montgomery employed in the second battle of El Alamein and the battle of Alam el Halfa, victories that enabled him to overcome Rommel and his Afrika Korps. Montgomery took credit for Dorman-Smith's good work and then tried to push him aside by busting him in rank. This explains the hostility of Cantwell's remarks about Montgomery in Hemingway's novel. In the Hotel Gritti bar, the colonel orders "two very dry martinis. . . . Montgomerys. Fifteen to one" (82). Cantwell tells Renata, "Monty was a character who needed fifteen to one to move, and then moved tardily." "I always supposed he was a great General," Renata says. "He was not," Cantwell replies. "The worst part was he knew it. I have seen him come into a hotel and change from his proper uniform into a crowd-catching kit to go out in the evening to animate

211

———

Mary,

Adriana, and

Across the

River and into

the Trees

the populace." "But he beat General Rommel," Renata says. "Yes," Cantwell replies. "And you don't think any one else had softened him up?" (125–26). It was Dorman-Smith who "softened him up," of course.[25] A month later, Hemingway sent Dorman-Smith proofs of the novel, and Hemingway reported radiantly to Charles Scribner that his friend had read the manuscript three times and said "it was the best thing I'd written." The two men stayed in touch thereafter, Dorman-Smith being a frequent visitor at Hemingway's home in Cuba.[26]

Cantwell is also based in part on Stonewall Jackson, the best known of Civil War generals after Robert E. Lee. Jackson gained his nickname (and a promotion to major general) by standing like a stone wall against Union troops at the Battle of Bull Run. Ironically, Jackson was felled by friendly fire: approaching a line of his own sentries, he was shot by mistake. Cantwell, too, is a victim of "friendly fire" in being wrongfully demoted because he has not followed the party line; he becomes a scapegoat. The title of Hemingway's novel comes from Stonewall Jackson's suggestion to an aide in the last moments of his life, "Let us cross over the river and rest under the shade of the trees."

Across the River began a pattern that prevailed in the final phase of Hemingway's career: returning to the past, experimenting stylistically, and allowing bitterness to overtake optimism in his view of human progress. In his last years, Hemingway became fond of returning to places from his past, reliving his experiences there, and remaking earlier works into a new series of novels, stories, and journalistic pieces. *Across the River* covers much of the same territory that Hemingway traversed in *A Farewell to Arms*. Hemingway's second African safari, in 1953–54, produced what was published posthumously as *True at First Light*, a book that bears many similarities to *Green Hills of Africa*. *The Dangerous Summer*—an expansion of a series of articles he wrote for *Life* magazine about the bullfights between Antonio Ordóñez and Luis Miguel Dominguín in 1960—concerns the same subject as *Death in the Afternoon* and themes and characters first introduced in *The Sun Also Rises* (Ordóñez was the son of the bullfighter who was the model for Pedro Romero). *A Moveable Feast* carries the reader down the same Paris thoroughfares traveled in Hemingway's first novel. "Chasing yesterdays is a bum show," Hemingway had written after revisiting Fossalta in 1922, but the perspective of age altered that view.[27]

Across the River and into the Trees is, however, strikingly different from *For Whom the Bell Tolls*. While the earlier novel is based primarily on action, *Across the River* dwells almost entirely on memory. Cantwell's memories cover quite a lot of history in which his life experiences and world events intersect. The novel also strikes out into fresh territory stylistically. Hemingway once described his method of storytelling with two metaphors: billiards ("three-cushion shots") and mathematics (calculus, as opposed to geometry or algebra).[28] If the critics did not appreciate his achievement, he thought, it was because they lacked the intelligence or the literary sophistication to follow what he was doing. Hemingway was trying to grow in his craft and experiment with new ways of storytelling.[29]

Cantwell is unlike earlier Hemingway characters in the bitterness that comes through in virtually all of his interactions with others. He is not the stoical hero who is mindful of form, shows no emotion, and realizes that life is an unwinnable game, but a deeply emotional man who is angry about all the injustices he has suffered, past and present. The only exception, of course, is Renata. The Cantwell character foreshadows Hemingway's own deepening bitterness, paranoia, and depression. More sadly, Cantwell's life closely parallels the way in which Hemingway came to live in his own invented world. Cantwell resides in an imagined realm of private jokes and private clubs, of inside knowledge and arcane rituals that are important only to him and his inner circle. He has become increasingly disconnected from the world around him. His acquaintances all have titles and behave according to an elaborate, predetermined code of manners. Ritual exists only for ritual's sake.

Because Hemingway had not published a novel in ten years, there was a good deal of prepublication hype about the new book. A major profile of Hemingway by Lillian Ross appeared in the *New Yorker* in May 1950, just four months before the novel came out. Hemingway said the new book would be a major work and would build to an almost unbearable tension. Sales of the book were huge, but the reviews all had the air of eulogies. Morton Zabel called it feeble and dull in the *Nation,* full of "routine mechanism and contrivance"; Alfred Kazin lamented that such an excellent writer had produced such poor work late in his career and called the book a travesty. Joseph Warren Beach considered the subject too slight to warrant a novel. Northrop Frye remarked that the novel was similar in theme to Thomas Mann's *Death in Venice* but that Hemingway's attempt was amateurish compared to Mann's.[30] The most sympathetic comments came from Evelyn Waugh, who acknowledged Hemingway's technical faults and personal excesses but recognized that the novel was animated by "decent feeling." Waugh observed that in the current critical environment, such a notion was "quite un-forgivable" and that Hemingway had been unduly ridiculed for his "sense of chivalry—respect for women, pity for the weak, love of honour."[31] E. B. White made his review in the *New Yorker* a parody of the book and titled it "Across the Street and into the Grill." The novel was not among Hemingway's best work, but neither did it deserve the contempt that most critics heaped on it. *For Whom the Bell Tolls* had been applauded loudly in part because it was seen as a return to what Hemingway did best, but when no new novel followed that book for ten years, the critics seemed almost glad that the author had supplied them with a mediocre book that they could use to write his epitaph. In all the shrill laughter at Hemingway, however, there was little serious consideration of what he had tried to do with the technique of the book.

Matters were made worse by a clumsy but well-intentioned review by John O'Hara, who had always idolized Hemingway and felt (as he naïvely did with many writers) that they were close friends and like-minded artists. In a claim that has since become infamous, O'Hara, trying to defend Hemingway from his detractors, maintained that Hemingway was the greatest writer since Shake-speare.[32] This irritated Hemingway, who naturally felt that he did not need to be defended. Moreover, it only gave the critics additional fuel for their ridicule. Letters to the editor showed up in major newspapers mocking O'Hara's statement. Cartoons appeared in the media showing Hemingway standing atop a pile of authors' corpses. O'Hara's review, however, was not read carefully; he did not claim that *Across the River* was a great or profound work, or one that would rival the works of Shakespeare or other great masters. He only claimed that Hemingway was a tremendously important writer, which was true, and that as such he deserved respectful attention, even if the book in question was not his best. It was no consolation to Hemingway, but at least it was true.

213

Mary,
Adriana, and
Across the
River and into
the Trees

––––––

The fallout from the novel was significant. The reviews sickened Hemingway, and the Ivanciches also suffered, as salacious rumors swirled about the nature of Hemingway's relationship with Adriana. When the Ivanciches visited Hemingway in Cuba, the press speculated that Hemingway had even asked Adriana to marry him. Mary later denied this, when her memoir *How It Was* appeared; she acknowledged that her husband was fond of Adriana, as he was fond of quite a few young women, but dismissed the rest as nonsense. Hemingway himself took pains to safeguard Adriana's reputation in her native country. He prohibited the novel from being published in Italy for ten years.

Bootleg copies had surfaced in Venice, however, and Adriana was hurt by the implication that she had had a sexual relationship with Hemingway (in one scene in the novel, Renata and Cantwell make love under a blanket in a gondola). The gossip columnist Louella Parsons even reported that Mary and Ernest were breaking up and that Adriana (who was in Italy at the time) was living in sin with Hemingway at the Finca.[33] This was hard for Adriana's mother, Dora, to overlook. Then, in January 1951, on another visit to Finca Vigía, Dora apparently received a letter from one of her friends in Venice that included a newspaper clipping featuring a large picture of Adriana and the caption "Renata, Hemingway's new love." This proved to be too much for Dora to take, and she and her daughter quickly returned home.

Hemingway remained devoted to Adriana, despite their separation. In the remaining ten years of his life, he wrote nearly a hundred letters to her—intimate, confiding letters like the ones he had written to Jane Mason, in which he was painfully honest about his feelings for her. From Nice in 1954, after two plane crashes in Africa in two days had left him with severe internal injuries, he wrote, "I love you more than the moon and the sky and for as long as I shall live. Daughter, how complicated can life become? The two times I died I had only one thought: 'I don't want to die, because I don't want Adriana to be sad.' I have never loved you as much as in the hour of my death."[34] The letters also show his interest in Adriana's well-being, her maturation, and her nascent skills as a writer and artist. He gave her one of his old Royal typewriters and a Rolleiflex camera. Hemingway also persuaded his publishers to use Adriana's drawings for the dust jacket illustrations for *Across the River*.

Hemingway's teacher-student relationship with Adriana also resembled a parent-child relationship. His most common form of address with her, both in person and in correspondence, was "daughter." The nurturing aspect of his personality that (contrary to some perceptions) often surfaced in his relationships with women emerged most fully in his relationship with Adriana. He saw her as the innocent that she was and tried to protect her from the vicissitudes of young life. He was probably remembering his own youthful infatuation—and its painful emotional cost—with Agnes von Kurowsky. And, given the difficult realities of his own fractured family life, Hemingway also was alert to the emotionally debilitating effects on Adriana of her father's death, and to how susceptible she must have been to the charms of a powerful older man.

Adriana tried to bear up under the rumors and the glare of public scrutiny, and she did so for a time, although her later life was unhappy. She was twice jilted by suitors, and then, after Hemingway's suicide in 1961, she married an older Greek man who mistreated her. After divorcing him in 1963, she married a German count, Rudolf von Rex, with whom she had two sons, they lived on a farm at Orbetello, on the coast northwest of Rome. But this marriage, too, turned sour, and Adriana grew deeply depressed, suffered from hypertension and nervous ailments, and drank herself into precarious health. She became increasingly hostile to her family, and then one day in March 1983, she committed suicide by hanging herself from a tree outside her home.

Revisiting the Past

AFRICA AND PARIS

Through all the storm and stress of the Ivanciches' stay at the Finca that winter of 1950–51, however, one benefit did emerge. With Adriana present, Hemingway was inspired to continue writing, despite the negative reviews of *Across the River and into the Trees*. Adriana broke down his defenses; he even stopped drinking when she asked him to. At Finca Vigía, Hemingway would rise in the morning and write, while Adriana would go to the upper story of the tower and work on her drawings. Together they developed a disciplined, productive routine that benefited them both creatively.

Hemingway returned to work on *Islands in the Stream,* which he had laid aside in 1948 to concentrate on the *Garden of Eden* narrative, and then *Across the River.* As he gained momentum with the revision of *Islands,* he found himself thinking about an event that had occurred more than fifteen years earlier. The April 1936 issue of *Esquire* had carried Hemingway's "On the Blue Water," a report on an old fisherman famed for fighting sharks and marlins.[1] As Hemingway told it, "An old man fishing alone . . . hooked a great marlin that . . . pulled the skiff far out to sea. Two days later the old man was picked up by fishermen sixty miles to the eastward with the head and forward part of the marlin lashed alongside. What was left of the fish, less than half, weighed eight hundred pounds. The old man stayed with him a day, a night, a day, and another night while the fish swam deep and pulled the boat. When he had come up the old man had pulled the boat up on him and harpooned him." The fisherman, however, was evidently mentally unstable and was crying uncontrollably when rescued. Hemingway reworked and expanded this piece into what he envisioned as the fourth section of *Islands in the Stream,* although it would end up being a stand-alone work—*The Old Man and the Sea,* one of his most famous novels, an instant classic and winner of the Pulitzer

Prize, and the work that is generally credited with his being awarded the Nobel Prize for Literature in 1954.

By 17 January 1952, Hemingway was six thousand words into this story, and on 6 February he claimed to be producing a thousand words per day. Indeed, he was writing so swiftly that by 17 February he had finished a first draft of 26,531 words. A few months later, however, Hemingway decided that *The Old Man and the Sea* should be published separately as a short novel—a decision that may have been motivated by a desire to strike back quickly at the critics who had panned *Across the River and into the Trees*. Hemingway knew he had a winner in the novella. "It will be nice to win after the shit I had to eat about that last book," Hemingway wrote to Wallace Meyer, who had replaced Max Perkins as his editor at Scribner's. "Tactically, publishing it now will get rid of the school of criticism that I am through as a writer. It will destroy the school of criticism that claims I can write about nothing except myself and my own experiences. . . . I am tired of not publishing anything. Other writers publish short books. But I am supposed to always lay back and come in with War and Peace or Crime and Punishment or be considered a bum."[2]

Hemingway continued to draw top dollar for his work, despite the bad reviews of *Across the River*. The Book of the Month Club guaranteed him a princely $21,000 for the rights to *The Old Man and the Sea* and ordered 153,000 copies. *Life* magazine paid $40,000 for the story, to appear in its September issue under unprecedented circumstances: a single story by Hemingway would take up the entire issue. So high was the level of anticipation among readers that 5.3 million copies of the issue were printed. The magazine came out on 1 September 1952 and sold out within two days. (George Plimpton recalled being in Grand Central Station late at night on 31 August and seeing a crowd of people around the kiosk where the issue was to be displayed.)[3] Scribner's ordered a first printing of fifty thousand copies of the novella that fall, and the book remained on the best-seller list for more than six months.

The Old Man and the Sea tells an inspiring story of epic struggle and resolve, emphasizing what is noble about human character. It also ties man's nature to the natural world that surrounds him, with which he must live in balance and harmony—a concept that Hemingway learned as a young boy and that stayed with him through all his experiences and is clear in much of his writing. Santiago, an old Cuban fisherman modeled in part on Hemingway's friend Gregorio Fuentes, has gone eighty-four days without hooking a fish. His failure is such that the parents of the boy who fishes with him, Manolin, force their son to abandon Santiago and sign on with a more successful fishing crew. Undaunted, Santiago decides the next day to sail his skiff beyond the shallow coastal waters and out into the Gulf Stream. He baits his hooks and drops his lines, and at noon a giant marlin strikes, the largest the old man has ever seen. Santiago has the fish expertly hooked, but he fears that if he lashes a taut line to the boat the fish will snap it, so he drapes the line over his shoulders, ready to give the fish slack if it decides to make a run. For three days the marlin pulls the boat northwest, until Santiago's arms and hands bleed from the abrasions of the fishing line. Finally, the marlin tires, and Santiago, who has gone without food, water, and sleep for three days, is able to pull it in close enough to kill it with a harpoon. Victorious at last, he ties the line to the boat and makes for home. Along the way, however, sharks smell the trail of blood left by the dead fish, and although Santiago is able to kill one and keep some of the others at bay, they are too much for him. The sharks devour the marlin, and when Santiago finally comes ashore at his village, all that remains of the great fish is the skeleton. He chastises himself for going out too far and for sacrificing the fish, but he stumbles into his hut and falls into a deep sleep. The next day, he and Manolin resume their partnership.

One of the main features of the story is its religious symbolism. Santiago (whose name derives from San Diego, or Saint James the Apostle) is a Christ figure. His right hand is strong; his left is useless—perhaps an image of the split in man's nature between the spiritual and the earthly. When he sees the first of the sharks, he cries out in physical agony, "as a man might . . . feeling the nail through his hands and into the wood" (118). He carries the mast of the boat up the hill to his home, stumbling under its heavy burden, just as Jesus carried the cross on which he was killed. Santiago then sleeps for three days, during which he is presumed dead, but, metaphorically, he is resurrected in the end.

A key line in the story—"a man can be destroyed but not defeated"—suggests that Hemingway intended the book as a personal allegory as well. Hemingway, like Santiago, had endured a long dry spell without reward or acclaim and had been derided and ridiculed by the critics. The two tourists who see the skeleton on the beach and mistake it for a shark may represent the reading public, who Hemingway believed did not fully grasp what he was trying to do in *Across the River and into the Trees*. In his Nobel Prize acceptance speech in 1954, Hemingway made an implicit connection between Santiago and himself when he said that the writer's goal was to try to attain something beyond his grasp, and that he accomplishes nothing unless he risks going far beyond his safety zone, where no one can help him if he fails.

The novel also provides continuity between Hemingway's earlier and later work. In such novels as *The Sun Also Rises* and *A Farewell to Arms*, Hemingway was concerned with corruption. In *Across the River* and *The Old Man and the Sea*, he wrote instead about the attempt to remain pure. One could argue that the ultimate purity is found in religious faith and devotion, which may at first seem an unusual topic for Hemingway. In his famous interview with George Plimpton for the *Paris Review*, Hemingway said bluntly that he never discussed religion or politics. But this did not stop him from writing about them.

Hemingway left his conventional religious upbringing behind when he left Oak Park. As he grew older, he fashioned himself as a brooding humanist, unconcerned with the bourgeois pieties of middle America. As a young writer in Europe, he did not convert to Catholicism for social reasons, as many of his friends there did. Some of these friends had superficial "conversion experiences" in Rome, which he regarded as silly fantasies. An early verse, "Neothomist Poem," makes fun of their ersatz epiphanies: "The Lord is my shepherd, I shall not / want him for long." In 1926, he satirized religion in the privately printed playlet *Today Is Friday,* in which the Roman soldiers who oversee the crucifixion of Jesus describe his struggles to climb the hill under the burden of his cross as though describing down-and-out football players who are not playing up to their level of ability. Hemingway's famous story "A Clean, Well-Lighted Place" has the old man cynically replacing the key words of the Lord's Prayer with the Spanish word for nothing, "nada." Another story, "The Light of the World," about prostitutes, takes its title from passages in the Gospels (Matt. 5:13 and John 8:12), and "God Rest You Merry, Gentlemen," about the fanaticism of a young boy who tries to castrate himself in the name of religion, takes its name from the title of a Christmas carol.[4]

Hemingway's thoughts about religion changed, however, when he proposed to Pauline Pfeiffer and was required to convert to Catholicism in order to be married. After being wounded in Fossalta, he had been blessed by an Italian priest. In a letter of January 1926, he told Ernest Walsh, "If I am anything I am a Catholic. Had extreme unction administered to me as such in July 1918 and recovered. So I guess I'm a super-catholic." Hemingway went on to call Catholicism "the most comfortable religion for anyone soldiering." He said that there was "a lot of nonsense about the church" but that he could not "imagine taking any other religion seriously."[5] To prove to the church that he'd been baptized, Hemingway got the equivalent of a religious affidavit from a Florentine priest, Giuseppe Bianchi, in Rapallo, while driving through Italy in March 1927.[6]

While married to Pauline, Hemingway had to follow church teachings about contraception. Both of Hemingway's sons by Pauline, Patrick and Gregory, were christened in the Catholic Church and both attended parochial school. Throughout his marriage to Pauline, Hemingway attended Mass regularly at St. Mary Star of the Sea in Key West. He was also known to wear a scapular regularly, and to make the sign of the cross each time he went swimming. During the Spanish Civil War, Hemingway began to question the wisdom of the Church, since it supported Franco, and in *The Fifth Column,* Philip Rawlings blasphemes Christianity by pretending to bless people with saliva from a cuspidor. In Cuba, however, a Hispanic country, Hemingway continued to maintain his connection to the Church. A frequent visitor to the Finca, Carlos Baker reported, was a Basque priest who had served with the Loyalists and been given a poor parish in Cuba. He came to lunch at the house every Wednesday, leading everyone to think that the Hemingways were "the biggest catholic family in the district," although he and Mary no longer went to church regularly.[7] In his correspondence with Carlos Baker while he was working on *The Old Man and the Sea* and afterward, Hemingway always referred to Jesus as "Our Lord." And although Hemingway committed suicide, he was given a Catholic burial.

Ultimately, though, as Matthew Nickel has commented, Hemingway "aimed to write as truly as he could with the knowledge he had gained about the world and its mysteries."[8] Truth could be approached through language, but never fully pinned down. As Hemingway said in *Death in the Afternoon,* "Mysticism implies a mystery, and there are many mysteries" (54). Given the wide range of his reading and travel, Hemingway was as much a mystic as a true believer.

——

The success of *The Old Man and the Sea* made Hemingway an attractive subject to academic critics and would-be biographers, who had been interested in him for some time but now renewed and increased their attempts to become friendly with him. Hemingway had also recently been the subject of high-profile feature stories by Malcolm Cowley in *Life* and Lillian Ross in the *New Yorker.* Cowley, who interviewed Hemingway at the Finca in 1948, constructed a portrait of the author that emphasized his physical activity—his travels, his skill at shooting and fishing, his agility in the boxing ring. His heroic view of Hemingway was close to how Hemingway saw himself. Hemingway cooperated with Cowley, but after the article, "A Portrait of Mister Papa," appeared in January 1949, he wrote to the editor that it was "a very bad thing for me" that Cowley's article had been published: "there has been too damned much written about my personal life and I am sick of it."[9]

A few months later, in November, Lillian Ross came to the Finca to research a profile of Hemingway for the *New Yorker.* Her essay, "How Do You Like It Now, Gentlemen," which was published in May 1950, was the opposite of Cowley's. Ross argued that Hemingway had succumbed to a life of wealth and luxury that had corrupted his talent—an old theme that Hemingway himself at times believed. Hemingway had apparently boasted to Ross that he would whip Turgenev, de Maupassant, and Stendhal in the boxing ring but was not yet sure he could handle Tolstoy. Such remarks made him sound like a boor and a braggart. Hemingway read the proofs of Ross's article before it went to press, and told Marlene Dietrich that he was "shocked" by how it portrayed him, and that it made him feel "awful." But he would not intervene: "since she was a friend of mine and I knew that she was not writing in malice she had a right to make me seem that way if she wished."[10]

The curious mix of cooperation and contempt that defined Hemingway's interactions with Cowley and Ross seems to have continued as academics began to write about him in scholarly works—in particular, Charles Fenton, an English instructor at Yale, and Philip Young, a professor at New York University. These scholars were mostly interested in Hemingway's outsized life and less in his writing; Hemingway had told Cowley, "I truly think we suffer in our times from an exaggerated emphasis on personality, and I would much rather have my work discussed than the offence of my life. That's why I don't want any biography. Literary, yes. I have written it and stand by it, but unless I check on everything and told you what was true and what was false you would run into all kinds of shit, printed as well as verbal."[11] Academics, Hemingway thought, tended too readily to associate authors with their characters, yet he had been encouraging the public to view him that way for years.

Hemingway had never much cared for college professors. He made the hero of *For Whom the Bell Tolls,* Robert Jordan, an academic at a university in the American West, but that was a tangential detail, derived from his model for the character, Robert Merriman, an economics professor at Berkeley who became an influential figure in the International Brigades in Spain. For most of his life, Hemingway affected an anti-intellectual hostility to academic critics who, he told one friend, could dehumanize a work of literature with their sterile, reductionist overanalysis. He probably also resented what he saw as the academic's coddled life in the ivory tower, removed from the problems of people in the real world. Hemingway had, after all, chosen to work as a journalist and then go to war instead of getting a college education.

Fenton was completing a book on Hemingway's early years as a writer and had been corresponding with many people from Hemingway's time in Oak Park, Toronto, and Kansas City. He had also been soliciting information from Hemingway's sisters, news that, when it reached Hemingway, made him angry. He told Fenton that he would not give him permission to quote from his early writing—work he said was no good and did not want to see reprinted—or to invade his privacy by "go[ing] into my family, etc." He threatened Fenton with legal action and instructed his lawyer, Alfred Rice, to be ready to move against Fenton should the need arise. "Naming actual people with their real names," Hemingway said, "makes it impossible for me to write fiction and by saying that so and so was such and such a real person he exposes me to any amount of libel suits." Further, Hemingway blasted Fenton for forcing him to respond to Fenton's quest for information: "I average between fifty cents and a dollar a word for everything that I write and [then] I write you letters between five hundred and fifteen hundred words long which you in-corporate in material which you sell for 2 1/2 cents a word."[12]

Curiously, however, Hemingway kept up his correspondence with Fenton for almost two years, and in each letter Hemingway let fall bits of information that he had never revealed to anyone else, which Fenton eagerly soaked up for his book. He may have actually been considering Fenton as a candidate for his official biographer, but he decided against him. Fenton's eventual book, *The Apprenticeship of Ernest Hemingway,* was serialized in the *Atlantic Monthly* in the spring of 1954 and was later brought out in book form. But Hemingway did not encourage Fenton further. In 1961, the year he committed suicide, Hemingway was in Saint Mary's Hospital in Rochester, Minnesota, suffering from severe depression, when he learned that Charles Fenton had killed himself by jumping from a hotel window in Durham, North Carolina.[13]

His angry exchanges with Fenton made matters nearly impossible for Philip Young. The professor's book on Hemingway had been accepted by Rinehart pending permission from Hemingway to quote from his works. But Hemingway would not give permission, as he had gotten hold of a paper that Young had read to the Modern Language Association meeting in which he argued that all of Hemingway's fiction was inspired by his wounding in July 1918. To Hemingway, this smacked of amateur psychoanalysis and, worse, confused the fiction with the life. He found it "shocking" that critics "lightly used medical terms without, as far as I [know] being medically qualified to pronounce such judgments even in private."[14] He told Young that "to accuse a man of mental disorder in his lifetime is as serious as to accuse him of physical disorder. You damage him, his wife and his children. You do it gratuitously and without necessity."[15] Writing to Harvey Breit, Hemingway summarized Young's thesis: "P. Young: It's all trauma."[16] Nonetheless, as he had with Cowley, Ross, and Fenton, Hemingway relented and allowed Young to quote from his work, so long as he promised "that the book is not biography disguised as criticism and that it is not a psycho-analytical study of a living writer." He also felt bad for Young, who was just starting out in the profession and trying to support his family on a teacher's salary. Hemingway said he did not want to imperil someone's living and even offered to write him a check as charity. But it is likely that Hemingway knew there was no stopping the biographers and thought he should have as much say in what was written as he could, rather than try to stop people from writing.

What was most curious in all of these exchanges with critics was Hemingway's obvious interest in who would write about him, what they would say, and what he wanted his literary legacy to be. Hemingway was only in his early fifties—still relatively young—but he was clearly negotiating how his posthumous reputation would be defined. Did he not expect to live much longer? He felt creatively drained by his labors on *The Garden of Eden* and *Islands in the Stream* and sometimes said offhandedly that he would publish no more work of any significance.

This reasoning may have been behind the help he offered to Carlos Baker, who would eventually, after Hemingway's death, become his authorized biographer. It was unusual for Baker, an Ivy League–educated professor at Princeton University, to be interested in Hemingway as a scholarly subject. Baker's training was in the English romantic poets, and his previous book was on Percy Bysshe Shelley. Nonetheless, Baker contacted Hemingway in early 1951 requesting permission to quote from his works for a study to be called *Hemingway: The Writer as Artist*. Hemingway took Baker to mean that the book was a biography, and he immediately balked, using the arguments he had earlier used with Fenton and Young. Baker replied that Hemingway had misunderstood him, that the work would be focused "directly and analytically" on Hemingway's writing. Hemingway, in turn, told Baker that he never wanted anyone to write about his father's suicide:

This is the best story I never wrote. Then comes Pauline moving in on Hadley; which I would never write. Then comes, in a true story, coitus interruptus, with Pauline after the two Caesarians because the doctor said you could not have another and birth control barred. Then Martha moving in on Pauline. Then lots of stuff I don't want to remember and whores and nice girls and whores until I run into Mary. Can you see why I do not want dates and hotel registers, etc.?[17]

Having received permission, Baker published his study in October 1952. Thereafter, he maintained a friendly and fruitful correspondence with Hemingway. Baker flattered Hemingway in his letters, especially with an analysis of *Across the River,* which Baker compared to Thomas Mann's *Death in Venice.* Hemingway must have liked Baker's comments, because he sent him the typescript of *The Old Man and the Sea* and asked for his opinion. Baker read the story twice and responded within two days, sending him a positive critique and querying him on a few minor points. Baker also enclosed a copy of a recent piece he had published in the *New York Times,* an appreciation of *The Sun Also Rises* on the occasion of the twenty-fifth anniversary of its publication. Hemingway continued to correspond with Baker, eventually addressing him as Carlos, keeping him up to date on his medical conditions, and chatting informally about what was going on in his life.

Hemingway may have been happy to have a sympathetic ear, especially after the loss of such intimates as Max Perkins and, on 11 February 1952, Charles Scribner. Less than a year earlier, in June 1951, his mother had died, after falling and injuring her head while in Oak Park Hospital, at the age of seventy-nine. He had supported Grace financially for many years, but Hemingway still blamed her for his father's suicide and had kept his distance ever since the Paris days. Hemingway repeated the old charges against her when he talked with friends about her passing—that she had spent his college money on herself, that she had ruined his father, and that she had refused to take financial advice and wasted her inheritance. He did not attend her funeral, but he must have grieved her loss.

More traumatic than the death of his mother and two friends, however, was the sudden trouble in which his youngest son, Gregory, became involved in California—events that Hemingway would claim caused the death of Gregory's mother, Pauline. In 1950, Greg had begun his freshman year at St. John's College in Annapolis, Maryland. Unmotivated, however, he dropped out after only one semester. He then began experimenting with drugs and was briefly involved in studying Dianetics, the pseudoscience popularized by pulp fiction writer L. Ron Hubbard, which would eventually evolve into the Church of Scientology. In early 1951 (when Adriana Ivancich was staying at the Finca), Greg brought his girlfriend, Jane Rhodes, home to meet his father. Hemingway took an immediate dislike to her and began insulting her in front of the family and guests. He also boasted—again, in front of everyone—of breaking up his son's relationship with his previous girlfriend.

Greg then moved to California and worked briefly as an aircraft mechanic. Against his father's wishes, he became engaged to Jane, cabling his father about his intentions. Hemingway, furious, tried to reach Pauline by phone in Los Angeles, but apparently did not have the correct number. He then cabled Greg that he did not give permission, but Greg married Jane anyway. In September 1951, Greg was arrested in Los Angeles for entering a women's restroom at a movie theater dressed as a woman. Pauline was extremely distressed and tried to cover up the incident, doing her best to keep the Hemingway name out of the papers. But word leaked out, and on 30 September she called her ex-husband in Cuba. The ensuing argument was loud and bitter. "See how you've brought him up!" Hemingway shouted. Pauline shouted back at him and then started crying uncontrollably. Both slammed the phone down. Eight hours later, at about 1:00 a.m., Pauline woke up with severe abdominal pain. Rushed to the hospital, she was found to be bleeding internally. The doctors operated, but she died on the table.

In an autopsy, it was discovered that Pauline had a rare tumor on one of her adrenal glands. Hemingway's furious lashing out at her about Greg may have caused a surge of adrenalin, the shock of which could have contributed to her sudden death. Hemingway at least tacitly accepted responsibility for what had happened; he must have been consumed with guilt. He vacillated between rage and inconsolable worry, writing to his friend Marlene Dietrich, "as divorced and [with] the children in her custody, I have no authority to do a hell of a lot of things I should do to safe guard the children's interests."[18]

Angry with himself, Hemingway tried to pin the blame on his son. He told Greg that his troubles in California had killed Pauline, although Greg wisely did not take the bait; he said later that it was Hemingway's brutal phone conversation with Pauline that had upset her and made the gland malfunction. Depressed, Greg left to live in Africa, where he drank too much and hunted with a fury, as if he had something to prove. In one month, he shot a total of eighteen elephants—a strangely impressive achievement by any standard, and one of which his father must have been ironically proud.

____

Unable to push through on the sea book or *The Garden of Eden,* Hemingway began again to revisit his past, as he done in writing *Across the River* after his trip to Venice with Mary. He returned to Spain and to Africa, both places that had served as a balm to the anxieties in his personal life and had also led to two very good works of nonfiction. On 24 June 1953, Hemingway and Mary sailed for Spain by way of France. After a brief stay in Paris, they spent six weeks in Pamplona, Madrid, Valencia, and then Paris again. Hemingway wanted to gather material for a projected "appendix" to a new edition of *Death in the Afternoon,* an update on the art of the corrida with new material on emerging figures in the sport. He must have felt unsettled, a Republican supporter entering Franco's country, and probably half-expected armed guards to greet him at the airport. When there was no unfriendly reception, he concluded that "they would not harm Mary who had never been there and it was [too] late to shoot me."[19]

As he wandered through Spain, he was struck by the staying power of public interest in bullfighting and became convinced that there was plenty of material for a new book on the subject, a sequel to *Death in the Afternoon*. Gathering new material became his mission, as he picked up his usual crowd of followers and friends in Pamplona and returned to the scene of his first triumph, *The Sun Also Rises*, for the Fiesta of San Fermín. The mood, however, was vastly different than it had been those many years ago. Pamplona had none of the galvanizing energy he had felt as a young American expatriate discovering European culture for the first time. The town had become a tourist destination (thanks, ironically, to *The Sun Also Rises*), the bullfight just another stop on a sightseeing tour. It was a place he had helped make famous, but Hemingway could barely find a decent hotel room.

In Pamplona, Hemingway saw Niño de la Palma's son, Antonio Ordóñez, perform as a matador, and he became a devoted Ordóñez fan. After the fiesta, he and Mary traveled to Burgos and Madrid, making detours to Sepulveda, Segovia, and San Ildefonso. On his birthday, 21 July, Hemingway revisited the Prado, built in 1785 by King Charles III of Spain, who wanted to put his country on an equal cultural footing with the other great capitals of Europe. Later, he and Mary visited Ordóñez and his brother-in-law, Luis Miguel Dominguín, at Villa Paz ranch near Saelices. From there they traveled to Valencia to see more bullfights before returning to Paris to pick up their luggage and leave for a five-month safari, departing Marseilles on 6 August and landing at Mombasa, Kenya, at the end of the month. They were met by Philip Percival, then in his late sixties, who had come out of retirement to lead Hemingway's group.

The trip was well publicized, although, ironically, one of Hemingway's motives in taking it was to escape the pressures at home: his family concerns, health worries, visibility as a public figure and professional author, inability to complete the sea book or *The Garden of Eden,* and the pestering of academic critics who were trying to interview him for their studies. We must remember how difficult it was for him to be "Ernest Hemingway"—how the author must have come to feel that everyone wanted something from him, yet he rarely knew exactly what that was. The reviewers had at first chastised him for departing from his trademark style, for the self-indulgences of writing about himself (in *Death in the Afternoon,* in the *Esquire* articles, in *Green Hills of Africa*), and then for not writing at all. Africa was a place far removed from the demands of professional authorship. He could avoid the problems associated with celebrity, hide from the professors, and be something other than an icon. Tribalization and racial differentiation were new territory for him, and he was thrilled by the prospect of being someone different (he would even go native on the trip and "wed" a Wakondah woman).[20]

Despite his quest for privacy, however, Hemingway was earning a good bit of money from the trip and thus had plenty of company. To document the safari—and to compete with *Life,* which had earlier run *The Old Man and the Sea—Look* magazine sent along a photographer, Earl Theisen, who took many photographs of the writer and the landscape. At one point, an editor from *Look* arrived to keep an eye on the progress. Mario Menocal, Hemingway's Cuban friend, also accompanied them on the trip. Finally, there was Percival's assistant, Roy Home, a somewhat dodgy character who had spent time in prison after shooting his wife when he caught her in bed with another man.

Hemingway commanded very large fees for his work from the trip: $15,000 for a slight commentary, "Safari," to appear with Theisen's photographs, $10,000 for a thirty-five-hundred-word travel article, and $20,000 for an autobiographical essay, "The Christmas Gift." The magazine was particularly keen on having a picture of Hemingway with one of his trophies, and problems arose when Hemingway could not land a big enough specimen. This was not necessarily because Hemingway was no longer as good a shot as he had been in 1933, though that may have been part of it. He was simply not as interested in killing and collecting trophies as he had once been. He was more interested in studying the animals, learning their habits and habitats, and in watching the birds. He was content simply to explore and observe.

This put Theisen in a dilemma, as he had to return home to his bosses with a "classic" Hemingway image. There is a famous photo from the trip of the white-bearded author, cross-legged and relaxed, sitting behind the inert body of a beautiful leopard and staring off into the middle distance, but it quickly became known that the picture had been staged—Hemingway had not shot the animal, although the photograph implied that he had. In fact, Hemingway and Menocal were walking to the bait tree when they spotted the leopard, but Menocal fired first and killed it. Theisen persuaded Hemingway to pose with it for the publicity photo. Even the usually loyal and quiescent Mary made a moral issue of it, however, as she recalled in her autobiography: "'It's wrong,' I contended. 'All right,' Hemingway responded. 'I'll get a leopard to salve your conscience, then.'" Hemingway thus connived with his adulators as well as with himself.[21]

In October, Hemingway was on his way to see his son Patrick in Tanganyika when he fell out of a Land Rover that had swung out on a sharp curve. He cut his face and sprained his shoulder badly, but was still able to make the trip. After Pauline's death, Patrick had bought a twenty-three-hundred-acre farm at Sao Hill with his inheritance; he loved Africa as much as his father did.[22]

In Kenya, Hemingway's group had been given permission to shoot in two areas: on the banks of the Salengai River and near the Kimana River and swamp. Hemingway was made an honorary game warden for the region by the Kenyan government, which was eager for the Hemingway party to be there and happy about the attendant publicity; there had been a violent uprising among the Mau Mau, a militant African nationalist movement, beginning in 1952 that attracted unfavorable press coverage. Hemingway and his group were relatively safe, but they also had to take precautions against a rumored attack on the Salengai camp by a group of Wakamba tribesmen who had sworn an oath to the Mau Mau. While there, Hemingway bagged a lion—the one trophy he really desired. It was not a clean killing; it took him and a guide half an hour to track the wounded animal, and then it was the guide, not Hemingway, who brought it down. But he had what he wanted. Watching the animal being skinned, Hemingway bent down, took out his pocketknife, and cut out a bit of the tenderloin along the spine. He chewed some and pronounced it delicious.

They struck camp in mid-September and drove east into the Tsavo region, home to the Waliangulu tribe, the greatest elephant hunters in Africa and the most adept at tracking. The famously warlike Maasai also lived there. But by 1953, in Hemingway's view, the Maasai had lost their fierceness: he sadly recorded seeing a group retreat in fear when faced with a cattle-killing lion. In *Under Kilimanjaro,* he called them a "syphilis-ridden, anthropological . . . curiosity" (230).

Hemingway's behavior during this trip became increasingly bizarre. Age and drink had much to do with his physical deterioration, but his mental state was also in steep decline. He seemed to have lost confidence in himself; he was a changed man. Mary withstood ever more abusive behavior, which swelled and crested on the waves of Hemingway's by now typically abrupt mood swings. She never knew, from one hour to the next, his state of mind.

At one point, Hemingway decided to go native. He dyed his clothes the rusty-brown color of the Maasai, shaved his head, and began hunting with a spear. As he tells it in his "African Journal," a two-hundred-thousand-word text published after his death, he also began courting a native named Debba, whom he apparently seriously intended to take as a second wife. Well aware of the effect his erratic actions were having on Mary, Hemingway seemed to accept his own mental instability: "she just stays the hell away from it and is understanding and wonderful."[23]

In January 1954, Hemingway's characteristic bad luck struck once again when he was nearly killed in not one but two plane crashes. Although only fifty-five years old, Hemingway had aged rapidly. He had subjected his body to much physical and mental abuse and was no longer able to recover easily from such injuries. Like his wounding in Italy in 1918, this run of physical misfortune was a turning point in his life. Already suffering from paranoia, delusions, emotional instability, and general physical infirmity, the injuries from the plane crashes, particularly to his head, had permanent effects. Hemingway was never the same again.

The Hemingways had been "hedge-hopping"—making low-flying excursions over the plains so that they could observe the wildlife. They were piloted by Roy Marsh, whom Mary described as "a cheery spic and span young man who flew charter flights out of Nairobi in small planes."[24] Hemingway was initially nervous about flying so low, but he soon got caught up in Mary's enthusiasm and forgot the danger. On 21 January, they took off in a blue and silver single-engine Cessna, skimming over the lakes and often coming close to bumping into hippos, buffaloes, and elephants who had come to the shore to bathe and drink. They headed north to Entebbe and then over marshland along the Victoria Nile before reaching the Upper Nile near Murchison Falls.

Mary wanted to get photographs, so Marsh angled the plane for a better shot, circling over the cliffs and cascading falls. All of a sudden, he had to dive at low altitude to avoid hitting a flock of ibises—black and white jungle birds big enough to pose a threat to the plane. As he swerved, he ripped into an almost invisible telegraph wire, which tore the rudder and radio antenna. "There was the usual sound of rending metal," Hemingway wrote in "The Christmas Gift," the autobiographical article for *Look* magazine that was published in the April–May 1954 issue, and the Cessna rapidly lost altitude and had to make an emergency landing. The options were to land on a sandpit where crocodiles lay basking in the sun, or on an elephant track through thick scrub. The pilot chose the scrub and "plopped right into" it, landing the plane in thick brush with minor damage. However, so much vegetation "made it impossible to discover any signs of human life nearby," and with no radio and surrounded by dangerous animals in the night, the scene was frightening. The trio had to set up backfires to protect themselves and the plane, and at twilight they were forced to move back from the banks of the Nile in order to avoid the swarms of mosquitoes that had descended with the darkness. They spent the night around a campfire surrounded by an elephant herd.[25]

A search plane was sent out to rescue them, but the deafening roar of the falls obliterated the drone of the plane's engine; they neither saw nor heard it. The pilot of the rescue plane saw the wreckage and reported them dead. In the morning, however, they were spotted by a passing sightseeing boat and taken to Butiaba on Lake Albert.

Not forty-eight hours later, they were on a de Havilland airplane headed for Entebbe when, just after takeoff, the plane ground-looped into a sisal plantation, took a nosedive to the ground, and instantly caught fire. The pilot, Reginald Cartwright, and Mary were able to squeeze through a cabin window, but Hemingway was too large to do so. Moments before the fuel tank burst into flames, Hemingway butted open the rear door with his head and scrambled out. In seconds, the plane was a bonfire, their cameras, money, and passports destroyed.

The injuries from the second crash were even more serious than those sustained in the first. Hemingway sprained his right shoulder, right arm, and left leg, had yet another grave concussion, temporarily lost vision in his left eye and the hearing in his left ear, and suffered paralysis of the spine, a crushed vertebra, a ruptured liver, spleen, and kidney, and first-degree burns on his face, arms, and leg. His most embarrassing injury was paralysis of the sphincter, which forced him to defecate standing up for more than five months. Did any other American writer live with so many difficult, painful, and extraordinary ailments? Admitted to the hospital in Masindi, Uganda, Hemingway was at first thought to be holding up pretty well, but when he awoke the next morning, his pillow was drenched with fluid from his brain.

Some American newspapers mistakenly published his obituary when the search plane reported that there were no survivors. The headline in the 25 January *New York Herald* read, "Hemingway, Wife Killed in Plane Crash," thus giving Hemingway the macabre pleasure of reading his obituary while still very much alive. Always fascinated by mortality, he got more than a small thrill from this turn of events. He collected all the obituaries and preserved them in two scrapbooks, bound in zebra hide and lion skin. He read and reread the obituaries obsessively, day and night. His lamplight bothering Mary, he would get up from bed and go into the bathroom to pore over the accounts with fascination and awe, long into the night. A statement that appeared in many of the obituaries—that he had sought death all his life—he found particularly interesting. "Can one imagine that if a man sought death all of his life," Hemingway asked rhetorically, "he could not have found her before the age of 54?"[26]

Hemingway's brushes with death in Africa, however, did not end with the spectacular second plane crash. In February, he was fishing in the Kenyan village of Shimoni, south of Mombasa on the Indian Ocean. A brush fire broke out, and Hemingway rushed into the woods to help fight it. He fell down, caught fire himself, and suffered second- and third-degree burns—on top of the first-degree burns, still healing, from the plane crash. When doctors in Venice took the toll of the damage in March, he had lost twenty pounds. His speech was slow and hesitant, his hair white, and his movements slow and shaky. His eyesight was worse, and skin ailments bothered him. He seemed to have shrunk into himself, both physically and mentally.

When Adriana Ivancich received word that the Hemingways were in Venice, she implored her mother to allow her to visit them. Her mother consented, reasoning that it was better to give her permission than to have Adriana sneak out and see Hemingway on the sly. Hemingway was overjoyed to see Adriana, wrapping her in a big bear hug when she entered his room. He repeated that he loved her and held back tears, apologizing for the emotional upset that *Across the River* had caused her. "I'm sorry about the book," he said. "You are the last person I would have done any harm to. You are not the girl in the book . . . and I am not the colonel that died in the car that went on the road from Codroipo to Latisana."[27] He tried to tell her how to steel herself against the gossip but conceded in the end that it would probably have been better had they never met.

Finally back in Cuba in June 1954, Hemingway began work on his "African Journal" the following month, though there is little mention of this work in his extant correspondence. In one letter, however, to Robert Morgan Brown, a faculty member at Fordham University who wanted to write his doctoral dissertation on the religious structure of Hemingway's fiction, Hemingway did reveal that "the story is so rough and I am trying to write it so delicately that it is quite difficult."[28] One characteristic of this book is his attempt to blend fiction and nonfiction. This narrative strategy attempted to create the most truthful depiction of human experience—something that was, in his famous phrase, "truer than true." He also had to put the manuscript aside for at least two periods, the first when he learned that he had won the Nobel Prize for Literature in October 1954 and the public clamored for his attention, and then again in the spring of 1956, when he flew to Peru to be on hand for the filming of *The Old Man and the Sea*.

By 10 February 1956, Hemingway had completed 856 manuscript pages of the
"African Journal." From that point onward, however, he apparently made no attempt to write more of the book. He even later believed that it had been lost during the Cuban revolution, but when Mary went back to retrieve their belongings
in August 1961, she found it, wrapped in cellophane and apparently untouched
since February 1956. Hemingway evidently could not arrive at a satisfactory ending for the book—the same difficulty he had had in trying to write *Islands* and
The Garden of Eden. Perhaps for that reason—and in spite of the peril in which he
had placed himself on the previous trip—Hemingway and Mary had planned to
go on a third African safari, in August 1956, this time with Patrick. Hemingway
hoped he would be able to check details and descriptions in the manuscript and
perhaps find some way to close the story. But political disruption over the closing of the Suez Canal in Egypt quashed plans for a third African trip, and the
manuscript remained in a state that never completely satisfied Hemingway.

The manuscript contains many good passages, among them a description of
the hunt for a particular leopard that had been condemned to die by the game
department for killing sixteen goats. Hemingway spots the leopard in a tree and
shoots, knocking it off the branch and onto the ground; it lurches off into the
bush. Hemingway and his party follow the leopard's blood. Ngui, a guide, at one
point reaches down and picks up something out of the bloody trail—it is a part
of the animal's shoulder blade. Hemingway takes it and puts it in his mouth: "I
did it without thinking. But it linked us closer to the leopard and I bit on it and
tasted the new blood which tasted about like my own, and knew that the leopard
had not just lost his balance" (326–27). Eventually, the animal gives its position
away and is killed. But very little in the journal comes close to the quality of the
writing in *Green Hills of Africa*. What is noticeable about the later narrative is its
nostalgic—in places even elegiac—tone. Hemingway was searching for a corridor
into his past, a path that would lead him to happier memories. He would eventually achieve this in *A Moveable Feast,* his account of his years in Paris.

Under the title "African Journal," portions of the manuscript appeared in
three issues of *Sports Illustrated* in late 1971 and early 1972. Almost thirty years later,
the narrative appeared as a book-length work in two very different editions. In
1999, the centennial of Hemingway's birth, his son Patrick published his version
of the narrative under the title *True at First Light: A Fictional Memoir* (Scribner).
Patrick Hemingway's edition is about half the length of the original unfinished
manuscript. In 2005, through an agreement with the Hemingway family that
the work should also be made available in fuller form for the benefit of scholars
and other interested readers, Kent State University Press brought out *Under Kilimanjaro,* edited by veteran Hemingway scholars Robert W. Lewis and Robert E.
Fleming. Their edition is a transcription of the latest stage of Hemingway's draft,
and thus put a wealth of material in print (unlike the unpublished portions of
The Garden of Eden, which are still available to readers only in the Hemingway
Collection at the Kennedy Library).

The numerous injuries Hemingway had received in Africa did nothing to ease his dependence on alcohol. In fact, he began drinking even more heavily in order to ease his aches and pains. Patrick estimated that in the last part of his life, his father was drinking the equivalent of a quart a whiskey a day, plus beer or wine at lunch and dinner. Without drink, one acquaintance remarked, Hemingway was less companionable and merry, more depressed and morose. He had once been a "good" drinker who could hold his liquor and not have his thinking impaired. He was now a depressed alcoholic who needed drink to distract him from his problems and keep him relatively happy.

His physical deterioration was remarkable. His movements were slow, his speech slurred; he complained of double vision and an inability to concentrate; his blood pressure was alarmingly high, his hair snow white. He gained weight from lack of exercise and overconsumption of drink; he suffered back pain from the plane wrecks. He appeared a good fifteen years older than he was, and depression seeped into him like water into rotting wood.

But tremendous news arrived one evening at the Finca while Hemingway was visiting with friends in the living room. It was 28 October 1954, and Hemingway heard on the radio that he had won the Nobel Prize for Literature. The next day, Mary threw a party at the house and invited the staff and all their acquaintances. The award, with its munificent cash payment of $35,000, added to Hemingway's already overflowing coffers, and he beamed with pride upon acknowledging it. Things turned festive very quickly when an interviewer from Cuban television came out to the house with a camera crew and asked Hemingway about the prize. Hemingway's reply, given in halting Spanish, praised Cuba and the Cuban people for their influence on his art.

> First, I've experienced a feeling of happiness, then a bit more joy and then even more. I am very happy to be the first Cuban to have won this prize and happy because authorities have said that it was based on a Cuban landscape, which is Cojimar, more or less my town. . . . I believe it's an influence in the sense of getting to understand the sea. We who love the sea call it "la mar" but it is the same. But when there is a cold front, the word "sea" is used in the feminine sometimes. But the sea is the great influence in my life and in what I have tried to do in literature, and above all the sea on the north coast of Cuba, where there are such noble people . . . nobler than the one I tried to describe in *The Old Man and the Sea*. The state of Cojimar . . . is a very serious thing.[29]

Hemingway's elation at winning the Nobel Prize, however, was short-lived, owing to his excruciating physical pain and depression. Pleading poor health, he declined the invitation to go to Stockholm, but he wrote an insightful speech, which was read by the American ambassador to Sweden at the formal ceremony.

"Writing," Hemingway said, "at its best, is a lonely life. Organizations for writers palliate the writer's loneliness but I doubt if they improve his writing." The remarks threw his own insecurities and lack of confidence into somber relief and foreshadowed his deterioration in the years to come. "He grows in public stature as he sheds his loneliness and often his work deteriorates. For he does his work alone and if he is a good enough writer he must face eternity, or the lack of it, each day." "There's fame," noted the novelist Norman Lewis, who met Hemingway in Cuba shortly after the award was announced: "Saddest man I ever met."[30] Hemingway dedicated the gold medallion he received to the fishermen of Cojimar and gave it to the Cuban government, which kept it at the shrine of the Virgin of Cobre—the patron saint of Cuba.

Hemingway's separation from Adriana, his inability to finish the African book, and a severe kidney infection that left him bedridden for nearly two months in late 1955 and early 1956 conspired to compound his creative struggles. With no luck on the African narrative, Hemingway thought he could perhaps finish *The Garden of Eden*. A third and final period of work on that book took place from late 1957 through early March 1959. But, once again, Hemingway could not push through with the story. He apparently laid the manuscript aside at this point, unable to polish it to his satisfaction, and never returned to it.[31]

Why could he not complete the book? One answer is the bizarre newness of the material and its relation to his own personal and professional identity. Given the novel's concern with gender reversals, it may be that Hemingway could not bring himself to make the book public, as it would show him to be something other than the trademarked code hero—long oversold to his reading public by then—and would bring to light his long struggle with his own androgynous inclinations.[32] Hemingway's ideas about twinning and the sharing and exchange of identities can be seen in his letters to Adriana Ivancich, whom he never "got over." Hemingway often addressed her as "Adriana Hemingway" and signed himself "Ernest Ivancich." Further, as Rose Marie Burwell points out, in the early manuscript pages of *Across the River and into the Trees,* Renata is named "Nicola," an avatar of Hemingway's early self in its reference to a female incarnation of Nick Adams.[33]

Hemingway was intrigued by the idea of lesbianism. Both Hadley and Pauline had apparently had lesbian encounters, and perhaps his mother as well. Hemingway had been exposed to numerous homosexual relationships during his years in Paris and elsewhere; and we know that the hair fetish in the novel has an analogue in Hemingway's desires that his wives cut and/or bleach or dye their hair in accordance with his wishes at the time. In what was a shocking gesture, even in his own eyes, while writing *Islands / The Garden of Eden* in May 1947, Hemingway impulsively dyed his hair a bright copper color while his third wife, Martha Gellhorn, was traveling, then explained it away by saying he picked up the wrong bottle, thinking it was shampoo.[34]

But the most painful reason for Hemingway's interest in alternative sexual identities may have been his relationship with Gregory, who from a young age had experienced gender dysphoria and had experimented with cross-dressing. The types of gender games that Hemingway conceptualized in *The Garden of Eden* came very close to Greg's real life, and Hemingway, who at this point in his career was ever more concerned about privacy, would not have wanted these concepts to be associated with his son. Gregory's life began to follow a trajectory that would create a sad cycle of constant critique, injury, recrimination, and contrition with his father that carried him through a largely unhappy existence. Apart from one visit to Finca Vigía with his new wife, about six months after Pauline's death, Greg rarely saw his father again.

For a while, Greg retreated to Africa, where he tried to become an apprentice professional hunter, but he drank so heavily that he could not obtain his license. He then did a stint in the army in the 1950s, but depression forced him out and into institutionalized treatments for depression, culminating in his receiving at least a dozen electroshock treatments (as his father would soon do as well).[35] He eventually resumed his medical studies, graduating from the University of Miami Medical School. He practiced medicine for a while in New York and then took a job as a family physician in rural Montana, where he lived in the 1980s. He continued his cross-dressing, presenting in public as a man but living his private life as a woman. By the early 1990s, Greg's finances were so precarious—he was routinely spending every dime of the monthly checks he received from the family estate—that at one point he lived in his car, a beat-up Volkswagen. Apparently considering gender-reassignment surgery, he went so far as to have a single breast implant, leaving the other side of his chest flat.

Like his father, Greg was to marry four times. His third wife, an Irish woman born in Dublin in 1940 named Valerie Danby-Smith, was for a while his father's secretary in Cuba. After he and Valerie divorced in 1989, Greg moved to Coconut Grove, near Miami, a bohemian enclave where he made many friendships and was well known at the local bars. But, like his father, his mood swings were abrupt and could be dangerous. He was usually compassionate and kind, and he cared about what people thought of him, yet in his manic or euphoric state he could be reckless and violent. His life unraveled, and he always blamed his father for the mess he was in. When Hemingway biographer Jeffrey Meyers visited him in Montana in the early 1980s, Greg purportedly tried to kill them both by driving at dangerously high speeds.[36]

"I don't know how it was done, the destruction," Greg said in a 1987 interview in the *Washington Post*. "What is it about a loving, dominating, basically well-intentioned father that makes you end up going nuts?" He spoke in this interview about the pressures of trying to live up to his father's expectations. "Yes, I had the most talent. I was the brightest, I could do so many of the things he loved most," he said. He also said his father knew about his cross-dressing. "I've spent hundreds of thousands of dollars trying not to be a transvestite. It's a combination of things. . . . First you've got this father who's supermasculine, but who's somehow protesting it all the time, he's worried to death about it."[37]

The first two sentences of his 1976 book, *Papa: A Personal Memoir,* read: "I never got over a sense of responsibility for my father's death. And the recollection of it sometimes made me act in strange ways."

Whether or not it was a public slap at his father's hypermasculinity, Greg sometimes seemed more interested in creating a spectacle than in completing a process of sincere self-transformation. Perhaps the most dramatic example of this ambivalence occurred in 1995, when Greg, then sixty-four, boarded a Miami city bus, made a series of sexual advances toward the male driver, and then threatened to break his jaw. When police arrived, Hemingway was standing outside a gas station, dressed in women's clothing and talking incoherently. Pulling up his skirt, he said to one of the officers, "Let me show you that I'm a woman." The police officer reminded him he was in public and told him to put down his skirt. Hemingway responded by kicking the officer in the groin; it took three men to handcuff him. He pleaded guilty to a felony charge of battery on a police officer but was never convicted.

On the evening of 26 September 2001, Greg went to a cocktail party at a neighbor's house in Coconut Grove, appearing, for the first time in front of friends, as a woman. He introduced himself as "Vanessa" and seemed happy and agreeable. He was dressed in a black cocktail dress and high-heeled pumps. But at about four o'clock the following afternoon, he was seen walking down a street in Key Biscayne in the nude. A pedestrian phoned the police, and when the officer arrived, she found Gregory incoherent—apparently intoxicated—and struggling to put on a woman's thong. He was arrested on charges of indecent exposure and taken to the Miami-Dade Women's Detention Center, where he was jailed on a $1,000 bond. Gregory could have called any number of friends to come down and post the $100 (10 percent of the bond) it would have taken to get him released, but he did not. His daughter, Lorian, who sympathized with his problems, said that she did not bail her father out because she thought he needed help. Gregory remained in cell 3-C2, on a floor reserved for high-profile inmates, for four nights. On the morning of 1 October (exactly fifty years to the day after his mother's death in Los Angeles), he rose early and dressed for his court appearance, but moments later a guard found him collapsed in a heap on the concrete floor. He died from a combination of hypertension and cardiovascular problems and was buried in the town cemetery in Ketchum, Idaho, next to his father.

In *The Garden of Eden,* Hemingway had written, "When you start to live outside yourself, it's all dangerous" (54). It is possible, perhaps even likely, that Hemingway had his son in mind when he wrote these words. He had once said that Greg had "the biggest dark side" of anyone in his family "except me." In his memoir of his father, Gregory had written, "What I really wanted to be was a Hemingway hero."[38] Perhaps in some ironic way, he really was.

———

Because international disputes prevented Hemingway from returning to Africa for a third safari in 1956, he and Mary ended up spending two months watching the end-of-the-season bullfights in northern Spain. In their leisure time, they hunted partridge, walked in the pine-scented forests, read, and rested. They left Madrid on 17 November and drove an overloaded Lancia toward France. They followed the back roads, thick with sycamores, poplars, red oaks, and rusty beeches in an array of colors. When they reached Paris, they checked into the Ritz Hotel and were assigned suite 56, with a tiny sitting room and a smoky fireplace. The manager told Hemingway that some trunks belonging to him from the 1920s were still stored in the hotel's basement. Hemingway asked to have them brought up to the room. They were two small, fabric-covered rectangular boxes, both opening at the seams. The baggage carriers pried open the rusty locks to reveal the remains of Hemingway's early adulthood: blue and yellow notebooks and sheaves of typed papers, ancient newspaper cuttings, bad watercolors done by old friends, and a pair of withered sandals.

Once, a few years earlier in Paris, Hemingway had been sharing a meal with George Plimpton, who was then starting up a new publication called the *Paris Review*. Plimpton was keenly interested in Hemingway's early years in Paris and suggested that they take a walk around the city and visit the places associated with Hemingway's time there in the 1920s: the sawmill apartment, the Café des Deux Magots, and so on. When they stopped at each place, Plimpton suggested, Hemingway could say a little about the figures he remembered from that time: Ezra Pound, Gertrude Stein, and others. "That's the damn silliest idea I ever heard of," Hemingway responded. He had no interest, he claimed, in the past.

But in his melancholy cast of mind in the late 1950s, he relished the idea of reliving his youth. When he pulled the pages from the trunks, he smiled at Mary. "It's wonderful," he told her.[39] The trunk contained written sketches of Fitzgerald, Pound, and other Paris compatriots. Delighted by the discovery, Hemingway went up the Champs-Élysées to the luggage shop of Louis Vuitton and spent a month's income on new bags. He and Mary then sat on the floor of the hotel room and transferred all of the papers into the new luggage.

In retrospect, the Ritz Hotel papers were probably more of a catalyst than an actual base text from which Hemingway began to work. The remembrance of things past is a strong motive for writing, but a stronger one was probably the persistence of those academic critics who were still pestering Hemingway for permission to record his life. Writing the memoir was probably Hemingway's way of telling his own story in the manner he chose and not leaving it to others to muck up, as he felt Young and Fenton had done.

At the same time that he took up the sketches that would become *A Moveable Feast,* he was also trying to revise *The Garden of Eden.* These two texts intersect in the same manner in which *Islands in the Stream* and *The Garden of Eden* occasionally intersect. Both are portraits of the artist and are concerned with personal and professional identity; wives lose (or destroy) their husband's manuscripts in both; and writing figures prominently as an act of authority and, as Rose Marie Burwell puts it, "sexual possession."[40] And, like the African book, *A Moveable*

Feast enabled Hemingway imaginatively to occupy a space in his consciousness
that was not exactly memory or nostalgia but more neutrally authorship, before
success and celebrity had arrived and distracted him from the pure pursuit of art.

Back in Cuba, Hemingway worked on the Paris sketches from May 1957
through November 1958. Working mostly at the typewriter, Hemingway began
to revise and order the material. Mary then retyped it for him, correcting spelling
and punctuation and consulting him about wording that she thought needed
rephrasing. She told him that it was, unusually so, not much about him, but
mostly about other people. "It's biography by remate," Hemingway replied. Remate was a two-wall shot in jai alai: in other words, biography by reflection.[41] As
he wrote, Hemingway warmed to his subject. By the fall of 1957 he had at least
three sketches done to his satisfaction—one based on a Ford Madox Ford section
cut from the 1925 first draft of *The Sun Also Rises,* one about Gertrude Stein, and
one about writing in the café at Place Saint-Michel. By July 1958, he could report
that he had finished a total of eighteen of the sketches. But Hemingway's creative
energies were at their most scattered in this period. He was not only working
alternately on *The Garden of Eden* and *A Moveable Feast,* but in February 1959 he
had also contracted with *Life* to write a ten-thousand-word article on bullfighting—what became the posthumously published *Dangerous Summer* (1985).

All the while, the Castro revolution was simmering in Cuba (the actual takeover of power occurred in the first two days of January 1959), and Hemingway
felt additional anxiety about whether he would be able to remain in the country
he had come to love during a time of such intense political turmoil. His health
continued to decline. His blood pressure was too high, he slid into valleys of dark
depression from which he could barely climb back out, and he also developed
paranoia, believing that government agents were watching him. As biographer
Michael Reynolds puts it, "Hemingway's life alternated between ever-shortening
cycles of euphoric writing and paranoia-ridden depression."[42]

The subtitle that Patrick gave to *True at First Light* could fit *A Moveable Feast* as
well: a fictional memoir. The stories that Hemingway tells in the book are based
lightly on fact but are heavily embellished by his imagination, reconstructing
his life to fit the personal mythology that he had for years been constructing
and re-creating as his own version of the past. Much of the book is devoted to
Hemingway's retelling of how he became a writer and how he had lived in Paris
with Hadley in poverty. Much of the recollection is distorted. Looking back on
those long-ago years, the Hemingway writing the memoir is not the early master
but an old impostor, projecting his tastes, interests, and views of the 1950s onto
the 1920s. Ever one to hold a grudge, Hemingway also used the book to get back
at erstwhile friends who had become enemies. But he presented the vast majority
of his compatriots—among them Pound, Joyce, Sylvia Beach, Jules Pascin, and
Evan Shipman—in a positive light.

Miraculously, given the state of his health, Hemingway managed to forge
ahead on *A Moveable Feast* and was satisfied enough with its quality to deposit

the book with his publishers in New York in late October 1959. But he dithered over releasing it for more than a year, fearing libel lawsuits. Because of the
sometimes unclear distinction between fact and imagination in this book (as in
the African book), critics have long debated whether Hemingway intended it as
memoir or fiction; he indicated at various times that it was both. Hemingway
was again blurring the boundaries between fiction and nonfiction as a strategy
by which he could separate himself from his narrative alter egos. Opinions vary
as to whether Hemingway felt the manuscript was complete. His health was so
poor that perhaps none of his statements from the period can be entirely trusted.
But he delivered his last word on the book on 18 April 1961, just a few months
before his death, when he wrote to Charles Scribner Jr. that the Paris book could
not be published. Mary, however, did not mail the letter, apparently feeling that
Hemingway was making a poor decision.

A Moveable Feast, edited by Mary Hemingway, A. E. Hotchner, and Harry
Brague (a staff editor at Scribner's), was the first book to appear after Hemingway's death. Passages from eleven of the twenty chapters were published in *Life*
in April 1964, and Scribner's issued its edition in May, with a first printing of
eighty-five thousand copies. In 2009, Gregory Hemingway's son, Sean Hemingway, with the assistance of his uncle Patrick Hemingway, reedited the book, and
Scribner's brought out a new edition based on the last draft of the book, a typed
manuscript with original notations in Hemingway's hand, according to its editor. This new version claims to be less edited and more comprehensive than the
previous text.

The 2009 text contains more material than the 1964 version. There are several
additional sections, and many existing chapters are longer and fuller. The most
significant changes appear in the final, dark passages of "There Is Never Any End
to Paris"; these detail Hemingway's cheating on Hadley. In the first edition, Hadley is the victimized heroine; Pauline is the conniving interloper, befriending the
lonely wife while the husband is busy working. In passages not published in the
1964 text, Hemingway shows himself to be as much responsible for the breakup of
his marriage to Hadley as Pauline was. He writes not in a confessional tone but in
an almost analytical, instructional mode, attempting, in Robert Trogdon's words,
"to explain how a man could be in love with two people at the same time, and
to describe the exhilaration and pain of the experience. Here we have a complex
Hemingway who is both victim and villain in the story of his life."[43] For example,
Pauline's reputation is clearly improved by such passages as the following, which
Mary ignored but which were included in the revised edition: "For the girl [Pau-
line] to deceive her friend was a terrible thing, but it was my fault and blindness
that this did not repel me. Having become involved in it and being in love I accepted all the blame for it myself and lived with the remorse" (219).

Most readers and reviewers have found the 2009 version better than the first.
A. E. Hotchner, however, objected vociferously, contending that when Hemingway died, the manuscript was no longer a work in progress, as some have said,

but was ready for publication. What was published in 1964, according to Hotchner, was what Hemingway wanted published. "The book was a serious work that Ernest finished with his usual intensity, and . . . he certainly intended it for publication," Hotchner wrote in an article for the *New York Times*.[44] According to Hotchner, the 2009 edition was a betrayal of Hemingway's intentions.

In 1933, Gertrude Stein had published *The Autobiography of Alice B. Toklas,* a book about her own life presented in the guise of her lover's autobiography. Writing in *Esquire* magazine that year, and perhaps thinking of Stein's cunningly constructed memoir, Hemingway noted that "legendary people usually end by writing their memoirs."[45] This would turn out to be a prophetic statement as Hemingway entered his final years, a period of disintegration marked by desperate wanderings from place to place and a fatal combination of physical and mental illness that would make it impossible for him to do what he loved most: write.

This last period of Hemingway's life produced some of the most remarkable—and misunderstood—works of art in the canon. He was never so uncertain of himself as he was at this time, yet he was also never more alive creatively in his daring to take aesthetic risks. His final years were characterized by creative struggle and artistic nomadism. They were years of imaginative wandering and revisiting the past, of trying to stimulate creativity through remembrance of things past but also of stretching the boundaries of genre and of growing aesthetically through personal, sometimes sexual, metamorphosis. They were also years of contemplating his legacy and wondering why his once copious creative flow had been reduced to a trickle, why writing was so much harder now. They were years of anxiety and eventual paranoia, of feeling hounded by the critics and the academic "vultures" and what they might dig up about his personal life. Ultimately, as his posthumous work reveals, they were years of second-guessing who he really was, years when first tiny, then larger rips began to appear in the finely filamented scrim that he had draped between his public and private selves. He still seemed to the world the man of action, trekking in the green hills of Africa and plying the blue waters of the Gulf Stream. But beneath those surfaces, like the iceberg he had famously described, Hemingway was an aging, bookish man in wire-rimmed glasses, trying to find satisfaction in writing, and finding it harder to do so with each passing year.

14

Dangerous Summers

SPAIN, CUBA, IDAHO

Hemingway spent a good portion of the last two years of his life in Spain. Having seen how interest in bullfighting had surged there on his most recent trip, he contracted with *Life* magazine in the summer of 1959 to write some articles on a highly publicized series of bullfights that were to pit one legend against another. Instead of the usual corrida, with three bullfighters in the ring, there was to be a mano a mano—a contest between two bullfighters, dueling for the title of the best matador in Spain. The contestants were Luis Miguel Dominguín and Antonio Ordóñez, generally reckoned the best matadors since the death of Manuel Laureano Rodríguez Sánchez (known as Manolete). Ordóñez was the son of the bullfighter who had fought under the name Niño de la Palma, the model for Pedro Romero in *The Sun Also Rises*. Dominguín had risen to prominence in August 1947 during a mano-a-mano competition with Manolete in Linares, when Manolete was killed by a Miura bull. Dominguín had retired but was enticed back into action by Ordóñez's challenge in 1958.

Both Ordóñez and Dominguín were handsome celebrities well known in Spain and other parts of Europe. Of the two, Hemingway seems to have identified more with Ordóñez. He was young and fit, had a beautiful wife, and probably provided Hemingway with a way to recapture the spirit of his youth in Spain. He told his son Patrick that Ordóñez "has thirteen cornadas [wounds inflicted by the bull's horns] altogether and not one of them has spooked him. He is spooked sometimes in the night the way we all are and prefers to sleep in the daytime . . . but he loves his work truly and he loves bulls too." In contrast to Hemingway's own badly abused body and failing health, Ordóñez also, according to Hemingway, was the type of person who "by their actual physical conduct gave you a real feeling of admiration."[1] Dominguín, for his part, was extroverted, witty, and led a somewhat flamboyant life. He was gossip-magazine copy, had a much-publicized affair with Ava Gardner, and even went big-game hunting in Africa—an almost exact parallel of the path of celebrity that Hemingway had taken but of which Hemingway, in typically paradoxical fashion, disapproved. Willfully blind to their similarities, Hemingway disdained Dominguín for his dissolute and unprofessional way, and he admired Ordóñez for his pure devotion to his professional art.

On 26 April 1959, Hemingway and Mary sailed for Spain on the *Constitution,* and they were in Spain for the bullfights through September. They saw contests in Valencia, Málaga, Ciudad Real, and elsewhere. Both Ordóñez and Dominguín were seriously gored in different contests but were able to continue in the bullring after medical treatment. When Ordóñez was gored and had to spend two nights in a hospital, Hemingway sat up with him in his room. The Hemingways spent the summer crisscrossing the country by car, following the matadors from place to place, watching the contests, and interviewing the participants. As a home base between fights, they had been given the use of a luxurious estate called La Cónsula in Churriana, a village near the Málaga airport, which was much like Finca Vigía. It gave Hemingway a measure of privacy, which he appreciated, and felt like home. The residence was owned by a wealthy American, Nathan (Bill) Davis, whom Pauline had introduced to Hemingway in Sun Valley in 1941. The two men shared an interest in bullfights, and Davis became both Hemingway's host and his driver. Also along for the trip were A. E. Hotchner and Valerie Danby-Smith, the Irish woman who served Hemingway as a companion and secretary and with whom he would conduct another flirtation, à la Adriana, on their tour through Spain (she would also end up marrying Gregory, five years after his father's death, though they would divorce in 1989).

They left Spain in mid-October, Mary returning to Cuba and Hemingway going to Paris, where he worked on his bullfight article for a couple of weeks. He then returned to Cuba via New York, and in mid-November he and Mary went on to Ketchum, Idaho. Hemingway had first visited Idaho in 1939 at the invitation of Averell Harriman, an officer of the Union Pacific Railroad and a partner in the development of the Sun Valley Lodge, a new resort. Hemingway returned several times over the years and became fond of the lush scenery and the plentiful opportunities for quality hunting and fishing. In the fall of 1958, he had rented a house in Ketchum. When the lease expired at the end of the year, he had moved to another rental property, which he ended up purchasing in early January 1959, when the Batista government in Cuba fell and Fidel Castro came to power. Hemingway was probably unsure how long he might be able to remain in the revolutionary country and wanted somewhere to go if he had to leave Cuba in a hurry. Idaho reminded Hemingway of Spain, and Ketchum was small and remote enough to provide a buffer from the negative trappings of his celebrity.

The house in Ketchum at 400 Canyon Run Boulevard, one mile northwest of the town center, overlooked the Big Wood River and was sited on a spacious seventeen acres. But the home was oddly fortresslike in its architecture—cold and unappealing, in contrast to the warmth and lush vegetation of the Finca. The house was sheathed in faux-wood siding, which covered a cinder-block frame. The décor was spare and contemporary in design; the ceilings hung low and the many rooms were quite small. The whole structure seemed more like a series of monastic cells than like rooms designed to live and entertain in. Mary thought the Ketchum house was depressing but went along, as always, with her husband's wishes. Patrick wondered if his father had bought the house as a place in which to die.

Although he suffered from hypertension and insomnia, Hemingway continued to work on the bullfight articles in Ketchum and then later at the Finca in the spring of 1960. But the size of the manuscript swelled by the day, to alarming proportions: in April, at 63,000 words, it was already ridiculously longer than the 10,000 words *Life* had requested, and by the end of May, when Hemingway stopped writing, it had reached a gargantuan 120,000 words. A. E. Hotchner arrived at the Finca in June to help cut the baggy manuscript down to size, and together he and Hemingway were able to pare it down to 70,000 words. It appeared in the magazine in three installments, in September 1960, under the title "The Dangerous Summer." (Hemingway had earlier sold another section, "A Matter of Wind," to *Sports Illustrated* in August 1959.) The articles were intended to be a supplement to a new edition of *Death in the Afternoon,* but no such book was ever published. Instead, after Hemingway's death, Scribner's brought out *The Dangerous Summer,* a book-length version of the articles, in 1985. The narrative was bloated, fuzzy, and plainly uninteresting in places. Hemingway struggled to find a focus in the manuscript but failed, most probably because of his rapidly deteriorating mental health.

Meanwhile, Hemingway's behavior became ever more bizarre. At a sixtieth birthday party that Mary threw for him at La Cónsula on 21 July 1959, his friend Ordóñez was in attendance. Hemingway drank heavily and took uncharacteristic risks, like shooting cigarettes out of Ordóñez's mouth with pellets from an air gun—and then with bullets. Buck Lanham had flown in especially for the festivities; he infuriated his old friend when he accidentally grazed the top of Hemingway's head with his hand. Hemingway turned on Lanham in a fury and shouted that no one was allowed to touch his head. Events worsened after the party was over. While driving Hemingway and Valerie Danby-Smith to Madrid, Bill Davis lost control of the car and bounced off a concrete barrier. Hemingway again suffered bruises; fortunately, however, no one was seriously injured in the wreck.

As Hemingway's cavalcade moved across Spain that summer, Hemingway picked up friends and followers wherever he stopped, assembling an entourage that came to number more than twenty people. At mealtime, a festive but reckless atmosphere prevailed, with Hemingway paying everyone's tab. Mary was repelled by the dirty tables, the sour smell of wine, and her husband's reckless behavior. At one hotel, Hemingway charged naked into the women's quarters,

waving a bottle of whiskey and making lewd gestures. At one of the bullfights,
Hemingway turned on Mary when she did not immediately fulfill a request he
had made of her, comparing her to his mother, who he said had driven his father
to suicide.

Signs of his mental blankness occurred regularly. He became utterly indifferent to others' feelings. At a picnic on the banks of the Irati River, Mary cracked a
toe as she scrambled across some jagged rocks. Hemingway merely nodded to her
as she passed him, in obvious pain, then turned back to Hotchner to comment
on how good the food was. It is possible that he had not even recognized Mary,
that he had blanked out for a moment. Yet privately he boasted to friends of his
sexual potency and his wife's submissiveness as a lover. At the birthday party,
he crudely told Lanham with contempt that he had "irrigated her four times the
night before."[2] Mary wrote in her diary that she felt she had become "inaudible"
and "invisible" to him.[3] Soon she wondered if she would be able to stay married
to him.

To make matters worse, Hemingway had fallen for Valerie Danby-Smith, a
nineteen-year-old reporter who had sought out Hemingway for an interview. She
had found him at a hotel in Madrid, and Hemingway had consented to speak with
her. He then commanded her to come to Pamplona in July for the fiesta, which
she did. She soon wearied of the endless rounds of café trolling, however, the
heavy drinking and late hours. As if to prevent her from running away from him,
Hemingway, like a possessive lover, hired her as his secretary, and after they left
Spain she continued to work for him in Cuba and Ketchum. Valerie also worked
briefly for Mary, helping her with the estate after Hemingway's death.

Valerie was a comely young woman, fair-skinned and dark-haired. Hemingway was attracted to her as he had been to Adriana, who had also been nineteen
when they met. Adriana, however, was an aristocrat, whereas Valerie was decidedly middle-class—and less noble-looking and exotic. Nonetheless, the relationship quickly assumed a familiar shape. As with his obsession with Adriana, Mary
accepted Hemingway's infatuation because it made him more manageable and
reduced his cruelty to her. Like Adriana, Valerie dismissed speculation that she
and Hemingway were lovers.

Back in Cuba that fall and the following spring, the abuse continued. Although they lived together, Mary would write Hemingway letters, afraid to approach him in person. She would itemize his cruelties to her and offer to move
out. Yet then they would reconcile, Hemingway begging her forgiveness and
promising that the abuse would stop. He could not live without her, he insisted.

The madness was an illness that he could not control. He felt that the forced
labor of finishing the bullfighting articles had caused tremendous mental strain
and left his eyesight further weakened. He feared that he might be losing some
of his reason. His general attitude had become markedly more negative, even
despairing. He had bad nightmares, cramps, extreme anxiety, even delusions
of persecution. He began acting unusually hesitant and indecisive about things

as important as planning a trip and as trivial as which shirt to wear. He became increasingly concerned with how he looked. Skin problems had erased the mature handsomeness of his facial features; he had grown a beard to cover up the white scaling around his chin and mouth. He had always associated a full head of hair with virility; now he was balding, a cause for further insecurity. Almost everyone was shocked at how quickly Hemingway had aged. Only sixty-one years old, he looked closer to ninety.

High blood pressure was the ostensible cause of many of his health problems, but two other factors played a part: Hemingway's hypochondria and the conflicting medications prescribed by his Cuban doctors. Strangely, Hemingway always exaggerated his minor illnesses and downplayed his major ones. He worried throughout his life that a minor malady would be—in the phrase he typically used—"the death" of him. Common viruses sent him to his bed, sometimes for weeks, where he spent days consulting medical books. Hemingway's library at Finca Vigía contained an unusually large number of medical texts, one about liver disease, another about sedatives, and still another about electroshock therapy, which he acquired after Patrick underwent the treatments in 1947. Conversely, his serious physical injuries, like the numerous concussions he suffered during World War II and in Africa, he tended to discount, rarely seeking medical attention. Yet these injuries to the head affected his mental balance.

The medications that Hemingway took also ruined his physical and mental health. Reserpine, a drug he was prescribed for hypertension, was later shown to have significant depressive effects. But it appears to have been the combination of drugs—with their respective side effects—that did Hemingway in. According to a document (perhaps a summary of Hemingway's health written at the request of Mary or another family member), dated shortly after Hemingway's death, 20 July 1961, written in the hand of his Cuban physician, one Dr. Herrera, Hemingway was taking a potentially deadly daily cocktail of Wychol, Ritalin, Serpasil, Equanil, and Seconal—in addition to the Reserpine.[4] Dr. Howard Rome, one of his physicians at the Mayo Clinic, discontinued the use of the Ritalin and Serpasil, concluding that these drugs "compounded" and "accelerated" the depression.[5] Another attending physician made the terse determination "Psychoses: Schizophrenia," at the bottom of one page of his medical records.[6]

———

In July 1960 Hemingway left Cuba for the last time for a return visit to Spain, via New York, ostensibly to fact-check his "Dangerous Summer" articles and still contemplating a sequel to *Death in the Afternoon* (Mary remained in Manhattan). The political climate in Cuba had changed since Castro's takeover. Although Hemingway supported the revolutionary government, he could not support the atrocities committed during the overthrow of Batista—such as the public executions of former police officers—and, moreover, the American ambassador there, Philip Wilson Bonsal, told him that if he remained in Havana, he would be considered a traitor.

Hemingway arrived in Spain in August 1960. Even before leaving, things had been chaotic. Crossing from Havana to Key West, Valerie discovered that she had not renewed her visitor's visa. Hemingway became frantic, fearing that immigration officials would not allow her remain in Cuba, but the incident was soon resolved and Hemingway was temporarily mollified. In Madrid, matters deteriorated quickly: Hemingway became extremely worried and agitated about everything, and Mary had to arrange for Valerie, who had stayed behind in Havana, to go to Madrid to help her husband. In Madrid, Valerie mislaid her passport, and when she asked Hemingway if it was in his room, he began yelling at her to phone the immigration office at once (as he had done in Havana) and follow their directions to the letter. He thought he could somehow be held liable if she broke any immigration rules. Compounding his anxiety, he was convinced that Davis would try to kill them again in another car accident, and he ranted to Valerie about this, too.

Then, as if to confirm his fears, on 8 August a Spanish radio station reported that Hemingway had taken ill in the bullring at Málaga. When Mary heard the news, she immediately booked a flight to Madrid, but moments later a cable arrived from Hemingway in Granada correcting the error: "Reports False Enroute Madrid Love Papa." Still, his letters from Madrid sounded more and more desperate. "I wish you were here to look after me and help me out and keep me from cracking up," he told Mary bluntly in a letter of 23 September.[7] Mary, however, remained in Cuba, apparently not realizing that something was seriously wrong with her husband's mental state. He would do outrageous things, as when he wrote Hotchner instructing him to ask for $900,000 for the film rights to the Nick Adams stories. Hotchner was soon sent over to bring Hemingway home safely. Hemingway agreed to go with him but insisted on booking passage on an ancient propeller airplane that took fourteen hours to cross the Atlantic. He explained to Hotchner that the slower plane offered better security than the newer, faster jet aircraft.

This was a new manifestation of Hemingway's mental problems: paranoia. Irritable beyond belief, withdrawn, and deluded, Hemingway began to fear that everyone was out to get him. At dinner with friends one night in Ketchum, he noticed that lights were on in the bank building down the hill. He stared out the window and told everyone that "they" were checking his accounts. When pressed to explain who "they" were, Hemingway said that the FBI was tailing him—a suspicion he had harbored for several years. In 1955 at the Floridita, he was speaking with a group of students from Miami University in Ohio when he "stated that a certain person in the bar was an FBI man who was keeping him under surveillance."[8] Toby Bruce recalled that Hemingway thought the FBI was also wiretapping the phone at the Finca. In fact, since his counterespionage activities in the Caribbean had first been brought to J. Edgar Hoover's attention in the early 1940s, Hemingway *had* been investigated by the FBI—but no more seriously than any of the other suspected Communists in America during that period, especially those who had supported the Loyalist cause in the Spanish Civil War.[9] Later, at the Mayo Clinic, he told his physician that one of the interns there "was a Fed in disguise." Sadly, Hemingway was unravelling, like a length of coarse rope frayed at both ends.

He was also in anguish about money, pleading poverty and worrying that at any moment he would land in the poorhouse. Even when Mary phoned a vice president at their New York bank, Morgan Guaranty Trust, and had him tell Hemingway personally how much money he had in the bank, Hemingway was unconvinced, and thought that the banker was "covering up something." He had also feared for years that he was paying too much in income tax, that he was being persecuted by the government for his success. Bizarrely, he began to think that by living in Idaho they were subjecting themselves to higher taxes. In her memoir, Mary described how Hemingway would stand in the doorway after she'd gone to bed for the night and upbraid her for spending too much money on groceries: she did not understand the "danger" of living in Idaho, nor was she helping him find a tax haven.[10] At this point, Mary was finally willing to admit that Hemingway was terribly ill.

_____

Hemingway ended up in the Mayo Clinic in Rochester, Minnesota, on 30 November 1960. The gaunt man who walked unsteadily down the white-tiled corridors of the hospital that autumn evening might have been mistaken for a recent widower or a grieving relative. The vacant look in his eyes bespoke confusion, or even disbelief, brought on by the trauma of loss. But in fact the frail man with the uncertain stride had few feelings of any kind. He was completely passive, almost insensate, for he was captive to a black depression that had tightened its grip on him so firmly that he couldn't wriggle away.

Accidents, illness, hypochondria, depression, alcoholism, and finally paranoia had settled around him like a fog that would not lift. No longer physically robust, his "capital," as he called it—his writing—had gone through a similar process of diminishment, to the point where it now cost him an entire day's labor to complete three or four simple sentences. It was a sign of his mental incapacity that he could start a sentence but not complete one, or he could produce a sentence, but it would make no sense when he read it back. As early as January 1958, in a letter to Gianfranco Ivancich, he had reported that three times he had tried to send him a letter but in each case he "could no[t] place the words correctly."[11] Invited by the newly elected president John F. Kennedy to attend his inauguration in January 1961, Hemingway begged off for reasons of ill health but tried to write a note of congratulations to send instead. It took him days to write a few words. His last telegram to Valerie from Ketchum in October read: "Goodbye. Have good luck whatever you do. Forever go."[12]

By Thanksgiving, he was suffering from terrible nervous anxiety and soaring blood pressure. It was clear that he would have to be hospitalized. His physician in Ketchum, George Saviers, thought that if his fears could be calmed, his blood pressure would fall, and so it was arranged, in the utmost secrecy, that he be flown to Rochester, Minnesota, to be admitted to the Mayo Clinic at Saint Mary's Hospital—a grim, cheerless place in the midst of a drab, gray city. Registering under the name George Saviers, Hemingway was searched when he entered his room on the sixth-floor psychiatric ward, which had double-locked doors and iron-barred windows. Hemingway did not like doctors in general, psychiatrists even less. Recalling Dr. Lawrence Kubie's attempts to psychoanalyze him on the basis of the information he drew from Jane Mason, Hemingway harbored a lifelong distrust of such physicians. Nor did he like the Mayo Clinic. It was there that Pauline had gone in 1951 complaining of headaches and dizziness; the Mayo doctors had diagnosed blocked arteries and hypertension but had failed to discover the tumor on her adrenal gland, thus precipitating her early death. After an initial consultation, his doctors determined that Hemingway's depression was so severe that more substantial methods had to be attempted to bring him back to normal, and they ordered a course of electroshock treatments.

Electroconvulsive therapy (ECT) was in widespread use in psychiatric circles in the United States in the 1940s, '50s, and '60s. The technique delivered relatively low levels of power, ranging from 70 to 150 volts, to the brain for about one minute. The pulse was supposed to unsettle whatever unfavorable brain patterns were causing aberrant behavior so that more positive ones could take their place. That was the theory; the reality was quite different. In many cases, ECT was later found to make the mental illness worse, creating in patients hostility and delusions more marked than before. Because of such extreme side effects, ECT eventually was discredited and stopped being used (although recent modifications have brought it back into use today).

Hemingway received between eleven and fifteen ECT treatments at the Mayo Clinic. For the procedure, the patient lies on a table with his wrists and ankles clamped down. Electrodes are attached to his scalp, and he is given a piece of rubber hose to bite on. An electrical current is then passed through the skull and into the brain. When the pulse is turned off, an acrid, burning smell lingers in the air. Many writers and artists underwent ECT treatments, including Sylvia Plath, Anne Sexton, Vladimir Horowitz, Paul Robeson, and Vaslav Nijinsky. The poet Robert Lowell, whose mental problems were far more severe than Hemingway's and who also received ECT, compared it to "a trolley-pole sparking at contact."[13]

Although Hemingway was irreversibly damaged by these treatments, he still found the kindness and empathy to write an emotional letter to his doctor's nine-year-old son. The boy, Fritz Saviers, was terminally ill with a viral heart disease, and he had been hospitalized off and on in Denver, where he underwent treatments by specialists in the hope of saving his life. Hemingway wrote to Fritz on 15 June 1961, just days before he took his own life. He encouraged the boy to picture the beautiful country around him and the abundance of bass jumping in the river, and the pheasants and ducks that would appear in the fall. "But not as many as in Idaho and I hope we'll both be back there shortly and can joke about our hospital experiences together. Best always to you, old timer from your good friend who misses you very much / (Mister) Papa."[14] Without question, Hemingway liked, respected, and trusted his physician, although he knew that the illness that gripped him would never be shaken. He was done for. But, much worse, so was nine-year-old Fritz. Yet Hemingway still thought he could do something to save him—an encouraging word, a deflection of the tragedy that would inevitably come. He probably saw himself in the young boy, fond of the outdoors, eager to go hunting, breathing the mountain air, and tramping through the brush with a fly rod in one hand and a string of bass in the other.

Inside, however, Hemingway's depression remained, centered around his inability to write. On a sheet of cheap paper, he carefully printed in block letters the following message: "Former writer engaged in preparation of scheduled full scale news conference as promised in the P-D [publicity department] by our spokesman. Please do not disturb unless absolutely necessary to obtain photographs or confirmation of treatment given exclusively to the PD. It is necessary that his privacy be respected and that he have the benefit of rest and quiet."[15] *Former writer:* the message was later cleaned up a bit, to make it sound more positive, and put out as a press release.[16]

The ECT treatments were assumed to have worked, because Hemingway was released from the Mayo Clinic on 22 January 1961. But it quickly became apparent that his delusions had not disappeared. As January turned into February, he became more and more of a recluse in the gray concrete house on the hilltop. He no longer invited friends to watch the Friday night fights on television. He rarely went into Ketchum or Sun Valley. He said little and often stood gazing out the front window across the river toward the cemetery, the snow piled deep. He wrote nothing, locked in a cage of despair. He began obsessively keeping track of how much he weighed, penciling the numbers on the bathroom wall beside the scales. He had lost weight dramatically—dropping from 250 pounds to only 155—and looked ravaged. Bill Walton, visiting him in the spring, found him scarcely recognizable. The critic Leslie Fiedler, who had made a pilgrimage to visit Hemingway the previous autumn, thought him "broken beyond repair. . . . [He feared] that he had done nothing of lasting worth" and was convinced that "he must die."[17] When Hemingway heard news of the Bay of Pigs fiasco in April, he probably realized that he would never see Cuba and his beloved Finca again—or other things that were dear to him: his boat, paintings, library, and the manuscripts he had been trying to finish.

Toward eleven o'clock one April morning, Mary came downstairs to find Hemingway standing in the front vestibule holding a shotgun. On the windowsill were two shells and a note he had written her. Mary told him quietly that he must not give up. She mentioned that they might go to Mexico on the *Pilar* and told him there was marvelous fishing off the Yucatan Peninsula. Or they could sublet a little flat in Paris. They had been "awfully happy" there. All the while Mary was talking quietly, Hemingway gave no response. "Honey, you wouldn't do anything harmful to me as well as you," she told him, and reminded him of his courage and bravery in the war and elsewhere. She told him she needed him.[18] The minutes ticked away. Mary knew that Dr. Saviers was due at noon to take her husband's blood pressure, a daily routine. She continued to wait. After about fifty minutes, mercifully, she heard Saviers's car pull into the driveway. The physician persuaded Hemingway to come with him to Sun Valley Hospital, where he was put under heavy sedation.[19]

Set to be readmitted to the Mayo Clinic a few days later, Hemingway was first driven back to the house to collect some clothes before the flight to Rochester. His neighbors, Don Anderson and Joanie Higgons, a nurse at the local hospital, accompanied him. When they reached the house, Hemingway looked at them with a cunning smile and said not to bother coming in, that he could handle things himself. He then walked swiftly through the house to the foyer, where the gun rack stood, and, despite Anderson's being close behind him, managed to grab a shotgun and ram in two shells before having the weapon wrested away from him. He was taken back to the hospital and sedated again.

Two mornings later, Anderson flew him in a private plane to Rochester. At a refueling stop in Cedar Rapids, Iowa, Hemingway climbed out of the plane and made a hurried tour of the hangar. He may have been looking for a gun, Anderson later surmised; crazily, Hemingway ran from unlocked car to unlocked car in the airport parking lot, rummaging through glove compartments, before Anderson could restrain him. As another plane taxied toward them after landing, Hemingway walked purposefully toward its whirling propellers but then veered away when the pilot cut the engines.

Back at the Mayo Clinic, Hemingway submitted to another series of shock treatments. Little changed. Friends sent notes of encouragement. "Hem," wrote John Dos Passos, "Hope this isn't getting to be a habit. Take it easy there." A telegram from Gary Cooper (himself dying of cancer) and his wife read, "Whats [sic] There To Say Except That You Have Our Love?" An ominous letter from Marlene Dietrich read, "What is it? Whatever it is I don't like it." Mary, advised to stay behind in Ketchum, locked all the guns in a storage room in the basement.[20]

The great sadness deepened. Hemingway felt the sick, dirty ache of something spoiled. Once again, however, he talked his doctors into releasing him. Mary flew to Rochester to collect him, and on 26 June they set off, with George Brown, an old friend, on the drive back to Ketchum. It took them five days to cover the fifteen-hundred-mile route because they had to stop so often to calm Hemingway. His delusions were as bad as ever. At one rest stop, he became frantic with fear that state troopers would arrest them for drinking wine with their picnic lunch.

They arrived in Ketchum on Friday, 30 June. George Brown stayed in a cinderblock guesthouse next to the parking area beside the kitchen door. The next morning, Hemingway saw George Saviers and called on Don Anderson at his office but found that he was out. In the evening, he and Mary took George

Brown to a local restaurant for dinner. Hemingway thought that two men in suits at a nearby table were FBI agents, again on his trail. He said little else but did not seem morose. When they got home, Hemingway went to bed early.

Sunday morning, 2 July, saw a bright sun just starting to pierce a clear blue sky. July was a ritual month for Hemingway. It was his birth month and the month in which his family had always set out for Michigan. It was the month in which he had been wounded on the Italian front, and the month of the yearly fiesta in Pamplona. All of these things now in the past, never to come again. Hemingway woke early, as always. He knew that the guns had been locked up, but he also knew that the keys were stored on the window ledge above the kitchen sink. Taking the keys, he went down to the basement, unlocked the storage room, and chose a W. & C. Scott & Son Monte Carlo B shotgun.[21] He took some shells, closed and locked the door behind him, and climbed the steps back up to the living room. He crossed over to the foyer, slipped two shells into the chamber, and then gently balanced the butt against the floor. He leaned forward, put the twin barrels in his mouth, and pulled both triggers.

Mary was awakened by what she later said sounded like "a couple of drawers banging shut." She went downstairs to find a crumpled, bloody heap of bathrobe on the floor of the foyer. Bone, teeth, hair, and flesh were scattered around the floor and stuck to the ceiling and walls. Shattered parts of her husband's head lay on the steps. The upper half of his skull was gone. She screamed for George Brown, who came running from the guesthouse. He telephoned Don Anderson. Anderson said only, "Papa's finally got the job done." He then phoned the police.[22]

Mary had to be sedated, and she spent the night in the local hospital. She did not believe her husband capable of killing himself—despite all his previous attempts. The following day, she returned to the house and cleaned the area where Hemingway had died. When she finished, she had restored it to pristine condition; not a speck or stain remained. She then talked to reporters. For Mary's sake, the coroner initially stated, "I can only say at this stage that the wound was self-inflict-ed. . . . I couldn't say it was accidental and I couldn't say it was suicide."[23] When reporters pressed Mary, she insisted that Hemingway's death had been accidental, spinning the improbable story that her husband was going out to hunt and had been cleaning the gun with the barrels pointed at his face, when it accidentally discharged. No one, of course, believed that Hemingway, experienced with fire-arms, would clean a loaded gun—or, for that matter, that he would be hunting in July. But in deference to Mary, the matter was not pursued. Under Idaho law, an inquest was not required unless there was suspicion of foul play.

Almost incredibly, the ruse that Hemingway's death was an accident was perpetuated for five years, until the publication of A. E. Hotchner's *Papa Heming-way,* in 1966, with its many new revelations.[24] Mary filed suit to try and prevent the book from being published, but she was unsuccessful.[25] When the truth was finally made public, Mary grudgingly gave an interview to *Look* magazine in which she admitted that her husband had killed himself. Asked why she had denied it for so long, Mary replied that it probably "had something to do with self-defense"—a reasonable position, given all that she had endured with her husband, especially in the last three or four years of his life.

Although Hemingway had not been to Mass in many years, the local Catholic priest allowed the body to be buried in hallowed ground.[26] (The Catholic burial was also intended to confirm that Hemingway had not committed suicide.) The funeral took place on 5 July, giving Patrick, Jack, and Gregory time to travel to Ketchum. Also in attendance were Bill Horne and his wife, Gianfranco Ivancich, Clara Spiegel, Leicester, and all of Hemingway's sisters except Carol. The burial, for obvious reasons, was closed to the public, but people still thronged outside the chain-link fence that enclosed the cemetery. The grave in which the body was placed, between two towering pine trees, faced the Sawtooth Mountains.

Mary industriously oversaw Hemingway's literary estate until her death in 1986. She retrieved his papers and belongings from Cuba, consented to the transfer of his manuscripts to the Kennedy Library in Boston, and carefully regulated the posthumous publication of his unfinished work. She kept his reputation alive, but she did more than that. Her shield of protection taken from her, Mary was left raw and exposed—as vulnerable as her husband had taken care not to be for most of his life, until poor health and mental illness had eroded his defenses. Mary compared her loss of Ernest to wandering down an endless tunnel of darkness, an image that would fit Hemingway's final journey of despair, and wrote of being left "alone with my loneliness."[27] In her husband's death, Mary had assimilated his lifelong fear of emptiness and solitude. It was as though his anxieties and insecurities had not died with him but had merely been passed on to someone else, someone who would continue to promote the legend and the myth.

NOTES

INTRODUCTION

1. With the exception of Linda Wagner-Martin's excellent *Ernest Hemingway: A Literary Life* (2007), which is not a biography in the traditional sense but a condensed volume that is part of Palgrave Macmillan's Literary Lives series, giving a critical reading of his best-known works and focusing on Hemingway's writing and publishing career. Any biographer of Hemingway would also be sorely remiss not to mention the late Michael S. Reynolds's masterly and impeccably researched five-volume life of the author, published between 1986 and 1999. Reynolds uncovered much new material that has since become an accepted and often drawn-on part of the official biographical record.

CHAPTER 1

1. David M. Sokol, *Oak Park: The Evolution of a Village* (Charleston, S.C.: History Press, 2011), 24, 30.
2. For a reassessment of Bruce Barton's career, and of the ways in which his book appealed to communities like Oak Park, see Wayne Elzey, "Jesus the Salesman: A Reassessment of *The Man Nobody Knows,*" *Journal of the American Academy of Religion* 46, no. 2 (1978): 151–77.
3. Stein, *Autobiography of Alice B. Toklas,* 270.
4. Hilary K. Justice, "Music at the Finca Vigia: A Preliminary Catalog of Hemingway's Audio Collection," *Hemingway Review* 25 (Fall 2005): 96–108. See also Hilary K. Justice, "Alias Grace: Music and the Feminine Aesthetic in Hemingway's Early Style," in Broer and Holland, *Hemingway and Women,* 221–38.
5. Quoted in Sanford, *At the Hemingways,* 7.
6. "Abba" is also Aramaic for "father," and is a biblical term expressing filial affection. Hemingway's famous nickname, "Papa" (which he reportedly bestowed on himself in the mid- to late 1920s), may have come from his recollection of his maternal grandfather.
7. Sanford, *At the Hemingways,* 15.
8. "Celebrated His 82nd Birthday," *Oak Leaves,* Saturday, 28 August 1926, Marcelline Hemingway Sanford Collection, Hemingway Family Papers, Clarke Historical Library, University of Michigan, box 28, folder 7. Typed transcriptions of Anson Hemingway's diaries from the Civil War are also preserved in this collection.
9. Carol Hemingway to Bernice Kert, 8 May 1979, quoted in Kert, *Hemingway Women,* 22.
10. Ben F. Meyer, "Hemingway Novel of Venice Completed at Home in Cuba," quoted in Bruccoli, *Conversations with Ernest Hemingway,* 55.

11. Delmore Schwartz, "The Literary Situation of Ernest Hemingway," in *Ernest Hemingway: The Man and His Work,* ed. John K. M. McCaffrey (New York: World, 1951), 127.

12. Hemingway, *My Brother, Ernest Hemingway,* 22. For the bleaker aspects of Hemingway's childhood, see Morris Buske, "Hemingway Faces God," *Hemingway Notes* 22, no. 2 (2002): 72–87. Buske quotes unpublished portions of Marcelline Hemingway Sanford's *At the Hemingways* that refer to corporal punishment and various instances of public humiliation.

13. Gregory Hemingway spoke about this "title" and the competition for it in an interview for *Ernest Hemingway: Wrestling with Life,* a documentary film produced for A&E television in 1997.

14. Hemingway to Coates, 5 October 1932, in Baker, *Selected Letters, 1917–1961,* 369.

15. See, for example, the 7 December 1966 letter of Buck Lanham to Carlos Baker, quoted in Kert, *Hemingway Women,* 21: "From my earliest days with Ernest Hemingway, he always referred to his mother as 'that bitch.' He must have told me a thousand times how much he hated her and in how many ways."

16. Sanford, *At the Hemingways,* 23.

17. Young, *Hemingway: A Reconsideration,* 136.

18. Hemingway, *My Brother, Ernest Hemingway,* 23.

19. "In those days there was the North Prairie," unpublished item, box MS 51, folder 514, Hemingway Collection, John F. Kennedy Presidential Library and Museum, Boston, Massachusetts (hereafter Hemingway Collection).

20. Sanford, *At the Hemingways,* 69.

21. "Scrapbook II," 52, Hemingway Collection.

22. "Inventory of Personal Property," 21 March 1915, in "Other Materials," ibid.

23. "[Hemingway] goes to the Agassiz of which he is a member and makes observations with the big boys." "Scrapbook II," 76, ibid. For the importance of the Agassiz Clubs in America, see Robert E. Fleming's introduction to *Hemingway and the Natural World,* 1–6. See also Harlan H. Ballard, "History of the Agassiz Association," *Swiss Cross* 1 (January 1887): 4–7.

24. See Beegel, "Eye and Heart," 54.

25. Sanford, *At the Hemingways,* 79.

26. Meyers, *Hemingway: A Biography,* 12.

27. Montgomery, *Hemingway in Michigan,* 51.

28. Hemingway, "No Worse Than a Bad Cold," unpublished play, box MS 55, folder 623, Hemingway Collection.

29. For more detail about Prudence Boulton, see *Sweetgrass and Smoke* (2002), by Constance Cappel (the author of *Hemingway in Michigan,* writing here under a slightly different name), a self-published study, with some fictional parts, by an assiduous researcher of Hemingway's connections to the Native Americans of northern Michigan. Hemingway variously refers to this person in his fiction as Prudence Mitchell, Prudie, and Trudy Boulton. See also Strong, *Race and Identity in Hemingway's Fiction*; and Peter L. Hays, "Hemingway's Use of a Natural Resource: Indians," in Fleming, *Hemingway and the Natural World,* 45–54. Hays focuses on the twin themes of promiscuity and loss in the stories involving Native Americans.

30. Parenthetical citations of Hemingway's short stories are to *The Fifth Column and the First Forty-Nine Stories* (New York: Charles Scribner's Sons, 1938).

31. Box MS 59, MS 729, Hemingway Collection.

32. Box MS 44, MS 382, ibid.

33. For an interesting discussion of this topic, see Christian K. Messenger, *Sport and the Spirit of Play in American Fiction* (New York: Columbia University Press, 2013), especially chapter 10.
34. Quoted in Meyers, *Hemingway: A Biography*, 17.
35. See Fenton, *Apprenticeship of Ernest Hemingway*, 6–10.
36. See ibid., 261; also see Donaldson, *Fitzgerald and Hemingway*, 309–25.
37. H. L. Mencken, *The American Language* (1919) (New York: Cosimo, 2010), 210.
38. For the statement about *Huckleberry Finn,* see Hemingway, *Green Hills of Africa,* 22.

CHAPTER 2

1. See Robert Fleming, "Hemingway's Chicago: The Iceberg Beneath the Water Line," *North Dakota Quarterly* 70, no. 1 (2004): 81–87.
2. "Back to His First Field," *Kansas City Times,* 26 November 1940, reprinted in Bruccoli, *Conversations with Ernest Hemingway,* 21–24.
3. Jim Fisher, "Of 'Star' Style and a Reporter Named Hemingway," *Kansas City Star,* 27 September 2007, 1–2.
4. Hemingway, *My Brother, Ernest Hemingway,* 45.
5. Bruccoli, *Ernest Hemingway: Cub Reporter,* 7.
6. "Back to His First Field," 1.
7. Scott Donaldson, "Introduction," in *The Cambridge Companion to Hemingway,* ed. Scott Donaldson (Cambridge: Cambridge University Press, 1996), 22.
8. Hemingway, interview by George Plimpton, in "Ernest Hemingway: The Art of Fiction, No. 21," *Paris Review* 5 (Spring 1958): 60–89, reprinted in Bruccoli, *Conversations with Ernest Hemingway,* 109–29 (quotation on 125).
9. Hemingway to "Dad and Mother," 6 December 1917, Hemingway Collection.
10. See Fenton, *Apprenticeship of Ernest Hemingway,* 51–53, for a discussion of the many humanitarian organizations that worked there with the wounded.
11. This was the nickname of the Episcopal Church of the Transfiguration, a well-known Gothic Revival edifice at 1 East 29th Street, between Fifth Avenue and Madison Avenue. Its storied history and blend of unusual architectural elements made it a tourist destination at the time, and it had a reputation for performing weddings for out-of-towners.
12. Ed Hemingway to Ernest Hemingway, 19 May 1918, quoted in Griffin, *Along with Youth,* 58.
13. Quoted in Roselle Dean, "First Lieutenant Hemingway," *Oak Parker,* 1 February 1919, newspaper clippings, box NC 01, Hemingway Collection.
14. Hemingway to Hemingway family, [ca. 31 May] and 2 June [1918], in Spanier and Trogdon, *Letters of Ernest Hemingway,* 1:107.
15. Quoted in Griffin, *Along with Youth,* 64.
16. Diary of Milford Baker, entry for 7 June 1918, Carlos Baker Papers, Firestone Library, Princeton University.
17. Hemingway, *Moveable Feast: The Restored Edition,* 62.
18. Among them, perhaps, John Dos Passos, although there is some haziness as to when the two men first met. In his memoir *The Best Times,* Dos Passos recalls being in Schio in May 1918, "when Ernest had just arrived with Section 4 of the Red Cross Ambulance in Italy" (141). In *The Hemingway Log,* Brewster Chamberlin argues that the chronology indicates that Dos Passos had left Schio for another part of Italy before Hemingway arrived. He concludes that the meeting was "mythological rather than factual" (21).

19. Hemingway to Fitzgerald, 15 December 1925, in Spanier and Trogdon, *Letters of Ernest Hemingway,* 1:446.

20. Hemingway to Ruth [Morrison?], [ca. late June–early July 1918], ibid., 1:113.

21. Theodore Brumback to the Hemingways, 14 July 1918, Hemingway Collection, reprinted in Sanford, *At the Hemingways,* 162.

22. "Has 227 Wounds, but Is Looking for Job," *New York Sun,* 22 January 1919, reprinted in Bruccoli, *Conversations with Ernest Hemingway,* 1; "Wounded 227 Times," *Oak Leaves,* 5 October 1918, 12. See also Villard and Nagel, *Hemingway in Love and War,* 212–19. For a good complement to the Villard-Nagel volume, see John J. Festermaker, "Agnes and Ernest: A Decade Before Catherine," *North Dakota Quarterly* 70, no. 1 (2004): 19–39.

23. Hemingway himself made this claim. See Spanier and Trogdon, *Letters of Ernest Hemingway,* 1:118. Villard and Nagel point out, however, that one Lt. Edward M. McKey was actually the first American to be wounded. See *Hemingway in Love and War,* 210.

24. Spanier and Trogdon, *Letters of Ernest Hemingway,* 1:130.

25. The quotations in this and the following seven paragraphs are from Villard and Nagel, *Hemingway in Love and War,* 24, 11, 14, 30–31, 22.

26. Dos Passos, *Best Times,* 156.

27. The voice of the "interchapters" in Hemingway's *In Our Time* is also often attributed to Dorman-Smith. Hemingway was fond of borrowing Britishisms from his friend.

28. Quoted in Villard and Nagel, *Hemingway in Love and War,* 260.

29. William D. Horne, interview by Peter Griffin, 7 July 1979, in Griffin, *Along with Youth,* 241.

30. Quoted in Villard and Nagel, *Hemingway in Love and War,* 144, 148, 154.

31. Ibid., 135–38.

32. Hemingway to Horne, 13 March 1919, quoted in Griffin, *Along with Youth,* 113.

33. Ibid., 122.

CHAPTER 3

1. *New York Sun,* 22 January 1919, 8, quoted in Bruccoli, *Conversations with Ernest Hemingway,* 1–2.

2. Sanford, *At the Hemingways,* 177.

3. See Leo van Bergen, *Before My Helpless Sight: Suffering, Dying, and Military Medicine on the Western Front, 1914–1918* (London: Ashgate, 2009), 241.

4. Reynolds, *Young Hemingway,* 85–86.

5. Sanford, *At the Hemingways,* 184.

6. For a reading of Hemingway's work through this lens, see Young, *Hemingway: A Reconsideration.*

7. "Lt. Hemingway Talks," 22 March 1919, and "War Hero to Address Club," [25 March 1919], photograph collection, grandparents' scrapbook, box NC 01, Hemingway Collection.

8. Frank Platt, transcript of a Hemingway panel discussion at Triton College, River Grove, Illinois, 24 September 1974, Carlos Baker Papers, Firestone Library, Princeton University.

9. Hemingway to Gamble, 3 March 1919, in Spanier and Trogdon, *Letters of Ernest Hemingway,* 1:169.

10. Grace Hemingway to Clarence Hemingway, [spring 1919], box, 6, folder 5, Hemingway Family Papers, Harry Ransom Center, University of Texas, Austin (hereafter Hemingway Family Papers, Harry Ransom Center).

11. Sanford, *At the Hemingways,* 198.

12. Little is known of Ruth Arnold. See Reynolds, *Young Hemingway,* 78–81, for some information. Other relevant background detail is provided by John Sanford (Marcelline's son) in an interview with Allie Baker at thehemingwayproject.com.

13. Ruth Arnold to Grace Hemingway, [1909], box 8, folder 6, Hemingway Family Papers, Harry Ransom Center.

14. Ruth Arnold to Grace Hemingway, 4 August 1919, ibid.

15. Grace Hemingway to Clarence Hemingway, n.d., ibid.

16. As late as 1934, Grace felt compelled to try to silence the wagging tongues that were still insinuating that there was something "abnormal" about her attachment to Ruth Arnold. "Ruth tells me that you have been misinformed by the repetition of an old malicious story," Grace wrote to two former neighbors in Oak Park. "In the first place, Ruth never had such a thought; and in the second place, Dr. Hemingway and his wife were never separated. They were loving and sympathetic every day of their lives. . . . As for Ruth, I have known and loved her for nearly 30 years, and she has always been loyal and true to the Hemingway family. Every one of my children come to see her and are grateful for all her many kindnesses. I trust you will hasten to make amends for hurting her feelings with the repetition of an old untrue story." Grace Hemingway to Marjorie Andree and Clara Harell, 10 July 1934, ibid.

17. Hemingway to Harvey Breit, 3 July 1956, in Baker, *Selected Letters, 1917–1961,* 861.

18. Reynolds, *Young Hemingway,* 250–51.

19. Hemingway did publish a humorous piece titled "Condensing the Classics" in the *Star Weekly* issue of 20 August 1920, in which he satirically summarized such well-known works of literature as *Don Quixote* and *Othello* in pithy, newslike paragraphs. Reprinted in Trogdon, *Ernest Hemingway: A Literary Reference,* 16–17.

20. Quoted in Bill Smith to Carlos Baker, 17 September 1965, Carlos Baker Papers, Firestone Library, Princeton University.

21. Paula McLain's novel *The Paris Wife* (2012) treats Hadley as a fictional subject with great accuracy; the majority of my information about Hadley (and Hemingway's other wives) comes from Kert, *Hemingway Women,* and from Diliberto, *Hadley.*

22. Hadley Richardson to Hemingway, 20 and 22 April 1921, Hemingway Collection.

23. Hadley Richardson to Hemingway, 25 November 1920, ibid.

24. Meyers, *Hemingway: A Biography,* 60.

25. Hadley Richardson to Hemingway, 17 December 1920, Hemingway Collection.

CHAPTER 4

1. Spanier and Trogdon, *Letters of Ernest Hemingway,* 1:316.

2. See Eric Hazan, *The Invention of Paris: A History in Footsteps* (New York: Verso, 2011), 163–65.

3. "American Bohemians in Paris," *Toronto Star Weekly,* 25 March 1922, reprinted in Hemingway, *By-Line,* 25.

4. Claude McKay, *A Long Way from Home* (1937; reprint, New Brunswick: Rutgers University Press, 2007), 192.

5. Stein, *Paris France,* 11.

6. F. Scott Fitzgerald would later say, "Ernest would always give a helping hand to a man on a ledge a little higher up."

7. Ernest Walsh, "Ernest Hemingway," *This Quarter* 2 (Autumn–Winter 1925–26): 67.

8. Hemingway, *A Moveable Feast: The Restored Edition,* 24. The best general biography of Stein is Linda Wagner-Martin, *Favored Strangers: Gertrude Stein and Her Family*

(New Brunswick: Rutgers University Press, 1997). See also Lyle Larsen, *Stein and Hemingway.*

9. Mabel Dodge Luhan, *Intimate Memories: European Experiences* (1935), ed. Lois Palken Rudnick (Albuquerque: University of New Mexico Press, 1999), 90.

10. Ray Lewis White, ed., *Sherwood Anderson / Gertrude Stein: Correspondence and Personal Essays* (Chapel Hill: University of North Carolina Press, 1972), 32.

11. Stein, *Autobiography of Alice B. Toklas,* 262.

12. Mellow, *Hemingway: A Life Without Consequences,* 70.

13. For a different reading of this story, see Nancy R. Comley and Robert Scholes, "Reading 'Up in Michigan,'" in *New Essays on Hemingway's Short Fiction*, ed. Paul Smith (Cambridge: Cambridge University Press, 1998), 19–45, which argues that the sexual intercourse need not be construed as a rape but as "a classic confrontation between female tenderness and male sexual drive," that "Hemingway's sympathies are enlisted on the female side of the equation, though he clearly understands how it looks from the male side as well" (44), and that, while Hemingway sympathizes with the woman, he leaves the story open to interpretation.

14. In addition, while Hemingway was on assignment in the Ruhr in March 1923, Bernice Kert notes, Hadley, who had a lesbian fling before she met Hemingway, spent a good deal of time with the pianist Renata Bergatti. *Hemingway Women*, 448.

15. Baker, *Selected Letters, 1917–1961,* 650.

16. Gold quoted in Michael J. Hoffman, "Introduction," in *Critical Essays on Gertrude Stein,* ed. Michael J. Hoffman (Boston: G. K. Hall, 1986), 1; and Wyndham Lewis, "Tests for Counterfeit in the Arts and the Prose-Song of Gertrude Stein," in *Time and Western Man* (1927; reprint, Boston: Beacon Press, 1957), 49–51, reprinted as "The Work of Gertrude Stein," in Hoffman, *Critical Essays on Gertrude Stein,* 55.

17. Hemingway, *Moveable Feast: The Restored Edition,* 27.

18. Stein, *Autobiography of Alice B. Toklas,* 267.

19. Baker, *Selected Letters, 1917–1961,* 649–50.

20. For biographical information on Beach, see Shari Benstock, *Women of the Left Bank: Paris, 1900–1940* (Austin: University of Texas Press, 2010); and Beach's autobiography, *Shakespeare and Company.*

21. Spanier and Trogdon, *Letters of Ernest Hemingway,* 1:331.

22. Hemingway's forays into stream-of-consciousness prose are also indebted to Joyce, although they are usually not as successful as Joyce's, except perhaps in "The Snows of Kilimanjaro."

23. Hemingway to Arthur Mizener, 1 June 1950, in Baker, *Selected Letters, 1917–1961,* 696.

24. Quoted in Robert Manning, "Hemingway in Cuba," *Atlantic Monthly,* August 1965, 106.

25. Quoted in Valerie Danby-Smith, "Reminiscences of Hemingway," *Saturday Review,* 9 May 1964, 31.

26. Hemingway, "Homage to Ezra," *This Quarter* (Spring 1925), reprinted in Peter Russell, ed., *Ezra Pound: A Collection of Essays to Be Presented to Ezra Pound on His Sixty-Fifth Birthday* (London: P. Nevill, 1950), 74.

27. Hemingway, *Moveable Feast,* 87.

28. Hemingway, "Homage to Ezra," 75–76.

29. Hemingway to Sherwood Anderson, 9 March [1922], in Spanier and Trogdon, *Letters of Ernest Hemingway,* 1:331.

30. Quoted in John Cohassey, *Hemingway and Pound: A Most Unlikely Friendship* (Jefferson, N.C.: McFarland, 2014), 97.

31. Hemingway, "Homage to Ezra," 74.

32. The Hemingway-Fitzgerald relationship has been written about copiously, the most recent volume being Scott Donaldson, *Fitzgerald and Hemingway*. Another foundational work is Donaldson's *Hemingway vs. Fitzgerald*; see also Bruccoli, *Fitzgerald and Hemingway*. For a more specific discussion of Fitzgerald's steering Hemingway to Scribner's, see Donaldson, "Fitzgerald's Blue Pencil," in Kennedy and Bryer, *French Connections*, 15–29.

33. Hemingway to Fitzgerald, 13 September 1929, in Baker, *Selected Letters, 1917–1961*, 306.

34. Hemingway to Fitzgerald, 28 May 1934, ibid., 408.

35. Quoted in Matthew J. Bruccoli, *Some Sort of Epic Grandeur: The Life of F. Scott Fitzgerald* (New York: Harcourt, 1981), 229.

36. Hemingway, *Moveable Feast*, 163.

37. Quoted in Vaill, *Everybody Was So Young*, 114.

38. Quoted in Barbara Gamarekian, "In the Circle of a Charmed Life," *New York Times*, 6 February 1983.

39. Vaill, *Everybody Was So Young*, 165.

40. Murphy to Fitzgerald, 31 December 1935, in *Letters from the Lost Generation: Gerald and Sara Murphy and Friends*, ed. Linda Patterson Miller (New Brunswick: Rutgers University Press, 1991), 151.

41. Quoted in Honoria Murphy Donnelly, with Richard N. Billings, *Sara and Gerald: Villa America and After* (New York: Holt, Rinehart and Winston, 1984), 171.

42. Quoted in Nicholas Joost, *Ernest Hemingway and the Little Magazines: The Paris Years* (Barre, Mass.: Barre Publishers, 1968), 41.

43. Dos Passos, *Best Times*, 143.

44. Beach, *Shakespeare and Company*, 80.

45. Callaghan, *That Summer in Paris*, 211–19.

46. Quoted in Matthew J. Bruccoli, *Scott and Ernest: The Authority of Failure and the Authority of Success* (Carbondale: Southern Illinois University Press, 1980), 93.

47. Arnold Gingrich, "Horsing Them in with Hemingway," *Playboy*, September 1965, 123.

48. Hemingway to Pound, 23 January 1923, in Spanier, DeFazio, and Trogdon, *Letters of Ernest Hemingway*, 2:6. James Mellow argues that Hemingway exaggerated the enormity of the loss, claiming that he had not yet had time to produce as much work as he said was in the suitcase. Mellow also points out that Hemingway took his time in returning to Paris to search for the manuscripts, the lack of urgency suggesting that their number was not very large. *Hemingway: A Life Without Consequences*, 208–11.

49. Sanford, *At the Hemingways*, 221.

50. Spanier, DeFazio, and Trogdon, *Letters of Ernest Hemingway*, 2:6.

51. See Tom Dardis, *Firebrand: The Life of Horace Liveright* (New York: Random House, 1995), for the complete story of Liveright's life and career. A helpful supplement to this biography is Charles Egleston, *The House of Boni and Liveright, 1917–1933: A Documentary Volume* (Detroit: Gale Research, 2003), which reprints much of the author-publisher correspondence in facsimile.

52. Liveright famously won an obscenity case, lodged against him by Vice Society flag-bearer John Sumner, for publishing Maxwell Bodenheim's rather tawdry *Replenishing Jessica* (1925), thus cementing his reputation as a publisher willing to take risks with unorthodox material.

53. Fitzgerald, *A Brief Autobiography*, ed. James L. W. West III (New York: Simon and Schuster, 2011), 89–91, reprinted in the May 1926 issue of the *Bookman*.

54. Robert Paul Lamb makes an interesting argument, however, that Hemingway's innovation in dialogue was spurred by William Dean Howells's "realist mandates

of fidelity to experience and probability of motive." See Lamb, *Art Matters: Hemingway, Craft, and the Creation of the Modern Short Story* (Baton Rouge: Louisiana State University Press, 2010), 173. Lamb also notes that Hemingway learned from Henry James the art of indirection and ambiguity. A more recent book by Lamb—*The Hemingway Short Story: A Study in Craft for Writers and Readers* (Baton Rouge: Louisiana State University Press, 2013) (something of a sequel to *Art Matters*)—presents extremely close, tightly argued readings of several classic Hemingway tales.

55. Quoted in Stephens, *Ernest Hemingway: The Critical Reception*, 7.

56. Jack Hemingway interviewed in *Ernest Hemingway: Wrestling with Life*, documentary film produced for A&E television, 1997.

CHAPTER 5

1. What Hemingway referred to as "the first bullfight I ever saw," in an account published in the *Toronto Star Weekly* on 20 October 1923 ("Bullfighting a Tragedy"), was actually the conflation of a pair of corridas from July 1923, according to Miriam B. Mandel in "The Birth of Hemingway's *Afición:* Madrid and 'The First Bullfight I Ever Saw,'" *Journal of Modern Literature* 23, no. 1 (1999): 127–42.

2. See Matthew J. Bruccoli, "The Hemingway/Fenton Correspondence," in *Dictionary of Literary Biography Yearbook 2002,* ed. Matthew J. Bruccoli and George Garrett (Detroit: Gale Research, 2003), 282–85.

3. Donald Ogden Stewart, "An Interview," *Hemingway-Fitzgerald Annual, 1973* (Washington, D.C.: NCR Microcard Editions, 1974), 85.

4. Hemingway to Pound, [30 November 1925], in Spanier, DeFazio, and Trogdon, *Letters of Ernest Hemingway,* 2:422–23.

5. Fitzgerald to Horace Liveright and T. R. Smith, before 30 December 1925, in *The Correspondence of F. Scott Fitzgerald,* ed. Matthew J. Bruccoli and Margaret Duggan (New York: Random House, 1980), 183.

6. Hemingway to Liveright, 7 December 1925, in Spanier, DeFazio, and Trogdon, *Letters of Ernest Hemingway,* 2:435.

7. Hemingway to Pound, [30 November 1925], ibid., 422.

8. Quoted in Walker Gilmer, *Horace Liveright: Publisher of the Twenties* (New York: D. Lewis, 1970), 123.

9. Welford Dunaway Taylor proposes that the book was more than a way out of his obligation to Liveright; it also shows the "anxiety of influence" that bore down on Hemingway through his intensive reading during this period. See Taylor, "A Shelter from *The Torrents of Spring,*" in Kennedy and Bryer, *French Connections*, 101–19. Although seldom mentioned, *The Torrents of Spring* is also the title of a novel by the Russian writer Ivan Turgenev.

10. Catherine Turner advances a fascinating theory about Scribner's wooing of Hemingway, in "Changing American Literary Taste: Scribner's and Ernest Hemingway," in her book *Marketing Modernism Between the Two World Wars* (Amherst: University of Massachusetts Press, 2003). Turner paints a compelling picture of the publisher's institutional exploitation of a willing Hemingway, a strategy designed to permanently alter middlebrow literary tastes.

11. Callaghan, *That Summer in Paris,* 216. Perkins was not, however, without weaknesses. For one thing, he was not a good copyeditor. Fitzgerald's work was poorly proofread and marred by errors, earning him a reputation for sloppiness with details. Hemingway's later novel *To Have and Have Not,* in particular, is riddled with typographical mistakes and internal inconsistencies.

12. Hemingway once wrote Perkins, "please remember that when I am loud mouthed, bitter, rude, son of a bitching and mistrustful I am really very reasonable and have great confidence and absolute trust in you." Hemingway to Perkins, 27 April 1931, in Bruccoli, *Only Thing That Counts,* 157.

13. Hemingway to Anderson, 21 May 1926, in Baker, *Selected Letters, 1917–1961,* 205.

14. Anderson to Hemingway, [14 June 1926], in Charles E. Modlin, *Sherwood Anderson: Selected Letters* (Knoxville: University of Tennessee Press, 1984), 78–80.

15. Hemingway to Anderson, 1 July 1926, in Baker, *Selected Letters, 1917–1961,* 210.

16. Box ms 53, ms KL/EH 535, Hemingway Collection.

17. Ibid., 536a.

18. See Michael S. Reynolds and Judy Jo Small, "Hemingway v. Anderson: The Final Rounds," *Hemingway Review* 14 (Spring 1995): 1–17. Hemingway may have taken satirical aim yet a third time at Anderson. There is an unpublished manuscript fragment at the Kennedy Library titled "Back When $40 a Week Was Good Money"; the story concerns one Eugene Dawes, who gives up a well-paying job as a theatrical electrician to become a copywriter for an ad agency. The character seems to be modeled closely on Anderson.

19. Hemingway made these comments in the preface to a projected collection of his stories for classroom use, a project broached to him by his publisher in 1959. Hemingway wrote the preface, but for various reasons the project was dropped. Titled "The Art of the Short Story," it was first published in volume 79 of the *Paris Review* in 1981. The passages here are taken from its appearance in *New Critical Approaches to the Short Stories of Ernest Hemingway,* ed. Jackson J. Benson (Durham: Duke University Press, 1990), 12.

20. Sherwood Anderson, *Sherwood Anderson's Memoirs: A Critical Edition,* ed. Ray Lewis White (New York: Harcourt, Brace, 1942), 475.

21. Box ms 38, ms 295, Hemingway Collection.

22. Dos Passos, *Best Times,* 155.

23. Hemingway to Heap, [ca. 23 August 1925], in Spanier, DeFazio, and Trogdon, *Letters of Ernest Hemingway,* 2:383.

24. Dorman-Smith to Hemingway, 16 December 1925, Hemingway Collection.

25. Item 194, notebook III, ibid.

26. See Hemingway, *The Sun Also Rises: The Hemingway Library Edition* (New York: Simon and Schuster, 2014), appendix 2, 226.

27. Svoboda, *Hemingway and "The Sun Also Rises,"* 105.

28. Hemingway to Perkins, 5 June 1926, in Bruccoli, *Only Thing That Counts,* 40–41.

29. Meyers, *Hemingway: A Biography,* 152–53.

30. Quoted in Harold Loeb, "Ernest Hemingway: A Life Story," *Southern Review,* new ser., 5 (Autumn 1969): 1214–15.

31. Hadley Richardson Mowrer, interview by Carlos Baker, quoted in Reynolds, *Hemingway, The Paris Years,* 290–91.

32. Ibid., 289.

33. Kitty Cannell (1963), quoted in Bertram D. Sarason, *Hemingway and the Sun Set* (Washington, D.C.: Microcard Editions, 1972), 149.

34. Quoted in Brian, *True Gen,* 58.

35. *New Yorker,* 23 October 1926, 82.

36. For these reviews, see Meyers, *Hemingway: The Critical Heritage.*

37. Conrad Aiken, review of *The Sun Also Rises, New York Herald Tribune Books,* 31 October 1926, 4; Herbert Gorman, review of *The Sun Also Rises, New York World,* 14 November 1926, both reprinted in Meyers, *Hemingway: The Critical Heritage,* 90–91 and 92, respectively.

38. Unsigned review of *The Sun Also Rises, Chicago Daily Tribune*, 27 November 1926, 18.

39. Unsigned review of *The Sun Also Rises, Time* magazine, 1 November 1926, 48.

40. Edwin Muir, review of *The Sun Also Rises, Nation and Athenaeum*, 2 July 1927, 450, 452, reprinted in Meyers, *Hemingway: The Critical Heritage*, 96.

41. Dos Passos, "A Lost Generation," *New Masses*, December 1926, 26.

CHAPTER 6

1. Hemingway, *Moveable Feast: The Restored Edition*, 215–16.

2. Dos Passos, *Best Times*, 204.

3. Hawkins, *Unbelievable Happiness and Final Sorrow*, 65–67.

4. Quoted in Kert, *Hemingway Women*, 176, 178–79.

5. Quoted in ibid., 182.

6. Lynn, *Hemingway*, 347.

7. Baker, *Selected Letters, 1917–1961*, 217.

8. Baker, *Hemingway: A Life Story*, 591.

9. Baker, *Selected Letters, 1917–1961*, 222.

10. Hadley Richardson to Hemingway, 16 November 1926, Hemingway Collection.

11. Quoted in William Bird to Carlos Baker, in Baker, *Hemingway: A Life Story*, 178.

12. Baker, *Selected Letters, 1917–1961*, 222.

13. Quoted in Meyers, *Hemingway: A Biography*, 179.

14. Ruth Hawkins, to the contrary, contends that Pauline actually helped Hemingway with his writing. As an accomplished writer herself and a graduate of the Missouri School of Journalism, Hawkins argues, she was his best editor. *Unbelievable Happiness and Final Sorrow*, 44.

15. Hemingway, *Moveable Feast: The Restored Edition*, 219.

16. Hemingway to Hadley Richardson, 18 November 1926, in Baker, *Hemingway: A Life Story*, 227–28.

17. In 1929, Mowrer won the first Pulitzer Prize for foreign correspondent reporting, for his stories on efforts to create the League of Nations.

18. Meyers, *Hemingway: A Biography*, 183.

19. Dos Passos, *Best Times*, 199.

20. Chief among them Jacqueline Tavernier-Courbin, in *Ernest Hemingway's "A Moveable Feast."*

21. George Plimpton, *Shadow Box: An Amateur in the Ring* (New York: Putnam, 1977), 143.

22. Hemingway to Martha Gellhorn, [August 1942], Hemingway Collection.

23. Bruccoli, *Conversations with Ernest Hemingway*, 181.

24. Hemingway to Perkins, 13 June 1933, in Bruccoli, *Only Thing That Counts*, 190.

25. For discussions of the homoeroticism in Hemingway's work and in his circle, see Spilka, *Hemingway's Quarrel with Androgyny*. Andrew Hoffman, in *Inventing Mark Twain: The Lives of Samuel Langhorne Clemens* (New York: Harper Collins, 1998), delves deeply into Twain's close relationships with male friends during his years as a reporter in California and Nevada.

26. *Time* magazine, 18 October, 1937. The saturnine Peirce was once called "the Ernest Hemingway of American painters," to which he replied, "They'll never call Ernest Hemingway the Waldo Peirce of American writers."

27. Hemingway to Malcolm Cowley, 14 November 1945, in Baker, *Selected Letters, 1917–1961*, 605.

28. See Hemingway, *My Brother, Ernest Hemingway,* 190.

29. MacLeish, "His Mirror Was Danger," *Life,* 14 July 1961, 171.

30. William Walton, interview by Rose Marie Burwell, oral history transcript, 12, Hemingway Collection.

31. Hemingway to Martha Gellhorn, 25 August [1942], ibid.

32. Elizabeth Bishop to Robert Lowell, 18 November 1947, in *Words in Air: The Complete Correspondence Between Elizabeth Bishop and Robert Lowell,* ed. Thomas Travisano and Saskia Hamilton (New York: Farrar, Straus and Giroux, 2008), 13.

33. Quoted in Eugene Ehrlich and Gorton Carruth, *Oxford Illustrated Literary Guide to the United States* (New York: Oxford University Press, 1982), 263.

34. Quoted in Brian Burnes, "In 1928 in Kansas City, Hemingway Gained a Son and a Novel Insight," *Kansas City Star,* 27 June 1999, 2.

35. Hemingway to Peirce, 17 and 19 June 1928, Waldo Peirce Papers, Colby College, Waterville, Maine.

36. See Reynolds, *Hemingway's First War,* 138, 142, 144–45.

37. Hemingway to Peirce, 17 and 19 July 1928, Waldo Peirce Papers, Colby College, Waterville, Maine.

38. Hemingway to Peirce, 6 July 1928, ibid.

39. Quoted in Reynolds, *Young Hemingway,* 349.

40. Hemingway to Jane Mason, 16 October 1933, Hemingway Collection.

41. Sanford, *At the Hemingways,* 179.

42. Quoted in Fenton, *Apprenticeship of Ernest Hemingway,* 35.

43. Hemingway to Peirce, 23 July 1928, Waldo Peirce Papers, Colby College, Waterville, Maine.

44. Hemingway to Peirce, 9 August 1928, ibid.

45. Ibid.

46. Hemingway to Martha Gellhorn, 31 July 1942, Hemingway Collection.

47. Hemingway to "Mouse and Gigi," [1944], ibid.

48. Hemingway, *My Brother, Ernest Hemingway,* 111.

49. John Sanford documents Ed's real-estate dealings in "A Garden of Eden, or, Hemingway's Last Lot," *North Dakota Quarterly* 66, no. 2 (1999): 101–12.

50. Quoted in Morris Buske, "The Soldier's Home Again," *Hemingway Review* 15 (Spring 1996): 104–7.

51. Paul Hendrickson, in *Hemingway's Boat,* points out that Ed had had to go away for a "rest cure" in 1912, and that Hemingway always regarded his father with a certain mixture of anxiety and pity (381).

52. Clarence E. Hemingway to Grace Hemingway, 18 July 1920, Hemingway Family Papers, Harry Ransom Center.

53. Meyers, *Hemingway: A Biography,* 48.

54. "He was quite thin and blonde," ms fragment, box ms 50, ms 471, Hemingway Collection.

55. Quoted in Hawkins, *Unbelievable Happiness and Final Sorrow,* 96.

56. Hemingway to Mary Pfeiffer, 13 December 1928, Carlos Baker Papers, Firestone Library, Princeton University.

57. Jack Hemingway, panel discussion, Hemingway Centennial Literary Conference, Oak Park, Illinois, 19–21 July 1999.

58. Hemingway, *My Brother, Ernest Hemingway,* 111.

59. For a good comparison of the two novels, see William Adair, "*The Sun Also Rises:* The Source of *A Farewell to Arms,*" *American Notes and Queries* 12, no. 4 (1999): 25–28. Adair contends that Hemingway found the structural source of *A Farewell to Arms* in the earlier novel "more consciously than unconsciously" (25).

60. Joan Didion, "Last Words," *New Yorker,* 9 November 1998, 74.

61. Michael S. Reynolds discusses this in *Hemingway's First War.* See also "The Sense of an Ending," in Bernard Oldsey, *Hemingway's Hidden Craft: The Writing of "A Farewell to Arms"* (University Park: Pennsylvania State University Press, 1979).

62. Hemingway, interview by George Plimpton, in "Ernest Hemingway: The Art of Fiction, No. 21," *Paris Review* 5 (Spring 1958): 60–89, reprinted in Bruccoli, *Conversations with Ernest Hemingway,* 113.

63. Fitzgerald to Hemingway, 1 June 1934, in *The Correspondence of F. Scott Fitzgerald,* ed. Matthew J. Bruccoli and Margaret Duggan (New York: Random House, 1980), 264.

64. See James B. Meriwether, "The Dashes in Hemingway's *A Farewell to Arms,*" *Papers of the Bibliographical Society of America* 57 (October–December 1964): 451–54.

65. Bruccoli, *Only Thing That Counts,* 122.

66. James Aswell, "Critic Lavishes Praise on New Hemingway Novel," *Richmond Times-Dispatch,* 6 October 1929, 3.

67. Henry Seidel Canby, "Story of the Brave," *Saturday Review of Literature,* 12 October 1929, 231.

68. Dos Passos, "A Farewell to Arms," *New Masses,* 1 December 1929, 16.

69. Burton Rascoe, *A Bookman's Daybook* (New York: H. Liveright, 1929), quoted in Reynolds, *Hemingway, The 1930s,* 28.

70. Quoted in ibid., 28.

71. Robert Herrick, "What Is Dirt?" *Bookman* 70 (November 1929): 258–62.

72. MacLeish to Hemingway, 1 September 1929, in *Letters of Archibald MacLeish, 1907 to 1982,* ed. R. H. Winnick (Boston: Houghton Mifflin, 1983), 230.

73. Hemingway to Perkins, 17 November 1929, in Bruccoli, *Only Thing That Counts,* 125.

CHAPTER 7

1. Josephine Herbst, "The Hour of Counterfeit Bliss," 7, in Josephine Herbst Papers, Yale Collection of American Literature, Beinecke Rare Book and Manuscript Library, Yale University.

2. Josephine Herbst to Katherine Anne Porter, 1 April 1930, ibid.

3. Hemingway to Perkins, 16 November 1933, in Baker, *Selected Letters, 1917–1961,* 400.

4. Gregory Hemingway interviewed in *Ernest Hemingway: Wrestling with Life*, documentary film produced for A&E television, 1997.

5. Hemingway to Perkins, 15 April 1925, in Baker, *Selected Letters, 1917–1961,* 156.

6. Meyers, *Hemingway: A Biography,* 230.

7. Hemingway to Strater, 20 May 1930, ibid., 322.

8. See G. A. Pfeiffer to A. M. Teixidor, 3 and 4 June 1930, Hemingway Collection.

9. Brian, *True Gen,* 83.

10. *Key West Citizen,* 30 April 1931, quoted in Chamberlin, *Hemingway Log,* 108.

11. Hemingway to Peirce, 4 May 1931, Hemingway Collection.

12. Juanito Quintana to Hemingway, 25 June 1931, ibid.

13. Hemingway to Louis Henry Cohn, [16 November 1931], Special Collections, Morris Library, University of Delaware.

14. Hemingway to Peirce, ca. 12 November 1931, in Baker, *Selected Letters, 1917–1961,* 343.

15. Hemingway to Perkins, 9 December 1931, Scribner Archive, Firestone Library, Princeton University.

16. Hemingway to Hickok, 12 December 1931, Yale Collection of American Literature, Beinecke Rare Book and Manuscript Library, Yale University.

17. Hemingway to MacLeish, 9 December 1931, Archibald MacLeish Papers, Library of Congress, Washington, D.C.

18. Dos Passos to Hemingway, [February 1932], in Dos Passos, *Fourteenth Chronicle,* 402–3.

19. Hemingway to Perkins, 28 June 1932, in Baker, *Selected Letters, 1917–1961,* 362.

20. Perkins to Hemingway, 25 January 1932, in Bruccoli, *Only Thing That Counts,* 158.

21. Trogdon, *Lousy Racket,* 117. Hemingway had a famous outburst when the galley proofs arrived with the running head "hemingway's death." He fired off a telegram to Perkins: "Did it seem very funny to slug every galley Hemingways death or was that what you wanted. Have been plenty sick." Intensely superstitious, Hemingway told Perkins in a letter the following day, "You know I am superstitious and it is a hell of a damn dirty business to stare at that a thousand times. . . . If I would have passed out would have said your godamned lot put the curse on me." See also Robert W. Trogdon, "The Composition, Publication, Revision, and Reception," in Mandel, *Companion to Hemingway's "Death,"* 30.

22. Trogdon, *Lousy Racket,* 108–10.

23. Laurence Stallings, review of *Death in the Afternoon, New York Sun,* 23 September 1932, 34; Ben Ray Redman, "Blood and Sand, and Art," *Saturday Review of Literature,* 24 September 1932, 121; H. L. Mencken, "The Spanish Idea of a Good Time," *American Mercury,* December 1932, 506–7.

24. Robert Coates, review of *Death in the Afternoon, New Yorker,* 1 October 1932, 61–63 (quotation on 61); Granville Hicks, review of *Death in the Afternoon, Nation,* 9 November 1932, 461.

25. Herschel Brickell, review of *Death in the Afternoon, New York Herald Tribune Books,* 25 September 1932, 3, 12 (quotation on 12).

26. See Nancy Bredendick, "Death in the Afternoon as Seen by Tomás Orts-Ramos," *Hemingway Review* 24 (Spring 2005): 56.

27. Hemingway to Perkins, 13 June 1933, in Baker, *Selected Letters, 1917–1961,* 394.

28. Hemingway to Perkins, 17 November 1933, in Bruccoli, *Only Thing That Counts,* 203.

29. Perkins described the event in a letter to F. Scott Fitzgerald, 24 August 1937, in F. Scott Fitzgerald and Maxwell E. Perkins, *Dear Scott / Dear Max: The Fitzgerald-Perkins Correspondence* (New York: Scribner, 1971), 238–40.

30. Max Eastman, *Great Companions: Critical Memoirs of Some Famous Friends* (New York: Farrar, Straus, 1959), 46–47.

31. Hemingway to Murphy, ca. 27 February 1936, in Baker, *Selected Letters, 1917–1961,* 439.

32. Sanford, *At the Hemingways,* 225–26.

33. Baker, *Selected Letters, 1917–1961,* 126–28. Paul Hendrickson also mentions this event in *Hemingway's Boat,* 243.

34. Hemingway, *Papa: A Personal Memoir,* 18–19.

35. Hemingway to Mrs. Paul Pfeiffer, 26 January 1936, in Baker, *Selected Letters, 1917–1961,* 436.

36. Quoted in Barbara Gamarekian, "In the Circle of a Charmed Life," *New York Times,* 6 February 1983. See Hendrickson, *Hemingway's Boat,* for a detailed account of the lives of Samuelson and Houk and their relationships with Hemingway.

37. See Gail Sinclair, "Carol and Ernest Hemingway: The Letters of Loss," *Hemingway Review* 24 (Fall 2004): 37–48.

CHAPTER 8

1. Quoted in Meyers, *Hemingway: A Biography,* 243.

2. Quoted in Kert, *Hemingway Women,* 265.

3. Meyers, *Hemingway: A Biography,* 243.

4. Jane Mason to Hemingway, [1933], Hemingway Collection.

5. Quoted in Reynolds, *Hemingway: The 1930s,* 130. More information on Jane Mason is available in *Hemingway Notes* 21, no. 2 (2002), a special issue with an introduction by Susan F. Beegel to Mason's play, *Safari.* See especially the introduction to the issue (13–21) by Alane Salierno Mason, Jane Mason's adoptive granddaughter, who found the manuscript of "The Short Happy Life of Francis Macomber," along with letters and telegrams, in steamer trunks belonging to Mason. These discoveries formed the basis for two articles (one in *Vanity Fair* in July 1999 and one in the *Boston Review* in February/March 2001) by Alane Mason that give fully detailed pictures of the Hemingway-Mason relationship and the ways in which Hemingway used Mason as a model for Margot Macomber.

6. Hemingway to MacLeish, 27 July 1933, Archibald MacLeish Papers, Library of Congress, Washington, D.C.

7. Interestingly, in the manuscript version, Tommy is much more likable and far from impotent—a Hemingway surrogate; he avoids Helene because he feels that he can do better.

8. Hemingway to Jane Mason, 19 September [1932], Hemingway Collection.

9. Jane Mason to Hemingway, [1932?], ibid.

10. Hemingway to "Poor dear old daughter," [1932], ibid.

11. Hemingway to Jane Mason, 16 October 1933, ibid.

12. Quoted in Meyers, *Hemingway: A Biography,* 246.

13. Hemingway to Jane Mason, 9 July 1932, ibid.

14. Hemingway to Jane Mason, 12 November 1932, ibid.

15. See Meyers, *Hemingway: A Biography,* 247–52. Hemingway was still involved with Jane as late as December 1936, just a few weeks before he met Martha Gellhorn.

16. Hemingway, *Dateline: Toronto,* 147.

17. See Kevin Maier, "Hemingway's Ecotourism: *Under Kilimanjaro* and the Ethics of Travel," *Interdisciplinary Studies in Literature and Environment* 18, no. 4 (2011): 717–36.

18. Isak Dinesen, *Out of Africa* (London: Putnam, 1947), 21.

19. See Brian Herne, *White Hunters: The Golden Age of African Safaris* (New York: Henry Holt, 1999), 71–74.

20. Theodore Roosevelt, *African Game Trails* (New York: Charles Scribner's Sons, 1910), 47.

21. Quoted in Meyers, *Hemingway: A Biography,* 262.

22. Hemingway, "Notes on Dangerous Game: The Third Tanganyika Letter," *Esquire,* July 1934, reprinted in Hemingway, *By-Line,* 167–71 (quotations on 168).

23. Hemingway to Cadwalader, 13 December 1934, reprinted in Lawrence H. Martin, "Ernest Hemingway, Gulf Stream Marine Scientist: The 1934–35 Academy of Natural Sciences Correspondence," *Hemingway Notes* 20, no. 2 (2001): 5–15.

24. See Errol Trzebinski, *The Lives of Beryl Markham* (New York: W. W. Norton, 1993), 191–95.

25. Hemingway to Perkins, 27 August 1942, in Baker, *Selected Letters, 1917–1961,* 541. See also Barry Shlachter, "A Life of Adventure Rediscovered: Beryl Markham's 1942 Book, Lauded by Hemingway, Reprinted," *International Herald Tribune* (Paris), 16 June 1983.

26. Stewart Edward White, *The Undiscovered Country* (New York: Doubleday, Page, 1915), 113.

27. Hemingway, "A. D. in Africa: A Tanganyika Letter," *Esquire,* August 1934, reprinted in Hemingway, *By-Line,* 161.

28. "Karl" was Hemingway's fictional name for Thompson. Hemingway had initially invited Archibald MacLeish and Mike Strater to go on the trip instead, but both had refused, perhaps sensing that it would turn into a contest that, one way or the other, neither could win.

29. John H. Patterson, *In the Grip of the Nyika: Further Adventures in British East Africa* (New York: Macmillan, 1909), 296, 302. For information on Patterson, see his obituary in the *New York Times,* 20 June 1947, which refers to the Blyth incident, and Meyers, *Hemingway: A Biography,* 268–72.

30. Hemingway to Dos Passos, 13 February 1934, Dos Passos Papers, Alderman Library, University of Virginia, Charlottesville.

31. Perkins to Hemingway, 28 November 1934, in Bruccoli, *Only Thing That Counts,* 217.

32. Hemingway to Perkins, 20 November 1934, ibid., 214–16.

33. Hemingway to Perkins, 16 November 1934, ibid., 213.

34. Quoted in Trogdon, *Lousy Racket,* 153. Peter Fleming's nonfiction *Brazilian Adventure* was a best seller for Scribner's in 1933. For an interesting interpretation of *Green Hills,* see Lawrence H. Martin, "Hemingway's Constructed Africa: *Green Hills of Africa* and the Conventions of Colonial Sporting Books," in Fleming, *Hemingway and the Natural World,* 87–97.

35. Edmund Wilson, "Ernest Hemingway: Gauge of Morale," *Atlantic Monthly,* July 1939, 36–46, reprinted in Meyers, *Hemingway: A Biography,* 305; Bernard DeVoto, "Hemingway in the Valley," *Saturday Review of Literature,* 26 October 1935, 5; and Granville Hicks, "Small Game Hunting," *New Masses,* 19 November 1935, 23, reprinted in Meyers, *Hemingway: A Biography,* 215.

CHAPTER 9

1. Quoted in Lynn, *Hemingway,* 464. For details on Gellhorn's life, see Carl S. Rollyson, *Nothing Ever Happens to the Brave: The Story of Martha Gellhorn* (New York: St. Martin's Press, 1990). See also Caroline Moorhead, *Martha Gellhorn: A Twentieth-Century Life* (New York: Macmillan, 2007).

2. Graham Greene, "Short Stories," *Spectator,* 22 May 1936, 950.

3. Quoted in James McLendon, *Papa: Hemingway in Key West* (Miami: Seeman, 1972), 165.

4. Martha Gellhorn to Eleanor Roosevelt, 8 January 1937, in *Selected Letters of Martha Gellhorn,* 45.

5. Archibald MacLeish to Carlos Baker, 9 August 1963, Carlos Baker Papers, Firestone Library, Princeton University.

6. H. L. Salmon amplifies this idea in "Martha Gellhorn and Ernest Hemingway: A Literary Relationship" (master's thesis, University of North Texas, 2003).

7. See A. Scott Berg, *Max Perkins: Editor of Genius* (New York: Scribner, 1978), 399.

8. Quoted in Brian, *True Gen,* 144. In a 1981 article, "On Apocryphism," she wrote that her career "had started long before I ever met Ernest Hemingway. It should be noted that I never used his name or my association with him, not when I was married to him or ever after." Ibid.

9. See Sandra Whipple Spanier, "Rivalry, Romance, and War Reporters: Martha Gellhorn's *Love Goes to Press* and the *Collier's* Files," in Broer and Holland, *Hemingway and Women,* 275.

10. Scholarship suffers from a dearth of attention to *To Have and Have Not,* although a fairly recent collection of essays on the novel can be found in Curnutt and Sinclair, *Key West Hemingway.*

11. Hemingway to Perkins, 19 April 1935, in Bruccoli, *Only Thing That Counts,* 242–43.

12. Hemingway to Perkins, 11 July 1936, ibid., 243–44.

13. Hemingway to Perkins, 26 September 1936, quoted in Trogdon, *Lousy Racket,* 174.

14. Hemingway to Perkins, 2 December 1936, quoted in ibid., 175.

15. See Robert W. Trogdon, "'Their Money's Worth': The Composition, Editing, and Publication," in *One Man Alone: Hemingway and "To Have and Have Not,"* ed. Toni D. Knott (Lanham, Md.: University Press of America, 1999), 47–63.

16. See Hemingway to Perkins, 19 April 1936, in Bruccoli, *Only Thing That Counts,* 243.

17. Trogdon, *Lousy Racket,* 183.

18. Sinclair Lewis, "Glorious Dirt," *Newsweek,* 8 October 1937, 34; Louis Kronenberger, review of *To Have and Have Not, Nation,* 23 October 1937, 439–40, reprinted in Meyers, *Hemingway: The Critical Heritage,* 236–38; V. S. Pritchett, review of *To Have and Have Not, Now & Then* 58 (Winter 1937): 29–30; and George Stevens, "Two Kinds of Life," *Saturday Review of Literature,* 16 October 1937, 6–7.

19. Bernard DeVoto, "Tiger, Tiger!," *Saturday Review of Literature,* 16 October 1937, 8.

20. For an interesting perspective on Hemingway and literary politics, see Brock Clarke, "What Literature Can and Cannot Do: Lionel Trilling, Richard Rorty, and the Left," *Michigan Review* 41 (2001): 523–39. Clarke observes that it was "not that Hemingway could not write political literature, but rather that Hemingway, aided and abetted by left-wing critics, had forgotten how expansive such literature had been and might still be" (528).

21. Stanley G. Payne, *Spain's First Democracy: The Second Republic, 1931–1936* (Madison: University of Wisconsin Press, 1993), 12.

22. W. H. Auden to E. R. Dodds, December 1936, quoted in Auden, *Early Auden,* ed. Edward Mendelson (New York: Farrar, Straus and Giroux, 2000), 195–96. For a recent analysis of writers' involvement in the Spanish Civil War, see Vaill, *Hotel Florida.* Alex Vernon provides an impressively detailed account of Hemingway's involvement in the Spanish war, drawing on numerous primary sources, in *Hemingway's Second War.* See also Phillip Knightley's classic history of journalism in wartime, *The First Casualty,* 3rd ed. (Baltimore: Johns Hopkins University Press, 2004). Writing of Hemingway's North American Newspaper Alliance dispatches, Knightley argues that Hemingway saved his best material from his reporting for *For Whom the Bell Tolls*: "For a novelist this was understandable. For a war correspondent, it was unforgivable" (232). Scott Donaldson offers a more positive analysis of the NANA pieces in *Fitzgerald and Hemingway,* 424–39.

23. Laurie Lee, *A Moment of War* (New York: Free Press, 1994), 46.

24. Quoted in Brian, *True Gen,* 118.

25. For an excellent discussion of how Hemingway "transformed himself from a propagandist with Stalinist inclinations into a political novelist of the first magnitude," see John Raeburn, "Hemingway on Stage: *The Fifth Column,* Politics, and Biography," *Hemingway Review* 18 (Fall 1998): 5–16 (quotation on 16).

26. Gellhorn, *Face of War,* 20.

27. Ibid., 37.

28. Martha Gellhorn, interview by Kevin Kerrane, "Martha's Quest," *Salon* magazine, 12 March 1998, www.salon1999.com/archives/1998/media.html.

29. George Orwell, *Homage to Catalonia* (New York: Harcourt, Brace, and World, 1952), 9.

30. Quoted in Brian, *True Gen,* 115.

31. Quoted in Cecil D. Eby, *Comrades and Commissars: The Lincoln Battalion in the Spanish Civil War* (University Park: Pennsylvania State University Press, 2007), 123.

32. Amanda Vaill, *Hotel Florida,* 173.

33. Quoted in Brian, *True Gen,* 109–10.

34. "Fascism Is a Lie," 4 June 1937, reprinted in Bruccoli, *Conversations with Ernest Hemingway,* 193.

35. See Scott Donaldson, *Archibald MacLeish* (Boston: Houghton Mifflin, 1992), 264–65.

36. Folsom, *Days of Anger, Days of Hope: A Memoir of the League of American Writers, 1937–1942* (Boulder: University Press of Colorado, 1994), 9.

37. Quoted in Baker, *Hemingway: A Life Story,* 314.

38. See Stephen Koch, *The Breaking Point: Hemingway, Dos Passos, and the Murder of José Robles* (New York: Counterpoint, 2005).

39. See Hans Schoots, *Living Dangerously: A Biography of Joris Ivens* (Amsterdam: Amsterdam University Press, 2000).

40. Quoted in Meyers, *Hemingway: A Biography,* 311.

41. Hemingway, "Afterword," *Spanish Earth,* 55–56.

42. Quoted in Meyers, *Hemingway: A Biography,* 312.

43. Quoted in ibid., 314. The voiceover was recorded on 13–14 July 1937 at Paramount Studios in Hollywood.

44. Hotchner, *Papa Hemingway,* 78.

45. Quoted in Meyers, *Hemingway: The Critical Heritage,* 258.

46. William Walton, interview by Rose Marie Burwell, oral history transcript, Hemingway Collection. Linda Stein challenges the conception of Philip Rawlings as a stoical stereotype by tracing Hemingway's changes in prepublication drafts of the play. See Stein, "Hemingway's *The Fifth Column*: Comparing the Typescript Drafts to the Published Play," *North Dakota Quarterly* 68, nos. 2–3 (2001): 233–44. For the problems Hemingway encountered in having the play produced, see Richard Allan Davison, "Hemingway and the Theater," *North Dakota Quarterly* 70, no. 1 (2004): 166–77.

CHAPTER 10

1. For a recent comprehensive cultural history of immigration and immigrants in Cuba and North America, see Louis A. Perez Jr., *On Becoming Cuban: Identity, Nationality, and Culture* (Chapel Hill: University of North Carolina Press, 1999), 73–74, 88–89, 414–32. For the specific influence of Cuban culture in Hemingway's fiction, see Bickford Sylvester's excellent "The Cuban Context of *The Old Man and the Sea,*" in *Ernest Hemingway's "The Old Man and the Sea,"* ed. Harold Bloom (London: Chelsea House, 1999), 165–84; and Larry Grimes and Bickford Sylvester, eds., *Hemingway, Cuba, and the Cuban Works* (Kent: Kent State University Press, 2014).

2. Graham Greene, *Ways of Escape* (New York: Simon & Schuster, 1980), 240.

3. Hemingway, "Marlin Off the Morro: A Cuban Letter," *Esquire,* Autumn 1933, reprinted in Hemingway, *By-Line,* 137.

4. Quoted in Dos Passos, *Fourteenth Chronicle,* 421.

5. See Eduardo Zayas-Bazan, "Hemingway: His Cuban Friends Remember," *Fitzgerald/Hemingway Annual* (1975): 153–90.

6. For more information on Menocal and Elicio Arguelles, see Meyers, *Hemingway: A Biography,* 330–32.

7. Hemingway, *My Brother, Ernest Hemingway,* 117.

8. Quoted in Meyers, *Hemingway: A Biography,* 331.

9. Quoted in Hemingway, *How It Was,* 381–82.

10. Hemingway, interview by George Plimpton, in "Ernest Hemingway: The Art of Fiction, No. 21," *Paris Review* 5 (Spring 1958): 60–89, reprinted in Bruccoli, *Conversations with Ernest Hemingway,* 128.

11. Robert van Gelder, "Ernest Hemingway Talks of Love and War," *New York Times,* 11 August 1940, reprinted in ibid., 17.

12. Hemingway to Perkins, 25 March 1939, in Baker, *Selected Letters, 1917–1961,* 82. See Trogdon, *Lousy Racket,* 199–217, for a complete history of the composition, revision, and publication of the book.

13. Hemingway to Perkins, 27 October 1939, quoted in Trogdon, *Lousy Racket,* 201.

14. Hemingway to Perkins, mid-November 1939, quoted in ibid., 201.

15. Perkins to Hemingway, 19 December 1939, quoted in ibid., 202.

16. Hemingway to Perkins, [ca. 14 January 1940], in Bruccoli, *Only Thing That Counts,* 277.

17. Galley proofs, *For Whom the Bell Tolls,* Cohn Collection, University of Delaware Special Collections.

18. Robert Manning, "Hemingway in Cuba," *Atlantic Monthly,* August 1965, 101–8, reprinted in Bruccoli, *Conversations with Ernest Hemingway,* 180.

19. MS 198–99, 200 (box MS 10, folder 83), 566 (box MS 11, folder 83), Hemingway Collection.

20. See Thomas Gould, "Authorial Revision and Editorial Emasculation in Ernest Hemingway's *For Whom the Bell Tolls,*" in *Blowing the Bridge: Essays on Hemingway and "For Whom the Bell Tolls,"* ed. Rena Sanderson (New York: Greenwood Press, 1992), 67–82.

21. See Robert W. Trogdon, "Money and Marriage: Hemingway's Self-Censorship in *For Whom the Bell Tolls,*" *Hemingway Review* 22 (Fall 2003): 6–18, for a fuller discussion of Hemingway's possible rationale for rendering the profanities in the novel in this way.

22. However, lest the novel be considered mere fantasy, it is worth noting that the book had a profound impact on the young revolutionary Fidel Castro. "We had to develop ideas to overcome the immense obstacle of defeating a government that was backed by an army of eighty thousand heavily armed men. We had very few resources, and we had to optimize our use of them, as well as the deployment of weapons and men." Fidel Castro and Ignacio Ramonet, *My Life: A Spoken Autobiography*, trans. Andrew Hurley (New York: Scribner, 2007), 205–6. Castro explained that in such circumstances, one man alone, if well placed, could stop an army, and so he hid out in the mountains with his small band of men and triumphed over overwhelming odds. At least to Castro, then, Hemingway's plot was not so unrealistic.

23. For representative reviews, see Meyers, *Hemingway: The Critical Heritage,* 314–65. Only Albert Camus, writing in 1947 for the resistance newspaper *Combat,* critiqued the love story subplot inserted into the tale of world-altering events. Camus said that *For Whom the Bell Tolls* was "a children's book" compared to Malraux's *Man's Hope,* and quipped, "you can't mix Hollywood with Guernica." Camus, *Camus at "Combat": Writing, 1944–1947,* ed. Jacqueline Lévi-Valensi (Princeton: Princeton University Press, 2006), 279.

24. Alvah Bessie, "Hemingway's 'For Whom the Bell Tolls,'" *New Masses,* 5 November 1940, 25–29.

25. Dwight Macdonald, "Reading from Left to Right," *Partisan Review* 8 (January 1941): 24–28.

26. Mary evidently did not retrieve everything; some items ended up in the Florida Research Room of the Monroe County Public Library. Toby Bruce's son, Dink, later turned up various odds and ends (including some Walker Evans photographs smuggled out of Cuba) in the family work shed in Key West.

27. Hemingway, *Papa: A Personal Memoir,* 23.

28. Pauline's sister Jinny, also a lesbian, was later involved in a polygamous relationship with Aldous Huxley.

29. Quoted in Hemingway, *My Brother, Ernest Hemingway,* 226.

30. "The Monument," box ms 54, ms 580.5, 14, Hemingway Collection.

31. Quoted in Mario Menocal to Carlos Baker, 10 April 1950, Hemingway Family Papers, Harry Ransom Center.

32. Hemingway to Perkins, ca. 16 November 1943, in Baker, *Selected Letters, 1917–1961,* 553–54.

33. Hemingway named the *Pilar* after the patron saint of Zaragoza, Spain. In a.d. 40, the apostle James, traveling in this area, was supposed to have seen a vision of the Virgin Mary on a pillar asking him to build a church on that spot. As a consequence, the Basilica-Catedral de Nuestra Señora del Pilar was erected there in the late seventeenth century.

34. Hemingway to Martha Gellhorn, 25 August [1942], Hemingway Collection.

35. Hemingway to Patrick and Gregory Hemingway, 14 July 1939, Special Collections, Alderman Library, University of Virginia, Charlottesville.

36. Hemingway to Martha Gellhorn, 27 July [1942], Hemingway Collection.

37. Hemingway to Gregory Hemingway, 16 November 1942, ibid.

38. Undated miscellaneous manuscript, outgoing correspondence, 1 June 1942–31 July 1942, ibid.

CHAPTER 11

1. Hemingway to Martha Gellhorn, 25 August [1942], Hemingway Collection.

2. Moreira, *Hemingway on the China Front,* 18. Moreira gives a complete discussion of this episode in Hemingway's life, although the term "spy" in the subtitle of the book (*His WWII Spy Mission with Martha Gellhorn*) is a bit of a stretch. Hemingway was asked to, and did, gather information and report it to the U.S. government, but there was nothing cloak-and-dagger about it.

3. Harry Dexter White to Hemingway, 27 January 1941, Hemingway Collection.

4. I use modern spellings of Chinese place-names, though the old Western spellings (Peking, Chungking, etc.) were still in use during Hemingway's time there.

5. Gellhorn, *Travels with Myself and Another,* 30, 32.

6. Ibid., 35.

7. Hemingway to Henry Morgenthau, 30 July 1941, Hemingway Collection.

8. Hemingway to Martha Gellhorn, 2 May 1941, ibid.

9. Hemingway to Morgenthau, 29 May and 14 August 1941, ibid.

10. Reynolds, *Hemingway: The Final Years,* 56–57.

11. See Braden, *Diplomats and Demagogues: The Memoirs of Spruille Braden* (New Rochelle, N.Y.: Arlington House, 1971), 284.

12. Hemingway, *Papa: A Personal Memoir,* 70–71.

13. Quoted in Reynolds, *Hemingway: The Final Years,* 70–71; "Miscellaneous Accessions file HEM-55," Hemingway Collection, 10–11.

14. Robert P. Joyce, memorandum to secretary of state, no. 2875, 24 April 1943, and enclosures nos. 1–4 to despatch from embassy at Havana, 2 December 1942–13 April 1943, General Records of the Department of State, Central Decimal File, 1910–1963, National Archives and Records Administration, College Park, Maryland.

15. Braden, *Diplomats and Demagogues,* 284.

16. In a letter to Pauline's mother, Hemingway claimed that Jinny had spoken ill of him behind his back and made sure that word got around of his bad behavior.

"Virginia's version of my life and conduct is a very fantastic one," he wrote. Hemingway to Mrs. Paul Pfeiffer, 12 December 1939, in Baker, *Selected Letters, 1917–1961,* 499. See also Meyers, *Hemingway: A Biography,* 345.

17. Quoted in Kert, *Hemingway Women,* 391.

18. Hemingway to Edna Gellhorn, 31 January [1945], Hemingway Collection.

19. See Reynolds, *Hemingway: The Final Years,* 83.

20. Hemingway to Martha Gellhorn, [1942], Hemingway Collection.

21. Quoted in Kert, *Hemingway Women,* 391.

22. Hemingway to Archibald MacLeish, quoted in Honoria Donnelly, with Richard N. Billings, *Sara and Gerald: Villa America and After* (New York: Holt, Rinehart and Winston, 1984), 178.

23. Quoted in Meyers, *Hemingway: A Biography,* 352.

24. After the war, Jack worked for a time as a stockbroker but found he did not much like the profession. He went into selling fishing supplies and made a living from his lifelong love of fly-fishing. He later became a conservationist, environmental activist, and patron of the Nature Conservancy. In June 1949, in Paris, he had married Byra Louise Whittlesey (called Puck), and they settled in Ketchum, Idaho. Despite his gregarious and bibulous manner, Jack had a rather sad life, abetted in part by alcohol abuse and perhaps also by traces of mental illness that trickled down through the family tree. A son died in infancy; he and Puck went on to have three daughters: Joan, born in 1950 (called Muffet), Margot (born in 1954), and Mariel (born three months after her grandfather's suicide, in October 1961). Joan currently lives in semiseclusion near Ketchum and paints watercolors, which have been exhibited locally. As a youth, she endured spells of mental illness and has spent some of her life in treatment for bipolar schizophrenia. Margot changed the spelling of her first name to "Margaux" and became a successful model and actress before succumbing to suicidal impulses and dying in Los Angeles from an overdose of barbiturates on 1 July 1996, one day before the thirty-fifth anniversary of Ernest Hemingway's suicide. Mariel is an Academy Award–nominated actress, model, fitness expert, and mental health advocate who has often spoken in public about her life growing up as a Hemingway. Her 2015 memoir, *Out Came the Sun,* and a documentary film, *Running from Crazy,* explore the Hemingway history of alcoholism, addiction, and mental illness. The film, which debuted on the Oprah Winfrey Network in 2014, contains lengthy footage of the family at home filmed by Margaux in 1983, and also the revelation that Mariel believes that her father sexually abused her two older sisters when they were girls. She says, "When I was really small, I shared a room with Margaux. My dad came in the room. I don't recall what it was, but it wasn't right. It's hard to have a visual of that. I know what happened. I think my dad sexually abused the girls when they were young." The girls' mother, who apparently protected Mariel by allowing her to sleep with her from "about age seven to sixteen," died of cancer in 1988. Jack died in New York on 1 December 2000, at age seventy-seven, from complications following heart surgery. An earlier, little-known documentary sheds more light on the history of the troubled family. Thirteen years before her suicide, Margaux Hemingway and her husband, the film director Bernard Foucher, made a documentary—*Winner Take Nothing,* released in 1998—following Hemingway's footsteps in Paris, Pamplona, and Venice. The film contains interviews with such figures as former French prime minister Jacques Chirac, the actress Jane Seymour, and two World War II correspondents, who share their memories of Hemingway. These parts of the film are intercut with footage from the home movies that Margaux shot, featured in *Running from Crazy.*

25. Hemingway to Martha Gellhorn, 25 August [1942], Hemingway Collection.

26. Quoted in Kert, *Hemingway Women,* 392.

27. Martha Gellhorn to Hortense Flexner, 17 May (?) 1944, in *Selected Letters of Martha Gellhorn,* 163.

28. Hemingway to Patrick Hemingway, 15 September 1944, and remark to Lanham, both quoted in Kert, *Hemingway Women,* 409.

29. Quoted in Bruccoli, *Conversations with Ernest Hemingway,* 33.

30. Hemingway to Perkins, ca. 1 May 1940, in Baker, *Selected Letters, 1917–1961,* 505.

31. Quoted in Shirrel Rhoades, "One on One with the Author: John Hemingway," *Saturday Evening Post,* 29 June 2009.

32. Quoted in Vernon Klimo, *Hemingway and Jake: An Extraordinary Friendship* (Garden City, N.Y.: Doubleday, 1972), 79–80.

33. *Time* magazine, 2 November 1953, quoted in Hendrickson, *Hemingway's Boat,* 196.

34. Quoted in ibid., 257–58.

35. Hemingway, *My Brother, Ernest Hemingway,* 117.

36. Martha Gellhorn, interview by Kevin Kerrane, "Martha's Quest," *Salon* magazine, 12 March 1998, www.salon1999.com/archives/1998/media.html.

37. William Walton, interview by Rose Marie Burwell, oral history transcript, 44, Hemingway Collection.

38. Hemingway to Mary Welsh Hemingway, 27 August 1944, ibid.

39. Hemingway, *By-Line,* 382.

40. Irving Krieger to Jeffrey Meyers, 23 February 1983, quoted in Meyers, *Hemingway: A Biography,* 406.

41. Undated letter from David Bruce to a war correspondent, ca. 1947–48, Hemingway Collection.

42. J. D. Salinger, who had already written several stories that he would integrate into *The Catcher in the Rye,* was also there. He and Hemingway later met again at the battle of Hürtgen Forest. Salinger, a sergeant, was working in counterintelligence.

43. William Walton, interview by Rose Marie Burwell, oral history transcript, 74–76, Hemingway Collection. For an analysis of Hemingway's combat role in World War II, see William E. Cote, "Correspondent or Warrior? Hemingway's Murky World War II 'Combat' Experience," *Hemingway Notes* 22, no. 1 (2002): 88–104.

44. William Walton, interview by Rose Marie Burwell, oral history transcript, 36, Hemingway Collection.

45. Ibid., 51–52.

46. "Citation for Bronze Star Medal," typescript, enclosed in letter of Charles Trueman (Buck) Lanham to Hemingway, 18 July 1947, Hemingway Collection.

47. Martha Gellhorn to Jeffrey Meyers, 30 July 1983, quoted in Meyers, *Hemingway: A Biography,* 414.

CHAPTER 12

1. Hemingway, *How It Was,* 106.

2. Mary Hemingway to Bernice Kert, September 1979, quoted in Kert, *Hemingway Women,* 399.

3. Hemingway, *How It Was,* 106, 108.

4. Quoted in William Walton, interview by Rose Marie Burwell, oral history transcript, 126, Hemingway Collection.

5. Hemingway to Mary Welsh Hemingway, 13 September 1944, in Baker, *Selected Letters, 1917–1961,* 569–70.

6. Quoted in Fuentes, *Hemingway in Cuba,* 86.

7. Hemingway to Lanham, 30 June 1945, Hemingway Collection.

8. Hemingway to Thomas Welsh, 19 June 1945, in Baker, *Selected Letters, 1917–1961,* 592–93.

9. Burwell, *Hemingway: The Postwar Years,* 6.

10. For a useful interpretation of *Islands* as being about the creative process, see Donald Junkins, "Rereading *Islands in the Stream,*" *North Dakota Quarterly* 68, nos. 2–3 (2001): 109–22.

11. Hemingway to Perkins, 5 March 1947, in Baker, *Selected Letters, 1917–1961,* 616.

12. Hemingway to Lanham, 15 April 1948, ibid., 629, 633.

13. Hemingway to Walton, 4 August 1951, Hemingway Collection.

14. Hemingway to Marlene Dietrich, 21 November 1951, ibid.

15. Hemingway to Charles Scribner III, 5 October 1951, in Baker, *Selected Letters, 1917–1961,* 739.

16. See Susan M. Seitz, "The Posthumous Editing of Ernest Hemingway's Fiction" (PhD diss., University of Massachusetts, 1993).

17. Inspired in part by Kenneth S. Lynn's psychoanalytic biography of Hemingway in 1987 and the publication of *The Garden of Eden* the year before, a focus of Hemingway criticism since the early 1990s has been the representation of polymorphous sexual experiences in his fiction. Among the major works in this vein are Spilka, *Hemingway's Quarrel with Androgyny*; Comley and Scholes, *Hemingway's Genders*; Eby, *Hemingway's Fetishism,* Moddelmog, *Reading Desire*; and Strychacz, *Hemingway's Theaters of Masculinity.* The fixation with the body has found a positive legacy in Hemingway's granddaughter Mariel, who has spent much of her life as an advocate of fitness, healthful eating, yoga, and the like, even co-authoring a recipe book. In the film *Running from Crazy,* Mariel talks at length about her heightened sensitivity to all things physical. She recounts, for one thing, the numerous diets she followed in different phases of her life, including one where she ate only popcorn and another where she ingested only coffee in different forms. Sexuality and the body have also figured in subtle, perhaps ironic, ways in Mariel's film career. Her first appearance onscreen, at age sixteen, was in the role of Tracy, the seventeen-year-old lover of the much older adult character played by Woody Allen in 1979's *Manhattan.* In 1982, she played a bisexual track-and-field athlete in *Personal Best,* which featured lesbian love scenes. And for the film *Star 80* (1983), a biopic about *Playboy* model Dorothy Stratten (murdered at age twenty), she underwent surgery for breast implants in order to fill out her bust and thus more closely resemble Stratten. The implants later ruptured, sending silicone traces into her bloodstream and necessitating several painful procedures in order to restore her to good physical health.

18. Hemingway to Mary Welsh Hemingway, [11 February 1951], Hemingway Collection.

19. Bruccoli, *Conversations with Ernest Hemingway,* 177.

20. Hemingway, *How It Was,* 189; Hemingway to Lanham, 25 August 1946, in Baker, *Selected Letters, 1917–1961,* 610.

21. Quoted in Jeffrey Meyers, *Gary Cooper: American Hero* (New York: Morrow, 1998), 75.

22. Hemingway, *How It Was,* 283.

23. Adriana Ivancich to Bernice Kert, quoted in Kert, *Hemingway Women,* 443.

24. Quoted in ibid., 450–51.

25. Meyers, *Hemingway: A Biography,* 472.

26. See ibid., 470–77, for a full discussion of how Dorman-Smith was a model for Cantwell.

27. Hemingway, *Dateline: Toronto,* 233.

28. Hemingway to Owen Wister, ca. 25 July 1929, in Baker, *Selected Letters, 1917–1961,* 301.

29. See James H. Meredith, "The Later Hemingway in War and Peace," *North Dakota Quarterly* 66, no. 2 (1999): 93–100, esp. 99–100.

30. Morton Zabel, review of *Across the River and into the Trees, Nation,* 9 September 1950, 230; Alfred Kazin, review of *Across the River and into the Trees, New Yorker,* 9 September 1950, 101; Joseph Warren Beach, "How Do You Like It Now, Gentlemen?," *Sewanee Review* 59 (Spring 1951): 311–16; Northrop Frye, review of *Across the River and into the Trees, Hudson Review* 3 (Winter 1951): 611–12.

31. Evelyn Waugh, review of *Across the River and into the Trees, Tablet,* 30 September 1950, 290.

32. John O'Hara, "The Author's Name Is Hemingway," *New York Times Book Review,* 10 September 1950, 1.

33. Reynolds, *Hemingway: The Final Years,* 230–31.

34. Hemingway to Adriana Ivancich, 9 May 1954, in Baker, *Selected Letters, 1917–1961,* 830–31.

CHAPTER 13

1. "On the Blue Water" is very similar to an earlier piece, "The Great Blue River," which had appeared in *Holiday* magazine in 1949.

2. Hemingway to Meyer, 4 and 7 March 1952, in Baker, *Selected Letters, 1917–1961,* 758.

3. George Plimpton, *The Best of Plimpton* (Boston: Atlantic Monthly Press, 1994), 128–29.

4. Meyers, *Hemingway: A Biography,* 186.

5. Hemingway to Ernest Walsh, quoted in Reynolds, *Hemingway: The Paris Years,* 345.

6. For Hemingway's religious views, see H. R. Stoneback, "In the Nominal Country of the Bogus: Hemingway's Catholicism and the Biographies," in *Hemingway: Essays of Reassessment,* ed. Frank Scafella (New York: Oxford University Press, 1991), 105–40; and John Clark Pratt, "A Sometimes Great Notion: Ernest Hemingway's Roman Catholicism," in *Hemingway in Our Time,* ed. Richard Astro and Jackson J. Benson, (Corvallis: Oregon State University Press, 1974), 145–57.

7. Hemingway to Marlene Dietrich, 26 September 1951, Hemingway Collection.

8. Matthew Nickel, "Religion," in Moddelmog and del Gizzo, *Hemingway in Context,* 355. For a fuller treatment, see Nickel's *Hemingway's Dark Night.*

9. Hemingway to Thomas Bledsoe, 9 December 1951, in Baker, *Selected Letters, 1917–1961,* 744.

10. Hemingway to Marlene Dietrich, 23 May 1950, Hemingway Collection.

11. Hemingway to Cowley, 10 June 1949, quoted in James D. Brasch, "Invention from Knowledge: The Hemingway-Cowley Correspondence," in *Ernest Hemingway: The Writer in Context,* ed. James Nagel (Madison: University of Wisconsin Press, 1984), 207.

12. Hemingway to Fenton, 29 July 1952, in Baker, *Selected Letters, 1917–1961,* 776. Fenton's life and career is analyzed by Scott Donaldson in *Death of a Rebel: The Charlie Fenton Story* (Lanham, Md.: Rowman and Littlefield, 2011).

13. Most commentators on this incident quote Hemingway's remark about Fenton's death to Carlos Baker: "Wonder what he thought about on the way down." But Hemingway continued, "He was supposed to have had some trouble when he was in the R.A.F. and that may have had something to do with it. Never met him but

feel very sorry for him." The latter part of the remark mitigates the harshness of the first part somewhat. Hemingway to Baker, 16 January 1961, Hemingway Collection.

14. Hemingway to Philip Young, 6 March 1952, in Baker, *Selected Letters, 1917–1961,* 760.

15. Hemingway to Philip Young, 27 May 1952, Hemingway Collection.

16. Hemingway to Harvey Breit, 23 July 1956, in Baker, *Selected Letters, 1917–1961,* 867.

17. Hemingway to Baker, 17 February 1951, Hemingway Collection.

18. Hemingway to Marlene Dietrich, 21 November 1951, Hemingway Collection.

19. Hemingway to Bernard Berenson, 11 August 1953, in Baker, *Selected Letters, 1917–1961,* 823.

20. For a discussion of Hemingway's concept of racial identity in the African works, see, most recently, Dudley, *Hemingway, Race, and Art.* See also Suzanne del Gizzo, "Going Home: Hemingway, Primitivism, and Identity," *Modern Fiction Studies* 49 (2003): 498–523.

21. Hemingway, *How It Was,* 412.

22. Patrick became a farmer and gradually made a reputation for himself as one of the elite white hunters in the area. In 1955, he started his own successful safari tour company, with encouragement from Philip Percival, but he had to sell the business when his wife became ill in 1963. He then worked briefly for the United Nations in Arusha, in northern Tanzania. Later, he returned to the United States, taking up residence in Montana, where he still lives today.

23. Hemingway to Harvey Breit, 3 January 1954, in Baker, *Selected Letters, 1917–1961,* 826.

24. Hemingway, *How It Was,* 100.

25. "Hemingway and His Wife Crash in Africa; Plane Is Seen in Jungle, No Word on Fate," AP clipping, 25 January 1954, box SB 08, Hemingway Collection.

26. "Invulnerable Papa," *New York Post,* 25 January 1954, 3.

27. Quoted in Kert, *Hemingway Women,* 479.

28. Hemingway to Robert Morgan Brown, [summer] 1956, Hemingway Family Papers, Harry Ransom Center. See also Burwell, *Hemingway: The Postwar Years,* 138.

29. Transcription of a taped television interview accessed at http://www.youtube.com/watch?v=TGZNE5VWBjk. As far as I can determine, the text has never appeared in print.

30. Quoted in Caroline Moorehead, "Stories of Survival," *Times* (London), 8 December 1983, 15.

31. Scribner's brought out *The Garden of Eden* in 1986, edited by a fiction editor there named Tom Jenks. Jenks took a hatchet to what was arguably Hemingway's most complex creative work, reducing it in length by almost 80 percent and conflating chapters in the process. A major casualty was the loss of a second plot involving a painter named Nick Sheldon, his wife, Barbara, and their mutual friend, a writer named Andy Murray. Jenks sought to create a unified narrative with commercial appeal, a book that would, as he later put it, "stand up for a reader who had never heard of Hemingway, a book that wouldn't require an introduction by way of explanation, or footnotes, or any other mediation between the author and his readers." This was, then, basically a commercial decision, resulting in a text that was in many ways untrue to Hemingway's artistic intentions. For that reason, most scholars who have written about the book have relied on the unpublished manuscript and related papers at the Kennedy Library in Boston. These materials have in fact been the catalyst for a large number of critical studies in which *The Garden of Eden* figures prominently. Indeed, this work has become central to much of the current critical conversation about Hemingway's views on gender and sexuality. Chris L. Nesmith provides a complete list of Jenks's emendations to the novel in ""The Law of an

Ancient God' and the Editing of Hemingway's *The Garden of Eden:* The Final Corrected Typescript and Galleys," *Hemingway Notes* 20, no. 2 (2001): 16–36. Nesmith
avers that Jenks's line editing was even more harmful to the novel than his cutting
of the entire subplot.

32. Hendrickson, in *Hemingway's Boat,* offers the fullest and best examination of this
topic.

33. Burwell, *Hemingway: The Postwar Years,* 131.

34. A curious variation on the hair fetish also appears in an unpublished manuscript
fragment at the Kennedy Library titled "A Dark Young Man," in which the central
character goes to a barber in France and is intrigued by the man in the chair next to
him, who is wearing "a net of some sort over his head."

35. Gregory's electroshock treatments are documented in Valerie Hemingway, *Running
with the Bulls,* 235, 241–42, 264. Hemingway's middle son, Patrick, also underwent
electroshock treatments, in 1947. Meyers, *Hemingway: A Biography,* 422.

36. Jeffrey Meyers, "The Hemingways: An American Tragedy," *Virginia Quarterly Review*
75 (Spring 1999): 276.

37. Quoted in Hendrickson, *Hemingway's Boat,* 504–5.

38. Hemingway, *Papa: A Personal Memoir,* 101.

39. Mary Hemingway, "The Making of the Book: A Chronicle and a Memoir," *New
York Times Book Review,* 10 May 1964, 26–27. A. E. Hotchner, in a different retelling,
claims that it was he who was with Hemingway when the trunks were brought up;
they had just had lunch with Charles Ritz, the owner, and learned of the trunks in
the hotel basement. Hotchner, "Don't Touch 'A Moveable Feast,'" *New York Times,* 19
July 2009.

40. Burwell, *Hemingway: The Postwar Years,* xxiv.

41. Mary Hemingway, "Making of the Book," 27.

42. Michael Reynolds, "Ernest Hemingway, 1899–1961: A Brief Biography," in Wagner-
Martin, *Historical Guide to Ernest Hemingway,* 46.

43. Robert W. Trogdon, "*A Moveable Feast: The Restored Edition;* A Review and a Colla-
tion of Differences," *Hemingway Review* 29 (Fall 2009): 27.

44. Hotcher, "Don't Touch 'A Moveable Feast.'"

45. Hemingway, *By-Line,* 158.

CHAPTER 14

1. Hemingway to Patrick Hemingway, 5 August 1959, in Baker, *Selected Letters,
1917–1961,* 895.

2. Lanham, interview by Scott Donaldson, quoted in Meyers, *Hemingway: A Biography,*
530.

3. Hemingway, *How It Was,* 140.

4. Untitled document signed by Dr. Herrera, box OM 12, "Medical Records, 1958–
1961" folder, 20 July 1961, Hemingway Collection.

5. Howard Rome to Hemingway, 21 January 1961, ibid.

6. Memorandum of Richard M. Steinhilber, MD, Mayo Clinic, Rochester, Minnesota,
"Medical Records, 1958–1961" folder, ibid.

7. Quoted in Kert, *Hemingway Women,* 498.

8. Quoted in John De Grot, "FBI vs. Papa," *Palm Beach News-Sun-Sentinel,* 9 October
1983, 6A.

9. For an account of Hemingway's FBI history, see Mitgang, *Dangerous Dossiers,* 63–69.

10. Hemingway, *How It Was,* 572.

11. Hemingway to Gianfranco Ivancich, 31 January 1958, Hemingway Collection.

12. Hemingway to Valerie Danby-Smith, 25 October 1960, ibid.

13. Lowell described this in a poem, "A Mad Soldier Confined at Munich," quoted in Paul Mariani, *Lost Puritan: A Life of Robert Lowell* (New York: W. W. Norton, 1996), 216.

14. *Life* published the letter nearly two months after Hemingway's death, under the title "Papa's Last Words." *Life,* 25 August 1961, 7.

15. Box OM 12, "Medical Records, 1958–1961" folder, Hemingway Collection.

16. "Ernest Hemingway Being Treated for Hypertension," *Rochester (MN) Post Bulletin,* 11 January 1961.

17. Leslie Fiedler, "An Almost Imaginary Interview: Hemingway in Ketchum," *Partisan Review* 29 (Summer 1962): 404, 400, 402.

18. Hemingway, *How It Was,* 573.

19. See Mary Welsh Hemingway to Ursula Hemingway Jepson, 25 April 1961, Hemingway Collection.

20. Dos Passos quoted in Virginia Spencer Carr, *John Dos Passos: A Life* (New York: Doubleday, 1984), 522; Cooper quoted in Jeffrey Meyers, *Gary Cooper: American Hero* (New York: Morrow, 1998), 319; Marlene Dietrich to Hemingway, 16 May 1961, Hemingway Collection.

21. Until recently, it was thought that Hemingway had killed himself with a gun made by the bespoke London gunsmith Boss & Co., but the authors of *Hemingway's Guns* (2010), through exhaustive research, travel, correspondence, and interviews, conclude that Hemingway never owned a Boss. After the suicide, the gun that Hemingway used was handed over to a welder in Ketchum to be destroyed, and the mangled parts were then buried in a field nearby. Roger Sanger, while researching *Hemingway's Guns,* found the welding shop still in business; the proprietor, the grandson of the person who had owned the shop in 1961, had fragments of the destroyed gun in a matchbox. Analysis revealed that it was a Scott, not a Boss. See Silvio Calabi, Steve Helsley, and Roger Sanger, *Hemingway's Guns: The Sporting Arms of Ernest Hemingway* (Camden, Maine: Down East Books, 2010), 150–53.

22. Hemingway, *How it Was,* 579.

23. "Hemingway Dead of Gunshot Wound," *New York Times,* 2 July 1961.

24. In fact, the fiction persisted even longer than five years for some of the younger Hemingways. Mariel Hemingway recalled recently that when she and her older sister Margaux were children, their father led them to believe that their grandfather's death was an accident. In the film *Winner Take Nothing,* Margaux said she was in her teens before she realized that her grandfather had committed suicide.

25. When Hotchner published *Papa Hemingway* in 1966, he omitted a good deal of material because he thought it might be injurious to Mary and others then living. In October 2015, Hotchner published *Hemingway in Love: His Own Story* (New York: St. Martin's Press, 2015), in which, on the basis of taped conversations with Hemingway at Saint Mary's Hospital, he asserts that Hemingway never actually loved Pauline, that the marriage was a disaster, and that throughout their years together Hemingway constantly pined for Hadley. (Given Hemingway's mental state at the time, these are dubious claims at best. Even when lucid, he was prone to revising history.) Hotchner also argues that Mary engineered the cover-up of Hemingway's suicide.

26. "Simple Farewell to Hemingway," *Newsday,* 7 July 1961, 42.

27. Hemingway, *How It Was,* 599.

SELECTED BIBLIOGRAPHY

WORKS BY HEMINGWAY

FICTION, NONFICTION, AND POETRY
References to Hemingway's works are to these editions.

Hemingway, Ernest. *Across the River and into the Trees.* New York: Charles Scribner's Sons, 1950.

———. *By-Line: Ernest Hemingway, Selected Articles and Dispatches of Four Decades.* Edited by William White. New York: Charles Scribner's Sons, 1967.

———. *The Dangerous Summer.* New York: Charles Scribner's Sons, 1985.

———. *Dateline: Toronto; Hemingway's Complete Toronto Star Dispatches, 1920–1924.* Edited by William White. New York: Charles Scribner's Sons, 1985.

———. *Death in the Afternoon.* New York: Charles Scribner's Sons, 1932.

———. *A Farewell to Arms.* New York: Charles Scribner's Sons, 1929.

———. *The Fifth Column and the First Forty-Nine Stories.* New York: Charles Scribner's Sons, 1938.

———. *For Whom the Bell Tolls.* New York: Charles Scribner's Sons, 1940.

———. *The Garden of Eden.* New York: Charles Scribner's Sons, 1986.

———. *Green Hills of Africa.* New York: Charles Scribner's Sons, 1935.

———. *in our time.* Paris: Three Mountains Press, 1924.

———. *In Our Time: Stories by Ernest Hemingway.* New York: Boni & Liveright, 1925.

———. *Islands in the Stream.* New York: Charles Scribner's Sons, 1970.

———. *Men Without Women.* New York: Charles Scribner's Sons, 1927.

———. *A Moveable Feast.* New York: Charles Scribner's Sons, 1964.

———. *A Moveable Feast: The Restored Edition.* Edited by Sean Hemingway. New York: Scribner, 2009.

———. *The Old Man and the Sea.* New York: Charles Scribner's Sons, 1952.

———. *The Spanish Earth.* Cleveland: J. B. Savage, 1938.

———. *The Sun Also Rises.* New York: Charles Scribner's Sons, 1926.

———. *Three Stories and Ten Poems.* Paris: Contact Publishing, 1923.

———. *To Have and Have Not.* New York: Charles Scribner's Sons, 1937.

———. *The Torrents of Spring.* New York: Charles Scribner's Sons, 1926.

———. *True at First Light: A Fictional Memoir.* Edited by Patrick Hemingway. New York: Scribner, 1999.

———. *Under Kilimanjaro.* Edited by Robert W. Lewis and Robert E. Fleming. Kent: Kent State University Press, 2005.

———. *Winner Take Nothing.* New York: Charles Scribner's Sons, 1933.

Baker, Carlos, ed. *Ernest Hemingway: Selected Letters, 1917–1961.* New York: Charles Scribner's Sons, 1981.

Bruccoli, Matthew J. *The Only Thing That Counts: The Ernest Hemingway / Maxwell Perkins
Correspondence, 1925–1947.* New York: Scribner, 1996.

DeFazio, Albert J., III, ed. *Dear Papa, Dear Hotch: The Correspondence of Ernest Hemingway
and A. E. Hotchner.* Columbia: University of Missouri Press, 2005.

Spanier, Sandra, Albert J. DeFazio III, and Robert W. Trogdon, eds. *The Letters of Ernest
Hemingway.* Vol. 2, *1923–1925.* Cambridge: Cambridge University Press, 2013.

Spanier, Sandra, and Robert W. Trogdon, eds. *The Letters of Ernest Hemingway.* Vol. 1,
1907–1922. Cambridge: Cambridge University Press, 2011.

Villard, Henry S., and James Nagel, eds. *Hemingway in Love and War: The Lost Diary of
Agnes von Kurowsky, Her Letters, and Correspondence of Ernest Hemingway.* Boston:
Northeastern University Press, 1989.

OTHER SOURCES

Arthur, Anthony. *Literary Feuds: A Century of Celebrated Quarrels—From Mark Twain to Tom
Wolfe.* New York. Thomas Dunne / St. Martin's Press, 2002.

Baker, Carlos. *Ernest Hemingway: A Life Story.* New York: Charles Scribner's Sons, 1969.

———. *Hemingway: The Writer as Artist.* Princeton: Princeton University Press, 1972.

Beach, Sylvia. *Shakespeare and Company.* 1951. Introduction by James Laughlin. Reprint,
Lincoln: University of Nebraska Press, 1991.

Beegel, Susan F. "Eye and Heart: Hemingway's Education as a Naturalist." In *A Historical Guide to Ernest Hemingway,* edited by Linda Wagner-Martin, 53–92. New
York: Oxford University Press, 2000.

———. "Hemingway and Hemochromatosis." *Hemingway Review* 10 (Fall 1990): 57–65.

Berenson, Bernard. *Sunset and Twilight: From the Diaries of 1947–1958.* Edited by Nicky
Mariano. New York: Harcourt, Brace and World, 1963.

Brasch, James, and Joseph Sigman. *Hemingway's Library: A Composite Record.* New York:
Garland, 1981.

Braudy, Leo. *The Frenzy of Renown: Fame and Its History.* New York: Oxford University
Press, 1986.

Brian, Denis. *The True Gen: An Intimate Portrait of Ernest Hemingway by Those Who Knew
Him.* New York: Grove Press, 1988.

Broer, Lawrence R., and Gloria Holland, eds. *Hemingway and Women: Female Critics and
the Female Voice.* Tuscaloosa: University of Alabama Press, 2002.

Bruccoli, Matthew J., ed. *Conversations with Ernest Hemingway.* Jackson: University Press
of Mississippi, 1986.

———, ed. *Ernest Hemingway: Cub Reporter.* Pittsburgh: University of Pittsburgh Press,
1970.

———. *Fitzgerald and Hemingway: A Dangerous Friendship.* New York: Carroll and Graf,
1993.

Bruccoli, Matthew J., and Judith S. Baughman. *Hemingway and the Mechanism of Fame:
Statements, Public Letters, Introductions, Forewords, Prefaces, Blurbs, Reviews, and
Endorsements.* Columbia: University of South Carolina Press, 2006.

Burwell, Rose Marie. *Hemingway: The Postwar Years and the Posthumous Novels.* Cambridge:
Cambridge University Press, 1996.

Callaghan, Morley. *That Summer in Paris: Memories of Tangled Friendships with Hemingway, Fitzgerald, and Some Others.* New York: Coward-McCann, 1963.

Chamberlin, Brewster. *The Hemingway Log: A Chronology of His Life and Times.* Lawrence: University Press of Kansas, 2015.

Cohen, Milton A. *Hemingway's Laboratory: The Paris in Our Time.* Tuscaloosa: University of Alabama Press, 2005.

Comley, Nancy R., and Robert Scholes. *Hemingway's Genders: Rereading the Hemingway Text.* New Haven: Yale University Press, 1994.

Crowley, John. *"The White Logic": Alcoholism and Gender in American Modernist Fiction.* Amherst: University of Massachusetts Press, 1994.

Curnutt, Kirk. *Literary Topics: Ernest Hemingway and the Expatriate Modernist Movement.* Vol. 2. Farmington Hills, Mich.: Gale, 2000.

Curnutt, Kirk, and Gail D. Sinclair, eds. *Key West Hemingway: A Reassessment.* Gainesville: University of Florida Press, 2009.

Diliberto, Gioia. *Hadley.* New York: Ticknor and Fields, 1992.

Donaldson, Scott. *By Force of Will: The Life and Art of Ernest Hemingway.* New York: Viking, 1977.

——. *Fitzgerald and Hemingway: Works and Days.* New York: Columbia University Press, 2009.

——. *Hemingway vs. Fitzgerald: The Rise and Fall of a Literary Friendship.* Woodstock, N.Y.: Overlook Press, 1999.

Dos Passos, John. *The Best Times: An Informal Memoir.* New York: New American Library, 1966.

——. *The Fourteenth Chronicle: Letters and Diaries of John Dos Passos.* Edited by Townsend Ludington. Boston: Gambit, 1973.

Dudley, Marc Kevin. *Hemingway, Race, and Art: Bloodlines and the Color Line.* Kent: Kent State University Press, 2011.

Eby, Carl. *Hemingway's Fetishism: Psychoanalysis and the Mirror of Manhood.* Albany: State University of New York Press, 1999.

Fantina, Richard. *Ernest Hemingway: Machismo and Masochism.* New York: Palgrave Macmillan, 2005.

Fenton, Charles. *The Apprenticeship of Ernest Hemingway: The Early Years.* New York: Farrar, Straus and Young, 1954.

Fitch, Noel Riley. *Sylvia Beach and the Lost Generation: A History of Literary Paris in the Twenties and Thirties.* New York: W. W. Norton, 1983.

Fleming, Robert E. *The Face in the Mirror: Hemingway's Writers.* Tuscaloosa: University of Alabama Press, 1994.

——, ed. *Hemingway and the Natural World.* Moscow: University of Idaho Press, 1999.

Fuentes, Norberto. *Hemingway in Cuba.* Translated by Consuelo E. Corwin. Secaucus, N.J.: Lyle Stuart, 1984.

Gajdusek, Robert E. *Hemingway in His Own Country.* Notre Dame: University of Notre Dame Press, 2002.

Gellhorn, Martha. *The Face of War.* Rev. ed. New York: Atlantic Monthly Press, 1988.

——. Introduction to *Love Goes to Press,* by Martha Gellhorn and Virginia Cowles. Lincoln: University of Nebraska Press, 1946.

——. *Selected Letters of Martha Gellhorn.* Edited by Caroline Moorhead. New York: Macmillan, 2007.

——. *Travels with Myself and Another.* London: Allen Lane, 1978.

Griffin, Peter. *Along with Youth: Hemingway, the Early Years.* New York: Oxford University Press, 1985.

——. *Less Than a Treason: Hemingway in Paris.* New York: Oxford University Press, 1990.

Hanneman, Audra. *Ernest Hemingway: A Comprehensive Bibliography.* Princeton: Princeton University Press, 1967.

———. *Supplement to Ernest Hemingway: A Comprehensive Bibliography.* Princeton: Princeton University Press, 1975.

Hawkins, Ruth A. *Unbelievable Happiness and Final Sorrow: The Hemingway-Pfeiffer Marriage.* Fayetteville: University of Arkansas Press, 2012.

Hays, Peter L. "Hemingway's Clinical Depression: A Speculation." *Hemingway Review* 14 (Fall 1995): 50–63.

Hemingway, Carol. "Jane Mason's *Safari.*" *Hemingway Review* 21 (Spring 2002): 117–20.

Hemingway, Gregory. *Papa: A Personal Memoir.* Boston: Houghton Mifflin, 1976.

Hemingway, Hilary, and Jeffry P. Lindsay. *Hunting with Hemingway.* New York: Riverhead, 2000.

Hemingway, Leicester. *My Brother, Ernest Hemingway.* New York: World, 1962.

Hemingway, Mary Welsh. *How It Was.* New York: Knopf, 1976.

Hemingway, Patrick. Introduction. In *True at First Light*, by Ernest Hemingway, 7–11. New York: Scribner, 1999.

———. "*Islands in the Stream:* A Son Remembers." In *Ernest Hemingway: The Writer in Context,* edited by James Nagel, 13–18. Madison: University of Wisconsin Press, 1984.

Hemingway, Valerie. *Running with the Bulls: My Years with the Hemingways.* New York: Ballantine, 2004.

Hendrickson, Paul. *Hemingway's Boat: Everything He Loved in Life, and Lost.* New York: Knopf, 2011.

Hotchner, A. E. *Papa Hemingway: A Personal Memoir.* New York: Random House, 1966.

Justice, Hilary K. *The Bones of the Others: The Hemingway Text from the Lost Manuscripts to the Posthumous Novels.* Kent: Kent State University Press, 2006.

Kennedy, J. Gerald. *Imagining Paris: Exile, Writing, and American Identity.* New Haven: Yale University Press, 1993.

Kennedy, J. Gerald, and Jackson R. Bryer, eds. *French Connections: Hemingway and Fitzgerald Abroad.* New York: St. Martin's Press, 1998.

Kert, Bernice. *The Hemingway Women.* New York: W. W. Norton, 1983.

———. "Jane Mason and Ernest Hemingway: A Biographer Reviews Her Notes." *Hemingway Review* 21 (Spring 2002): 111–16.

Knoll, Robert E. *Robert McAlmon.* Lincoln: University of Nebraska Press, 1957.

Kubie, Lawrence. "Ernest Hemingway: Cyrano and the Matador." *American Imago* 41 (Spring 1984): 9–18.

Larsen, Lyle. *Stein and Hemingway: The Story of a Turbulent Relationship.* Jefferson, N.C.: McFarland, 2011.

Larson, Kelli A. *Ernest Hemingway: A Reference Guide, 1974–1989.* Boston: G. K. Hall, 1990.

Lynn, Kenneth S. *Hemingway.* New York: Simon & Schuster, 1987.

Mandel, Miriam B., ed. *A Companion to Hemingway's "Death in the Afternoon."* Rochester, N.Y.: Camden House, 2004.

———, ed. *Hemingway and Africa.* Suffolk, UK: Camden House, 2011.

Mason, Alane Salierno. "An Introduction to Jane Mason's *Safari.*" *Hemingway Review* 21 (Spring 2002): 13–21.

———. "To Love and Love Not." *Vanity Fair,* July 1999, 108–18, 146–52.

Mellow, James. *Hemingway: A Life Without Consequences.* New York: Houghton Mifflin, 1992.

Meyers, Jeffrey, ed. *Ernest Hemingway: The Critical Heritage.* London: Routledge, 2003.

———. *Hemingway: A Biography.* New York: Harper and Row, 1985.

Miller, Madelaine Hemingway. *Ernie: Hemingway's Sister "Sunny" Remembers*. New York: Crown, 1975.

Mitgang, Herbert. *Dangerous Dossiers: Exposing the Secret War Against America's Greatest Authors*. New York: D. I. Fine, 1988.

Moddelmog, Debra A. *Reading Desire: In Pursuit of Ernest Hemingway*. Ithaca: Cornell University Press, 1999.

Moddelmog, Debra A., and Suzanne del Gizzo, eds. *Hemingway in Context*. Cambridge: Cambridge University Press, 2013.

Montgomery, Constance Cappel. *Hemingway in Michigan*. New York: Fleet Publishing, 1966.

Moorehead, Caroline. *Gellhorn: A Twentieth-Century Life*. New York: Henry Holt, 2003.

Moreira, Peter. *Hemingway on the China Front: His WWII Spy Mission with Martha Gellhorn*. Washington, D.C.: Potomac Books, 2006.

Morrison, Toni. *Playing in the Dark: Whiteness and the Literary Imagination*. Cambridge: Harvard University Press, 1992.

Mort, Terry. *The Hemingway Patrols: Ernest Hemingway and His Hunt for U-Boats*. New York: Scribner, 2009.

Nickel, Matthew. *Hemingway's Dark Night: Catholic Influences and Intertextualities in the Work of Ernest Hemingway*. Wickford, R.I.: New Street Communications, 2013.

Ondaatje, Christopher. *Hemingway in Africa: The Last Safari*. Woodstock, N.Y.: Overlook Press, 2004.

Ott, Mark P. *A Sea of Change: Ernest Hemingway and the Gulf Stream, a Contextual Biography*. Kent: Kent State University Press, 2010.

Raeburn, John. *Fame Became of Him: Hemingway as Public Writer*. Bloomington: Indiana University Press, 1984.

Reynolds, Michael. *Hemingway: The American Homecoming*. Cambridge: Basil Blackwell, 1992.

——. *Hemingway: An Annotated Chronology*. Detroit, Mich.: Omnigraphics, 1991.

——. *Hemingway: The Final Years*. New York: W. W. Norton, 1999.

——. *Hemingway: The 1930s*. New York: W. W. Norton, 1997.

——. *Hemingway: The Paris Years*. Cambridge: Basil Blackwell, 1989.

——. *Hemingway's First War: The Making of "A Farewell to Arms."* Princeton: Princeton University Press, 1976.

——. "Hemingway's Home: Depression and Suicide." In *Ernest Hemingway: Six Decades of Criticism*, edited by Linda Wagner-Martin, 9–17. East Lansing: Michigan State University Press, 1987.

——. *Hemingway's Reading: 1910–1940*. Princeton: Princeton University Press, 1981.

——. "A Supplement to *Hemingway's Reading: 1910–1940*." *Studies in American Fiction* 14, no. 1 (1986): 99–108.

——. *The Young Hemingway*. Cambridge: Basil Blackwell, 1986.

Rovit, Earl, and Arthur Waldhorn, eds. *Hemingway and Faulkner in Their Time*. New York: Continuum, 2005.

Samuelson, Arnold. *With Hemingway: A Year in Key West and Cuba*. New York: Random House, 1984.

Sanford, Marcelline Hemingway. *At the Hemingways: With Fifty Years of Correspondence Between Ernest and Marcelline Hemingway*. Boston: Little, Brown, 1962. Reprint, Moscow, Idaho: University of Idaho Press, 1999.

Scribner, Charles, Jr. *In the Company of Writers: A Life in Publishing*. New York: Scribner's, 1990.

Smith, Paul. *A Reader's Guide to the Short Stories of Ernest Hemingway*. Boston: G. K. Hall, 1989.

Sojka, Gregory S. *Ernest Hemingway: The Angler as Artist.* New York: Peter Lang, 1985.

Spilka, Mark. *Hemingway's Quarrel with Androgyny.* Lincoln: University of Nebraska Press, 1990.

Stein, Gertrude. *The Autobiography of Alice B. Toklas.* New York: Charles Scribner's Sons, 1933.

———. *Paris France: Personal Recollections.* New York: Charles Scribner's Sons, 1940.

Stephens, Robert O., ed. *Ernest Hemingway: The Critical Reception.* New York: Burt Franklin, 1977.

———. *Hemingway's Nonfiction: The Public Voice.* Chapel Hill: University of North Carolina Press, 1968.

Strong, Amy. *Race and Identity in Hemingway's Fiction.* New York: Palgrave Macmillan, 2008.

Strychacz, Thomas. *Hemingway's Theaters of Masculinity.* Baton Rouge: Louisiana State University Press, 2003.

Svoboda, Frederic J. "The Great Themes in Hemingway: Love, War, Wilderness, and Loss." In *A Historical Guide to Ernest Hemingway,* edited by Linda Wagner-Martin, 155–72. New York: Oxford University Press, 2000.

———, ed. *Hemingway and "The Sun Also Rises": The Crafting of a Style.* Lawrence: University Press of Kansas, 1983.

———. *Hemingway: Up in Michigan Perspectives.* East Lansing: Michigan State University Press, 1995.

Tavernier-Courbin, Jacqueline. *Ernest Hemingway's "A Moveable Feast". The Making of a Myth.* Boston: Northeastern University Press, 1991.

Trogdon, Robert W., ed. *Ernest Hemingway: A Literary Reference.* New York: Carroll and Graf, 1999.

———. *The Lousy Racket: Hemingway, Scribners, and the Business of Literature.* Kent: Kent State University Press, 2007.

Vaill, Amanda. *Everybody Was So Young: Gerald and Sara Murphy; A Lost Generation Love Story.* New York: Broadway Books, 1998.

———. *Hotel Florida: Truth, Love, and Death in the Spanish Civil War.* New York: Farrar, Straus and Giroux, 2014.

Vernon, Alex. *Hemingway's Second War: Bearing Witness to the Spanish Civil War.* Iowa City: University of Iowa Press, 2010.

Viertel, Peter. *Dangerous Friends: At Large with Huston and Hemingway in the Fifties.* New York: Doubleday, 1992.

Wagner-Martin, Linda. *Ernest Hemingway: A Literary Life.* New York: Palgrave Macmillan, 2007.

———, ed. *A Historical Guide to Ernest Hemingway.* New York: Oxford University Press, 2000.

Yalom, Irvin D., and Marilyn Yalom. "Ernest Hemingway—A Psychiatric View." *Archives of General Psychiatry* 24 (June 1971): 485–94.

Young, Philip. *Ernest Hemingway.* Pamplets on American Writers, no. 1. Minneapolis: University of Minnesota Press, 1959.

———. *Ernest Hemingway: A Reconsideration.* New York: Harcourt, Brace, 1966.

INDEX